Vasileios Liotsakis
Plato's Proto-Narratology

Trends in Classics –
Supplementary Volumes

Edited by
Franco Montanari and Antonios Rengakos

Associate Editors
Stavros Frangoulidis · Fausto Montana · Lara Pagani
Serena Perrone · Evina Sistakou · Christos Tsagalis

Scientific Committee
Alberto Bernabé · Margarethe Billerbeck
Claude Calame · Kathleen Coleman · Jonas Grethlein
Philip R. Hardie · Stephen J. Harrison · Stephen Hinds
Richard Hunter · Giuseppe Mastromarco
Gregory Nagy · Theodore D. Papanghelis
Giusto Picone · Alessandro Schiesaro
Tim Whitmarsh · Bernhard Zimmermann

Volume 153

Vasileios Liotsakis
Plato's Proto-Narratology

Metanarrative Reflections and Narrative Paradigms

DE GRUYTER

ISBN 978-3-11-221545-6
e-ISBN (PDF) 978-3-11-130782-4
e-ISBN (EPUB) 978-3-11-130845-6
ISSN 1868-4785

Library of Congress Control Number: 2023942329

Bibliographic information published by the Deutsche Nationalbibliothek
The Deutsche Nationalbibliothek lists this publication in the Deutsche Nationalbibliografie;
detailed bibliographic data are available on the Internet at http://dnb.dnb.de.

© 2025 Walter de Gruyter GmbH, Berlin/Boston
This volume is text- and page-identical with the hardback published in 2023.
Editorial Office: Alessia Ferreccio and Katerina Zianna
Logo: Christopher Schneider, Laufen
Printing and binding: CPI books GmbH, Leck

www.degruyter.com

... to Semina, Antonis and Myrto

Foreword

This book was written somewhere between September of 2019 and December of 2022 in Προσήλιο (Prosilio), a small, beautiful village of West Mani laying at the foot of Taygetus. During this period of time I was very often not in a position to visit libraries due to the quarantine imposed by the Greek government in their effort to confine the transmission of covid-19. Despite these difficulties — or, to be precise, exactly because of them — I am very proud that I managed to collect the bibliography required for this project. I am also deeply indebted to my dear friends and colleagues Professor Ioannis Konstantakos, Marietta Zacharioudaki, Andreas Panoutsopoulos, Stelios Perakis, Professor Mario Baumann and Michalis Vgontzas for providing me with a number of monographs and papers. I am also especially grateful to Professors Stephen Halliwell, David Konstan and Jonathan Griffiths for their kind willingness to read a draft of this book and for generously providing me with their invaluable comments and encouragement. All remaining errors are my own. Finally yet importantly, I wish to thank Professors Antonios Rengakos and Franco Montanari for hosting my third monograph too in their excellent series *Trends in Classics Supplementary Volumes*.

Prosilio, July 12th, 2023
V.L.

Contents

Foreword —— VII
Introduction —— XI

1	**The *Statesman*: A Formalist Approach to Narrative —— 1**
1.1	The narrative arrangement of the myth —— 3
1.2	The Visitor's speculations on turning raw material into a coherent narrative whole —— 12
1.2.1	Selectivity —— 15
1.2.2	Causality —— 24
1.2.3	Temporality —— 30
1.3	Narrating/listening time —— 36
1.3.1	The digression on the two types of measurement —— 38
1.3.2	The myth's narrating/listening time and the audience's anticipation —— 45
1.4	Conclusion —— 50
2	***Timaeus* and *Critias*: Plato's 'Proto-Theory' of Fictional Worlds —— 55**
2.1	The possibility of fictional worlds —— 59
2.2	Fictional worlds are incomplete and indeterminate constructs —— 68
2.3	The author's and audience's immersion in the fictional worlds —— 80
2.4	Fictional worlds as products of our sociocultural background —— 88
2.5	Fictional worlds and intertextuality —— 99
2.6	Conclusion —— 107
3	**The *Laws*: Formalism and Reception Theory Intermingled —— 108**
3.1	Narration as a means of persuasion and the audience's psychology —— 112
3.1.1	The 'teaser' reflections in Books 1–2 —— 115
3.1.2	The connections between Books 1–2 and the accounts of Book 3 —— 132
3.1.3	The connections between the accounts of Book 3 and the preludes of the laws of Books 4–12 —— 143
3.2	The poetics of intentional history —— 159
3.2.1	Selectivity and temporality —— 162
3.2.2	The ideological 'coating' of the material —— 171

3.2.3	Creating questions and answering them —— 181
3.2.4	The narrator's political views as the backbone of the plot —— 190
3.3	Conclusion —— 195

4	**General Conclusions —— 196**
4.1	The emergence of a proto-narratology: the typicality of the interaction between metanarrative reflections and narrative paradigms —— 196
4.2	Plato's sociological perspective on narrative realities —— 205

Bibliography —— 211
Index Nominum et Rerum —— 225
Index Locorum —— 229

Introduction

Any attempt to reconstruct a coherent theory of narrative in the Platonic oeuvre and to compare it with modern systems of narrative theory is faced with a number of intimidating and, in most cases, insurmountable hindrances. First and foremost, we possess no Platonic work which is strictly devoted to the art of narrating, either in prose or poetry. Ancient studies of this kind, not only of narrative theory but generally of literary criticism, such as Aristotle's *Poetics*, Horace's *The Art of Poetry* and Pseudo-Longinus' *On the Sublime*, with all their obvious differences from their modern counterparts, undoubtedly constitute the first attempts in western civilisation to describe the features of a text with clarity and on the basis of a relatively stable terminology. Such treatises of Greco-Roman literature provide modern scholars with greater confidence to engage with the theories that emerge from them and to trace points of accordance or deviation between these theories and modern ones.[1] In these cases, we often do not even need to schematise the views of an ancient critic because the latter offers us his thoughts almost on a plate, i.e. in a consolidated and relatively straightforward form.[2] On the other hand, Plato, despite the abundance of the views about poetry, myths and narration he here and there exposes in his dialogues, has not attracted the interest of modern theorists of narrative, narratologists and classicists who are engaged with these fields. Plato, it seems, does not satisfy our high expectations to find a clear-cut conceptualisation of narrative phenomena and a systematic approach by which to describe them.[3] Hence, the absence of a study on Plato's 'theory of narrative', a gap certain parts of which I aspire to fill in this book.

---

[1] On Aristotle and narratology see Rösler 1980 and Eco 1996 on Aristotle and fiction; Kirby 1991, who examines Plato and Aristotle as forefathers of aesthetics in the theory of narrative; Belfiore 1992 and 2000 on the differences between Aristotle's *mythos* and the narratological term "plot"; de Jong 2005, 19–22; Frangakis 2016. For discussion from a narratological perspective, see Appelrot 1893; Trowbridge 1944 on Aristotle and New Criticism; Bal 1981; Ogata 2016, 3, 6–8, 10, 18, 27; Liveley 2019, 25–62 and *passim*. On Horace and narratology see Liveley 2019, 63–73. Herrick 1946 and Cronk 1999 on Aristotle, Horace and Longinus and reader-response criticism.
[2] Although Horace's *The Art of Poetry* is marked by a "generic hybridity" (Liveley 2019, 72 and 63–73 *passim*), it still constitutes a far more focused mode of expression of literary criticism than the scattered statements we find in Plato.
[3] See Liveley 2019, 11 and with n. 1 for further bibliography on this tendency in narratological circles.

Plato's most clear-cut schematisation of a narrative aspect, and consequently the most popular one in the circles of both classicists and narratologists, is Socrates' classification of the three modes of narration in Book 3 of the *Republic* (392c7–397b5). On the one hand, according to Socrates, we have the recitation in which the narrator relates a story from the past, the present or the future (392d3) in a third-person narration, thereby rendering his presence constantly perceptible to the reader (392d5: ἁπλῇ διηγήσει; 393d6: ἁπλῆ διήγησις; 394b1: ἄνευ μιμήσεως ἁπλῆ διήγησις). Socrates mentions dithyramb as the literary genre that represents this mode of narration (394c2–3). In a second mode, the narrator weaves the plot of a story by means of representation (392d5: διὰ μιμήσεως; cf. 393c8: διὰ μιμήσεως τὴν διήγησιν; cf. 394c1), namely through dialogue or/and monologue (393a1–c9). Socrates finds that drama (tragedy and comedy) exemplifies this narrative mode (394b7–c2). Last, in a third type of narration, storytellers combine the two aforementioned modes (392d6 and 394c3–4: δι' ἀμφοτέρων), i.e. they relate the events both in a third-person narration and *via* dialogue or/and monologue. Socrates mentions the Homeric epics as representative of this narrative mode (394c3–5).

As is the case with most subjects discussed in the *Republic*, Socrates addresses these three kinds of narration in order to assess the suitability of each to the *kallipolis*' moral code and socio-political agenda. From this perspective, Socrates rejects narration by means of representation out of the belief that this mode of narration makes everyone involved in a dramatic performance (the poet, actors and audience) identify with the ideologies and emotions of the story's characters, some of whom sometimes adopt behaviours and moral codes incongruent with those which are proposed for the ideal city under construction. This state of affairs, Socrates argues, serves as an obstacle to the city founders' efforts for two reasons. First, people are led to immorality by being acquainted with the perspectives of unethical literary figures. Second, in contrast with the desired morality promised by the ethical and professional monomania which is proposed by the founders, to identify with many moral codes and behaviours generates an affective and moral pluralism, which is without doubt, in Socrates' mind, an unwelcome phenomenon. For these reasons, he reaches the conclusion that the founders should only approve of ἁπλῆ διήγησις or an almost ἁπλῆ διήγησις which is sparsely interrupted by monologues and dialogues of morally upright characters (394d1–397b5). In Book 10, Socrates returns to this subject and addresses the epistemological inadequacy of poetry (595–608).

These passages have served as the main basis for classicists who endeavour to reconstruct Plato's views on these modes of narration and on the audience's ideological and emotional identification with the characters of a story.⁴ Plato has also had an immense influence on narratological theories which consider the distance of the narrator from what she or he narrates and, depending on the range of this distance, the various kinds of narrators which emerge, as some of them have been classified by Gérard Genette and others have been added to the theory of narrative until today.⁵ On the other hand, the issue of a poetical performance's affective impact upon the audience is traditionally co-examined with the views expressed in the *Ion* by the eponymous character and Socrates. These views pertain to the reception of a mimetic narration and the audience's so-called immersion into the fictional world of a literary work, all of which have also been subjected to meticulous and in-depth analysis in recent decades in the fields of cognitive science and cognitive narratology.⁶

However, even this straightforward categorisation, despite its imposing imprint on narratologists, does not suffice to help us reconstruct Plato's "integrated" theory of narrative modes. As Stephen Halliwell has forcefully demonstrated, this schematisation is inadequate because it does not cover all kinds of narrators used by Plato in his surviving oeuvre, as these modes are defined by narratologists.⁷ Second, it does not offer a solid terminology of stable semiotic potential. To begin with, the terms διήγησις and μίμησις carry different meanings depending on the context in which they appear in the dialogues. For example, while in Socrates' tripartite scheme in the *Republic* the technique μίμησις denotes mainly dialogue and monologue and is taken as a sub-category to διήγησις, in other dialogues, such as in the *Timaeus*, *Critias* and the *Laws*, narration, in the way it is meant as ἁπλῆ διήγησις in the *Republic*, is presented as being a sub-category to μίμησις, which in these cases means representation and

---

4 On different kinds of narrators, see Morgan 2004; Halliwell 2009; Collobert 2013; Halliwell 2014; Brunschwig 2018; Finkelberg 2019. On the audience's identification with the characters of a (poetic) narrative, see Gould 1992; Greco 1994–1995; Janaway 1995, 80–102; Cohn 2000; Halliwell 2002, 40–41 and 49–50 for a reading of the *Republic* and *Ion*; Lear 2011.
5 Genette 1980, 162–185; Chatman 1990, 115; Walsh 1997; Kania 2005; Ryan 2005, 11–12; Gaudreault 2009, 38–51, who correctly challenges the conceptual identification of the dipole *diegesis vs. mimesis* with that of *showing vs. telling* (see, e.g., Willems 1989), cf. Halliwell 2012, 5. For a concise and thorough overview of Plato's influence on narratology and narrative analysis up to their time, see Alber/Fludernik 2009, 176–186; Currie 2010, 65–85; Schmid 2010, 7, 91 and 118–121 on the distinction between the narrator's discourse, which Schmid parallels with Plato's *diegesis*, and the character's discourse, which Schmid identifies with *mimesis*; Walsh 2010 on the conceptual inadequacy of this dipole; Brütsch 2017, 324–326; Liveley 2019, 189–203.
6 See, e.g., Menza 1972; Partee 1973; Gould 1992; Murray 1992; Grethlein 2021.
7 See Halliwell 2009, following Morgan 2004, and followed by Collobert 2013 and Finkelberg 2019.

not strictly dialogue or monologue.⁸ Similar problems also trouble those who trace a stable basis on which to examine Plato's theory of narrative in other terms as well, such as μῦθος or λόγος, both of which occasionally denote, apart from a narrative, other kinds of discourse.⁹

Apart from Socrates' division of narrative modes in the *Republic*, other aspects of storytelling are also addressed throughout the Platonic oeuvre, sometimes in a rather fleeting way and during the course of discussing topics irrelevant to narration or, in some other cases, in a more elaborately developed fashion and with a special interest in the nature of literature and narrativity. The question for those interested in tracing the seeds of Plato's 'narrative theory' is what we can make of these, in some sense, metanarrative statements. Furthermore, what is the point in drawing parallels between the views on narratives in Plato and the facets of modern theories of narrative and narratologies? What is the value, one can reasonably ask, of a comparison between, on the one hand, views that are merely mined from fragments and *are just believed to* belong to Plato or to the characters of his dialogues and, on the other, the ideas we today find in narratological studies, which are the results of years of speculation and have been systematically expounded? For many scholars, such Platonic passages betray nothing but instantaneous flares of metanarrative speculation on Plato's part and can at best contribute to the reconstruction of a theory of narrative only after they have been meticulously collected and categorised through a cherry-picking process. However, this method is in itself always a precarious way to approach matters. For even if we manage to offer in this way a detailed image of Plato's views on narrative issues, the result cannot definitively escape the limits of our subjectivism.¹⁰

One further methodological quandary, for those interested in not only the theory of narrative but in all facets of the Platonic thought, pertains to the crux issue of "who speaks for Plato".¹¹ Even if we may reach definitive conclusions about exactly what the views of the Platonic characters are on aspects of narra-

---

8 For *mimesis* as representation in Plato, see principally Halliwell 2002, 37–71. Cf. Auerbach 2003, 554, who states that he was inspired by Plato to explore literary representations of reality; Cain 2012; Gottschlich 2015; Feddern/Kablitz 2020.
9 Hildebrandt 1959; Capizzi 1989; Halliwell 2000; Morgan 2000, 15–37 and 132–289; Fowler (2011) estimates that the complicated way in which Plato uses these terms reflects his criticism of sophistic doctrines.
10 Cf. below Halliwell's (2009) view.
11 The collective volume edited by G.A. Press (2000) reflects on this multifaceted issue, with Press (2000, 1–10) offering a comprehensive overview of the literature. See, further, Blondell 2002, 19–20 with n. 55.

tivity, it could still be objected that we cannot say whether these views were also embraced by Plato himself. We are by no means justified, for example, to claim that the tripartite division of narration exposed in the *Republic* is not (only) Socrates' but (also) Plato's view. To such a claim one could counter-argue that no one can deny the contingency that it was indeed Socrates who recognised only these three narrative modes and that Plato merely records them without however agreeing that there are no others. As demonstrated by Halliwell, the fact that Plato employs an abundance of further other kinds of narrators renders this objection totally reasonable and hard to refute.[12]

Now, since not only this tripartite classification of narrative modes but also every other view on storytelling, including those which will be analysed in this book, are mainly expressed by Plato from a normative point of view, we may speak of two distinct perspectives from which to approach the issue of "who speaks for Plato" on narratives. Firstly, according to a normative point of view, one may focus on the thoughts expressed in the dialogues on what aspects of narrativity *should* be employed by a storyteller. It is with regard to this issue that it would make some sense to examine whether or not Plato embraces, rejects or is indifferent to the views of his characters. Secondly, from a purely descriptive point of view, one may explore what views are expressed not about what aspects of narrativity should be used but merely about what is their nature. From this angle, one needs not penetrate into whether or not Plato agrees with such views because it is obvious that, since he exposes them, he is fully aware of them.

For example, with regard to Socrates' thesis that, from the three types of narration, the one which is achieved by means of representation is ethically harmful for society, we may speculate on whether or not Plato agreed with Socrates' suggestion that drama be expelled from the *kallipolis*. Nonetheless, independently of whether or not we reach definitive conclusions on this issue, from the second perspective it is undeniable that Plato had schematised in his mind — at least — these three modes of narration and that he was interested in touching upon them in the *Republic*. This approach frees us from the pitfalls of opening our verdicts with the sentence "Plato believes that ..." and leads us instead to the more neutral and safer solution of claiming that "Plato was aware of" or "was interested in touching upon" a narrative phenomenon.[13]

I chose to open this book with this set of interpretive issues in order to underline how the exploration of elements of narrative theory in the Platonic corpus is

---

12 Halliwell 2009.
13 Halliwell (2009, 21) deliberately avoids discussing the question of whose views are expressed in metanarrative statements.

a venture which raises an abundance of methodological risks and challenges. To recapitulate: first, Plato did not bequeath to us any systematic treatise of narrative phenomena like the one Socrates builds on the three narrative modes in the *Republic*. Second, he reveals views on such matters through his characters' words. Third, these opinions are found scattered throughout the Platonic oeuvre and by no means cover the vastness of Plato's competence as a narrator, as this competence emerges from the profusion of narrative techniques he puts into effect in his works. Consequently, those interested in the seeds of narrative theory in Plato are inevitably invited (a) to reconstruct such seeds by co-examining the metanarrative statements of the Platonic characters and the narrative techniques used by Plato; (b) to decide what method to adopt in their effort to answer the question of whose — Plato's or his characters' — these metanarrative views are; and (c) to cautiously avoid anachronistic and loose connections between the non-systematically conveyed and conceptually incomplete views of the Platonic dialogues and facets of modern narratology. As Halliwell puts it,

> [...] the interest of Plato for narratology, as well as for the history of poetics in general, consequently lies not in the possibility of systematising certain views expressed in the dialogues into a putatively authorial theory. It lies, rather, in the challenge of coming to terms with the counterpoint between possibilities of 'theory' and 'practice' in the fabric of the works themselves and with the unresolved puzzles to which this counterpoint gives rise.[14]

Halliwell's suggestion that we co-examine the 'theory' and 'practice' of narrative in Plato represents, I think, the most fruitful solution for those interested in issues of narrative theory in Plato and is also the one followed in this book. The usefulness of such an approach lies in the fact that gaps created by the scarcity of theoretical statements on narration can be covered — of course up to a certain degree and not in every case — by what the techniques used by Plato can tell us about, if not his views, at least his attitude towards narration.

Nonetheless, despite its merits, the co-examination of 'theory' and 'practice' of narrative collides with the following obstacle. Although the narrative techniques traceable in the Platonic works are innumerable and relatively distinct, we have to be careful in determining what is to be taken as 'theory'. In particular, it is worth asking under what circumstances we are justified in using Plato's narrative techniques as reflecting his attitude towards narration. If we agree to do so, I believe that we are inevitably led to three interpretive methods that are

---

14 Halliwell 2009, 41.

often combined by critics. In what follows, I address each of them, progressing from the most to the least precarious.

First, one may trace Plato's views on narration exclusively by examining the narrative techniques employed in the dialogues. This practice frees us from the headache of solving the aforementioned puzzle of who speaks for Plato. Since Plato is unquestionably the author of the dialogues (leaving questions of authenticity in the case of some dialogues aside), it is he who must be credited with the techniques we find in them and with the attitudes towards narration that are mirrored by these techniques. If such an approach is conducted with the help of narratological conceptual agendas and terminologies, we can then produce fruitful studies that describe Plato's narrative practice in modern terms and in comparison with modern attitudes towards storytelling.[15] Even more importantly, whenever such studies manage to prove that a specific technique or particular narrative mode constitutes a pattern in Plato's writings, we can then with greater safety conclude that Plato had a consolidated view on the nature of this technique, given that he must have repeatedly reflected on its functionality in employing it. Last, although the recurrence of a technique is sometimes nothing other than an aesthetic quirk, in some other cases it may be taken to betray the author's intention to elicit our engagement with the way this technique is performed and its impact on how we perceive the structure and meanings of a literary composition.

However, the usefulness of the practice of narrative for those interested in unearthing Plato's views on narration, with all its advantages, is questionable. A distinctive feature of all theorists of narrative is their stated intention to communicate their views on the matter. In this respect, compared with clear-cut metanarrative statements, the use of a technique and the presence of narrative aspects are less revealing of the authors' *intention* to communicate their thoughts on narration. This is so because statements are unquestionably expressions of an author's intention to share with us their reflections on issues of narrative. On the other hand, the use of a technique might perhaps reveal an author's standpoint on narration but does not necessarily constitute an undeniable sign of her or his wish to share it with us. First, it is hard to believe that every single narrative feature we trace in the dialogues proves that Plato had

---

15 See, for example, Scarcella 1987, Gill 1996 and 2002 on dialogue form; Morgan 2004, Desclos 2006, Bowery 2007, Halliwell 2009, Ferrari 2010, Schultz 2013, and Finkelberg 2019 on different types of narrators; Morgan 2012 on space; Collins 2012 and 2015, 45–181 on the techniques (metalepsis, narrators) through which the dialogues invite readers to participate in the situations they read about.

reflected on it. Even the aforementioned high degree of repetition of a technique does not prove the existence of a theory and the author's wish to reveal it to us, but rather enhances the impression that the author has had some thoughts about it. More importantly, the presence of a narrative structure or, generally, a textual feature is commonly used by authors as a rhetorical means of manipulating their audiences. In this respect, it can reasonably be noted that the elaborate use of narrative schemes does not reveal the author's intention to highlight them, as she or he would thereby contradict her or his goal to manipulate us through them. For all these reasons, the use of narrative schemes as evidence of the author's intention to share with us his views about them cannot escape from being highly conjectural.

For this reason we return to Halliwell's suggestion, which takes narrative techniques and metanarrative statements as jointly reconstructing different segments of the same puzzle, i.e. Plato's attitude towards the phenomenon of narration. This approach can be adopted on both an intra-textual and intertextual level, or on both.

But again, how should such a co-examination be developed? One way to adopt this approach is the one introduced by Halliwell and followed by Finkelberg and others: we first trace a metanarrative statement and decode the views latent in it about a narrative phenomenon. We then put this statement's 'completeness' to the test by examining whether or not the views expressed in it about a narrative phenomenon cover the vastness of the ways in which Plato handles this phenomenon. According to this logic, in most cases, I imagine, we would reach the conclusion that statements on a narrative aspect fail to exhaust the pluralism of ways in which Plato uses this aspect. Were we to scrutinise the 'integrity' of Umberto Eco's theory about the various kinds of implied reader by comparing his views with the innumerable ways in which Eco plays with hypothetical readerships in his novels, I am quite confident that we would find his theory on the matter to fall short of his practice of narrative.

In this book, I do not examine the "counterpoint" between metanarrative comments and narrative schemes, a counterpoint which might emerge from *our* intended comparative eye independently of whether or not Plato was interested at all in inviting us to compare what we compare. Instead, I have chosen to explore passages in which I believe that theory and practice of narrative are deliberately placed together in an orchestrated coexistence, which is elaborated by Plato himself in order to draw our attention to narrative phenomena. My goals are three. First, I endeavour to demonstrate that in three cases – the *Statesman*, the *Timaeus/Critias* and the *Laws* – Plato uses a specific scheme with which he expresses his views on narrative issues. Specifically, I develop

Halliwell's thesis by specifying one way, although not the only one, of reading passages of 'theory' close to those of 'practice' of narrative. I argue that in the aforementioned three cases Plato invites us to do exactly what Halliwell says in the passage quoted above. In all these three cases, I recognise that Plato offers an abundance of metanarrative comments and invites us to read the narratives developed in these works (the cosmological myth in the *Statesman*, the two myths in the *Timaeus/Critias* and the narratives of Book 3 in the *Laws*) through the prism of these metanarrative comments. In each case, Plato proceeds with some reflections about how a narrative is or should be arranged or about how it is received by the audience, and then uses the aforementioned accounts as a set of narrative paradigms for the views expressed in the metanarrative comments. Second, I define the narrative aspects in question and analyse the views which are expressed by the Platonic characters about them. Third, I argue that these themes which are highlighted by Plato constitute some of the most celebrated narrative phenomena in modern narratology, and that Plato approaches them in a way that in many respects resembles established narratological standpoints.

It is for this reason that I intend the term "proto-narratology" in the title of this book.[16] If narratology is marked by its effort to provide a solid system of conceptualisation and description of narrative phenomena, then, I believe, one of the first such endeavours in the history of western civilisation is evident in what Plato does in the *Statesman*, *Timaeus/Critias* and the *Laws*. In these dialogues, I shall argue, we witness the birth of a proto-narratology which may indeed differ in many respects from what we today expect from a narratological handbook, but still demonstrates two foundational features of narratology: (a) a conscious focus on certain aspects of narrativity and narrative phenomena; and (b) a schematised mode of interaction between metanarrative reflections and textual bodies which serve as the paradigms through which to explore the interpretive potential of these reflections.

I would like to describe this scheme as a set of "metanarrative reflections and narrative paradigms". Its details will be exposed in the main body of this book and will be recapitulated in the General Conclusions. However, at this point one preliminary remark would be useful for the reader. In the *Statesman*, *Timaeus/Critias* and the *Laws* Plato employs a scheme of interaction between theory and practice of discourse that he also uses in other dialogues as well.

---

16 I borrow the term 'proto-narratology' from Liveley 2019 (11–23 for Plato and *passim* for Aristotle, Horace and Russian Formalism). As for the latter, see also Schmid's (2009) volume *Russische Proto-Narratologie*.

For example, this scheme is also used in the *Republic*. When Socrates tries to explain to Adeimantus the difference between a third-person narration and an act of storytelling in which the narrator, through dialogue or monologue, pretends to be a character of his story, Adeimantus asks him to explain further what he means (392d7). Socrates then decides to clarify his thoughts through an example. He takes a scene from Book 1 of the *Iliad*, in which Chryses is presented as asking Agamemnon to free his daughter. Agamemnon refuses to do so, which leads Chryses to ask Apollo to punish the Greeks. Socrates distinguishes two modes of narration in these verses: the parts in which Homer does not impersonate his characters and uses instead a third-person narration, and those segments in which Homer pretends to be Chryses and Agamemnon through direct speech. In order to make this distinction even sharper to Adeimantus, Socrates offers one further narrative paradigm, which is this time fabricated by himself. He says that Homer could have narrated the dialogue of Chryses and Agamemnon, as well as Chryses' subsequent prayer to Apollo, without direct speech but through a third-person story. Socrates then builds this third-person story by himself and Adeimantus seems to have now understood the difference between the two modes of narration (392d8–394b3). The parts in which Socrates describes the narrative phenomena of ἁπλῆ διήγησις and διήγησις διὰ μιμήσεως can be treated as metanarrative reflections, while the narrative bodies which Socrates uses as examples with which to clarify these reflections serve as what I describe as "narrative paradigms".

This scheme of interaction between meta-compositional statements and compositional paradigms is also found in other dialogues and, what is more, in a way that does not merely define one small segment of a dialogue, as is the case with the *Republic*, but rather shapes greater parts of its overall structure. This is what happens in the *Phaedrus*. In the first part of the dialogue, three paradigms of rhetoric are revealed: Lysias' speech against love, and Socrates' two speeches, the one against and the other in favour of love. Both between these speeches and in the later discussion about rhetoric and writing, Socrates addresses a number of issues pertaining to the content and structure of the aforementioned speeches. The *Phaedrus* exemplifies in the most characteristic way how the scheme of "meta-compositional reflections and compositional paradigms" defines the overall logic of a dialogue.[17] This is also the case, I believe, with the *Statesman*, the *Timaeus/Critias* and the *Laws*. However, while in

---

17 On this aspect of the *Phaedrus*' structure, see Hackforth 1952, 8–12; Burger 1980, 7–89; Ferrari 1990³, 37–85; Griswold 1996, 45–137 and 157–201; Nichols 1998, 15–18; Waterfield 2002, ix–xi; Yunis 2011, 2–7.

the *Phaedrus* Plato uses this scheme in order to highlight the art of rhetoric, in the three cases examined in this book, it will be argued, he employs it in order to present views on the nature of narration.

In Chapter 1, I analyse the way in which Plato employs the scheme of "metanarrative reflections and narrative paradigms" in his framing of the cosmological myth of the *Statesman* with a number of metanarrative statements of both the myth's narrator, the Eleatic Visitor, and his interlocutor, Young Socrates. Scholarly interest has traditionally focused on the myth's contribution to the realisation of the overall goal setting in the *Statesman*, both in terms of methodology and the definition of statesmanship. On a methodological level, commentators have elaborated the ways in which the myth contributes to the improvement, or at least the development, of the predominant method of inquiry in the *Statesman*, i.e. the method of division.[18] From a different but still intra-textual angle, the myth has also been read in relation to its immediate context, especially with what comes after the account and which pertains to the relationship of political knowledge with law.[19] In this respect, scholars conclude that the myth should also be taken to illustrate the view that political expertise is superior and thus preferable to legal systems.[20]

On an intertextual level, an equally well examined topic concerns the ways that the information of the mythical account is connected with ancient Greek literature in general and the Platonic oeuvre in particular. This is so because the myth includes some themes which were very popular in ancient Greek narrative tradition (both oral and literary), such as the parallelism between leadership and shepherding, the golden age of Cronus and autochthony. Such elements have already been examined in comparison with Homer, Hesiod and the Pre-Socratics.[21] Also, these themes of the myth, which cover a vast range of intellec-

---

18 Schröder 1935, 42–59; Zeise 1938, 53–58; Benardete 1963, 197–198, 203; Davis 1967, 319; Klein 1977, 160; Miller 1980, 35–53; Benardete 1984 III, 95, 100–103; Benardete 1992, 25 and 37–42; Hemmenway 1994, 259–263; Rowe 1995, 197–198; Lane 1998, 117–119; Cooper 1999, 78–79; Petrucci 2004, 110–111, 113–129; Blondell 2005, 31; Neiman 2007, 402–403; Crotty 2009, 174–178; Zuckert 2009, 186–187; Gill 2010, 185–197; Ionescu 2014, 42–45; White 2018.
19 Benardete 1984 III, 95; Cole 1991; Arends 1988, 155–156 and 165–166; Miller 1993, 225; Naddaf 1993, 126; Hemmenway 1994, 254; Cooper 1999; Michelini 2000, 185, 189; El Murr 2010, 130; Gill 2010, 192; Davenport 2011, 78–80; Horn 2012, 394; Márquez 2012; van Noorden 2015, 144; Naas 2018, 42–98.
20 González 2000, 173; Neiman 2007; Naas 2018, 42–98. See, *contra*, Speliotis' (2011, *passim* and mainly 301–310) unconvincing view.
21 On the Hesiodic (*Op.* 109–126) echoes of χρυσέον γένος in this myth, see Miller 1980, 39–53 (also on Homer); Rowe 1995, 187; Lane 1998, 111–112; Petrucci 2004, 115; Griswold 1989, 149–153; Tulli 1991, 99; Zuckert 2009, 189. On the parallelism between leadership and shepherding in

tual inquiries (anthropology, theology, cosmology, ontology and metaphysics), have been examined in relation with other Platonic myths, principally those we find in the *Timaeus*, *Phaedrus*, *Phaedo*, the *Republic* and the *Laws*.[22] In the same spirit, it has also been noted that not only the myth but also the *Statesman* as a whole constitute integral parts of both Platonic political views and the ancient Greek tradition of political theory.[23]

From an anthropological point of view, the myth has also been seen as reflecting the development of human civilisation and its social structures.[24] As far as this theme is concerned, scholars have often endeavoured to define the exact number and nature of the stages of human civilisation we may discern in the myth.[25] Scholarly interest has also been attracted by theological issues that

---

Homer, see Miller 1980, 40; Benardete 1992, 39–40; Zuckert 2009, 181 n. 9; El Murr 2010, 131–133; Gill 2010, 186 n. 23; van Noorden 2015, 143–167; Naas 2018, 50, 54, 56, 63. On elements of the Pre-Socratic doctrines in the myth, see Schuhl 1932, 50–51; Cordero 2002 on Empedocles; Naas 2018, 42–98, mostly on Heraclitus. See also Blondell's (2005) excellent discussion on the myth's affinities with ancient Greek literature, especially with Homer and Hesiod, and Livov 2011 on the myth as a reflection of Plato's criticism of Parmenidean principles. On the element of autochthony in Hesiod, Empedocles and Democritus, see Schuhl 1932, 55.

22 On similarities between this myth and those in the *Phaedrus*, *Timaeus* and *Laws*, see Stewart 1905, 173–195 (*Laws*) and 197–198 (*Timaeus*); Robin 1919, 71 ff.; Schuhl 1932, 47 and between the *Statesman*, *Timaeus* and the *Republic* ibid, 49–50 with n. 2. For a comparative examination of the *Statesman* and *Timaeus*, see also Herter 1958, 106, 110; Mohr 1978. On the *Statesman*, *Timaeus* and the *Laws*, see Herter 1957, *passim* and Herter 1958, 111–113; Mohr 1980 along with the *Phaedrus*; 1981 along with the *Phaedrus*, *Timaeus* and the *Laws*. Tulli 1991, 98–103 on the *Statesman*, *Gorgias*, *Timaeus* and the *Laws*; Kélessidou 1993; Dorter 1994, 192–194 with the *Timaeus*; Rowe 1995, 11–12 on the myth's differences from that of the *Protagoras* and 188 ff. on its connections to the myth of the *Timaeus*; Lane 1998, 116–117 for a short comparison with the cosmic myth in the *Laws*; McCabe 2000, 143 n. 10. On affinities and differences between the myths in the *Statesman* and *Timaeus*, see Robinson 2003; Petrucci 2004, 114–122; Carone 2005; Verlinsky 2009 and 2010–2011. Cf. Mason 2013 with the *Timaeus*, *Philebus*, *Laws* and the *Republic*.

23 In particular, it has been argued that the *Statesman* should be read in close association with the *Republic* and the *Laws*. Skemp 1952, 40; Davis 1967; Miller 1993; Annas in Annas/Waterfield 1995, xxii; Rosen 1995, 7; Lane 1998; Schofield 1999; Taylor 2000; Kamtekar 2004; Pradeau 2004; Meyer 2006, who reads the *Statesman*, apart from the *Republic* and the *Laws*, in association with the *Crito* as well; Neiman 2007; Kahn 2009; Zuckert 2009; Marshall/Bilsborough 2010; Livov 2011, 339–341; Cambiano 2012.

24 Rodier 1911; Naddaf 1993.

25 The less popular view that the myth describes three periods is supported by Lovejoy/Boas 1935, Rowe 1995, 13 and 189, and 2002, and Brisson 1995, 349–363; Carone 2004; Horn 2012; Naas 2018, 42–98. On the traditional view of the two ages, see, e.g., McCabe 1997; Lane 1998;

emerge from the Visitor's depiction of the divine creator, such as the identity of this god, with special emphasis being laid upon whether or not he is to be identified with Cronus, Zeus or a third god.[26]

In the first chapter, it will be argued that Plato in the *Statesman* leads the reader to associate the aforementioned themes with the procedures that a narrator-composer engages with in his effort to transform the raw material at his disposal (*fabula*) into a coherent narrative whole (*sujet*). Modern narratology recognises that organising the data into a narrative form (emplotment)[27] is a multilevel procedure, which is shaped by a plethora of factors. The material collected by every aspiring composer of a narrative is mostly, if not always, marked to a high degree by diversity, both in terms of the content of the information and its origin. As far as Platonic narrative is concerned, to compose a cosmological account such as the one in the *Statesman* requires that one take into account sundry facets of the current, oral and written, narrative tradition, such as mythology and the realistic representation of historical events. In parallel, the narrator of such a story has at his disposal material relating to theories of cosmogony, such as the data we trace in Hesiod's *Theogony* and Pre-Socratic natural science. In his effort to shape a 'hierarchy of usage' in this material, the narrator is invited to choose what parts of it he wants to use and what others he wants to omit, and, after selecting the data to be included in his story, he has to organise it in his mind into categories such as myths, historical events, conjectures, interpretations, etc. With particular regard to mythical material, the narrator is occasionally challenged to decode meanings latent in the symbolic texture of a myth, keeping only those meanings which are truly significant and getting rid of their mythical cocoon. Last but not least, after selecting the material, the narrator also has to organise it on the basis of temporal and causative relations which he establishes by himself. He should also be especially careful about the duration of his narration (narrating/listening time). As will be argued, Plato includes the cosmological myth in the *Statesman* exactly – and *inter alia* – in order to draw the reader's attention to these compositional challenges that a philosopher of his time was faced with in his effort to shape a narrative useful for his teaching.

Merrill 2003, 45; Blondell 2005, 23 n. 1; Verlinsky 2008 and 2009; El Murr 2010, 114; Speliotis 2011, 298 n. 5; Horn 2012, 394; Ionescu 2014, 37; van Noorden 2015, 147–153.

26 See Blondell 2005, 28 n. 28 with bibliography on the matter. Livov (2011, 338) and Mason (2013, 223) unconvincingly argue that the demiurge is identified with Cronus. See, *contra*, Dorter 1994, 193–194; Brisson 2000, 181–182; Márquez 2012, 159; Blondell 2005, 32 n. 41; Ionescu 2014, 38.

27 White 1973.

In Chapter 2, I trace the scheme of "metanarrative reflections and narrative paradigms" in the way that Plato frames the two myths in the *Timaeus* and *Critias* with the introductory discussions of each dialogue. Although the *Statesman* has historically been overlooked as a text suggestive of Plato's views on narrative issues, the *Timaeus* and *Critias* have attracted scholarly attention in terms of what they can tell us about three subjects related to narration: (a) Plato's interest in the construction of narratives; (b) his views on the way these narratives (the cosmological myth and the Atlantis tale) are aimed to be received by the audience; and (c) his concern about composing fictional accounts. In this last respect, countless studies have been written in pursuit of an answer as to whether the cosmological narrative of the *Timaeus* and the Atlantis narratives in both the *Timaeus* and *Critias* are aimed by Plato to be read as accounts that refer to reality or as mere fiction.[28] However, classicists who are occupied with this issue traditionally avoid drawing parallels between the views on fiction latent in these two dialogues and modern theories of fictional narratives.

In her book *Myth and Philosophy. From the Pre-Socratics to Plato*, Kathryn Morgan offers a literary rather than an analytic, as she puts it, interpretation of the ways in which philosophers, including Plato, used myths within the framework of their philosophical enquiries and expositions. In this context, she discusses a plethora of issues emerging in the two introductions of the *Timaeus* and *Critias* with regard to the way philosophers of the period were invited to construct a story and how they expected their tales to be received by the audience.[29] Still, Morgan is not interested in tracing any kind of connections between the views expressed by Plato in these works and modern theories of narrative and fiction. On the other hand, these two works have also been completely neglected by modern theorists of fiction.

In Chapter 2, following Morgan's point of view, I argue that the introductory parts of the *Timaeus* and *Critias* are indeed particularly revealing of Plato's speculations on the way that fictional worlds are conceived by their composers and received by their audiences. In this line of thought, I compare the views emerging from these Platonic texts with modern theories of fiction which are influenced by the philosophical concept of 'possible worlds'. These theorists of fiction treat Plato as the forefather of a realist approach of fiction, according to which what is taken as true or not and what is taken as possible or impossible in a verbally conveyed world, either of a historical or fictional work, should be

---

28 Gill 1993, who argues that the distinction between factual and fictional discourse is not discernible in Plato; Finkelberg 1998; Nesselrath 2002 and 2006.
29 Morgan 2000, followed by Desclos 2006.

decided on the basis of whether or not it refers to states of affairs that exist in the actual world. This way of thinking, object narratologists and theorists of fiction, overlooks the intuitive way in which audiences digest and assess the plausibility and truthfulness of fictional worlds. For audiences are taken by these critics to judge what is true or possible in a fictional world on the basis of whether or not what they read corresponds not to the actual world but to the rules which emerge from the overall structure of the fictional world itself. In the audience's minds, these logical rules of a fictional world are ontologically independent of those of the actual world.

Plato's treatment of literature as a representation of reality is inevitably rejected by modern theorists of fictional worlds who are not concerned with what is actually true or possible in a narrative world but with what is received as such by the audience. One of the pioneers of the possible-worlds theory in fiction, Thomas Pavel, comments in his book *Fictional Worlds*:

> In the medieval theater, the story of Creation and Salvation embodied the absolute truth in a universe with a definite structure and history. In a sense, the sacred medieval theater answered the Platonic requirement for good, truthful poetry better than any other literary project. It may also be surmised that the medieval image of the world was more or less foreign to the idea of alternative possibilities, even less to the feeling of fictional possibilities.[30]

In a similar line of thought, in his paper "Mimesis and Possible Worlds", Lubomir Doležel treats Plato as the forefather of what he defines as the 'mimetic' approach to fiction, which he endeavours to question in the rest of his article:

> From its origins, i.e., the writings of Plato and Aristotle, Occidental aesthetic thinking has been dominated by the idea of mimesis: Fictions (fictional objects) are derived from reality, they are imitations/representations of actually existing entities. During its long reign, the idea has been interpreted in many different ways and, consequently, the term "mimesis" has accumulated several distinct meanings. [...] My paper is intended to [...] offer a critique of the popular mimetic phraseology and to propose a promising alternative to mimetic theories of fictionality.[31]

Plato is also approached in this way by one further representative of the theory of fictional worlds, Ruth Ronen. In her book *Possible Worlds in Literary Theory*, she writes:

> Possible worlds provide for the first time a philosophical explanatory framework that pertains to the problem of fiction. This is an exception in view of the long philosophical tradi-

---

30 Pavel 1986, 83.
31 Doležel 1988, 475 with n. 1. Cf. Doležel 1998, 6 ff. and 2019, 53.

tion, from Plato to Russell, that has excluded fiction from the philosophical discussion (fiction has been viewed, for instance, as a sequence of propositions devoid of truth value).[32]

In Chapter 2, I argue that the *Timaeus* and *Critias* have much to say about the creation of a 'proto-theory' of fictional worlds by Plato. The latter, although indeed believing that narratives are nothing less than imitations of reality, in these dialogues does exactly what modern theorists of fiction do. He transfers the focal point of his interest from what is true or possible in a fictional world towards what is taken as such by the audience. What is more, in the discussions preceding the two myths between Socrates, Timaeus and Critias, Plato foregrounds certain themes which constitute the key elements of modern theories of fictional worlds that draw on the philosophical notion of 'possible worlds'. These themes are the following: (a) the possibility of fictional worlds; (b) their incompleteness; (c) the author's and audience's immersion into the fictional worlds; (d) fictional worlds as products of the author's and audience's cultural background; (e) and the way fictional worlds emerge from intertextual connections. This chapter focuses more on the metanarrative reflections on these issues and less on the narrative techniques through which Plato highlights these themes in the two narratives on the universe and Atlantis. However, I often try to explain, albeit not in a detailed way, that some distinctive features of the two accounts emerge as products of their narrators' speculation on the aforementioned five key elements.

In Chapter 3, I demonstrate how Plato employs the scheme of "metanarrative reflections and narrative paradigms" in the *Laws*. In his *requiem*, Plato endeavours to construct an ideal city and shape its legal system. The first two books of the dialogue offer the ideological basis on which the laws of Books 4–12 are decreed. However, between the first two books and the legislation of Books 4–12, Plato places Book 3, in which he composes an extensive narrative about the prehistory and history of the Mediterranean states and legal systems. Both throughout the dialogue and within these narratives themselves, Plato presents the three interlocutors, an anonymous Athenian Visitor, the Cretan Clinias and the Spartan Megillus, as delivering a number of statements on the composition and reception of narratives. In this chapter, I take the accounts offered by the Athenian Visitor in Book 3 as the main narrative paradigm.

---

32 Ronen 1994, 6–7. Cf. *ibid*, 20, 26–27, 214–215. For similar approaches to Plato by narratologists other than the theorists of fictional worlds, see Auerbach 2003; Schaeffer 2009, 103–104; Zipfel 2014, 109.

The *Laws* has traditionally been explored by scholars interested in ancient Greek literary criticism due to the plethora of views expressed by the three interlocutors on poetry.[33] Throughout the dialogue, the interlocutors criticise the way in which poets compose their works and the negative influence they exercise upon their audiences on an ethical level by representing morally questionable figures and states of affairs. The three elders' criticism also targets the fact that poetic artefacts are assessed not by experienced and virtuous individuals but according to the tastes of uneducated crowds. These views are often co-examined with similar theses found in the rest of the Platonic oeuvre as parts of Plato's attitude towards poetry and its place in Greek society.[34]

The narratives of Book 3 have been thoroughly examined in an abundance of studies, with the most seminal among them being Raymond Weil's book *L' "Archaeologie" de Platon*. Weil focuses on the similarities between the way Plato reconstructs the Greeks' prehistory and Thucydides' and Aristotle's works. However, he opts not to trace the ideological and thematic linkages between these narratives and the rest of the work, thus overlooking the main function of these accounts, which lies in how they offer to the legislators of the hypothetical Magnesia the historical exempla with which to validate in the citizens' minds the moral messages they wish to impose.[35] In the *Laws*, what is at stake is not only a legislator's competence in decreeing laws but also his persuasion skills, through which he has to convince the people of his city to obey the laws.[36] For this reason, Plato stresses, each law has to be accompanied by some kind of a prelude, in which the legislator explains the reasons why a law abiding way of life leads to happiness. Throughout the *Laws*, the main figure of the dialogue, the Athenian Visitor, composes a plethora of preludes for many categories of laws, which serve as a key vessel of communication through which the legislator's worldview is dispersed throughout the work. Although modern scholarship has meticulously analysed the content and persuasive role of the preludes, less attention has been paid to the ways in which the narratives of Book 3 contribute to

---

[33] Russell/Winterbottom 1972, 81–84; Ferrari 1993², 104–108; Halliwell 2006, 117 with n. 6, 119 with n. 11, 123–125; Emlyn–Jones 2008; Folch 2013.
[34] The bibliography is vast. See, for some examples, the precious discussions of the subject and the bibliographical overviews offered in the papers collected in Destrée's/Herrmann's (2011) and Peponi's (2013) volumes.
[35] Weil 1959. Cf. Prauscello 2017; Atack 2020.
[36] Bury 1937, 312; Morrow 1953; Fuks 1979, 34–35; Nightingale 1993, 285; Powell 1994; Stalley 1994; Clark 2003; Lisi 2017, 118–121.

the effectiveness of the preludes by endowing them with the necessary historical models to either follow or avoid.[37]

In Chapter 3, I first gather and analyse the metanarrative statements with which the three Platonic characters touch upon the effectiveness of narratives on the people's psychology. These statements are offered mainly in Books 1–2 and thereby serve as teasers of the rhetoric way in which the narratives of Book 3 will contribute to the legislator's efforts to convince the citizens of Magnesia to follow his will. I then trace the linkages between the narratives of Book 3 and the preludes of Books 4–12, linkages through which these accounts emerge as a basic ingredient of the legislator's rhetoric of persuasion. In the last part of the chapter, I analyse the structure of these narratives and argue that both the techniques through which they are arranged and the metanarrative statements made by the three men in the process of composing them draw the reader's attention to the way in which a narrative should be structured in order to be emotionally and logically effective. In essence, the two perspectives of the *Statesman* (structuralism) and the *Timaeus/Critias* (reception of a narrative) meet each other in the *Laws*.

In the General Conclusions, I recapitulate the typical modes through which the metanarrative reflections interact with the narrative paradigms and argue that the typicality of this scheme in all three cases shows that we are justified to think that Plato had consolidated in his mind a solid mode in which to express his speculations on narrative phenomena. In this line of thought, and also building on the fact that in all three cases these speculations are expressed within the framework of Plato's interest in socio-political matters, I re-address the place of Plato's proto-(socio)narratology on the archaeological map of modern narrative theory.

---

37 For an overview of the literature, see Chapter 3 n. 7.

1 The *Statesman*: A Formalist Approach to Narrative

The cosmological myth of the *Statesman* (268e4–274e3) is narrated by the central figure of the dialogue, the Eleatic Visitor (henceforth, the Visitor),[1] immediately after an initial and unsuccessful effort of the interlocutors to reach a definition of statesmanship. The conclusion which the Visitor and his conversation-partner, Young Socrates, reach before the myth is as follows: the statesman should be treated as the shepherd of humans. The latter is distinguished from the rest of the animals in being a two-legged, non-interbreeding species which lives on land. At this point, the Visitor complains that the aforementioned definition cannot stand, as it is marred by the following flaw. The parallelism between statesmanship and shepherding is methodologically inappropriate because the statesman is of the same nature as his herd (a human among other humans) and is therefore invited to deal with the competitiveness of citizens who act as pretenders of his power. On the contrary, the shepherd is of a nature superior to that of his herd and is therefore the unquestionable administrator of all the activities which aim at his animals' welfare. In order to make this difference between human statesmen and herdsmen more perceptible in Young Socrates' mind, the Visitor decides to relate the cosmological myth. In this way, he explains to the boy that only god is to be considered a true shepherd to humans, being superior to them in nature and their absolute ruler.

The narrative arrangement of the myth will be discussed at length in Sections 1.1 and 1.2. For the moment, let us offer a short summary of the story. According to the Visitor, the world moves in two periods which eternally follow each other. In the one period, which is named by the narrator "the Age of Cronus", the universe is moved by its divine creator, while the beings that live in the world (including humans) are governed as herds by some other deities, who are inferior to the demiurge. Similarly to all mortal beings, humans are abundantly provided by nature and their divine shepherds with food and all kinds of care. For this reason, in this phase of their history humans have not developed

---

[1] Scholars either translate the word ξένος as "Stranger" or "Visitor". I choose the second option for the three reasons stated by Blondell (2002, 319 n. 18): "(a) it captures this friendly yet liminal character more aptly; (b) it conveys the asymmetry of *xenos*, which is used only "by natives of the place in which it is spoken, to addressees who come from somewhere else" [...]; (c) it avoids the misleading resonances of the English "strange"." For the text of the *Statesman* I use the first volume of the OCT edition of Duke/Hicken/Nicoll/Robinson/Strachan 1995. I also use Benardete's (1984) translation.

yet any kind of civilisation or socio-political organisation. They do not breed but come directly out of the earth at an advanced age, and then, for the rest of their lives, gradually grow young and eventually return to the earth. In the other period, which is defined as the "Age of Zeus", the god-creator and his subordinate divinities decide to abandon the universe, while the latter subsequently begins moving by itself. Humans now breed through sexual intercourse and develop arts and political life in order to protect themselves from wild animals and the adversities of the natural environment, which ceases to offer them the abundance of goods they need for their survival. The Visitor ends his narration by explaining to Young Socrates that the message of the myth for the subject at stake (the definition of statesmanship) should be that the sole governor of humanity who can be taken to resemble a shepherd is the divine demiurge of the universe.

The myth is framed by the Visitor's introductory remarks (268d8–269c3) and an extensive digression that follows its narration and pertains to its narrating time (283b1–287b3). It also includes an abundance of authorial comments on the procedure through which it was composed. It thereby serves as a narrative paradigm that exemplifies the way in which the metanarrative reflections expressed in the opening statements and the excursus define the structuring of a narrative. The schemes on the basis of which this cosmological story unfolds and the metanarrative comments of the Visitor have been mostly overlooked by modern scholarship with regard to the picture they convey of Plato's view on the relationship between certain aspects of narrativity and the narrative's educational potential.

In this chapter, I argue that Plato builds an elaborate net of cross-references between, on the one hand, the plethora of metanarrative statements found both in the introductory remarks to the myth and after it, and, on the other hand, comments and narrative schemes within the myth. Through this cross-referencing Plato underlines (a) the three main aspects of narrativity that, according to formalist narratologists, distinguish a raw material from a coherent narrative whole (selectivity and creation of causal and temporal connections between the events of the plot) and (b) the issue of narrating/listening time and its relation to the audience's suspense, as defined by structuralist narratology. I first analyse the narrative arrangement of the myth (Section 1.1), and then present how the Visitor's reflections on the aforementioned aspects of narrativity define the myth's structure at its most pivotal points (Sections 1.2 and 1.3).

1.1 The narrative arrangement of the myth

One of the most distinctive characteristics of the myth lies in the spatial and temporal widening of the Visitor's gaze towards the universe.[2] On a temporal level, in order to juxtapose the limited capacity of humans in political affairs with the administrative perfection of the divine demiurge, the Visitor places the god in a period of time remote from that of the interlocutors. The narrator thereby leads Young Socrates to a distant past, in which the universe is administered by the god, and compares this phase with the present, which is marked by the imperfect self-administration of the *cosmos* and the inefficacy of human political life.[3] Young Socrates is thus invited not only to identify shepherding with an entity that is different from humans but also to search for it in a period beyond that of their own political existence. Furthermore, after structuring this antithetical relation between past and present, the Visitor broadens our temporal horizons further, by placing the *cosmos* in all three levels of time (past, present and future). This is so because, as he explains, these two phases of cosmic administration do not merely emerge from a temporal sequence which began in the past and was completed in the present; these two phases keep following each other *ad infinitum*.

This contrast between divine perfection and human deficiency in politics is accentuated even further by a simultaneous widening of the spatial horizon. The cosmic field of action, although being smoothly organised by its demiurge, cannot be fully controlled by humans in the absence of gods and troubles men through obstacles in their struggle for existence. One can easily perceive the contrast that Plato creates between the demiurge's competence in governing the universe in its entirety and the humans' difficulty in trying to cope with only the places they inhabit. By the end of this juxtaposition between divine and human nature within the space-time continuum, the Visitor's verdict that no man but only the god deserves the metaphor 'shepherd of humans' strikes Young Socrates as undoubtedly convincing. Scholars have exhaustively analysed the origins and meanings of this divergent material which the Visitor uses for the construction of his myth. It is thus today taken for granted that this account serves as the avenue for a plethora of information, which pertains to multiple fields such as

---

[2] Miller 1980, 36–37; Tomasi 1990, 355–356; Tulli 1991, 100; Rowe 1995, 11.
[3] Cf. Neiman 2007, 403; Speliotis 2011, 296. Lane (1998, 100 ff.) treats the two ages as an antithetical pair but in terms of human civilisation, so that they create a contrast between men and themselves in terms of how they live in each era and not an antithesis between gods and men, as I interpret it here.

cosmology, theology, anthropology and political theory.⁴ Nonetheless, what has not been much explored is the narrative structure of these elements' blending.

The account can be divided into two parts. In the first one, the Visitor presents what happens in the Age of Cronus (269c4–272d4), and in the second part what takes place in the Age of Zeus (272d4–274e3). Now, each of these segments is further divided into three sub-segments, which shape the route '*cosmos* → human nature into the *cosmos* → politics into the *cosmos*'.⁵ In essence, each time the Visitor initially sketches the universe as an all-encompassing whole (first sub-segment), into which he then places humanity, first in terms of biology (second sub-segment) and finally in terms of politics (third sub-segment).⁶

Let us begin with the Age of Cronus. From the very beginning of his narration, the Visitor broadens our gaze by realising a shift from the political microcosm of humans towards the wider movement of the universe. The world undergoes a circular movement around itself, initially under the guidance of its divine demiurge and, when the latter abandons it, by itself and in the opposite direction. The Visitor offers three reasons why the world changes direction. First, the world consists of soul and body. Its bodily nature is conditioned by an inherent tendency not to remain in the same state, in contrast to divine beings.⁷ Second, it is hard to believe that it is the god who changes direction in the world's movement, since the god can hardly do something opposite to what he had initially decided.⁸ Third, it is also hard to believe that the first movement is governed by a certain god and the opposite movement by another god, because such an assumption would entail the impossible condition that two gods act in an opposing way.⁹ So, according to the Visitor, what remains is that the one movement of the world is governed by the god and the other emerges as soon as the god abandons the world (269c4–270b2).

---

4 On the metaphysical and cultural-political nature of the myth, see Miller 1980, 35–53. See also Introduction.
5 Cf. Speliotis 2011, 297–298, who emphasises the transition in the myth from a macro- towards a micro-cosmic level of description. Cf. Gartner/Yau 2020, who describe this causal connection between what happens on these two levels as the "Correspondence Principle". For further bibliography, see Gartner/Yau 2020, 6 n. 13.
6 My division is closer to that of Verlinsky (2008, 58–60), who divides the story into six parts (apart from the introductory remarks of 268d5–269c2). Also, Benardete (1984 III, 96) divides the myth into seven parts. Rowe (1995, 12–13) offers, apart from the introduction, seven parts.
7 Rowe 1995, 189.
8 Rowe 1995, 189–190.
9 A typical view of Plato. Cf. *Ti.* 40a–b (on this parallelism, see Herter 1958, 108).

This stage (269c3–270b2) lacks any political colouring, although later on, as we will see, the divine demiurge is presented as a political entity. The absence of a political dimension in characterising the relationship between the universe and its creator is illustrated by the verbs with which the Visitor describes their activities. As far as the god is concerned, in total we find four verbs suggestive of the fact that he moves the world. The first two verbs are the συμποδηγεῖ and συγκυκλεῖ (269c5). The prefix σύν- in both these verbs mitigates the regulative role of the god over the world and rather foregrounds the auxiliary character of his activity ("joins in conducting this"; "he helps it revolve").[10] The other verbs used are also empty of any political connotation (269e6: κινεῖν; 270a2: στρέφειν). It is worth noting the co-ordinated fashion in which Plato uses half of them to denote merely the movement of the world (συμποδηγεῖ and κινεῖν) and the other half to explicate the nature of this movement (cyclic: συγκυκλεῖ and στρέφειν). Plato's special care for stylistic polishing is not oriented towards any kind of political relationship between the god and its creation but merely towards its global movement.

We find a single participle suggestive of the element of political power (269e6: ἡγουμένῳ). However, the Visitor does not use this verb to highlight the political dimension of the divine control over the *cosmos* but rather to assert that it is only the god (who controls all movements) who is able to move himself forever (269e5–6). Equally neutral in terms of political connotations are the two participles which refer to the process of the world's creation by the god (269d1–2: συναρμόσαντος; 269d9: γεννήσαντος). As already noted by modern scholarship, the first carries some kind of political load in that it anticipates the comparison which is made between the god and the human statesman as he will be defined in the last part of the dialogue (279a7–311c10).[11] However, up to this point there has been no link made between the act of fitting a number of elements together into a harmonious whole and statesmanship, so the Visitor should not be taken to use this verb in order to encourage Young Socrates to associate the god with how human statesmen were described in the investigation which preceded the myth.

The verbs referring to the universe are equally empty of political meanings (269c5: πορευόμενον; 269c7–d1: περιάγεται; 269d2, 270a6 and 270a9: ἰέναι; 269e3: κινεῖται; 269e5 and 269e9: στρέφειν; 269e9: στρέφεσθαι; 270a3–4: συ-μποδηγεῖσθαι; 270a6: ἀνεθῇ; 270a7: ἀφεθέντα; 270a7: πορεύεσθαι). Plato rather seems to use these words in order to create a cause-effect relationship between

---

10 The translation of συγκυκλεῖ is mine. Cf. Stewart 1905, 198; Herter 1958, 109.
11 On the divine demiurge as a political model for the statesman of the final definition, see Merrill 2003, 46–54 and Blondell 2005.

divine activity and global behaviour. This is at least evident in the pairs of verbs that emerge (269c5: the active voice συμποδηγεῖ for the god and 270a3–4: the passive voice συμποδηγεῖσθαι for the *cosmos*; 269c5: similarly, the active ἀνῆκεν for the god and 270a6–7: the passive ἀνεθῇ and ἀφεθέντα for the *cosmos*). We reach the same conclusion in assessing the phrase ὑπ' ἄλλης συμποδηγεῖσθαι αἰτίας (270a3–4), which stresses the causative quality of the relationship. Last, it is worth noting that Plato uses five verbs which have the god as their subject and thirteen verbs in which the subject is the world as such. The universal revolving is emphasised as a feature of the universe itself and less so as the work of its regulator. I do not infer that in this stage the Visitor underappreciates the god's absolute control over the world; my point is that he rather presents it from the natural scientist's point of view without sketching the god as the political being which he will become in the ensuing parts of the myth.

In the second stage, the Visitor shifts his interest towards human biology under the Age of Cronus.[12] In his opening remarks to the myth, he has revealed to Young Socrates that he will base his story, *inter alia*, on three myths: the one about the interchange of west and east, another about the rule of Cronus, and that on the earth-born men (268e8–269c2). He now explains to Young Socrates that the cause of the events described in the three myths is to be sought exactly at this change of direction in the world's circular movement, which is the greatest of all natural changes. The living beings, incapable as they are of remaining unaffected by such great changes, suffer certain alterations. In particular, in the period when the world is ruled by the god – a period which is defined as the opposite to the one in which the interlocutors live –, organisms cease to grow, become shorter and return to the earth. This is also the case for those who have an unnatural death. At this point, Young Socrates asks the Visitor how humans were born in this period, and the Visitor answers that they came directly out of the earth. Furthermore, the first men of the interlocutors' period, who partly coincided with the last earth-born men of the preceding era, preserved the stories about the earth-born men (270b3–271c2). Men are not only framed within the universe but are also presented as part of a wider category of living beings.

In the third and last stage of the narrative on the Age of Cronus (271c3–272d4), the interlocutors shift their interest for the first time towards the political implications of the aforementioned cosmological and biological details. The pivotal point lies in Young Socrates' question: he first asks the Visitor whether

---

12 Cf. Klein's (1977, 157 n. 27) comment that from this point onwards the Visitor shifts his interest exclusively towards men. He also discerns two further similar turning points at 273c8 and 274b2–4, on which see below in this chapter. Cf. Miller 1980, 37.

they should identify the popular phrase "the Age of Cronus" with the period of divine rule or with the one in which the universe revolves by itself. However, he expresses this question clearly from an anthropological perspective, since he essentially wants to know about men's way of life in that period (271c4–5: ἀλλὰ δὴ τὸν βίον ὃν ἐπὶ τῆς Κρόνου φῂς εἶναι δυνάμεως, πότερον ἐν ἐκείναις ἦν ταῖς τροπαῖς ἢ ἐν ταῖσδε; "but, more to the point, that life which you say was at the time of Cronus' power — was it in those revolutions or in these?").[13] This shift of interest is also evident in the Visitor's words. After Socrates' question, he begins to describe the way that the gods ruled the *cosmos* and its creatures under the Age of Cronus. Then, at the end of his description, he explains that he offered all this cosmological information because it will help them apprehend the state of human society in that time (271e3–5). With this comment the Visitor introduces his description of human society (see below).

Apart from Young Socrates' pivotal question and the Visitor's introductory comment, the shift of interest towards the political connotations of the myth is also achieved through a striking change in the vocabulary which the Visitor uses to describe the demiurge's regulative role in the universal motion. We saw that in the first stage the Visitor described the two modes of this motion by using verbs without any political content and cross-references between these verbs and the vocabulary he had used in his preceding definition of statesmanship. At this stage, he begins his narration by referring once again to this very relationship between the divine regulator and the revolving universe, replacing, however, the politically neutral verbs of the first stage with the words τότε γὰρ αὐτῆς πρῶτον τῆς κυκλήσεως ἦρχεν ἐπιμελούμενος ὅλης ὁ θεός (271d3–4: "at that time, the god who has it in his care first ruled the circling itself as a whole"). The verb ἦρχεν clearly has a political dimension, while the participle ἐπιμελούμενος echoes one of the distinctive activities of the human statesman/shepherd as it was delineated in the preceding chapters (261d6: ἐπιμέλειαν; 265e7: ὁ πολιτικὸς ἄρ' ἐπιμέλειαν ἔχειν φαίνεται; 267d8–9: ... ἦν ἡ πολιτικὴ καὶ μιᾶς τινος ἀγέλης ἐπιμέλεια; 268a2: ἐπιμελοῦνται on the pretenders of the statesman's power).

In the ensuing paragraphs of this stage, the Visitor penetrates further into the ways in which the gods govern the world and its beings. He offers clarifications about the hierarchy and the role of the co-governors, the nature of their administration, their relationship with the governed beings, and their duties. This description focuses generally, in terms of its content and style, on the polit-

---

13 On the pivotal role of this question between the different stages of the myth, see Rosen 1995, 52.

ical dimension of this relationship between gods and mortal beings. The leading god has assigned to his subordinate gods the rule of the earth, while they on their part are described as acting in obedience to his commands. These gods are also described as rulers, who administer separate areas of the world and govern the animals as if they are shepherds who take care of their herds. Each of these gods rules his region in a self-sufficient way, such that they can offer to their herds everything they need. As a result, the animals live in peace and are able to secure for themselves an abundance of goods necessary for their survival. They do not eat or fight with each other (271c8–e3).[14] Modern scholarship has elaborated on the vocabulary of political content with which the Visitor delineates the demiurge and the subordinate gods as divine shepherds.[15] However, it is also worth noting that this description appears only from the third stage of the Age of Cronus onwards.

At the end of this description of the divine rule, the Visitor proceeds in the way he suggested earlier, namely by revealing the anthropocentric goal of all this information (271e3–5: τὸ δ' οὖν τῶν ἀνθρώπων λεχθὲν αὐτομάτου πέρι βίου διὰ τὸ τοιόνδε εἴρηται "but, in any case, the story about the spontaneous livelihood (life) of human beings has been said on account of something of the following sort"). It is now time for him to explain what is useful about all these details on the god's rule for our understanding of what Young Socrates asked, namely the way that humans lived in that period. The ensuing narrative on humans' way of life (271e5–272d4) marks a shift of interest from the biological state of men we saw in the previous stage towards human civilisation, with special emphasis being laid on issues of socio-political organisation (or rather the lack thereof). The Visitor has just mentioned that there was no war between living beings, foreshadowing that this was also the case for humans both between themselves as well as against animals. Now, in focusing exclusively on humans, the Visitor adds the following: they had no families, as they came out from the earth, and no memory. Neither had they developed any kind of constitution, nor agriculture or any arts or sciences. They lived naked as animals, taking everything they needed from nature, which offered them all goods in abundance.

The Visitor narrates the Age of Zeus through the same scheme: '*cosmos* → human biology → human politics'. In this part of the account, the Visitor does not interrupt his narration in order to converse with Young Socrates. As previously demonstrated, up to this point of the myth the dialogue between the two

---

14 Gartner/Yau 2020.
15 Merrill 2003, 47; Miller 1980, 52–53. Blondell 2005, 31–44.

interlocutors does not interrupt the narration randomly but only marks the transition from the one stage to the next. Such transitions will from now on be effected by the comments of the Eleatic narrator. The first of these comments highlights the shift from the last stage of the account on the Age of Cronus to the first stage of the narrative on the Age of Zeus. After the Visitor completes his exposition on the absence of advanced socio-political structures in humans, he comments: "But the purpose for which we awakened the myth, this has to be said, in order that we may get on with the next thing that still lies ahead" (272d4–6).With these words we are introduced to the Age of Zeus and particularly the account's first stage (272d4–273e4), in which the Visitor describes the activities of the gods and universe. As soon as the period of the divine rule was completed, the story goes, the divine demiurge abandoned the universe and was followed by the subordinate gods who administered the individual areas of the world. The latter was now moved by fate and desire, but changed the direction of its rotation. During this transitional period, the world was disturbed by earthquakes, because of which every kind of mortal life suffered significant losses. However, when, after a great amount of time, the world's rotation was stabilised in its new direction, the world moved in such a way that it took care of itself and of the beings found in it. Now, since the universe partly consisted of a bodily nature, which it had already before the god put it in order, it is always prone to change and disintegration. For this reason, the world, remembering the excellent way in which it was governed by the god, administers itself and whatever exists in it in a smooth way only in the first period after it is abandoned by the demiurge. However, as time passes by, the world forgets the god's flawless rule and therefore leads itself and everything it consists of towards disorder and attrition. It is at this point that the god, fearing that the world will destroy itself, interferes periodically to take control of the world and move it again to the opposite direction.[16]

Contrary to the first stage of the account on the Age of Cronus, the focus on the wider universal canvas is not achieved by the absence of connections between the demiurge's and the universe's activity and the features of political conduct. Now, the divine creator, the subordinate gods, and even the universe itself, are all described by means of vocabulary which carries political connotations. The demiurge is presented as a governor (272e4: κυβερνήτης), specifically as the commander of a ship who abandons the handle of the rudder. The rest of the gods are sketched as co-governors (272e7: συνάρχοντες), while the Visitor once again stresses the fact that they take care of the world (273a1: τῆς αὑτῶν

---

[16] Miller 1980, 37 on 272b–d.

ἐπιμελείας), an act which, as we have seen, points to a statesman's duty to take care of his people, as explained by the Visitor in the definition that precedes the myth. Even the *cosmos* is delineated as administering itself (273a7–b1: ἐπιμέλειαν καὶ κράτος ἔχων αὐτός). The emergence of disorder after the demiurge's withdrawal is also expressed with a verb of political colouring (273c7: δυναστεύει). Nonetheless, the Visitor never refers to the political life of men. Similarly to the first stage of the account on the Age of Cronus, in this part of the Age of Zeus the narrator's goal is to focus on the macro-structure of the universe, which human nature and activity belongs to.

The transition to the developments in human biology is achieved through one further comment of the Visitor: "Now the end point of everything has been stated, and it's adequate for the showing forth of the king if we attach the speech to a remark previously made" (273e4–6). All the changes suffered by living organisms, humans included, are presented as being causally connected with the wider, universal developments which take place in the Age of Zeus. The direction of the world is now described from the perspective of how organisms give birth (273e7: τὴν ἐπὶ τὴν νῦν γένεσιν ὁδόν). As soon as the world followed this new rotation, the organisms' age started again and developed in the normal way. All the shifts that animals underwent in terms of pregnancy, birth and breeding (274a1–2: καὶ τὸ τῆς κυήσεως καὶ γεννήσεως καὶ τροφῆς μίμημα) are also presented as ramifications of the global evolution (274a2–3: συνείπετο τοῖς πᾶσιν ὑπ' ἀνάγκης). According to the Visitor, animals could no longer be born out of the earth, in the aid of nature. As the universe was now invited to organise itself, each species had to take care of its reproduction and perpetuation by itself.

The changes in the motion and organisation of the universe generate a new *status quo* in the biology of organisms, which, in turn, serves to bring about the emergence of humans' socio-political organisation. The transition from human nature in general towards politics is again realised by means of the narrator's transitional and introductory comment: "Now it's just here that we're at last at the point for the sake of which the whole speech set out" (274b1–2). As is commonly agreed by critics, the ensuing account resembles in many respects Protagoras' myth (*Prot.* 320c7–323a4) in the eponymous dialogue.[17] According to this myth, humans, without being now protected by their divine shepherds, fell prey to wild and much stronger animals. They also lacked those arts through which they could secure food for themselves, because, up to that point, there had been no need for them to search for goods by themselves, as they had been provided with them by the gods. So, in order to save them from extinction, the

---

17 See, e.g., Rowe 1995, 11–12.

gods offered humans celebrated gifts, such as fire by Prometheus and the arts of Hephaestus and Athena. Although in his myth Protagoras explicitly refers to specific facets of men's socio-political evolution, the Visitor offers no descriptions of this kind. In the *Protagoras*, we read that men, in their effort to save themselves from wild beasts, (a) begin establishing settlements, (b) develop the art of war, which belongs to the art of politics, and (c) are offered by Zeus shame and moderation as connecting bonds of harmony for their societies (*Prot.* 321c7–323a4). In the *Statesman*, however, the Visitor confines himself to the vague information that men should now take care of (274d4: τῆς ἐπιμελείας) and organise (274d5: διαγωγήν) themselves in compliance with the way in which the universe does so for itself. However, despite this vagueness, this stage, compared with the previous one's focus exclusively on human biology, brings to the fore issues such as crafts, material culture, self-preservation and organisation, all of which are inextricably related with men's socio-political organisation.

At this point, let us see what can be revealed by our structural analysis of the scheme '*cosmos* → human biology → politics' in terms of the way in which the myth serves as a narrative paradigm. If we read the myth through the prism of Socrates' digression about philosophers in the *Theaetetus* (172c3–177c5), we can observe how the myth exemplifies the way in which philosophers are described by Socrates to examine politics as part of the universe. In this digression, Socrates gradually reveals to the reader that philosophers zoom out on and broaden their gaze to the earth and sky, losing their interest in individual objects and organisms and conceiving the wider categories which the latter belong to. One from among these categories is human nature. A philosopher, in placing humans into the *cosmos*, realises the nonentity of their nature in comparison with the size of the world and shapes his view of human politics on the basis of exactly this realisation. The Visitor's myth in the *Statesman* constitutes a narrative paradigm of the way in which the scheme '*cosmos* → human biology → politics' can be conveyed through narrative discourse. It remains for us to see the Visitor's metanarrative reflections upon the process of this scheme's narrativization. In the ensuing section, it will be argued that, for the Visitor, the structuring of this kind of philosophical thinking in a narrative presupposes certain key principles which are also addressed by today's formalist narratologists.

1.2 The Visitor's speculations on turning raw material into a coherent narrative whole

The *Statesman* is indeed a special case within the Platonic corpus because it reveals how Plato regards narrative composition as a creative procedure in a formalistic fashion which heralds the ground-breaking narratological distinction between the so-called *fabula* and the *sujet*. The *Statesman* illustrates Plato's speculations on a central element of narrativity, and what for many is the very essence of narrative composition: the transformation of a raw mass of materials into a narrative whole. This narrative whole is marked by a specific temporal organisation of the events, clear-cut causative relationships between them, and a focused narrative goal. The Visitor's numerous metanarrative statements remind the reader how a gaze on human civilisation from a widened point of view can only be achieved after a careful and studied manipulation of countless stories of the past into a tight and coherent narrative.

Before examining these metanarrative comments in the *Statesman*, let us first touch upon some central aspects of modern narratological theories on the nature of narrative. Needless to say, a thorough *Forschungsbericht* of all versions of the dipole 'raw material (*fabula*) – plot (*sujet*)', as expressed by all schools or their most celebrated representatives, falls far beyond the goals of our analysis. I also find it unnecessary to adopt the terminology of a specific theory, as the terms with which the two parts of the dipole have usually been described differ from period to period. It is helpful, however, to examine those narratological observations on the matter which, independently of their terminology, constitute the common denominators of most versions of the theory in question and, most importantly, can be studied in conjunction with the Visitor's metanarrative comments in the *Statesman*.

Narratologists recognise that there are two distinguishable states in which the information which will contribute to a plot can be found. On the one hand, there is the state in which the material is found before being selected and incorporated into the plot by the composer/narrator. We may say that in this phase the material comprises all the events of a narrative in a temporally and causally unorganised form or in a form different from the one of the narrator's plot. This material may serve as the basis for different versions of a story as developed by different storytellers. For example, the events that took place during Socrates' trial served as the source of the two different versions of Plato's and Xenophon's *Apologies*. Furthermore, the fact that the *fabula* comprises all the events of a story entails that it includes *all* the events which happened to *all* the protagonists in a *plethora* of fields of action and in *countless* moments of time, whether simultaneously or in a temporal sequence. On the other hand, the *sujet* can be defined as the way in which these events are presented in an (oral or written) narrative form. In essence, this is an artificial representation of the *fabula*'s subject in the form of a plot; an elaborated version of the raw material of the *fabula*.[18]

It is noteworthy in this respect that the three basic principles on the basis of which the conversion of the raw material into organised narrative discourse is achieved are exactly those which are highlighted by Plato in the *Statesman*. These principles of narrative composition are: (a) selectivity, (b) the creation of a temporal organisation of the events, and (c) the moulding of causal relationships between them. With regard to selectivity, narratologists agree that a narrator is neither willing nor able to take advantage of all the information which may be included into a story.[19] The narrator chooses instead those details which, in her or his opinion, fit better with the narrative goals and the thematic orientation of the story she or he aspires to compose.[20] As soon as the composer distinguishes the data which is to be used from what is to be omitted, he or she is then invited to organise this material by its causal and temporal connections, none of which needs to follow the causal and temporal connections the events had at the state of the *fabula*.[21] It is worth noting that the narrator does not always create cause-effect relations and temporal sequences from scratch. She or he may indeed causally connect two incidents which had no such relationship in the *fabula*. Nonetheless, in some other cases the temporal and causal connections are not established out of nothing but replace other already existing ones. In such cases, we may speak of a temporal rearrangement and a reconsideration

---

18 The distinction between these two concepts was introduced by critics who represent what we today describe as Russian Formalism (for an overview see Schmid 2010, 175–185). Shklovsky (1929) distinguishes between *fabula* and *syuzhet*. He finds that "the fabula is, in fact, only material for syuzhet formulation" (1965, 57). Petrovsky inverts the meaning of the two terms (Schmid 2010, 180). Tomashevsky (Schmid 2010, 184–185). Cf. the distinction between *story* and *discourse* in Chatman 1978 and Schmid's (2010, 186–188) overview of the dipole *histoire/discours* in French Structuralism.
19 Russian Formalism: Shklovsky (1990, 206) notes that "The plot distorts the material by the very fact that it selects it"; Petrovsky 1987, 24–25: "above all, story (*syuzhet*) is selection"; Appelrot 1893, 75; Chatman 1978, 29–30; Todorov 1981, xi, 64; Pavel 1986, 68–69; Bal 1997^2, 182–183. For further examples of theorists of narrative who see narration as the product of selection, see Liveley's (2019) excellent study. Cf. Schmid 2010, 191–197.
20 Genette 1980, 187; Todorov 1981, xxii, xxviii; Schmid 2010, 197–198.
21 Causality: Genette 1980, 142–143, 232; Todorov 1981, 14, 41–46; Prince 1982, 66–67; Schmid 2010, 175–215. Temporality: Sternberg 1978; Genette 1980, 33–160; Todorov 1981, 27–32, 41–46; Prince 1982, 64–65; Bal 1997^2, 102–111; Schmid 2010, 175–215.

of the already existing cause-effect relationships. On a temporal level, some events which precede others in the *fabula* may be replaced at the end of the plot and *vice versa*. On a causal level, an event which survives in the *fabula* as the cause of another incident may be transformed from the cause to the result of an action. Narratologists traditionally trace the seeds of a proto-theory on the aspects of selectivity, causality and temporality to Aristotle's *Poetics*.[22] However, the *Statesman* (along with the *Laws*, see Chapter 3) shows that such a proto-theory may also be identified with Plato's views on narratives.

The Visitor explicitly recognises exactly these three aspects (selectivity, temporal arrangement and the creation of causality) as the main facets of narrativity, initially in his introductory remarks to the myth and, secondly, at some pivotal points of its plot. Let us begin with the opening statements (268d5–269c2):

> ΞΕ. Πάλιν τοίνυν ἐξ ἄλλης ἀρχῆς δεῖ καθ' ἑτέραν ὁδὸν πορευθῆναί τινα.
> ΝΕ. ΣΩ. Ποίαν δή;
> ΞΕ. Σχεδὸν παιδιὰν ἐγκερασαμένους· συχνῷ γὰρ μέρει δεῖ μεγάλου μύθου προσχρήσασθαι, καὶ τὸ λοιπὸν δή, καθάπερ ἐν τοῖς πρόσθεν, μέρος ἀεὶ μέρους ἀφαιρουμένους ἐπ' ἄκρον ἀφικνεῖσθαι τὸ ζητούμενον. οὐκοῦν χρή;
> ΝΕ. ΣΩ. Πάνυ μὲν οὖν.
> ΞΕ. Ἀλλὰ δὴ τῷ μύθῳ μου πάνυ πρόσεχε τὸν νοῦν, καθάπερ οἱ παῖδες· πάντως οὐ πολλὰ ἐκφεύγεις παιδιὰς[23] ἔτη.
> ΝΕ. ΣΩ. Λέγοις ἄν.
> ΞΕ. Ἦν τοίνυν καὶ ἔτι ἔσται τῶν πάλαι λεχθέντων πολλά τε ἄλλα καὶ δὴ καὶ τὸ περὶ τὴν Ἀτρέως τε καὶ Θυέστου λεχθεῖσαν ἔριν φάσμα. ἀκήκοας γάρ που καὶ ἀπομνημονεύεις ὅ φασι γενέσθαι τότε.
> ΝΕ. ΣΩ. Τὸ περὶ τῆς χρυσῆς ἀρνὸς ἴσως σημεῖον φράζεις.
> ΞΕ. Οὐδαμῶς, ἀλλὰ τὸ περὶ τῆς μεταβολῆς δύσεώς τε καὶ ἀνατολῆς ἡλίου καὶ τῶν ἄλλων ἄστρων, ὡς ἄρα ὅθεν μὲν ἀνατέλλει νῦν εἰς τοῦτον τότε τὸν τόπον ἐδύετο, ἀνέτελλε δ' ἐκ τοῦ ἐναντίου, τότε δὲ δὴ μαρτυρήσας ἄρα ὁ θεὸς Ἀτρεῖ μετέβαλεν αὐτὸ ἐπὶ τὸ νῦν σχῆμα.
> ΝΕ. ΣΩ. Λέγεται γὰρ οὖν δὴ καὶ τοῦτο.
> ΞΕ. Καὶ μὴν αὖ καὶ τήν γε βασιλείαν ἣν ἦρξε Κρόνος πολλῶν ἀκηκόαμεν.
> ΝΕ. ΣΩ. Πλείστων μὲν οὖν.
> ΞΕ. Τί δέ; τὸ τοὺς ἔμπροσθεν φύεσθαι γηγενεῖς καὶ μὴ ἐξ ἀλλήλων γεννᾶσθαι;
> ΝΕ. ΣΩ. Καὶ τοῦτο ἓν τῶν πάλαι λεχθέντων.
> ΞΕ. Ταῦτα τοίνυν ἐστὶ μὲν σύμπαντα ἐκ ταὐτοῦ πάθους, καὶ πρὸς τούτοις ἕτερα μυρία καὶ τούτων ἔτι θαυμαστότερα, διὰ δὲ χρόνου πλῆθος τὰ μὲν αὐτῶν ἀπέσβηκε, τὰ δὲ διεσπαρμένα εἴρηται χωρὶς ἕκαστα ἀπ' ἀλλήλων. ὃ δ' ἐστὶ πᾶσι τούτοις αἴτιον τὸ πάθος οὐδεὶς εἴρηκεν, νῦν δὲ δὴ λεκτέον· εἰς γὰρ τὴν τοῦ βασιλέως ἀπόδειξιν πρέψει ῥηθέν.

---

22 See Liveley 2019.
23 Instead of the OCT's (1995) παιδίας, I follow Campbell's reading παιδιὰς in agreement with the παιδιὰν of 268d8 (the verb ἐκφεύγεις is of no help in this case, as it can be followed by both a genitive and an accusative). For further versions of this passage, see OCT 1995, 494.

VIS: So we have to proceed again from a different beginning on some other way.
SO: What sort exactly?
VIS: By a mixture pretty near to child's play, for we have to make use of a large part of a big myth, and then afterwards, just as before, by continually removing part from part come at the summit to that which is being sought. Mustn't we?
SO: Yes, of course.
VIS: Well, then, pay very close attention to my myth, just as children do. It is in any case not many years since you've fled from child's play.
SO: You must speak.
VIS: Well, then, of ancient stories, there was, among many different ones which occurred and will recur, the particular case of the portent in the storied strife between Atreus and Thyestes. You've surely heard of it and remember what they say occurred at the time.
SO: Perhaps you're pointing at the sign about the golden ram.
VIS: No, not at all, mine pertains to the change in the setting and rising of the sun and the rest of the stars — the place, the story goes, from which it now rises was at that time where it set, and it rose from the opposite side, and that was the time when the god testified for Atreus and changed it into its present scheme.
SO: Yes, this too is indeed said.
VIS: And we've heard as well from many of the kingdom which Cronus ruled.
SO: From most, rather.
VIS: And what of this? That those before grew up earth-born and were not generated from one another?
SO: Yes, this too is one of the ancient stories.
VIS: Well, all these together are from the same state of affairs[24] (and besides these there are thousands of others still more astonishing than these), but, on account of the length of time, some of them have been extinguished and some have undergone a dispersal and been spoken of severally apart from one another. But no one has stated the state of affairs which is the cause for all these things, but it must at last be said, for once it's stated it will eminently fit in with the showing forth of the king.
SO: You put it most beautifully, and without omitting anything, speak.

In what follows, we will analyse the way in which each of the three aforementioned aspects of narrativity is foregrounded in these introductory remarks and then in the myth.

1.2.1 Selectivity

In the *Statesman*, the theme of selectivity shows itself in at least two stages of the composition of a narrative: (a) in the process of searching for the appropriate material in its raw form, and (b) in the process of incorporating the selected

---

[24] I replaced Benardete's "affect" with "state of affairs".

material into the overall arrangement of the plot under construction. In the build-up to the myth, the emphasis is clearly laid upon the first stage. Throughout this section several statements foreground the notion of selectivity as a fundamental factor for the composition of the ensuing account. The very first comment of the Visitor is that he will have to select only a part from a more extensive story (268d8–9: συχνῷ γὰρ μέρει δεῖ μεγάλου μύθου προσχρήσασθαι, "for we have to make use of a large part of a big myth"; cf. 277b4–5: θαυμαστὸν ὄγκον ἀράμενοι τοῦ μύθου). As mentioned above, some modern narratologists define the raw material as the totality of events which pertain to a story, and recognise that the eventual story emerges from the process of choosing only some events of the *fabula* (and omitting others). Similarly, Plato presents the myth to the reader as emerging from the selection of only a part of a story.[25] It is unclear, of course, whether the Visitor, by using the term μύθου, means a narrative which has already been composed by himself or someone else, or a story on the universe which circulated orally and could serve as a source of various versions.[26] It is not even clear whether the term suggests a narrative at all, given that in Plato it very often denotes the thoughts expressed by someone in oral or written discourse, whether expressed as a story, a lecture or a conversation.[27] Nonetheless, the Visitor here seems to treat this μῦθος as a body of material which could serve as a *fabula*, from which a composer can select those elements which fit with his philosophical goals.

Besides the information about where the myth came from as a whole, its individual details and episodes are also introduced as the result of selection. The Visitor allows Young Socrates to enter his compositional laboratory. He does not narrate to him the story immediately but first helps him understand that the creation of a myth requires material to be selected and then carefully incorporated into the plot.[28] So, he starts by listing three stories, in a deliberately unconnected and vague fashion: that of Atreus and Thyestes, another on the Age of Cronus and a last one that people were once born from the earth. It is as if the Visitor says to the boy: "Let us just pick some stories, which will serve as the three "basic ingredients"[29] for our myth; let us first take this one, then this one, etc."

---

25 Although many scholars believe (and I agree) that the myth is Plato's own fabrication. See Schuhl 1932, 47. See, *contra*, Herter 1958, 108.
26 Stewart (1905, 174) takes the term as meaning 'story' and thus translates as 'tale' (177).
27 Cf. Rowe 1995, 186. Robinson (2003, 47) takes μῦθος as meaning "narrative" ("racconto").
28 On the Visitor's emphasis in the build-up on his intention to incorporate the three stories in his myth, see Hemmenway 1994, 259.
29 To use Rowe's (1995, 12) wording. Cf. Lane 1998, 101 n. 3. Zuckert (2009, 186) also seems to take the myth as the Visitor's effort to rearrange the three stories of the build-up — at least this

The first story, on the quarrel of Atreus and Thyestes, is presented as one from among many other tales (268e8–10: ἦν τοίνυν καὶ ἔτι ἔσται τῶν πάλαι λεχθέντων πολλά τε ἄλλα καὶ δὴ καὶ τὸ περὶ τὴν Ἀτρέως τε καὶ Θυέστου ἔριν φάσμα, "well, then, of ancient stories, there were and there will be many others but also the particular case of the portent in the storied strife between Atreus and Thyestes"). This is also the case with the tale about the earth-born men, which is presented by Young Socrates as a single example from among a group of stories (269b4: καὶ τοῦτο ἓν τῶν πάλαι λεχθέντων, "yes, this too is one of the ancient stories"). Throughout the introductory section Plato also repeatedly underlines the multitude of material from which the teacher is invited to select the parts of his narrative (268d9: μεγάλου μύθου; 268e9: πολλά τε ἄλλα; 269b6: ἕτερα μύρια).[30]

The way in which the myth of Atreus and Thyestes is introduced (268e8–269a6) may help us to examine more clearly Plato's views on the procedure of selecting the data to be narrated. Based on the sources we have today on the story of the Pelopidae, the *fabula* from which the Visitor invites Young Socrates to select some material may be reconstructed as follows. Firstly, Atreus wished to offer a lamb as a sacrifice to Artemis. Then, while searching among his herd, he discovered that there was in the flock a golden lamb. He entrusted it to his wife to hide it from the goddess. His wife, however, gave it to her husband's brother and her lover Thyestes. Later, when the two brothers were in conflict over who should take the throne, Atreus argued that he should be the king because he had at his disposal a golden lamb, which was interpreted as a sign of divine favour. Thyestes, however, who had the animal, took the throne and told his brother that he would never bestow him his power unless the sun rises from where it sets. Zeus, in support of Atreus, changed the direction of the sun's route and Atreus thereby regained the throne.[31]

The theme of the two brothers' quarrel over the throne fits very well with the *Statesman*'s conversation at this point. In the previous chapters (257a1–268d4), the Visitor and Young Socrates' efforts to define statesmanship have reached a dead end. The Visitor determines that they should not identify the statesman with a shepherd because the latter is the unquestionable governor of a herd which is of nature inferior to his own, while the first is questioned by the people he governs and, what is more, some of them even claim his leadership.

---

is what I understand in her words that "he has retold and reinterpreted three old stories" (cf. *ibid*, 191). A similar approach is adapted by Speliotis (2011), who argues that "the Stranger's myth is constructed, or reported" (*ibid*. 297 n. 4).
30 Schmid 2010.
31 For the surviving sources about the myth and its different versions, see Gantz 1993, 545–548.

At the end of this exchange, the Visitor poses the question of what qualities distinguish a true statesman from his pretenders (267e1–268c11). Seen against this light, the myth of the Pelopidae as a story of two contenders to power is highly appropriate. First, it describes a claim of not just any kind of political power but what is discussed by the interlocutors, i.e. statesmanship or kingship. Second, the mythical example of the twin brothers also seems to strike at the heart of the issue. Atreus and Thyestes are not only brothers but also twins, so it is difficult for someone to decide which of them had the right to rule, since this cannot be decided by the question who was the firstborn son of Pelops. Third, the story includes two incidents which at first sight seem to help our understanding of the criterion whereby a statesman or king should be distinguished from other people: (a) the golden lamb, as a sign of potential supernatural origin and perhaps of divine favour, and (b) the change of the spots of west and east, which is explicitly presented as the expression of divine favour towards the true king.[32]

In this context, Young Socrates' association of the golden lamb with divine favour is a thought which many Greeks could have made if invited, as he is, to find what part of the story about Atreus and Thyestes is relevant to the question of what distinguishes a statesman from his pretenders.[33] At first sight, it seems that this is one of the many moments of Young Socrates' bluntness in investigation in the *Statesman*.[34] However, in this case Plato wishes to present the Visitor as remedying not the boy's inanity or his unwillingness to think, but a widely established way of approaching the mythical past in Greece.[35]

A principle followed by the Visitor is that one should only select material which will contribute to the definition of the category under examination. This view is strengthened by one further connection between the *Theaetetus* and the *Statesman*. Socrates, in his portrait of the philosopher, explained to Theodorus that the role of a philosopher in examining political issues is to help his interlocutor to move beyond the question of whether or not a ruler is happy or whether or not he possesses gold, and to lead him to the question of what kingship is (*Theaet.* 175b8–c8):

---

32 Dorter 1994, 194; Zuckert 2009, 187.
33 Dorter 1994, 195; Rowe 1995, 187; Zuckert 2009, 186.
34 On this theme, see Miller 1980, 7–34; Tomasi 1990, 350; Hemmenway 1994, 254–256. On Young Socrates' passive role in the conversation as a sign of Plato's indifference to the dramatic power of dialogic discourse in his late works, see Rowe 1995, 9–11; Blondell 2002, 328, 332.
35 See Miller's (1980, xiv) view that the discussants of Plato's dialogues are "his interpretive representations of aspects of contemporary culture", a view Miller expresses in a context where he refers to Young Socrates as well.

The Visitor's speculations on turning raw material into a coherent narrative whole — 19

ΣΩ. Ὅταν δέ γέ τινα αὐτός, ὦ φίλε," ἑλκύσῃ ἄνω, καὶ ἐθελήσῃ τις αὐτῷ ἐκβῆναι ἐκ τοῦ "Τί ἐγὼ σὲ ἀδικῶ ἢ σὺ ἐμέ;" εἰς σκέψιν αὐτῆς δικαιοσύνης τε καὶ ἀδικίας, τί τε ἑκάτερον αὐτοῖν καὶ τί τῶν πάντων ἢ ἀλλήλων διαφέρετον, ἢ ἐκ τοῦ "εἰ βασιλεὺς εὐδαίμων," "κεκτημένος τ' αὖ χρυσίον," βασιλείας πέρι καὶ ἀνθρωπίνης ὅλως εὐδαιμονίας καὶ ἀθλιότητος ἐπὶ σκέψιν, ποίω τέ τινε ἐστὸν καὶ τίνα τρόπον ἀνθρώπου φύσει προσήκει τὸ μὲν κτήσασθαι αὐτοῖν, τὸ δὲ ἀποφυγεῖν [...].

SO: But when, my friend, he draws a man upwards and the other is willing to rise with him above the level of "What wrong have I done you or you me?" to the investigation of abstract right and wrong, to inquire what each of them is and wherein they differ from each other and from all other things, or above the level of "Is a king happy?" or, on the other hand, "Has he great wealth?" to the investigation of royalty and of human happiness and wretchedness in general, to see what the nature of each is and in what way man is naturally fitted to gain the one and escape the other [...].[36]

In a similar vein, the Visitor helps Young Socrates to abandon his materialistic approach that associates kingship with the golden lamb and take up the more general issue of what statesmanship or kingship is. In both the *Theaetetus* and the *Statesman*, Plato dismisses people's conventional proneness to look for the very essence of statesmanship in the possession of material elements. In the *Theaetetus*, Plato's criticism of this practice among his contemporaries is expressed explicitly, through Socrates' words, while the part of the *Statesman* under examination constitutes a dramatisation of this criticism. What is more, in the *Statesman* the reader is led to the conclusion that, as soon as one realises that the essence of the political *techne* is not to be sought in the possession of material elements, one will cease to detect the political value of myths in their parts where a king's wealth is highlighted. In this way, one will be better primed to discern those parts of such myths which are truly significant for our apprehension of the political *techne*.

It is worth noting at this point that in the *Theaetetus* the philosopher is presented by Socrates as rejecting wealth as a sign of social prestige because he regards the quantity of a man's wealth (land) as trivial in comparison with the vast quantity of this natural element (earth) found in the *cosmos* (*Theaet.* 174e2-5). So, the philosopher may also reject gold with the same logic. Instead, he believes that the issue of a statesman's happiness should be examined from the broader perspective of the examination of statesmanship as a category. Last but not least, kingship a as category should in turn be examined as part of a wider category, i.e. human nature (175c5-6: βασιλείας πέρι καὶ ἀνθρωπίνης ὅλως εὐδαιμονίας καὶ ἀθλιότητος ἐπὶ σκέψιν). Hence, the logic which the philosopher

---

[36] Fowler's (1921) translation.

uses to reject wealth as an element suggestive of the statesman's nature should be traced in the philosopher's practice of examining categories through the route we demonstrated in the previous section: (a) examination of the *cosmos* → (b) examination of human nature as a part of the *cosmos* → (c) examination of statesmanship as a part of human nature, which is a part of the *cosmos*.

Now, in the prologue to the myth in the *Statesman*, the Visitor dissuades Young Socrates from treating the golden lamb as a means of distinguishing a statesman and his pretenders and thereby implies that it would be more appropriate for them to choose from the *fabula* the information about the alteration of the east and west. In essence, he encourages him to do exactly what a philosopher urges his student to do in the *Theaetetus* (175c4–6: ἐκβῆναι ... ἐκ τοῦ "εἰ βασιλεὺς εὐδαίμων," "κεκτημένος τ' αὖ χρυσίον," βασιλείας πέρι ... ἐπὶ σκέψιν, "to rise with him above the level of ... "Is a king happy?" or, on the other hand, "Has he great wealth?" to the investigation of royalty... in general").

Further, the alteration of west and east is treated throughout the myth as an element which reveals much about human nature and consequently about political expertise. As we have already seen, the change of the sun's direction belongs to those phenomena which manifest changes of the world's direction. This shift brought about radical changes in human nature with serious ramifications for men's political organisation in each age. The change of the sun's direction (examination of the *cosmos*) is therefore information from the Pelopidae *fabula* which offers answers about the category 'human nature' (examination of human nature as a part of the *cosmos*) and thus about the category 'political expertise' (examination of political expertise as a part of human nature which is a part of the *cosmos*). The selection of this material is motivated by the degree to which it contributes to the definition of the category in question.[37]

We may also discern one further procedure which Plato seems to take as being of crucial importance in the selection of the *fabula*'s material. Plato seems to recognise the fact that, in the process of selecting the material, the composer/narrator is sometimes invited to separate some events from consolidated narrative schemes of the tradition they belong to.[38] The shift of the sun's direction is detached from the story of Atreus and Thyestes. Now, in the cosmic myth this detail is not associated with the tale of the two brothers; it has been transformed into an element which is totally independent from the story from which it was drawn. In other words, this information has now been liberated from the role it

---

37 Cf. Rosen 1995, 41.
38 Cf. Miller 1980, 36.

had in the plot-development of the initial story.³⁹ In the *fabula* of Atreus and Thyestes the shift of the sun's direction has a special meaning in deciding who the legitimate king is, since it reflects the divine favour which the king enjoys.⁴⁰ However, the Visitor does not select this information in order to take advantage of this meaning; instead, he uses this element as a datum on the cosmic processes which affect human nature and not as the manifestation of divine favour. We may therefore trace one further principle which, in Plato's mind, defines the process of selecting the material from the *fabula*: the composer/narrator has to avoid being distracted by the seeming usefulness of some material in defining a category, as this usefulness seems to emerge from the role the material has in the economy of the story in which it is found.

Before turning to the main body of the myth, let us recapitulate our conclusions on Plato's views on selectivity as they are discerned in the myth's introduction. Plato highlights the following principles of selectivity: (a) the composer should select from the *fabula* material which contributes to the definition of the category in question; (b) she or he should also omit data which is of no help in this respect (e.g. golden lamb); (c) the composer sometimes breaks off such material from consolidated plots found in the *fabula*; (d) in such cases, the composer should free, if necessary, the selected material from its function in the plot development of the narrative it is taken from; and (e) she or he should also not be lured by the seeming usefulness of the selected material for examining the category in question, a usefulness which seems to emerge from the material's role in the story-line of the account in which it is found.

All these principles pertain to the stage in which the composer selects the material to be narrated from the *fabula*. On the other hand, as already noted, the aspect of selectivity also governs the composer's choices in a second phase, namely the process of narrating, when the composer of the plot turns into its narrator and is invited to proceed with a different kind of selection. Here, from the already selected material he will choose what he will narrate in detail and what he will pass by or mention in a fleeting way. This selection procedure is repeatedly underlined by the Visitor within the myth itself. At five points of his account he offers a self-referential comment, in which he shares with Young Socrates and the reader his concern about what events he should stress and what others to deemphasise. Even more importantly, the Visitor expresses his thoughts on the matter at the most pivotal moments of his account, in those

---

39 Benardete 1984 III, 96; Lane 1998, 113–114; Speliotis 2011, 297.
40 On this and other functions of the sun's μεταβολή in the mythical tradition, see Willink 1986, 254 followed by Rowe 1995, 187.

transitional parts from the one stage to the other. In the previous section, we saw that the Visitor marks most of these transitions with metanarrative comments. It is very interesting in this respect that the majority of these comments are accompanied by an additional statement that, in order to achieve the transition, the Visitor will have to omit some events and focus on others.

Let us present the passages in question. In the first shift of interest from the *cosmos* to human nature, the Visitor stresses the fact that the change of the subject requires the omission of much information and the selection of a single one. In particular, when he relates that the shift of the universe's direction causes certain changes in the humans' cycle of reproduction, the Visitor explains that he chooses this detail from among many others. What is more, he offers this explanation twice (270c11–d4). In the first case, he comments that the changes which humans suffer belong to a larger category of changes, which pertain to all living beings. In this way, he helps his audience understand that, in an account whose goal is to place humanity within the framework of natural environment, the narrator should zoom in on human nature over the effects caused to other animals. This message is evident in the words "the greatest destructions ... not only of the rest of the animals, but in particular the genus of human beings" (270c11–13: φθοραί ... μέγισται ... τῶν τε ἄλλων ζῴων, καὶ δὴ καὶ τὸ τῶν ἀνθρώπων γένος). Further, after moving from the general picture of animals to humans, he states that from all the changes that humans suffer he has now to choose again only one which is useful for the logic of the myth, i.e. humans' emergence from the earth (270d1–3: ἄλλα τε παθήματα πολλὰ καὶ θαυμαστὰ καὶ καινά ... μέγιστον δὲ τόδε, "many different circumstances, marvelous and strange ... but here is the greatest one"). These two comments create echoes of the introductory remarks: the τῶν τε ἄλλων ... καὶ δὴ καὶ τό (270c12) echo the τε ἄλλα καὶ δὴ καὶ τό of the build-up (268e9); the ἄλλα τε παθήματα πολλά (270d1–2) echo the πολλά τε ἄλλα of the introduction (268e9); and the ἄλλα ... πολλὰ καὶ θαυμαστά echo the ἕτερα μύρια ... θαυμαστότερα of the introduction (269b6–7).

The same principle is also evident in the transition from the political organisation of the *cosmos* towards that of the humans in the third stage in the description of the Age of Cronus. As we saw, according to the Visitor, the divine rule has certain effects on the state of the living beings (absence of war, peace, etc.). When the Visitor shifts his interest towards the political organisation of men, he says that "to tell of all the different things that are consequences of an arrangement of this sort would be to speak of thousands and thousands. But, in any case, the story about the spontaneous livelihood (life) of human beings ..." (271e2–4: ἄλλα θ' ὅσα τῆς τοιαύτης ἐστὶ κατακοσμήσεως ἑπόμενα, μυρία ἂν εἴη

The Visitor's speculations on turning raw material into a coherent narrative whole — 23

λέγειν. τὸ δ' οὖν τῶν ἀνθρώπων ...). The words ἄλλα ... μυρία (271e2–3) echo the words ἕτερα μυρία of the opening remarks (269b6). Similarly to the previous transition, the Visitor explains to Young Socrates that the route '*cosmos* — human nature — human politics' involves the omission of material which is irrelevant to this transition and the focusing on information which serves it, i.e. data on humanity.

In the transition from this last stage of the Age of Cronus to the one which opens the Age of Zeus, the Visitor once again touches upon the issue of selectivity. He has just completed his description of how men lived under the age of Cronus, and now he proceeds to give a digression concerning whether or not those men were engaged with philosophy. From the very beginning, he clarifies that he will express his own speculations on the matter, speculations which are difficult to prove due to the lack of evidence. For this reason, after revealing his understanding of the issue, he urges Young Socrates to abandon this theme and return to the main subject of the narrative: "But all the same, however this may be, let's disregard it, until some competent informant comes to light for us and reveals in which of the two ways those then had their desires about the sciences and the use of speeches. But the purpose for which we awakened the myth, this has to be said [...]" (272d1–5). With these words, the Visitor addresses one further criterion by which one should omit or choose the material to be narrated, i.e. the degree of its closeness to the truth.

In the transition from the universal picture of the Age of Zeus to the biological state of men, the Visitor proceeds with a comment similar to previous ones: "And everything else altered as well, in imitation and in consequence of the affect of the all, and in particular the imitation of conception, generation and nurture followed them all by necessity" (273e12–274a3: καὶ τἆλλά τε πάντα μετέβαλλε ... καὶ δὴ καὶ τὸ τῆς κυήσεως καὶ γεννήσεως καὶ τροφῆς). Finally, in the immediately ensuing transition from human biology to human civilisation and politics, he says again: "For about all the rest of the beasts, it would prove to be too much and too long to go through, from what and on account of what causes they have severally altered, but about human beings it's shorter and more appropriate" (274b1–5). In this example and in 271e2–4, the Visitor's choice of verbs shows how he fashions himself not as a composer but as a narrator (271e3: ἂν εἴη λέγειν; 274b3: ἂν ... διεξελθεῖν γίγνοιτο). Thus, in the myth itself selectivity is emphasised both when the aspiring storyteller selects his material from the *fabula* and when he incorporates it within his *sujet*. These verbs lay emphasis on the second procedure. All these passages may serve for us as strong evidence that in Plato's view selectivity has a central role in the structuring of the model 'cosmos – human nature – human politics' and, by extension, of narratives in general.

1.2.2 Causality

In the last part of his introduction to the myth, the Visitor claims that the three stories about the Pelopidae, the Age of Cronus and the earth-born men, as well as countless others, have either been lost or survived in a disconnected and fragmentary fashion (269b7–9: τὰ μὲν αὐτῶν ἀπέσβηκε, τὰ δὲ διεσπαρμένα εἴρηται χωρὶς ἕκαστα ἀπ' ἀλλήλων). He also promises that he will offer a narration of these events which will restore their true causal connection (269b9–c1: ὃ δ' ἐστὶν πᾶσι τούτοις αἴτιον ... νῦν δὲ δὴ λεκτέον). This metanarrative promise is the subject of this section. However, in order to be able to examine the subtle choices which Plato's narrators are expected to make in organising their material in a causally coherent way, we should first consider the emphasis given to the inability of human memory as one of the main reasons for the fragmentary state of the raw material. The Visitor argues that the three stories and many others circulate in a disconnected way due the enormity of time (269b7: διὰ δὲ χρόνου πλῆθος) and because people have forgotten the linkages between these events (269b8: ἀπέσβηκε).[41]

The view that memory explains the unorganised state of the material in the *fabula* in many respects resembles Mieke Bal's treatment of the *fabula* as a "memorial trace". According to Bal, "it is the way of the text that the reader has access to the story of which the *fabula* is, so to speak, a memorial trace that remains with the reader after completion of the reading".[42] There is no need to limit ourselves in our understanding of the scope of the terms "reader" and "reading". Bal would agree that these terms are used in a conventional fashion and may denote multiple kinds of narratees and many ways in which a story is received.[43] Thus, Bal seems to cite as the main reason for the *fabula*'s form the fact that the receivers of a narrative forget.[44] Yet, they do not forget everything because, in that case, we could preserve no story in the passing of time.[45] However, they

---

[41] Cf. *Phaedr.* 264b3–e2 on the lack of causal connections of different parts of a speech from a structural point of view.
[42] Bal 1997², Preface to the second edition, xv.
[43] See, e.g., Bal 1997², 38, 100 and 222, where she refers to listeners.
[44] Bal 1997², 115–118, 147–148.
[45] Schmid 2010, 178–180.

forget a sufficient amount that the *fabula* is no longer the same as the narrative whom it is a memorial trace of. Such an approach transfers, I would say, the focal point of our interest from the transformation of the *fabula* into *sujet* towards the converse procedure of turning the *sujet* into *fabula*. The *sujet* as a concept is no longer treated merely as the result of organising the material of the *fabula* in narrative form; the *sujet* also serves as the source of the *fabula*'s origin. With these words, Bal aptly illustrates the circular way in which these two states of a story's material constantly generate each other.[46]

In the introduction, the Visitor invites Young Socrates and the reader to realise that the myth is part of this circle '*sujet* — *fabula* — *sujet*'. We saw that the three stories which will be integral parts of his account are now arranged paratactically and lack any causal or temporal connection between each other (268e8–269b4). In essence, this paratactic exposition constitutes a short *fabula* which will later be turned into a coherent narration. This *fabula* goes as follows: "Once upon a time, the sun and the stars changed direction. And once upon a time there was also the Age of Cronus. And once upon a time there were also earth-born men." This simplistic *fabula* will be transformed into the following *sujet*: "Once upon a time the universe changed the direction of its revolving. For this reason, the sun and the stars changed direction and two ages emerged. One of these epochs is the Age of Cronus, in which the earth-born men lived."[47]

The Visitor explains that this *fabula*, which lacks any causal and temporal connection between its events, stemmed from the passage of time. All these events were once narrated, but this was a long time ago. As a result, humans throughout the centuries forgot the ways in which these stories were causally and temporally linked to each other, a fact from which the short *fabula* arrayed by the Visitor emerged. However, the latter programmatically clarifies his intention to gather these events and to narrate them in close association to one another.[48] He essentially explains that in composing his myth he will complete the circle '*sujet* — *fabula* — *sujet*'. The initial *sujets* should be traced in the old stories (268e8: τῶν πάλαι λεχθέντων) which once connected all these events to each other. Nonetheless, as time passed by, those remote stories were forgotten

---

[46] Cf. Schmid 2010, 178.
[47] On the Visitor's intention to causally connect these stories, cf. Schuhl 1932, 54; Rosen 1995, 40–42.
[48] Benardete 1984 III, 96.

and there were left only some 'memorial traces', i.e. paratactic *fabulas* of them, such as the list offered by the Visitor in 268e8–269b4.⁴⁹

As the Visitor claims, his myth's main contribution to the narrative tradition of these stories lies in the fact that it will restore the causal relationships which connect these three stories and others as well (269b5–c2):⁵⁰

> Ταῦτα τοίνυν ἔστι μὲν σύμπαντα ἐκ ταὐτοῦ πάθους, καὶ πρὸς τούτοις ἕτερα μυρία καὶ τούτων ἔτι θαυμαστότερα, διὰ δὲ χρόνου πλῆθος τὰ μὲν αὐτῶν ἀπέσβηκε, τὰ δὲ διεσπαρμένα εἴρηται χωρὶς ἕκαστα ἀπ' ἀλλήλων. ὃ δ' ἐστὶν πᾶσι τούτοις αἴτιον τὸ πάθος οὐδεὶς εἴρηκεν, νῦν δὲ δὴ λεκτέον· εἰς γὰρ τὴν τοῦ βασιλέως ἀπόδειξιν πρέψει ῥηθέν.

> Well, all these together are from the same state of affairs (and besides these there are thousands of others still more astonishing than these), but, on account of the length of time, some of them have been extinguished and some have undergone a dispersal and been spoken of severally apart from one another. But no one has stated the state of affairs which is the cause for all these things, but it must at last be said, for once it's stated it will eminently fit in with the showing forth of the king.

At this point, we may trace a distant forefather of formalist narratologists' interest in the fact that the main difference between the raw state of the material to be narrated and the narrative in which it is incorporated lies in that, in the latter, the narrator restores the causal linkages which are faint or even absent from the former. Although the Visitor seems at first sight to boast that the kind of causality which he will propose is totally original (269b9–c1: οὐδεὶς εἴρηκεν),⁵¹ it should be doubted whether or not he indeed means that no one in the past connected the three stories in the way that he does. All these stories are repeatedly presented as "old sayings" (268e8 and 269b4: τῶν πάλαι λεχθέντων). This phrase is of little help in our effort to penetrate into the circumstances under which those stories had circulated up to the moment the Visitor decided to narrate them as a whole. Had they *always* been narrated separately one from the

---

49 On memory as a prerequisite for the narration of past events, cf. *Parm.* 126b8–c3; *Symp.* 178a1–5 and 180c1–2; *Phaedr.* 227d6–228d5; *Euthyd.* 275c5–d4, 280b1–3, 290e1–291a7.
50 Plato was well aware of the fact mentioned by Stewart (1905, 173) that the myth of the *Statesman* has an 'aetiological' orientation. Although Petrucci (2004, 114) seems to treat this goal and that of restoring the errors of the preceding divisions as mutually exclusive, a more economical and realistic interpretation, which also takes into consideration the multi-layered goal setting of Plato's dialogues, is to accept that the myth serves both ends.
51 This is the view of Tomasi (1990, 349, 357), who describes the Visitor's introductory remarks as "fiction-presenting signals" (354). Rosen (1995, 2) describes the myth as "a bizarre fairy tale" and Rowe (1995, 187) claims that the story is to be taken as new.

other?[52] The Visitor argues that the passage of the centuries erased all causal relationships which those stories had. However, how had men narrated them before? Was there any period in which this material (the change of the sun's and stars' direction, the Age of Cronus and the earth-born men) was still narrated as part of a coherent narrative whole?

Perhaps the most economical interpretation, although not the most faithful to the text, would be to say that the words οὐδεὶς εἴρηκεν should not to be taken as meaning that no one *ever* related these elements together, but that no one did so since the way those stories were connected to each other was totally forgotten. In other words, those stories might have constituted causally interconnected parts of one or more *sujets* up to a certain point. However, as time passed by, they were only told in a fragmentary fashion and separately from each other. The Visitor now gathers them in a concise core, on the basis of which he will compose his own *sujet*, where he will restore those events' causal connections which once indeed took place and had perhaps been delineated in narrations of the tradition.

As is the case with the principle of selectivity, the importance of causality is also touched upon not just in the introductory remarks but also throughout the myth. By means of verbal echoes between his opening statements and his comments in the process of narrating the account, the Visitor repeatedly reminds Young Socrates that he remains aware of the promise he gave in the beginning to restore through the narrative arrangement of his account the causal relationships of the events.

The Visitor's first metanarrative statement concerning causality is found in the second stage of his description of the Age of Cronus (270b3–271c2). He has just described the way in which the world occasionally changes the direction of its movement. At this point, he says to Young Socrates: "On the basis, then, of the present remarks, let's figure out and get to understand the affect which, we said, was the cause of all the wonderful things. It is in fact this very thing" (270b3–5: λογισάμενοι δὴ συννοήσωμεν τὸ πάθος ἐκ τῶν νῦν λεχθέντων, ὃ πάντων ἔφαμεν εἶναι τῶν θαυμαστῶν αἴτιον. ἔστι γὰρ οὖν δὴ τοῦτ' αὐτό).[53] With these words, the Visitor reveals the purpose of what he has previously narrated about the two modes of universal movement: to explain the cause of the stories he introduced in the prelude. He does not merely state that he will causally connect a set of events; he reminds Young Socrates and the reader of the fact that the causal linkages he will create at this point will restore the absence of

---

52 As Rosen (1995, 41) seems to suggest.
53 Gartner/Yau 2020, 4.

these linkages from the *fabula* from which he selected those stories.⁵⁴ This reminder is further enhanced by strong verbal cross-references. The disconnected fragments of the introduction's *fabula* (268e8 and 269b4: τῶν πάλαι λεχθέντων) are juxtaposed with the logically interrelated segments of the present *sujet* (270b3–4: ἐκ τῶν νῦν λεχθέντων). The shift of the world's revolving is not merely presented as the cause of some events, but as the cause which connects into a narrative whole the disconnected stories mentioned in the lead-in (270b3–4: τὸ πάθος ... πάντων ... αἴτιον; cf. 269b5–6: σύμπαντα ἐκ ταὐτοῦ πάθους and 269b9: πᾶσι τούτοις αἴτιον τὸ πάθος of the lead-in). Also, the Visitor highlights the intellectual procedures which are required for the transformation of the *fabula* into *sujet* (270b3: λογισάμενοι δὴ συννοήσωμεν). There is also an explicit reference to their earlier exchange (270b4: ἔφαμεν). Last, all these stories which are now causally associated to each other are here, as previously, characterised as wonderful (270b4: τῶν θαυμαστῶν; cf. 269b7: θαυμαστότερα earlier on). However, the restoration of their interconnections eliminates the audience's wonder about them.

As in the build-up, the very cause of the events is described as a change (270b10: ταύτην τὴν μεταβολήν; cf. 269a1: τῆς μεταβολῆς on the shift of the sun's direction). It is also presented as the greatest of all changes (270b10–c1: τῶν περὶ τὸν οὐρανὸν γιγνομένων τροπῶν πασῶν εἶναι μεγίστην καὶ τελεωτάτην τροπήν), which echoes 269b9: πᾶσι τούτοις αἴτιον, while the περὶ τὸν οὐρανόν (270b10–c1) refers to the one of the three stories that the Visitor mentioned earlier, the change of the sun's direction (269a1–2: δύσεώς τε καὶ ἀνατολῆς ἡλίου καὶ τῶν ἄλλων ἄστρων).

When he decides to associate this great cosmic change with the second story of the introduction's *fabula*, the one about the earth-born men, the Visitor, as we have already seen, introduces this association with the words περὶ δὲ τούτους ἄλλα τε παθήματα πολλὰ καὶ θαυμαστὰ καὶ καινά [...] (270d1–2). The human breeding from the earth is here too presented as a marvellous subject (πολλὰ καὶ θαυμαστά), just as it was earlier (269b7: θαυμαστότερα). Through this verbal echo, the Visitor reminds Young Socrates that in composing his myth he intends to restore the causal connections of events which up to that point were treated as peculiar and thereby to expunge from people's minds any kind of wonder about the nature and origins of these events.

---

54 This is why I cannot accept Klein's (1977, 157) view that the first part of the myth, i.e. on the two motions of the universe, is a playful account which is not aimed by Plato to be taken seriously neither by Young Socrates nor by the reader. Cf. Hemmenway 1994, 267 n. 21, who follows a line of thought similar to that of the present analysis.

Equally rich in verbal echoes of the build-up is the Visitor's explanation why men were earth-born in the Age of Cronus. After he describes to the boy the way that humans and other living beings recycled themselves through the earth, the boy asks (271a3–4): "But what exactly, Visitor, was the genesis of animals then? And in what manner did they generate from one another?". The Visitor answers him that at that time there was no breeding through sexual intercourse but men came out of the earth (271a5–8). The words τὸ μὲν ἐξ ἀλλήλων οὐκ ἦν ἐν τῇ τότε φύσει γεννώμενον (271a5–6: "the generation from one another was not in their nature at that time") echoes the words of the earlier exchange μὴ ἐξ ἀλλήλων γεννᾶσθαι (269b2–3: "were not generated from one another?"). Also, the τὸ δὲ γηγενὲς εἶναί ποτε γένος λεχθέν (271a6–7: "the earth born genus that is reported to have once been") resembles the words γηγενεῖς (269b2) and καὶ τοῦτο ἓν τῶν πάλαι λεχθέντων (269b4) earlier. As was the case with the shift of the cosmic direction, the existence of the earth-born men is not merely presented as a piece of information but as the story (λεχθέν; cf. λεχθέντων) mentioned earlier, a story which is here incorporated into the causal canvas of the myth.

Especially interesting for our analysis is the information offered by the Visitor about the coexistence of the earth-born men with the first men of the Age of Zeus. After being told by the Visitor that the men of the Age of Cronus began getting younger and returning to the earth, Young Socrates asks him how these men were born. The boy's query is reasonable because the Visitor's description clarified only how men died and not how they were born. So, the Visitor answers Young Socrates' question with the following explanation: in the Age of Cronus reproduction was not achieved through sexual intercourse, but there were men who returned to the earth and who are today known as earth-born men. The latter were first mentioned by the first men of the next era, the Age of Zeus, who were born at the borderline between the two ages and therefore coexisted for a while with the men of the previous era, the Age of Cronus, which was near its end. These first men of the Age of Zeus are claimed by the Visitor to have been the first to compose and disseminate the tales about the earth-born men. Their tales are probably implied by the Visitor to have once gathered the three stories (about the Age of Cronus, the earth-born men and the alteration of the west and east) in close association to each other.

Exactly at this point, the Visitor returns to the fact he mentioned at the introduction to the myth that such stories cause people's bewilderment. As we have seen, in his opening remarks the Visitor implied that the reason why these stories, as well as those on the Age of Cronus and the change of the celestial bodies' rotation, strike people as unbelievable lies in the fact that they are now spread disconnected from one another. Now, at this point of the myth the Visitor does exactly what he promised in his opening remarks: he creates causal links between these stories in order to confirm their validity. For, when he argues that the first men of the Age of Zeus, who coexisted with the earth-born men, preserved the tales about them, the Visitor expresses the view that these tales are incorrectly distrusted by many (271b3–4: λόγων, οἳ νῦν ὑπὸ πολλῶν οὐκ ὀρθῶς ἀπιστοῦνται), introducing his explanation with a γάρ clause: "For I think we must reflect on what is implied by what we have said" (271b4: τὸ γὰρ ἐντεῦθεν οἶμαι χρὴ συννοεῖν). According to the Visitor, the stories about the earth-born men are true because the latter's existence is proved in the following way: the fact that these men used to die by returning to the earth entails that they were born from it, following the world's route which was opposite to that of the interlocutors' age.

The Visitor endeavours to prove the validity of one from among the three stories he introduced in his opening remarks (about the earth-born men) by causally connecting it with another from among these three stories (the one about the change in the stars' direction). It is worth noting the ring composition with which he frames this causal connection (271a6–7: τὸ δὲ γηγενὲς εἶναί ποτε γένος λεχθέν; 271c1: οὕτως ἔχειν τοὔνομα καὶ τὸν λόγον), a scheme which stresses the fact that he validates stories (λεχθέν and λόγον) which were disseminated in a disconnected way by logically linking them in his own narrative.

1.2.3 Temporality

In the opening remarks to the myth, when the Visitor explains to Young Socrates that the stories about the Age of Cronus, the change in the direction of the celestial bodies' motion and the earth-born men are narrated by his contemporaries disconnected from one another, he says, as we saw, that he will try to connect them by restoring their causal relationships. The Visitor does not explicitly clarify whether or not, with his words "in a scattered way, each separate from one another" (269b8–9: διεσπαρμένα ... χωρὶς ἕκαστα ἀπ' ἀλλήλων), he refers to the absence of temporal linkages as well. However, the way in which the myth unfolds in its first half and the discussion between narrator and receiver offer strong evidence in support of the view that Plato invites us to read the cosmological myth as the result of the narrator's deliberate effort to restore, apart from causal linkages, the temporal connections between the elements of the material he draws for his account. In this section, we will present and analyse the parts of the myth that prove this view.

Plato's goal is not merely to present the narrator as delineating temporal relations between seemingly disconnected events, but also to highlight how the techniques of structuring the narrative time help the receiver of the narrative, in this case Young Socrates, to apprehend the temporal relations under construction. The main technique through which the Visitor shapes narrative time is the alternation of present and past tenses. Let us first focus on how this scheme develops between the first and second stages of the Age of Cronus. We have seen that in the first stage of the divine rule the Visitor describes how the two inverse rotations of the world eternally follow one another. The Visitor uses the present tense and adverbs which do not denote the relationship exclusively between the past and the present but the perpetual repetition of certain phenomena in all three temporal levels (past, present, future). We do not read that the god *first* moved the world and *then* let it move by itself, but that these two phases *diachronically* (269c4–5: τοτὲ μέν ... τοτὲ δέ) alternate each other. All actions are offered in the present tense (269c5: συμποδηγεῖ, συγκυκλεῖ, ἀνῆκεν;[55] 269c7–d1: περιάγεται). Also, the subordinate clause "whenever its circuits have completed the measure of the time allotted to it" (269c6–7) is introduced by the conjunction ὅταν ("whenever"), which denotes a perpetual repetition. The Visitor also uses the present tense when he explains why it is reasonable that the universe is sometimes ruled by the god and some other times not. The whole first stage, which refers to the activity of the universe, describes a perpetually recurring state of affairs, but does not shed light on what is the temporal sequence between the Age of Cronus, the change in the celestial bodies' rotation and the age of the earth-born men. However, we are obviously led to the conclusion that one of these three elements, the change in the direction of the stars' motion, takes place in both periods, specifically whenever the world changes its direction either because it is abandoned by the god or because the latter takes again control of it. As will be explained, this is the very conclusion which Young Socrates is led to by this emphasis on all three temporal levels.

The shift from all three temporal levels towards the relationship between the two of them (past and present) coincides with the transition from the first stage of the Age of Cronus (269c4–270b2) to the second (270b3–271c2), in which the Visitor focuses on the biology of organisms, including humans. We have seen that in this stage the Visitor describes how organisms are born out of the earth and die by returning to it (270d6–271a2). While the preceding stage was entirely structured with present tenses, here the Visitor suddenly uses past tenses. With two aorists (270d7: ἔστη and ἐπαύσατο) he marks the change in the

---

55 This is a gnomic aorist, so it carries the force of a present tense (Rowe 1995, 187).

organisms' biology at the very moment when the god takes control of the *cosmos*. While this moment has hitherto been presented as taking place repeatedly in time, it is now presented as a point which belongs to the past in relation to the interlocutors' present. We do not read that, *whenever* the god takes over the guidance of the world, the beings cease to grow older but that they *ceased* to do so. This unexpected shift towards the past leads the reader and Young Socrates to the conclusion that, from among all the times that this shift takes place, the narrator chooses only one of them, which took place in the past. All the subsequent changes suffered by the animals are from now on offered in imperfects, which do not mark phenomena that took place only once but repeatedly in a long period of time in the past (270d8–e1: μεταβάλλον ... ἐφύετο; 270e3–4: λεαινόμεναι ... καθίστασαν; 270e6–7: γιγνόμενα ... ἀπῄει ... ἀφομοιούμενα; 270e8–9: μαραινόμενα ... ἐξηφανίζετο; 270e10–271a3: πάσχον διεφθείρετο).

This transition of the account towards the past is presented by Plato as being especially effective, since the receiver of the story, Young Socrates, is presented as taking notice of it. When he asks the Visitor about the reproduction of the animals in that period, he is not interested in what generally happens whenever the world is moved by the god, but he is swayed by the Visitor's past narrative and asks him how the animals *used to* give birth in the past (271a3: γένεσις δὲ δὴ τίς τότ' ἦν, ὦ ξένε, τῶν ζῴων;). The Visitor, by answering his question, offers him one further clarification about the temporal placement of the age of the earth-born men. As we saw, describing the perpetual alternation of the two motions of the world through the use of present tenses helps the receiver of the story to realise the repetitiveness of the shift in the celestial bodies' rotation in every change of the world's direction. At this point, the transition of the narrative on human biology towards the past forces Young Socrates to wonder about the temporal placement of one further story from among the three which the Visitor from the outset promised to organise causally and temporally in his account: the story about the existence of earth-born men.

That the delineation of the narrative time is up to this point aimed at temporally connecting the two of the three stories is made clear to us by Plato through the question with which Young Socrates introduces us to the third stage of the Age of Cronus. Let us see the boy's words (271c4–7):

ἀλλὰ δὴ τὸν βίον ὃν ἐπὶ τῆς Κρόνου φῂς εἶναι δυνάμεως, πότερον ἐν ἐκείναις ἦν ταῖς τροπαῖς ἢ ἐν ταῖσδε; τὴν μὲν γὰρ τῶν ἄστρων τε καὶ ἡλίου μεταβολὴν δῆλον ὡς ἐν ἑκατέραις συμπίπτει ταῖς τροπαῖς γίγνεσθαι.

But as for the life which you say there was in the time of Kronos' power — was it in those turnings or in these? For it is clear that it falls out that the change affecting the stars and the sun occurs in each set of turnings.

With these words, Plato proceeds with an implicit, dramatised, metanarrative statement to the reader that the goal of the narrative up to this point was, *inter alia*, to specify the temporal relations between the two of the three stories. The fact that the shift of the direction in the celestial bodies' motion takes place in both periods has become evident to the boy through the repetitive narrative on the first stage of the Age of Cronus. As for when the earth-born men existed, Young Socrates was offered a clear-cut answer from the Visitor, and what now remains is to temporally locate the Age of Cronus. The success of the Visitor's techniques through which he endeavours to help the boy apprehend the temporal relationships between the narrated events is underscored by the Visitor's commendatory words to the boy: "You have been keeping up with the argument well" (271c8: καλῶς τῷ λόγῳ συμπαρηκολούθηκας). He immediately afterwards answers Young Socrates' question by explaining that the Age of Cronus was the period preceding the one in which the interlocutors live.

In this way, by the time the Visitor has completed the narration of all three stages of the Age of Cronus, he has fulfilled his promise to restore through his account the temporal relationships of the three stories. The repetitive nature of the present-tense narrative on the first stage reveals that the change in the motion of the stars takes place in both periods. Second, the shift of the narrative on the biology of organisms towards the past leads the receiver of the story to wonder when the earth-born men lived. Last, the beginning of the third stage, the one about the political life of these men, coincides with the temporal placement of the third story, the one about the Age of Cronus.

So far, we have seen that the main technique through which the repetitiveness of the change in the star's rotation and the placement of the earth-born men in the past become evident to the receiver of the story is the alternation of present and past tenses from the first stage (*cosmos*) to the second (human biology) of the Age of Cronus. We also saw that, with regard to the delineation of narrative time, this scheme creates a distance between a wider approach of time on all its levels (past, present and future) and a limited focus on the relationship between past and present.

Exactly at this point, it is worth noting that the same distance emerges between the first and second stages of the account about the Age of Zeus. The widening of the narrator's gaze from the microcosm of humans towards a wider universal framework manifests itself on a temporal level, as the narrator does not merely offer a story of the past but expands the spectrum of the narrative time in the other two temporal levels as well (present and future). This scheme is realised through the following technique. The Visitor initially narrates the Age of Zeus using past tenses. The withdrawal of the gods, the universe's reaction and the phenomena that take place during the transitional period are all offered in aorists and imperfects (272d7: ἐτελεώθη, ἔδει; 272e1: ἀνήλωτο; 272e5: ἀπέστη; 272e5–6: ἀνέστρεφεν; 272e8: ἀφίεσαν; 273a4: ἀπηργάσατο; 273a7: ᾔει; 273b3: ἀπετέλει). However, when the Visitor mentions that the universe initially administered itself smoothly but was gradually leading itself to chaos, he explains this gradual decay in the present and perfect tense (273b8: κέκτηται; 273c1–2: γίγνεται, ἔχει, ἐναπεργάζεται): the universe *is* marked by an inherent proneness towards disorder, as it was such a state in which it existed before it was set up by the demiurge. After he offers this explanation, the Visitor brings his account back to the past by saying that the universe was producing more good things than bad ones as long as it was supported by the god, information which is offered in the imperfect (273c4: ἐνέτικτεν).

Although one expects the Visitor to continue his account in past tenses, he presents the remaining part of this stage on the gradual attrition of the universe and the demiurge's eventual interference using the present tense. After giving the aforementioned detail that the universe, aided by the god, was mainly producing good things, the narrator underlines that whatever he will from now on explain pertains to a process which takes place eternally. The initially smooth self-administration of the universe is presented as taking place forever (273c5: ἀεί). This adverb denotes an eternal repetition, indicating that, whenever god abandons the universe, it initially functions normally. With this adverb at the beginning of this present account, the narrator reveals that everything is described as taking place in 273c4–e4 recurs eternally. Through these alternations of the past and the present/future, the account of this first stage unfolds in the following route: past (272d6–273b4) → present/future (273b4–c2) → past (273c2–4) → present/future (273c4–e4). At this stage, the narrator offers the temporal canvas in which, in the next two stages, he will place human biology and politics by using past tenses.

We have seen that both parts of the myth (Age of Cronus and Age of Zeus) unfold on the basis of the scheme '*cosmos* → human biology → human politics'. In both cases the transition from the stage on the universe to the two next ones which pertain to men coincides with a transition from the three levels of time to two of them, or, to put it more simply, from an account of perpetually recurring procedures to a narrative of past events. The fact that Plato highlights this technique by repeating it and through the Visitor's commendatory words to Young Socrates show Plato's intention to stress the value of this technique in narratives such as the myth of the *Statesman*, in which the narrator is invited to present human nature as part of the *cosmos*.

Plato's interest in the procedure of delineating the causal and temporal relations between the narrated events is also shown by the fact that the interlocutors' conversations, which serve as the mainspring of the plot development in the account of the Age of Cronus, focuses exclusively on issues of causal relations and temporal clarifications. When the Visitor completes his description of the eternal alternation of the two inverse motions of the universe and is ready to explain the reason why the universe behaves in such a way, Young Socrates interrupts him by asking what the cause of all this is (269d4: διὰ τὸ ποῖον δή;). Then, after the Visitor offers his explanation, the boy is presented as finding it reasonable (270b1–2: φαίνεται γοῦν δὴ καὶ μάλα εἰκότως εἰρῆσθαι πάνθ' ὅσα διελήλυθας). When, immediately afterwards, the Visitor invites him to examine how the change of the world's motion generates biological changes in men, the boy interrupts him again and asks him what phenomenon he refers to (270b6: τὸ ποῖον;). Then, as soon as the Visitor explains to him the sequence of causal relations that lead from the universal motion to the earth-born men, Young Socrates again accepts the Visitor's thoughts as reasonable (270c6: καὶ τοῦτο εἰκός). The boy interrupts the Visitor on two further occasions and, as we saw, in both of them he asks him where in the temporal canvas of the myth they should place the three stories. The boy's willingness to apprehend the causal and temporal connections between the three stories which had initially been mentioned in a scattered way is by no means to be taken as reflecting his inability to reach by himself conclusions on these issues. As we saw, the Visitor is satisfied by the dexterity with which the boy receives what is narrated. The boy's interest in further clarifications rather mirrors the capacity of the myth to elicit the audience's interest in the causal and temporal connections between the events.

What is more, the boy is interested exclusively in these matters during the Visitor's narration. Apart from the aforementioned cases, there is also one further moment in which Young Socrates is presented as talking during the recitation of the myth. The Visitor has just completed his description of men's way of life at the Age of Cronus and asks the boy whether or not he wants to examine if the men of the Age of Cronus were happier than the men of the Age of Zeus. The boy answers with a striking unwillingness: "Not at all" (272b5: οὐδαμῶς). His indifference in exploring the comparison between the two eras is sharply contrasted with his keen interest in apprehending the causative and temporal logic of the account. The boy is presented as being interested only in asking about the "why" and "when" of the story.

The Visitor thus seems to fulfil his goal to offer a narrative which will emphasise the links between the three stories on the change in the star's motion, the Age of Cronus, and the earth-born men. His success is also stressed by the antithesis created by Plato between the perplexity with which Young Socrates is presented as initially listening to these stories, when they are arranged in a scattered way by the Visitor in the introduction to the myth, and the interest and success with which he is sketched as constructing, step by step, the connections between them while listening to the myth. In the section on the element of causality, we argued that the Visitor, through the disconnected, paratactic mention of the three tales, draws Young Socrates' attention to the way in which these stories were disseminated in that period. It is this scattered, paratactic circulation of the stories that the cosmological myth is juxtaposed with, in that it organises everything on both a causal and temporal level.

1.3 Narrating/listening time

So far, we have argued that the Visitor's myth serves as a paradigm of the way in which the scheme '*cosmos* → human biology → politics', which is introduced in the *Theaetetus*, can be conveyed in narrative discourse. Furthermore, we analysed the comments of the characters in the *Statesman* and the narrative arrangement of the myth itself and contended that the Visitor's metanarrative reflections and the techniques through which he narrates the myth deliberately shape a net of cross-references which emphasise three main, according to modern narratologists, aspects of narrative composition: the procedure of selecting and distributing the material and the construction of causal and temporal linkages between the events of the plot. In this last section, it will be argued that the Visitor highlights one further element of narrativity, narrating/listening time. While the three methods of the raw material's narrativisation are addressed in the opening remarks to the myth, the issue of narrating/listening time is touched upon long after the myth, in a digression offered by the Visitor about the two different modes of measuring. In particular, I will maintain that the Visitor is not only interested in this matter but also approaches it in a way similar to the one in which it is analysed by formalist narratologists.

Narrating time denotes the time needed for the narration of a story. This issue has traditionally attracted scholarly attention in most schools of narrative theory from the German formalists until today.[56] It is occasionally approached

---

[56] The concept was introduced by Günther Müller (1948; cf. Müller 1968) as "Erzählzeit" opposed to the narrated time ("erzählte Zeit"). Cf. Chatman 1978, 62–70; Genette 1980, 220; Todorov 1981, 30.

from the narrator's perspective, in the context of which scholarly discussion usually focuses on the time that a narrator consumes in narrating a story (narrating time).[57] On the other hand, this notion is also addressed from the receiver's point of view and is thus defined as the time which one needs to read or listen to an account (reading/listening time). These two kinds of time need not always coincide. For example, a narrator reasonably needs less time to narrate a story orally than the time a reader needs to read the same account. Nonetheless, in some cases these two times match. For example, in the present case of reciting an account within the framework of a dialogue, the duration of a story's production by the narrator coincides with the duration of its reception by the interlocutor who acts as a listener. In other words, whenever one from among the interlocutors relates a story, the rest of the interlocutors ideally begin listening to the story as soon as the narrator starts narrating it, and cease listening to it as soon as the narrator stops. This kind of time is the object of the present analysis, given that the myth is related by the Visitor in the same span of time as that in which Young Socrates listens to it. Therefore, for this description I chose to adopt the term "narrating/listening time", using a mixture of the two aforementioned terms.

The presence of the notion of narrating/listening time in the Platonic corpus has traditionally been neglected both by narratologists and classicists.[58] The *Statesman* is of great help in this respect, as we find in it the famous digression on the two modes of measurement, in which the Visitor quite systematically shares his reflections on the *proper* duration of a philosophical conversation, including the narrations of stories that might take place during such a dialogue. Although modern scholarship has analysed extensively this digression in terms of its relevance to the method of division[59] and the definition of statesmanship,[60] its connection to the cosmological myth's length and thus its significance for our understanding of Plato's views about narrating/listening time has been altogether neglected.

This digression (283b6–287b3) is marked by an intense normative orientation, as Plato is engaged not so much with what narrating time is but with how long it should be and for what reasons.[61] What is more, Plato interestingly addresses

---

[57] Fludernik 2009, 157.
[58] I have not found any narratological analysis of the concept that mentions Plato.
[59] Kucharský 1960; Klein 1977, 172–177; Miller 1980, 64–72; Benardete 1984 III, 113–119; Benardete 1992, 35 and 44–46; Dorter 1994, 202–209; Ionescu 2016; Smith 2018, 144–147.
[60] Hoffmann 1993; Petrucci 2004, 114–134; Harvey 2006, 99–114 and 2009 *passim*.
[61] For the deontic orientation of the second mode of measurement, which narrating/listening time is related to, in contrast with the descriptive nature of the first mode, see Harvey 2009, 2–3.

this issue from a psychological point of view as well, as he is also concerned with the narrator's and the audience's emotions elicited by the extent of the narrating/listening time. In this section I will examine Plato's views on narrating/listening time on two different but interconnected levels: (a) first, I will define Plato's views on the matter as they emerge from the digression of 283b6–287b3 on the two different modes of measurement; (b) second, I will analyse Plato's opinion on the effectiveness of the narrating/listening time's length upon the inner world of the interlocutors (both narrator and listener).

1.3.1 The digression on the two types of measurement

The digression on the two kinds of measuring and the proper extent of a philosophical discussion does not emerge out of the blue. Plato has already prepared us twice for the Visitor's interest in the duration of his conversation with Young Socrates. The Visitor reflects on the matter for the first time shortly after he completes his cosmological account. Explaining to the boy what the myth reveals to them about the mistake they made in their first attempt to define statesmanship, he argues that the myth shows that they should not have compared statesmen with shepherds because the sole governor of men who serves as a shepherd is god. The myth's contribution to the exploration of statesmanship thus lies in the fact that it leads to a new and useful division of statesmanship, the one between (a) divine and (b) human statesmen. The Visitor also suggests that they proceed with one further division of the human statesman and recognise (a) a governor who rules people against their will (a tyrant) and (b) a statesman whom his people willingly accept as their leader (a king). After these two divisions (divine–human statesman and tyrant–king), Young Socrates concludes that the definition of statesmanship has successfully been completed (274e1–277a2).

Exactly at this point, the Visitor advises the boy not to hurry to consider their examination complete and expresses the following thoughts on the extent of the cosmological narrative: the definition of statesmanship is not complete yet. Just as some sculptors, being in a hurry to complete their works, add too much material to it but do not elaborate on its details, so the interlocutors similarly took from an already sizable myth a part which was much more than needed in order to distinguish human statesmen from the greater example of the divine shepherd, without having penetrated the details of the nature of human statesman. For this reason, they should now employ a new kind of division, by means of which they are expected to distinguish a king from other groups of people who claim the right to be considered statesmen (277a3–c6). With these words, the Visitor essentially moves from the myth to the division of weaving and statesmanship.

Before employing this kind of division in the examination of statesmanship, the Visitor tests this method in the less significant art of weaving (277d1–283a8). He concludes this digression with similar reflections on the extent of a philosophical discussion. In particular, he poses the following question (283b1–3):

ΞΕ. Εἶεν· τί δή ποτε οὖν οὐκ εὐθὺς ἀπεκρινάμεθα πλεκτικὴν εἶναι κρόκης καὶ στήμονος ὑφαντικήν, ἀλλὰ περιήλθομεν ἐν κύκλῳ πάμπολλα διοριζόμενοι μάτην;

VIS: Good; so why ever, then, didn't we immediately reply that weaving was an intertwining of woof and warp, and instead went round in a circle defining a whole collection of things to no purpose?

He then proposes to the boy that they address the issue of the proper length of a conversation in order to clarify, once and for all, in what cases they should worry about the prolongation of their discussion (283b6–c1). It is in this context that he explains to the boy the nature of the two kinds of measuring.

In his digression on the two kinds of measuring ((283b6–287b3), the Visitor explains to Young Socrates the reasons why during a philosophical conversation one should not feel discontent to engage in deviations from the main subject in question. The trilogy *Theaetetus–Sophist–Statesman*, apart from its many other common features, is also marked by a series of digressions relating to questions of method.[62] In the *Theaetetus*, Socrates repeatedly interrupts the investigation of knowledge, with the most extensive interruptions being those about his meaiutic method (148e7–151d6) and philosophers (172c3–177c2). In the *Sophist*, the Visitor interrupted the investigation of the sophist's nature in order to examine questions of being and non-being (236d9–249d5).[63] In the *Statesman*, we are faced with two digressions, the myth and the paradigm of

---

62 On Plato's special interest in issues of methodology in the trilogy, see on *Theaetetus* Frede 1989, 20; Blondell 2002, 251 n. 2, 260, 298. On the *Statesman* see Ritter 1923, 135; Davis 1967, 320; Benardete 1992, 25; Arends 1993, 154–155, who treats the first two parts of the dialogue as exercises upon various methods of inquiry; Howland 1993, 15–16; Rowe 1995, 3, 8–9; Cooper 1999, 71; Michelini 2000, 181; Merrill 2003, 35, 39; Blondell 2005, 23; El Murr 2010, 109–116. See also Livov 2011, 331–332, who takes the *Sophist* and the *Statesman* as a "methodological unity". Horn 2012, 393; Naas 2018, 21. On the modes of exposition of ideas, see Poster 2005, 47. See also the conclusions to this chapter.

63 See, e.g., Priou 2013, who provides an exhaustive overview and discussion of the bibliography on the matter.

weaving. The Visitor here justifies the digressions which he has hitherto provided in the two dialogues in which he orchestrates the conversation, namely the *Sophist* and the *Statesman*.[64]

This is essentially a deviation in defence of deviations.[65] In this way, Plato essentially offers us a meta-digression and thereby reveals to us that digressive discourse is by no means a circumstantial feature of the trilogy but a deliberate choice on his part, with which he intends to highlight the educational value of this teaching tool. The focal point of interest in this meta-digression lies in the question of what one should consider as the proper length of a digression or of anything said in a philosophical discussion. Now, given that the Visitor explicitly includes the myth in these deviations, his points on the optimum duration of digressions pertains, *inter alia*, to the issue of narrating/listening time.

The Visitor opens his digression with the comment that what will be said will help the interlocutors to assess how certain parts of a discussion seem to last more, and other parts less, than is needed (283c3–6). Through this statement as well as the others that follow it, he offers us the opportunity to reach the conclusion that the views of the digression pertain to the art of conversation, including the cosmological myth.

According to the Visitor, the proper mode of assessing the length of what is said in a conversation should be explored through the method of division. He thus divides the art of measuring into two types. On the one hand, the extent of things can be measured as follows: the larger can be defined as such exclusively in relation to the smaller. Conversely, the smaller is defined as smaller exclusively in relation to the larger. This mode of measuring is exclusively based on the mutual relation between being larger and being smaller. On the other hand, the extent of both actions and words is also measured and assessed not only on the basis of whether something is larger or smaller than something else, but also on the basis of an effort to produce the mean. So, the Visitor concludes that there are two modes of measuring needed in assessing largeness and smallness (283d4–9):

ΞΕ. Διέλωμεν τοίνυν αὐτὴν δύο μέρη· δεῖ γὰρ δὴ πρὸς ὃ νῦν σπεύδομεν.
ΝΕ. ΣΩ. Λέγοις ἂν τὴν διαίρεσιν ὅπῃ.
ΞΕ. Τῇδε· τὸ μὲν κατὰ τὴν πρὸς ἄλληλα μεγέθους καὶ σμικρότητος κοινωνίαν, τὸ δὲ κατὰ τὴν τῆς γενέσεως ἀναγκαίαν οὐσίαν.

---

64 Blondell 2002.
65 And in this sense it is "self-justifying", as Blondell (2002, 369) notes.

VIS: Let's then divide it into two parts, for they're needed for what we're now striving for.
SOC: You must speak at what point the division is.
VIS: At this: one is to be characterised in terms of the mutually relative sharing in largeness and smallness, and one in terms of the necessary (indispensable) being of becoming.

It is worth noting that the Visitor makes this division not only with regard to the object of measurement but also in terms of the arts which adopt the one or other mode of the object's measuring. The Visitor discerns two categories of expertise: first, those arts which measure largeness and smallness on the basis of their mutually exclusive relationship; second, there are those arts which assess largeness and smallness by the criterion of their relationship with the mean. These arts, which include statesmanship and weaving, aim at producing deeds and sayings which are marked by the mean and avoid excess and deficiency. The practitioners of these arts, believing in the existence of the mean, endeavour to produce and preserve it through their products and thereby generate good and beautiful results. In this respect, if we accept that largeness and smallness can be measured only in relation to one another, then we should inevitably deny the existence of the mean. And if indeed the mean does not exist, then we are doomed to reach a conclusion that, given that there is no mean, there are neither the arts which pursue it, including statesmanship, which would be a dead end in the effort to define the political art (284a5–d9).

Now, in the Visitor's mind, the art of *logos*, including that of composing narratives, clearly belongs to those arts which assess the extent of their products on the basis of the mean. For, as we will see in what follows, both at the beginning and at the end of the digression the Visitor repeatedly emphasises that his purpose in dividing measurement into these two modes is to reveal the proper way to measure what is said and, especially, the proper way to measure and assess the digressions in the *Sophist* and the *Statesman*, including the cosmological myth.

The Visitor treats the myth as a product of an art and the art of narrating as a productive act. What is more, the products of discourse (the myth included) are strikingly placed at the end of the digression and thereby serve as the culmination of all the references to the arts which create their products on the basis of the mean. Let us examine all these references throughout the digression. While defining the first mode of measurement as one which is based on the mutual relation between largeness and smallness, the Visitor explicitly relates the second mode with the procedure of producing. This mode of measuring, which compares excess and deficiency with the mean, is immediately connected with "the necessary being of becoming" (283d8-9: κατὰ τὴν τῆς γενέσεως ἀναγκαίαν οὐσίαν), namely of producing.⁶⁶ The Visitor seems here to mean that the measuring arts which approach largeness and smallness from the perspective of their mutual relationship are invited to measure things which already exist. On the other hand, arts such as statesmanship, weaving and narrating, which define excess and deficiency in relation to the mean, do not measure something that exists but things which they will produce, and their goal is to produce things which will preserve the mean. The mean is thus presented as something which emerges along with the deeds and words which are marked by it (283e4-5: ἐν λόγοις εἴτε καὶ ἐν ἔργοις ... ὡς ὄντως γιγνόμενον, "in speeches or maybe in deeds ... as in its being a coming-into-being"). The Visitor's special emphasis not only on these arts but also on their products is also evident in his clarification that, if we accept that there is no mean, then we should also admit that neither the arts aiming at it nor their products exist (284a5-6: τὰς τέχνας τε αὐτὰς καὶ τἆργα αὐτῶν σύμπαντα).⁶⁷ These products are good and beautiful only on condition that they preserve the mean (284b2: μέτρον σῴζουσαι πάντα ἀγαθὰ καὶ καλὰ ἀπεργάζονται).⁶⁸ The Visitor concludes that all products of art are related to measurement (285a3-4: μετρήσεως ... πάνθ' ὁπόσα ἔντεχνα μετείληφεν), but some of them also pertain to the measuring which aims at the production of the mean.

The products (ἔντεχνα) of *logos*, including narrations, are placed at the centre of the Visitor's interest. Creating a ring composition with his introductory remarks of 283b6-c6, he says that he is noting all these examples in order for Young Socrates to understand how the large or small extent of sayings should be assessed (286b3-d2):⁶⁹

ΞΕ. Ὦν τοίνυν χάριν ἅπανθ' ἡμῖν ταῦτ' ἐρρήθη περὶ τούτων, μνησθῶμεν.
ΝΕ. ΣΩ. Τίνων;
ΞΕ. Ταύτης τε οὐχ ἥκιστα αὐτῆς ἕνεκα τῆς δυσχερείας ἣν περὶ τὴν μακρολογίαν τὴν περὶ τὴν ὑφαντικὴν ἀπεδεξάμεθα δυσχερῶς, καὶ τὴν περὶ τὴν τοῦ παντὸς ἀνείλιξιν καὶ τὴν τοῦ σοφιστοῦ περὶ τῆς τοῦ μὴ ὄντος οὐσίας, ἐννοοῦντες ὡς ἔσχε μῆκος πλέον, καὶ ἐπὶ τούτοις δὴ πᾶσιν ἐπεπλήξαμεν ἡμῖν αὐτοῖς, δείσαντες μὴ περίεργα ἅμα καὶ μακρὰ λέγοιμεν. ἵν' οὖν εἰς αὖθις μηδὲν πάσχωμεν τοιοῦτον, τούτων ἕνεκα πάντα τὰ πρόσθε νῷν εἰρῆσθαι φάθι.
ΝΕ. ΣΩ. Ταῦτ' ἔσται. λέγε ἑξῆς μόνον.
ΞΕ. Λέγω τοίνυν ὅτι χρὴ δὴ μεμνημένους ἐμὲ καὶ σὲ τῶν νῦν εἰρημένων τόν τε ψόγον ἑκάστοτε καὶ ἔπαινον ποιεῖσθαι βραχύτητος ἅμα καὶ μήκους ὧν ἂν ἀεὶ πέρι λέγωμεν, μὴ

---

66 Benardete 1984 III, 114-115.
67 Cf. Miller 1980, 66.
68 On the aesthetic perspective from which Plato treats this issue, see Kucharský 1960, 461, 480.
69 Miller 1980, 66.

πρὸς ἄλληλα τὰ μήκη κρίνοντες ἀλλὰ κατὰ τὸ τῆς μετρητικῆς μέρος ὃ τότε ἔφαμεν δεῖν μεμνῆσθαι, πρὸς τὸ πρέπον.

VIS: Then let's remind ourselves of that for the sake of which we have said all these things about them.
SOC: Which?
VIS: It's not least for the sake of this very disagreeableness with which we accepted disagreeably the lengthiness of speech about the art of weaving, about the unwinding of the all, and, in the case of the sophist, about the being of 'that which is not', in realising that they had got an excessive length. And we rebuked ourselves for all of this, out of fear that we were speaking superfluously as well as too lengthily. In order, then, that we may not undergo anything of the sort at a later time, do say that all the previous remarks have been stated by the pair of us for the sake of this.
SO: It shall be done. Just speak what's next in order.
VIS: Well, I'm saying that you and I ought to remember the present remarks and make our blame and praise of brevity and length about whatever we're speaking, not by judging their lengths relative to one another, but in accordance with the part of the art of measurement that we said at that time we must remember, relative to the fitting.

What the Visitor says here does not, of course, pertain exclusively to the procedure of composing a narrative. However, the latter issue is explicitly presented as counting among those phenomena which should be measured on the basis of their relation to the mean (286b7–8: περὶ τὴν μακρολογίαν ... τὴν περὶ τὴν τοῦ παντὸς ἀνείλιξιν).[70] Therefore, we may recapitulate our observations focusing only on narrating/listening time. The art of narration assesses the extent of its products (i.e. narrating/listening time) in terms of the degree to which the extent of a narration preserves the mean. In this respect, if a narrative is too small to preserve the mean, it is deficient. Conversely, if a narrative is too big and for this reason the mean is not preserved in the process of this narrative's composition, the narrating/listening time of such an account is too long.

At this point, the question arises as to what the Visitor takes as the mean in the case of narrating/listening time. In the last part of the digression, he answers this question. He clarifies to Young Socrates that what he has said proves the following: in case someone complains about the length of their conversation and their circular digressions, as in the myth, they should advise him not to worry about the largeness or the smallness of their sayings but about whether or not these sayings help the interlocutors to become more efficient in dialectic and more qualified in reaching the truth about the nature of things.[71] They

---

[70] Cf. ἀνειλίξει within the myth itself (270d3).
[71] Dorter (1994, 267 n. 20) too, although from a different point of view, argues that the myth is aimed by the Visitor to make Young Socrates better in dialectic.

should also say to such a man that, if he wants to measure and assess the size of a discussion, he should examine whether or not such a discussion would help people become better in dialectic in case it was shorter (286d4–287b2).

Based on the Visitor's words, we may reach the following conclusions about Plato's view on what is proper, excessive or deficient when it comes to the narrating/listening time of an account. When a narrator increases or decreases the narrating/listening time of her or his account and in this way renders the narrative less helpful in dialectic, the narrating/listening time of such an account secures the mean. However, if the narrating/listening time is increased to make the interlocutors better in dialectic, the narrating/listening time of such a narrative is deficient. Conversely, if the narrating/listening time of a story is decreased to become more helpful in dialectic, the narrating/listening time of such a story is excessive. Last but not least, the mean is identified with the notions of "the fitting, the opportune, and the needful, and everything settled toward the middle and away from the extremes" (284e6–8: πρὸς τὸ μέτριον καὶ τὸ πρέπον καὶ τὸν καιρὸν καὶ τὸ δέον καὶ πάνθ' ὁπόσα εἰς τὸ μέσον ἀπῳκίσθη τῶν ἐσχάτων).[72]

Although narrating/listening time emerges as the quality of a product, the Visitor also seems to pay attention to the compositional procedure itself, through which this product will be realised. In the process of narrating his story, the composer-narrator should constantly keep in mind not to relate less or more than what is required for the definition of the aspect in question. The notions of the fitting, the opportune and the needful serve the storyteller as criteria to increase or decrease the narrating/listening time of their accounts.

It is at this point that we can turn back to the way that the Visitor is presented by Plato as being particularly interested in the duration of his myth while he narrates it. We saw that at two remote points after the myth he expressed his dissatisfaction at the fact that he had to narrate a great part of an even greater myth (275a2–3: πάμπολυ παρηνέχθημεν; cf. 277b4–6: θαυμαστὸν ὄγκον ἀράμενοι τοῦ μύθου, μείζονι τοῦ δέοντος ἠναγκάσθημεν αὐτοῦ μέρει προσχρήσασθαι). This is also the way in which he introduces his cosmological account (268d8–9: συχνῷ γὰρ μέρει δεῖ μεγάλου μύθου). As already mentioned, his introductory remarks reflect his great concern over selectivity which compelled him to choose only one segment of a wider myth. However, apart from the notion of selectivity, the Visitor is also from the very beginning concerned with the long narrating/listening time of the myth and the segment he will make use of. From the very first moment he decides to engage with the myth, he is interested in the

---

[72] Harvey (2009, 3 n. 7) rightly observes that the Visitor seems here to identify the mean with all these criteria.

narrating time of his composition. What is more, he seems to assess the extent of his story on the basis of the criteria which he himself defines for the art of narrating in the digression on the modes of measuring (δέον, πρέπον and καιρός). He repeatedly stresses that this large myth is exactly what he *must* use in order to shed light on the nature of statesmanship (on the δέον see 268d2: ποιητέον; 268d5–6: δεῖ καθ' ἑτέραν ὁδὸν πορευθῆναί τινα; 268d9: δεῖ ... προσχρήσασθαι; on the πρέπον see 269c1–2: εἰς γὰρ τὴν τοῦ βασιλέως ἀπόδειξιν πρέψει ῥηθέν).

The Visitor expresses similar thoughts in the introductory comment made before the last stage of his account on the Age of Zeus. As we saw, this statement is particularly revealing of Plato's concern for issues of selectivity and the reconstruction of causality in the process of turning the raw material into a coherent narrative whole. However, this concern emerges together with the Visitor's aim to secure the proper narrating/listening time for the myth. He states that all those stories which he will omit by focusing on human politics would increase the narrating time (274b3: πολλὰ ἂν καὶ μακρὰ διεξελθεῖν γίγνοιτο). On the contrary, what pertains to human politics is shorter and more appropriate to the goals of the story (274b4–5: βραχύτερα καὶ μᾶλλον προσήκοντα). The notion of the fitting (πρέπον) which appears in the later discussion is here expressed by the participle προσήκοντα, which is a synonym of πρέπον.

1.3.2 The myth's narrating/listening time and the audience's anticipation

The Visitor does not treat narrating/listening time as a phenomenon disconnected from the receiver of a story. On the contrary, he repeatedly refers to the listeners' emotions elicited by the myth's length. We find two such references in the words with which the Visitor opens and ends his digression on the two modes of measuring. As we saw previously, he states that his intention is to teach Socrates to assess, either by giving praise or blame (283c4: ἐπαινῶμεν καὶ ψέγωμεν), the seemingly excessive duration of what is said by judging the degree to which what is said helps the interlocutors explore the truth on a subject. The Visitor also approaches the listener's attitude towards the length of what is said (including the narrating/listening time of the myth) from a psychological and emotional point of view. For he shares his wish to teach Young Socrates not merely to avoid complaining about the length of what is said, but also not to feel uncomfortable about it (286b6–8: ἕνεκα τῆς δυσχερείας ... ἦν ... ἀπεδεξάμεθα δυσχερῶς).[73] He also touches upon both the origin of this uneasiness and the way it manifests itself. As far as its origin is concerned, the Visitor explains that this kind of dissatisfaction emerges from one's fear that the discussion might deviate from its main goal (286c1–2: δείσαντες μὴ περίεργα ἅμα καὶ μακρὰ λέγοιμεν). This fear causes uneasiness, which is expressed as a rebuke (286c1: ἐπεπλήξαμεν ἡμῖν αὐτοῖς). The unpleasant nature of this emotional state is also denoted by its description as a disease (283b6–7: τὸ νόσημα τὸ τοιοῦτον) which one may suffer from (286c2–3: πάσχωμεν τοιοῦτον).

Elsewhere in the digression, the Visitor presents narrating/listening time as bringing about pleasant emotions. When he explains that the interlocutors should assess the length of what is said in terms of the mean, he says "well, but not everything relative to this either, for we'll have no need of any fitting length relative to pleasure, unless it's a by-product" (286d4–6: οὐ τοίνυν οὐδὲ πρὸς τοῦτο πάντα. οὔτε γὰρ πρὸς τὴν ἡδονὴν μήκους ἁρμόττοντος οὐδὲν προσδεησόμεθα, πλὴν εἰ πάρεργόν τι). In what follows, we can consider the meaning of all these statements.

Let us begin with the Visitor's thoughts on the displeasure caused by digressions. It was only the Visitor who complained about the length of the myth (275a2–3). When he asked Young Socrates if he also believes that the example of the weaving was superfluous, the boy answered that whatever was said was necessary (283b1–5). However, not even the Visitor himself is truly indignant at being forced to deviate from the main subject of the conversation, given that it is he himself who later explains (in 283b6–287b3) the reasons why one should not feel displeasure about lengthy deviations such as the myth and the paradigm of weaving.[74] Who, then, is dissatisfied with long speeches? No one of course. Plato merely refers to those who might be dissatisfied by such digressions in the process of a philosophical discussion.

Plato seems to define this kind of dissatisfaction as a kind of unpleasant anticipation that the digression will end and the discussion will return again to the task of defining the notion under examination.[75] Exactly at this point, we may

---

73 Rowe 1995, 212–213.
74 Klein 1977, 172. However, in a digression about the length of what is said, it can be argued that the Visitor traces the roots of the discussants' dissatisfaction in the long duration of the digressions and not merely in "the disorderliness, impreciseness, and faultiness of an account" (*ibid*).
75 Miller (1980, 65) defines it as "impatience", but not towards the myth but rather the paradigm of weaving. He also interprets the complaint of 283c as meaning that they deviated more

identify some connections between the Visitor's reflections on the effectiveness of narrating/listening time upon the receiver's emotions and modern theories of structural narratology and cognitive science.

To begin with structural narratology, the cosmological myth and the rest of the digressions in the *Sophist* and the *Statesman* are obviously treated as delays in conducting philosophical investigation.[76] Modern narratology indeed recognises digressive discourse as one from among many techniques of interruption and retardation of the plot development.[77] We say that a plot unfolds according to the degree that it leads us towards the realisation of the story's narrative goal.[78] In the *Statesman*, the narrative goal is announced from the very beginning of the dialogue: the definition of statesmanship. However, before the interlocutors reach an answer to this question, some retarding elements are inserted, such as the myth, the paradigm of weaving and the digression on the two types of measuring. Plato refers here to those readers who might champ at the bit to read the eventual definition of statesmanship, treating all the aforementioned deviations as unnecessary delays and therefore reproaching the Visitor for them.

However, exactly what is this feeling of anticipation which some people, according to Plato, might experience due to the retarding function of the myth's extensive narrating/listening time? At this point, the outcomes of another field, cognitive science, might be of help for us in our effort to answer this question. In daily life, people act not only as agents but also as observers of the situations which they are engaged in. In this way, they become acquainted with the order, frequency and duration of the events they experience. Consequently, people consolidate certain views about the structure of the events (plan schemas) and the stories they read or listen (story schemas).[79] On the basis of these plan and story schemas, people have certain expectations about when an action which they participate in will be completed. However, whenever this action is delayed, a contrast emerges between the expected time of the outcome and the real one (temporal contrast).[80] What is more, whenever people are impatient for the fulfilment of the desired outcome, they enter a state of anxiety and suspense, which is the result of the collision between their hope that the desired outcome

---

than needed from the main subject of their discussion. Rowe (1995, 3), on the other hand, defines this emotion as tedium.
76 For the myth as a delay of the investigation of statesmanship, see Lane 1998, 100.
77 Chatman 1978, 59–62; Sternberg 1978; Genette 1980.
78 Chatman 1978, 48 and 59–62; Sternberg 1978; Genette 1980.
79 Lichtenstein/Brewer 1980; Brewer/Lichtenstein 1981 and 1982; de Wied 1994, 114–115.
80 De Wied 1994.

will emerge and their fear, which is elicited by retarding elements, that the eventual resolution will not be reached.

The text does not allow us to argue with certainty that the displeasure which, according to the Visitor, some of his contemporaries experienced whenever the definition of a category was delayed should be identified with suspense or anxiety. This displeasure, however, clearly includes the element of anticipation towards a specific temporal point in which the desired outcome (the definition of a notion) is to come about. Plato touches upon the indignation elicited by extensive digressions such as the cosmological myth in the minds of those people who think that a philosophical conversation should consist of a plan schema free of retarding digressions. The latter generate fear in those people that they might deviate from the main subject of their discussion and so do not reach the truth about the subject under examination. Plato seems to treat his contemporaries' enthusiasm, if not excessive zeal, for the definition of a notion as an obstruction to conductive dialectic.[81] He seems instead to invite his readers to curb their yearning to discover what a category in question is, and to accept that the long narrating/listening time of a myth, although placing them in an unpleasant state of anticipation and insecurity about the outcome of their investigation, is occasionally a basic prerequisite for the valid definition of a notion. We are not surprised by the fact that Plato has such an attitude towards the matter, given that repeatedly in his works he says that the human soul cannot reach the truth unless it allows its reason to prevail over its emotions.

On the other hand, according to the Visitor, both the narrator and the listener of a story should pursue the proper narrating/listening time of an account, not only by controlling the unpleasant emotions caused by it but also by taming the pleasant ones which emerge from the story's recitation. Let us return to the Visitor's words mentioned above: "Well, but not everything relative to this either, for we'll have no need of any fitting length relative to pleasure, unless it's a by-product" (286d4–6: οὐ τοίνυν οὐδὲ πρὸς τοῦτο πάντα. οὔτε γὰρ πρὸς τὴν ἡδονὴν μήκους ἁρμόττοντος οὐδὲν προσδεησόμεθα, πλὴν εἰ πάρεργόν τι). We could interpret these words through the prism of the audience's anticipation elicited by the narrating/listening time of a myth. In this case, we may argue that the Visitor means here, *inter alia*, the following: one should not pursue a short narrating/listening time for a story due to the pleasure the story's shortness generates, as it contributes to the quick resolution of a dialogue.

---

81 On the Visitor's effort to criticise Young Socrates' enthusiasm in the *Statesman* (but not in this passage), see Miller 1980, 8 and 33; Benardete 1992, 33–34; Rowe 1995, 11; Blondell 2002, 328–329 and 338 with a more positive eye, and 333.

However, we could also enrich this interpretation by viewing 286d4–6 in association with the Visitor's introductory remarks to the myth. When he says to Young Socrates that he will narrate the myth in order to correct the mistakes of the preceding investigation, he also admits that the myth will serve as a "mixture pretty near to a child's play" (268d8: σχεδὸν παιδιὰν ἐγκερασαμένους).[82] Plato's conviction that myths can also — and should — be used as a means to console and entertain children will be further analysed in Chapter 3 on the narratives of the *Laws*. At this point, it is worth examining whether or not 268d8 contradicts 286d4–6. For, on the one hand, the Visitor seems to embrace the entertaining role of narratives (268d8), while, on the other hand, he rejects pleasure as a motive for composing accounts of long narrating/listening time (286d4–6). The coexistence of the two passages is defensible. Plato seems to recognise that a teacher occasionally has to include amusement of some educational means in a philosophical discussion with his students, provided that pleasure is not regarded as an end in itself and with no profit. On the other hand, Plato seems to believe that, in an amusing means of education such as the myth, one should not increase the narrating/listening time in order to intensify the audience's pleasure.

On a narrative level, to judge from the way the myth itself unfolds, Plato seems to lead us to the conclusion that narrating/listening time should not be increased either for the sake of the audience's pleasure or the narrator's. In the last stage of his account on the Age of Cronus, the Visitor interrupts his narration to speculate on whether or not the men of that epoch were engaged with philosophy. However, it is only he who is interested in answering this question. When he asks Young Socrates if he wishes to decide in which era humans were happier, the boy, as we saw, responds in a strikingly indifferent fashion: "In no way" (272b5: οὐδαμῶς). Then, without being discouraged by the boy's unwillingness and swayed by his own desire to further discuss this issue, the Visitor develops his conjectures about men's potential acquaintance with philosophy in the Age of Cronus. Plato presents here a philosopher as being carried away by his interest in the origins of his own field of expertise, and the question is why Plato presents the Visitor in this way.[83] A reasonable answer to this question,

---

[82] Cf. *Prot.* 320c with Stewart 1905, 174. Although the Visitor is serious in composing the myth, this does not necessarily mean that he ironically speaks here of the myth's entertaining nature, as Miller (1980, 36) believes. Pleasure and utility coexist in this case (cf. Tomasi 1990, 450; Rowe 1995, 186).

[83] Tulli (1991, 98–99) recognises Plato's own philosophical interest in this issue. Cf. Tomasi's (1990) view (inspired by Gill 1979) that in the myth of the *Statesman* Plato is infatuated by his own tale. In this respect, it might be said that Plato proceeds self-critically in terms of the

especially given the Visitor's rejection of pleasure as a motive for developing the narrating/listening time of a story (286d4–6), could be that in 272b–c Plato wished to convey the message that a narrator should not be lured by the pleasure elicited by superfluous penetration into matters which she or he is interested in.[84]

The thoughts expressed by the Visitor on the proper assessment of the duration of a philosophical discussion, including digressions such as the myth, should be treated as exemplifying the view we find in many Platonic dialogues about the necessity of leisure of time for the effectiveness of a philosophical discussion. With regard to the presence of this view in the trilogy *Theaetetus–Sophist–Statesman*, it is worth noting that leisure of time is one further issue that is first introduced by Socrates in the *Theaetetus*.[85]

1.4 Conclusion

Exactly because the *Theaetetus* is one from the prisms through which I analysed the myth of the *Statesman*, it is worth noting at this point some thoughts on the relationship of the two dialogues and its significance for our subject of tracing echoes of the one in the other. The *Theaetetus*, the *Sophist* and the *Statesman* constitute a trilogy not only in terms of having a common dramatic time, characters and field of action but also in exhibiting strong thematic, structural and methodological affinities. To begin with, the dramatic time is continuous from the one dialogue to the next. All three conversations take place during the last days of Socrates, shortly before his trial. In the *Theaetetus*, the discussion on the nature of knowledge is interrupted by Socrates, who informs his friends that he has to visit the Athenian authorities in order to be instructed about the accusations made against him. However, he suggests that they meet again in the next morning and at the same gymnasium. At the beginning of the *Sophist*, the geometer Theodorus, one of the main figures in the trilogy, welcomes Socrates, commenting that they indeed kept their promise from the previous day and are

---

restraint he should have while composing a narrative. For other explanations see Benardete 1992, 41 (*eudaimonia*). Dorter (1994, 195) finds that Plato wished to stress that wisdom is superior to pleasure. Hemmenway (1994, 260) believes that the Visitor expresses his uncertainty on the matter in order to expose Young Socrates' misconception of politics.

84 The pleasure the Visitor experiences in speculating on the possible engagement of the earth-born men with philosophy is also evident in the delightfully humorous style of his description. On the comical flavour of these paragraphs, see Klein 1977, 158.

85 Tulli 1991 *passim*. El Murr (2010, 117 n. 21) argues that in no other dialogue is Plato so interested in touching upon the time spent for the pursuit of truth.

now meeting.[86] From this information we may safely infer that in the *Sophist* and the *Statesman* the field of action too is the same as that of the *Theaetetus*.[87] Now, in the *Sophist*, Theodorus has brought with him a friend from Elea, an anonymous philosopher of Parmenides' school, who replaces Socrates in the *Sophist* and in the *Statesman* as the person who leads the course of the discussion. The characters agree to investigate the nature of three kinds of occupation, the sophist, the statesman and the philosopher. The first topic is discussed in the *Sophist*, the second in the *Statesman*, while no dialogue survives on the nature of the philosopher.

Some affinities between the three dialogues also pertain to methodological issues. In all three works the characters proceed to scrutinise the arguments and counterarguments exposed on each topic.[88] This elenctic procedure is marked by so abstruse a logic that it has occasionally been deemed unique in the Platonic oeuvre.[89] Also, the *Sophist* and the *Statesman* differ not only from the *Theaetetus* but also from the rest of the Platonic works on Socrates' last days in that only in them does Plato employ the method of division.[90] This method too, however, is in a way preluded by the *Theaetetus*, as Socrates introduces some thoughts there on how one should define the genus, a concept whose inception is the main precondition for the use of division. Even more importantly, in all three works Plato seems to pay particular attention not only to the methodology and content of the characters' argumentation but also to the modes in which the arguments are revealed. All three parts of the trilogy include extensive digressions, in which (especially those of the *Theaetetus* and *Statesman*) the interlocutors make a series of meta-methodological reflections on the communicative means by which a philosophical discussion should be conducted, with special emphasis being laid on the leisure of time.[91]

---

86 Apart from Rosen 1995, 12 and El Murr 2010, 130, the *communis opinio* is that the conversations of the *Sophist* and the *Statesman* take place on the same day. See, for example, Blondell 2002, 314; Poster 2005, 49.
87 Klein 1977, 4. See, *contra*, Blondell 2002, 317.
88 Campbell 1883, lv–lix;. Sayre (1992, 221 and *passim*) defines the *Theaetetus*, the *Sophist* and the *Statesman*, along with the *Parmenides* and the *Philebus*, as "the methodological dialogues". In these dialogues a conversation takes place between a seasoned philosopher and another discussant and the "methodological principles" of each dialogue are "explicitly proposed by the philosopher himself" (221).
89 Cooper 1990, 2; Rosen 1995, 1.
90 Benardete 1984, xvi; Bostock 1988, 3.
91 On Plato's special interest in issues of methodology in the trilogy, see on *Theaetetus* Frede 1989, 20; Blondell 2002, 251 n. 2, 260, 298; on the *Statesman* Ritter 1923, 135; Davis 1967, 320; Benardete 1992, 25; Arends 1993, 154–155, who treats the first two parts of the dialogue as

It is whithin this framework of meta-methodological reflections in the trilogy that I would like to read the metanarrative reflections of the *Statesman* and their linkages with the cosmological myth. Exactly because a key thesis of this chapter was that Plato's messages in the *Statesman* on certain issues of narrativity (the scheme '*cosmos — human nature — politics*', the aspect of selectivity and narrating/listening time) are preluded by the *Theaetetus*, it is of great significance at this point to stress the fact that the *Theaetetus* serves as a dramatic, thematic and methodological overture to the other two works. This is so because the main compositional technique by which Plato highlights certain themes in the trilogy lies exactly in his choice of introducing these themes in the *Theaetetus* and offering further analysis of them in the *Sophist* and the *Statesman*.[92] In this respect, the aspects of narrativity which are introduced in the *Theaetetus* and are further examined in the *Statesman* offer strong evidence for the following thesis: the educational potential of various modes of narration and the elements of narrativity which are useful for conducting a philosophical discussion are parts of Plato's main agenda of the trilogy. If this view holds true, it entails in turn that these seeds of narrative theory lie at the core of Plato's speculations and should therefore be treated as the fruits of a focused and systematic reflection on the matter to the same degree as, if not to a higher degree than, the views expressed in the *Ion* and the *Republic*.

To conclude this chapter, in the *Theaetetus*, *Sophist* and *Statesman* Plato forces us to experience the methodological complications that often emerge in the course of a philosophical inquiry. For this purpose, Plato presents the characters of the dialogues as putting to the test the potential of many methods, ranging from the Socratic maieutic, division, Protagoras' relativist doctrine of *homo mensura*, eristic arguments, and, of course, cosmological storytelling. All three dialogues are full of meta-methodological statements through which the two main instructors of the discussion, Socrates and the Visitor, explain to the boys and the other interlocutors the merits or the pitfalls of these methods.

Plato's preference for some of these methods over others is undoubtedly evident. However, what is mainly at stake in these dialogues is not so much to promote a single mode of inquiry but instead to teach the young boys of the

---

exercises upon various methods of inquiry; Howland 1993, 15–16; Rowe 1995, 3, 8–9 on the *Statesman*; Cooper 1999, 71 on the *Statesman*; Michelini 2000, 181; Merrill 2003, 35, 39; Blondell 2005, 23; El Murr 2010, 109–116 on the *Statesman*; See also Livov 2011, 331–332, who takes the *Sophist* and the *Statesman* as a "methodological unity". Horn 2012, 393; Naas 2018, 21. On the modes of exposition of ideas, see Poster 2005, 47.

92 Blondell 2002, 314; Merrill 2003, 38. See, *contra*, Lane 1998, 6–7.

dialogues, and along with them us, that philosophy entails an openness to a methodological pluralism, and that anyone who participates in a philosophical conversation is therefore invited to demonstrate patience whenever the discussion seems to reach a dead end. Interlocutors should, further, dedicate as much time as needed to find the proper method required for the discussion's goal, i.e. the definition of a concept. In the context of this intense focus on the pursuit of the proper method of inquiry, lengthy deviations are presented as inevitable solutions in cases where the interlocutors must reconsider their approaches and reorient their way of thinking towards more fruitful standpoints. In the trilogy, such therapeutic deviations are exemplified by Socrates' impersonation of Protagoras in the *Theaetetus*, the Visitor's digression on the being and non-being in the *Sophist*, and his cosmological account in the *Statesman*.

In this chapter, it was argued that modern scholarship has overlooked the fact that this general meta-methodological orientation of the trilogy includes Plato's plan in the *Statesman* to address the practicalities of structuring a cosmological account. Plato materialises this plan by creating an elaborate net of cross-references between a plethora of metanarrative reflections and the texture of the Visitor's myth. Plato depicts the challenges which a narrator is faced with in his effort to construct a narrative on the creation and function of the world, a narrative which is expected to place human affairs, including statesmanship, into the all-encompassing canvas of the universe. The structural scheme he chooses for his account begins with an overall image of the world and moves towards human biology and finally statesmanship. Plato prepares the reader for this structure in Socrates' digression in the *Theaetetus* about the way in which philosophers examine human nature as part of the *cosmos*.

The great challenge for the Visitor is presented as being the transformation of mythical material into a coherent narrative whole. He has to select specific parts from current myths and to incorporate them into his account in a way that restores the causal and temporal gaps between them created in centuries of oral and scattered dissemination of these myths. The views the Visitor expresses both in his opening remarks to the myth and within the myth itself highlight the main features that, for formalist narratologists too, differentiate the raw state of the material to be narrated and the organised form in which this material is transformed into a narrative. These features are selectivity and the creation of causal and temporal relationships between the events of the plot. One further narrative aspect that is approached by the Visitor from a structuralist point of view is narrating/listening time. Within the framework of the trilogy's overall focus on the value of leisure time in philosophical inquiry, the Visitor explains to Young Socrates that the length of what is said in a dialogue, including narratives such as the myth, should be assessed by the criterion of whether or not it contributes to the investigation of the matter in question. In this respect, participants in philosophical discussions should not complain about the length of deviations from the main course of the discussion, such as the cosmological account. The Visitor focuses on the place of the myth in a wider structure of discourse, which has its own goal, and treats the account as a digression which delays the desired outcome of the discussion and therefore elicits the audience's intense anticipation. This approach of narrating/listening time coincides with the formalist narratological approach of digressions as retarding narrative elements that generate readerly suspense.

2 *Timaeus* and *Critias*: Plato's 'Proto-Theory' of Fictional Worlds

In this chapter, moving beyond the 'time-honoured' interest in the three modes of narration and the audiences' emotional identification with a story's characters we read of in Book 3 of the *Republic*, I address the following two questions: (a) did Plato reflect on the *Republic* as a literary work that creates a fictional world? (b) And, if he did, do his reflections on the matter resemble in any respect modern narrative theories of fictional worlds? The views on the conception, narrativisation and reception of the *Republic*'s fictional world that I am interested in are not expressed in the *Republic* itself but in the prologues of the *Timaeus* (17a1–29d6) and *Critias* (106a1–108d8), two dialogues which can safely be treated as the thematic sequels of the *Republic*.

Before analysing these two introductions in detail, a summary of them would be useful. The *Timaeus* begins with Socrates greeting his three friends, Timaeus, Critias and Hermocrates. He talks to them about the discussion they all had on the previous day[1] about an ideal city. Although Timaeus, Critias and Hermocrates are never mentioned in the *Republic* as participants of the discussion at Cephalus' place and although in the *Timaeus* Socrates does not clarify whether he refers to the discussion of the *Republic* or to another occasion on which he had sketched the *kallipolis*, nonetheless the summary he offers of what he had said on the previous day (17b5–19b2) is essentially a concise presentation of the ideal city's three classes, as they are presented in Books 2–4 of the *Republic*.[2] Socrates also reminds his interlocutors of the agreement he had with them the day before. They agreed that Socrates would delineate the inner political organisation of an ideal city and his friends would then, on their part, describe how such a city would act at war with other cities in terms of both military enterprises and diplomatic negotiations (17a1–20c3).

Timaeus, Critias and Hermocrates reassure him that they will keep their promise. What is more, Critias confesses that, while listening to Socrates' description of the previous day, the *kallipolis* reminded him of Athens' political organisation in a remote period of the past, in which the Athenians are said to

---

[1] Although Critias claims that, after listening to Socrates' description of his *kallipolis* and returning to his residence, he spent the night reconstructing in his mind Solon's tale of Atlantis (26b1–2), we are never informed whether or not the preceding discussion with Socrates took place at night or during the day.
[2] Gill 2017, 2.

have defeated the people of Atlantis in a war and thereby secured the freedom of all the peoples expanding from Gibraltar to Asia. This story was told by the Egyptian priests of Sais to Solon during his visit to Egypt. Solon then recounted the tale to the elder Critias, Critias' grandfather, and the old man transmitted it to his grandson (20d7–26e1).

Socrates is thus told by his friends of their decision about how they will proceed. Timaeus will first describe the genesis and function of the universe, including humans. Critias will follow and narrate the story of Athens' victory over Atlantis. At this point, Critias urges his friends to pretend that Socrates' *kallipolis* is the Athens of this old tale (27a2–b6). Socrates accepts his friends' suggestion and Timaeus begins describing the universe in his well-known cosmological myth, after first saying to Socrates that, although his presentation cannot escape from being incomplete, he nonetheless will try to offer a likely version of the world (27b7–29d6). The *Timaeus* ends with the completion of this cosmological narrative and its dramatic sequel comes in the *Critias*, where the eponymous character relates the story about the war between Atlantis and Athens. Similarly to Timaeus, Critias introduces his account by expressing his scepticism about the degree to which listeners can treat his story as a faithful representation of reality (106b8–108a4).

For those familiar with literary theories of fictional worlds, even this concise summary of Socrates' discussion with his friends reveals some connections between the Platonic characters' views on the conception and reception of fictional worlds and modern theories of fiction influenced by the philosophical concept of 'possible worlds'. Socrates' thoughts on how his ideal city *could* behave at war dramatises a certain direction of speculations widespread in the narratology of fictional worlds about what parallel possible worlds can be taken to emerge from things that are not told but are inferred in the basic world of a literary work.

On the other hand, Timaeus' and Critias' introductory apologetic statements on their accounts' finite capacity to offer a complete representation of the worlds they aim to describe are related to one further popular claim of theorists of narrative fiction, namely the admission that fictional worlds, even those which emerge from especially detailed descriptions, are incomplete. In particular, Timaeus' and Critias' need to offer as faithful representations of reality as possible is contrasted with Socrates' humbler wish to listen to a possible extension not of the actual world but of the fictional one he himself has created. This antithesis resembles the following central assumption in the theory of fictional worlds: the alternative worlds which are inferred by the elements of a fictional world are taken by the audience as possible not because they constitute realistic representations of the actual world but because they logically conform to the rules defined by the global organisation of the fictional world they are alternative versions of.

Furthermore, Socrates' confession that, while describing his ideal city, was asking himself how this city would possibly conduct a war, and Critias' proposition that the interlocutors pretend that Athens of his narrative is Socrates' *kallipolis*, create the conditions for a make-believe game and the audience's immersion into the fictional world they are offered, elements which are also commonly treated by modern theorists of narrative and narratologists as the main prerequisites for the reception and apprehension of a fictional world. Last, the expansion of the fictional world of a literary work (the *Republic*) in other works (the *Timaeus* and *Critias*) foregrounds one further key theme in modern theories of narrative about fictional worlds, namely how a fictional world emerges on an intertextual level.[3] In this chapter, I compare the views of the Platonic characters about the aforementioned issues and those expressed by narratologists and theorists of fiction.

Plato touches upon these issues in the *Timaeus* and *Critias*, both of which are commonly considered to have been composed almost two decades after the completion of the *Republic*.[4] Consequently, if the metanarrative statements of the *Timaeus* and *Critias* should indeed be seen as reflections of Plato's speculations on issues of reception of the *Republic*'s fictional world, we are led to the following conclusion: the significance of the *Republic* for our understanding of Plato's thinking on the nature of narrative does not lie only in issues pertaining to the various kinds of the narrator, narrative techniques such as dialogue, monologue and third-person narration, and the audience's emotional immersion into the world of an account, but also in the audience's sense on issues of referentiality and narrative fiction's relationship with reality, possibility and necessity.

The concept of possible worlds debuts in philosophy, with its first seeds commonly being traced in Gottfried Leibniz's theological views expressed in his treatise *Essais de Théodicée sur la bonté de Dieu, la liberté de l'homme et l'origine*

---

[3] On the themes introduced by the opening discussion of the *Timaeus*, see Osborne 1996, 180 and *passim*. She notes as key motifs (a) the distance between the past and the present; (b) how many times a story has been told; (c) discussion of whether or not a story narrates true events; and (d) the degree to which language can represent reality.

[4] On the *Timaeus* see Taylor 1928, 3–13, who contends that the dialogue was written between 360 BCE and Plato's death in 347/346 BCE; Cornford 1937, 1; Lee 1965, 22–23; Brisson in Brisson/Patillon 2001[5], 72–73; Zeyl 2000, xvi–xx. On the *Critias* see Brisson in Brisson/Patillon 2001[5], 335–341. On both dialogues, see Rowe 1997, 52, who follows Kahn 1995, 49–60.

du mal.⁵ Leibniz argues that the divine demiurge conceived of all the possible worlds and from them chose to bring into being the one he considered as the best of all for humanity. The version of the possible-worlds theory that served as a source of inspiration and as the theoretical cornerstone for the theory of literature has been Saul Kripke's scheme of modal logic, which can be described as follows: there is a set of elements K, in which an element G exists. There is also a relationship R between G and other elements of K. Kripke encourages us to take the set K as a universe, which consists of countless worlds. He defines as G the privileged world of K, namely the world which we take as the actual world, while R is defined as the relationship of the actual world G with other possible worlds existing in K. The main principle of this kind of logic is that reality does not consist only of what exists but also of what we can imagine, including whatever does not exist or has not been realised yet but is considered logically necessary and possible. As possible existents are the sentences which do not conflict with the laws of contradiction and the mean.⁶ Modal logicians came up with this model of reasoning in order to attribute truth values to propositions and to include in their evaluative agenda also those propositions which are expressed by means of modal operators of necessity and possibility. For philosophers, possible worlds are innumerable and complete. However, they do not exist but are abstract logical concepts.⁷

The theory of possible worlds soon attracted literary theorists who had a keen interest in the nature of fiction and its difference with nonfiction. Distancing themselves from the introvert readings of literature proposed by formalists and structuralists (in their extreme form expressed by schools such as New Criticism), these theorists (Thomas Pavel, Lubomír Doležel, Marie-Laure Ryan and Ruth Ronen) placed at the core of their conceptual and research agenda questions on the referentiality of fictional worlds and their relationship with reality, possibility and necessity.⁸

The individual details of these critics' theories will be expounded in the rest of this chapter. However, it is worth clarifying from the outset that this approach to narrative worlds tips the scale in favour of issues pertaining to the

---

5 Leibniz 1710.
6 Kripke 1971.
7 Pavel 1975, 165–169; Lewis 1978, 39–40; Doležel 1979, 194–196; Pavel 1986, 32–51; Ryan 1991, 1–5; for a detailed overview of this approach, see Ronen 1994; Doležel 1998, 1–28.
8 Pavel 1975; Lewis 1978; Doležel 1979; Pavel 1986; Doležel 1988; Ryan 1991; Ronen 1994; Doležel 1998. For an overview of the theories of fiction and narrative which were affected by the philosophical concept of possible worlds, see the Introduction to Lavocat 2010; Fořt 2016; Ryan/Bell 2019, 1–28.

reception of literature, since the main question is not what is true, possible or necessary but what the audience takes as such. The reception of a work by its audience also involves the emotions elicited by a plot and the cognitive mechanisms through which we absorb and apprehend the data of a story. The theorists of fictional worlds do not overlook these issues but co-examine them with a special focus on how we use our imagination to reconstruct fictional worlds and how the structural properties of a text, filtered by our social background, enhance this reconstructionist activity of the human mind.

2.1 The possibility of fictional worlds

Athens of the distant past praised by Critias in the Atlantis story has been claimed by modern scholars to serve as a quasi-historical example which proves that what is described by Socrates in the *Republic* is not merely a constitutional chimera but existed once in the past and, what is more, demonstrated glorious and imposing feats in terms of foreign policy and military virtue.[9] However, less attention has been paid to the fact that what Critias does with his myth is certainly not what Socrates is presented as inviting him to do. For Socrates asks his friends to narrate to him the military feats of the *kallipolis* itself and not of an already existing polity which once resembled it.[10] These two different criteria of assessing a fictional world's plausibility resemble the ways in which, according to modern theorists of narrative, audiences weigh the truthfulness, possibility and necessity of fictional worlds. In this section, I will compare the thoughts expressed by the Platonic characters on this issue with those we find in modern theories and narratologies of fictional worlds.

Philosophers of modal logic offer the following axiom for the assessment of the truth or falsity of propositions: a proposition is taken as true only if it refers to an existing state of affairs. Philosophers propound the same criterion for the assessment of the possibility or impossibility of a fictional world. The latter is

---

9 Johansen 2004, 24; Haddad 2012–2013.
10 On the discrepancy between what Socrates asks his friend to do and what Critias does, see Johansen 2004, 27–29. Johansen and Morgan (2010, 269–270, inspired by Brague 1985, 53–54) take it for granted that Socrates' comparison of his *kallipolis* with both painted and alive animals (19b6–7) shows that he has no problem about listening to either a fictional or historical story of his ideal city's feats. I cannot accept this view, since Socrates is well aware of the fact that his *kallipolis* never existed and he has not been told yet by Critias that prehistoric Athens resembled his ideal city. Cf. Gill 2017, 3 (cf. p. 8), who describes Critias' offer as "unexpected", and his excellent discussion on pp. 14–17.

possible in the degree to which it represents characters, objects and states of affairs which can possibly exist in the real world. This approach, which is described by Doležel as the "correspondence theory",[11] entails an examination of fiction based on a theory of truth and possibility which intrudes fiction from the outside, i.e. the real world. In this case, we are invited to assess the ontology of fictional worlds on the basis of the nonfictional, real world's ontology. As a result, the ontological organisation of the real world logically prevails over that of the fictional world and all fictional statements end up being deemed as false or void of meaning.[12]

Theorists of fiction reject this, in their view, "naïve realist"[13] approach of literature and counter-argue that the truth or possibility of a fictional world is — or, at least, should be — assessed by the criterion of whether or not this world depicts elements that comply with its own rules and not with those of the real world. This is so because a fictional world does not constitute a random set of entities but has specific principles that emerge from its macro-structure (in Doležel's terms, "certain postulated global principles").[14] Most importantly, these rules are autonomous in respect to those of the actual world.[15] For example, in Tolkien's *Lord of the Rings*, Gandalf's usual practice of summoning the gigantic Eagles in the aid of a moth messenger is taken by the reader as reasonable and possible because in the world Gandalf belongs to there are indeed gigantic eagles and moths which communicate with men.

Audiences follow the same logic when they are invited to assess the possibility of fictional worlds that constitute expansions of a fictional protoworld. In such cases, theorists of fiction modify Kripke's scheme of modal logic in compliance with the nature of fiction. As said above, Kripke claims that in a set K there is the actual world, which serves as the point of reference for other, countless compossible worlds. Theorists of fiction replace the actual world with every fictional world, which, in their view, can be the point of reference for countless other, compossible, fictional worlds which constitute its possible extensions. On this logic, if we wish to assess the degree of possibility or impossibility of one from among the compossible fictional worlds, we should estimate the degree to which the compossible fictional world in question is shaped in accordance with

---

[11] Doležel 1979, 204–205 and 207.
[12] Pavel 1986, 15–16.
[13] This characterisation was coined by Pavel (1975).
[14] Doležel 1979, 196. Cf. Pavel 1975; Lewis 1978, 39; Pavel 1986, 14–17; Doležel 1988, 482–486; Ryan 1991; Ronen 1994, 9 and 50–54; Doležel 1998, 1–31.
[15] Pavel 1975; Lewis 1978; Doležel 1979; Pavel 1986; Doležel 1988; Ryan 1991; Ronen 1994; Doležel 1998.

the rules set by the fictional protoworld. As Ronen notes, fictional worlds are not possible in the sense that they represent alternative ways in which the actual world could stand. They have instead their own autonomous spheres of possibility and necessity because they show not what might happen in reality but what happened or could happen in fiction.[16]

However, critics also recognise the undeniable fact that people judge the possibility of fictional worlds according to the degree to which the latter represent the actual world. Doležel admits that fictional worlds, although autonomous logical systems and independent of reality, are inextricably connected with it. The actual world serves for fiction as a structural model and provides it with events and cultural elements. On this logic, Doležel propounds the following model of assessment of fictional worlds' possibility: he urges us to assume that there is a basic narrative world of a work, which has other compossible worlds. However, although the recognition of a fictional world as the point of reference to its imaginable compossible extensions leads to an 'esoteric' system of examination of fiction's possibility, this system in the final analysis relates to reality. This is so because Doležel urges us to take as the basic narrative word the one which logically and structurally corresponds to the actual world. For Doležel, the relationship between reality and fiction is marked by a structural restriction: the narrative statements which shape the basic narrative world should not contradict the statements which can be postulated for the actual world.[17] A similar line of thought is adopted by other critics as well. Pavel notes that the comparison of a fictional world with historical figures or events enhances its plausibility in the audience's minds. For example, if we hear that a civil war takes place in Greece, we find that such a development is likely to happen judging from the fact that Greece had faced civil wars in the past.[18] Similarly, Lewis and Ryan, in arguing that the deviations of fiction from the actual world are restricted by certain limits of our imagination, essentially recognise that fictional worlds' point of reference is the actual world.[19]

To schematise the aforementioned views, we can say that theorists of fiction unanimously recognise two elementary modes by which to assess the truthfulness and possibility of fictional worlds. According to the first one, we weigh the likeliness of a fictional world's elements and its imaginable extensions by using as a point of reference the fictional world itself, specifically by examining

---

16 Ronen 1994, 9.
17 Doležel 1979, 1988 and 1998.
18 Pavel 1975, 167–168 and 1986, 47–48.
19 Lewis 1978, 42–43; Ryan 1991, 48–60.

whether the explicitly stated parts and inferred extensions of this world comply with its own rules and not with those of the actual world. I would like to describe this attitude as an 'esoteric' approach to fictional worlds. Along with this esoteric way of thinking, audiences also adopt an 'exoteric' approach to literature, in that they are convinced by or reject what they read in a work according to the degree to which what they read corresponds to the features of the actual world.

Plato is treated by modern theorists as the forefather of the exoteric, and in their view naïve realist, approach to fiction, which should be avoided when it comes to issues of literature's referentiality.[20] In this section but also in the entire chapter, I will endeavour to demonstrate that, although Plato treated mimetic arts, including narratives, as insufficient reproductions of reality, he had no qualms about doing exactly what modern theorists do: he sidestepped the question of what is really true and shifted his interest towards the ways in which the audience considers parts and imaginable extensions of a fictional world as true or possible.[21] In particular, I will argue that in the *Timaeus* and *Critias* Plato brings to the foreground the two aforementioned modes of assessment of fiction's possibility, with Socrates representing the esoteric approach, Critias adopting the exoteric, and himself standing somewhere in the middle.

Let us begin with the esoteric approach of fiction, as this emerges from Socrates' words. Plato markedly lays emphasis upon Socrates' wish to be told not of what the *kallipolis* does but what it *is likely* to do. When he explains that the sophists are not able to conceive of what such a city would do at war, he says that "they may fail to grasp the true qualities which those who are philosophers and statesmen *would* (my italics) show in action and in negotiation in the conduct of peace and war" (19e6–8: ὅσ' ἂν οἷά τε ἐν πολέμῳ ... πράττοιεν καὶ λέγοιεν).[22] Most importantly, he repeatedly states that he expects the encomium of his *kallipolis*' military feats to base its plausibility on its correspondence not with the actual world but with the rules he himself has set in his fictional description. When he compares his desire to listen to this military praise with the desire of people to see a motionless animal moving, he says that people often wish to see an animal "moving and engaging in some of the activities for which they appear to be formed. That's exactly what I feel about the society we have de-

---

[20] See Introduction.
[21] This is the *communis opinio* among classicists specialised in the *Timaeus*. See, selectively, Taylor 1928, 19; Lee 1965, 11–12; Hadot 1983, 119–122; Osborne 1996, 186; Wright 2000; Zeyl 2000, xxxii–xxxiii; Casnati 2011; Morgan 2000, 261–280.
[22] For the texts of the *Timaeus* and *Critias* I use the OCT edition of Burnet (1978). I also use Lee's (1965) translations of both dialogues.

scribed." (19b8–c1: κινούμενά τε αὐτὰ καί τι τῶν τοῖς σώμασιν δοκούντων προσήκειν κατὰ τὴν ἀγωνίαν ἀθλοῦντα). Similarly, he does not wish to hear about a randomly sketched behaviour of his *kallipolis* but about an activity which is marked by "all the qualities one would expect from its system of education and training" (19c6: τὰ προσήκοντα ἀποδιδοῦσαν τῇ παιδείᾳ καὶ τροφῇ). Also, when he claims that his friends are the most suitable for the task of delineating the *kallipolis*' military feats, he once again expresses his hope that they could convey all the qualities that fit in with this city (20b5: ἅπαντ' αὐτῇ τὰ προσήκοντα ἀποδοῖτ' ἄν).

Socrates treats his *kallipolis* as an autonomous system of rules, which serves as the point of reference for its possible extensions. We may recognise in this way of thinking Ronen's view that fictional worlds do not describe what happened or what would be likely to happen in reality but what could possibly happen in a fictional world. We have seen that theorists modify Kripke's model and for them the privileged world G, according to which several other worlds are deemed possible in the set K, is not the actual world but a fictional protoworld. In this way, the issue of fiction's possibility obtains an autonomous ontological status and is dissociated from the actual world. Equally esoteric is Socrates' approach to the likeliness of the imaginary extension he asks his friends to build for the fictional world of his *kallipolis*. The world he searches for is not a random gathering of elements but a system of rules which follows (19c1: προσήκειν; 19c6: τὰ προσήκοντα; 20b5: τὰ προσήκοντα) the rules of the world he has created.

However, Critias connects the world he shapes with the world of the *kallipolis* in a different way from the one proposed by Socrates. As we saw in our summary of the opening chapters of the *Timaeus*, Critias tells Socrates that, while he was listening to him describing the *kallipolis*, he thought that this city resembles in its constitution Athens of the remote past, which is said to have defeated a superpower, Atlantis, in war. For this reason, he suggests that he describe Athens' constitution and narrate its military feats. He also urges his friends to take it for granted that Athens is identified with the Socratic state. Clearly, what Critias proposes is totally different from what Socrates asked in terms of how a fictional world emerges as likely. Socrates expects to hear about a fictional world, the plausibility of which would be based on the degree to which it would conform to the rules of his own fictional world. Critias, on the other hand, wants to defend the plausibility of a fictional world, the one of Socrates' *kallipolis*, by highlighting its resemblances to the actual world.

Of course, Critias' account is based on an ancient story, the details of which have disappeared due to its antiquity and because it came to Critias only after being disseminated by many other narrators (the Egyptians, Solon and Critias the elder). The first word we read about the Atlantis myth is that it is strange (20d7: ἄκουε δή, ὦ Σώκρατες, λόγου μάλα ἀτόπου). Also, the Egyptians explain to Solon that they will narrate some parts of the story in brief, while Critias himself confesses that he found it especially difficult to recollect the story (26a1–2: διὰ χρόνου γὰρ οὐχ ἱκανῶς ἐμεμνήμην). These passages, as well as others, have led some critics to the conclusion that Plato wishes to highlight the unreliability of the Atlantis tale.[23]

However, the validity of the tale is repeatedly defended by all its narrators. Critias, immediately after characterising it as strange, claims that it is a true story (20d8: παντάπασί γε μὴν ἀληθοῦς),[24] and this is also what the other narrators take for granted (cf. 23b8 for the Egyptians; Critias the elder's words ἔπραξε μέν, διὰ δὲ χρόνον …οὐ διήρκεσε δεῦρο ὁ λόγος in 21d5–7; and for Solon, Amynander's words ὡς ἀληθῆ ἀκηκοὼς ἔλεγεν Σόλων). Also, despite his difficulty in recollecting the story, Critias eventually assures Socrates that not only his grandfather (21c3: σφόδρα γὰρ οὖν μέμνημαι) but also he himself remembers it well and, after numerous rehearsals of narrating it throughout the previous night (26a2–c5), he is now in a position to offer not a summary but a detailed narrative of Athens' feats (26c6–7: λέγειν εἰμὶ ἕτοιμος, ὦ Σώκρατες, μὴ μόνον ἐν κεφαλαίοις ἀλλ' ὥσπερ ἤκουσα καθ' ἕκαστον). He also reassures Socrates that he would be surprised if he would miss something from what he had heard. The repetition of the preposition διά (26b6: διακήκοα; 26b7: διαπέφευγεν) shows Plato's intention to stress that Critias remembers everything he was told. Even if we accept the view that Plato wished to force us to doubt Critias' claims about the reliability of his account, it is still undeniable that Plato presents him as being convinced that the war between Athens and Atlantis is an actual event of the past, which took place in the actual world and not in the imagination of a narrator.[25]

Hence, independently of whether or not Critias' story is presented as corresponding to reality, in his words we can recognise the aforementioned view of modern theorists of fiction that in people's minds what takes place in a fictional world seems likely if it is believed to refer to events of the actual world. What

---

[23] Rosenmeyer 1956, 165. Osborne (1996, 181–183) believes that the multiple narrators of the Atlantis story diminish our trust in whether or not Critias' narrative is capable of representing reality. I disagree. Plato does not lay emphasis on the quantity but the quality of the narrators. Cf. Clay 2000, 11 and my analysis in Section 2.4.

[24] For an analysis of the coexistence of ἄτοπος and ἀληθής in the light of other cases from the Platonic corpus, see Haddad 2013.

[25] Clay 2000, 9–11; Broadie 2013, 250.

Socrates described about the *kallipolis* is plausible and likely to take place because there was once a polity similar to it. Also, a city so virtuous in its domestic politics is likely to be equally successful at war. Plato repeatedly has his characters relate Athens' ideal political life with its military feats. These two qualities of Athens are twice mentioned as the two sides of the same coin (23c3–d1; 23e5–6), so that the reader conveys the impression that Socrates' assumption that a city's virtuous political life brings about prudent handling of issues of foreign policy is reasonable.

However, Plato is well aware of the fact that the story on the Athenian triumph over Atlantis, in order to convince us about the feasibility of the political fiction of the *Republic*, should first defend its own plausibility. For this reason, the Atlantis account is not an exotic narrative of elements altogether foreign to the audience of Plato's age. On the contrary, it includes an abundance of events and situations that resemble the most celebrated moments of Greek history, and this is exactly the reason why this story leads its receivers to the conclusion that all that Critias describes, even if they did not really happen, could at least have taken place. First, the campaign of a superpower in pursuit of the conquest of the world resembles the Persians' enterprise against Greece. Second, the Athenians are not presented by Critias as merely participating in the war against Atlantis but as being the leaders of the anti-Atlantic coalition and the main defenders of freedom in the Mediterranean world (25b5–c6). Athens' central role in the Atlantis story alludes to their leading role in the Persian Wars. Furthermore, in Critias' story the patron goddess of Athens is Athena (23d4–24d6), as is also the case in the mythical tradition of the Athenians.

All these elements have been noticed by modern scholars.[26] What I would like to add is that they also lead us to the conclusion that the Athenian victory over Atlantis is by no means to be taken as impossible, since it fits well with the image which the Athenians and the rest of the Greeks had by then shaped for Athens. Consequently, if the Athenians did indeed defeat such an enormous superpower in the spirit of the ideological and political system of Socrates' *kallipolis*, the latter can then possibly exist in the future and prosper in terms of both domestic politics and its relationship with the rest of the world.

If we were to complete our analysis at this point, we could say that in the *Timaeus* and *Critias* we may discern two kinds of reasoning in which Plato's contemporaries took fictional worlds as likely. However, we should not confine our analysis only to what Socrates and Critias are presented as doing. We

---

[26] Vidal-Naquet 1986; Pradeau 1995; Dušanič 2002–2003; Johansen 2004, 11–13; Rowe 2007, 91–92; Garvey 2008; Broadie 2012, 130–140; Broadie 2013, 250 n. 3 and 253.

should also add to our interpretation what Plato himself, the creator of the dialogue, does. In the final analysis, Plato does what he presents Critias to suggest. He endeavours to convince his readers that the fictional world he has created in the *Republic* is likely to take place by connecting this imaginary utopia with the actual world of the past. If we embrace the view that Plato sincerely believed that the story of the Atlantis indeed referred to actual events,[27] we could say that Plato and Critias do exactly the same thing.

However, if we follow the more plausible view that Plato deliberately composes a fiction,[28] we are then led to a third mode in which to validate the likeliness of a fictional world, a mode that differs from those propounded by Socrates and Critias by combining them. On the one hand, Plato, by fabricating the Atlantis myth, does what Socrates is presented as asking: he composes one fiction on the basis of another. If it is true that the Athenians described by the Egyptians constitute the figment of Plato's imagination, we cannot but conclude that he, at least partly, structures the logic of the world delineated in the Atlantis story on the basis of the fictional protoworld of the *Republic*. However, Plato's goal is to promote the Atlantic fiction as a story that corresponds to reality, and exactly at this point there is a noticeable difference between Critias and Plato. While Critias indeed believes that the myth depicts actual events, Plato does not but pretends that he offers a true story.

In this respect, it can be argued that in the *Timaeus* and *Critias* we may discern not two but three modes of validation of a fictional world's possibility also mentioned by modern theorists. First, there is an esoteric mode, which is represented by Socrates and lies in the way we shape a world as an extension of a fictional protoworld and render this extension plausible by shaping it in a way that complies with the rules set by the macro-structure of the protoworld. Second, we may alternatively defend the plausibility and feasibility of a fictional world by demonstrating that what takes place in it has once taken place in the actual world (exoteric mode represented by Critias). Third, we may follow what Plato does in the *Timaeus* and *Critias*, and create a fictional world and, in order to convince the audience about its likeliness, we may shape one further fictional world on the basis of it. However, we promote the second fictional world as corresponding to actual historical events in order to present it not as what it

---

27 For an overview of the most influential studies of this kind, see Clay 2000, 1–2 and 4–9 on ancient readers who were convinced that the Atlantis story was not a fiction.
28 Clay 2000; Wright 2000, 3–4; Broadie 2013, 250; Gill 2017. For an overview of this view from antiquity up to his time, see Gill 2017, 40–45.

actually is, an expansion of the protoworld, but as a historical example in support of the plausibility of the protoworld.

The present analysis, if anything, shows that in the *Timaeus* and *Critias* the emphasis between a faithful representation of, on the one hand, reality and, on the other, mere possibility should not be exclusively sought in Timaeus' introductory comments to his cosmological myth. At the beginning of his treatise, Timaeus asks for Socrates' lenience and understanding in case he offers a self-contradictory description of the universe's function and its creation by the god, and explains that his goal is merely to offer a likely myth (29c4–d3). His words constitute one of the most discussed passages of the *Timaeus* and are traditionally taken as reflecting Plato's goal setting in terms of the logic he wished to structure for the myth.[29]

However, scholars mostly focus on the ways in which the logical coherence of the myth is achieved, while they overlook the fact that Timaeus' intention to offer an εἰκὼς λόγος should be contextualised within the framework of Socrates' and Critias' goals too.[30] The cosmological myth constitutes a part of a program of cooperative construction of a composite world, a program which has already been set by Socrates and Critias. The latter agrees to respect Socrates' wish that what he will describe comply with the logic of the *kallipolis*. He also, as we saw, announces to Socrates the decision he, Timaeus and Hermocrates made: Timaeus will speak first about the creation of the world, including humans. Critias will then take it that Athens of his myth acted in the universe delineated by Timaeus and was conditioned by the ethico-political principles of the Socratic state. Timaeus' myth is thus expected to contribute to the logical connection of what Socrates has presented and what will be exposed by Critias. The cosmological account belongs to Plato's rhetorical scheme through which he tries to convince the reader about the likeliness not only of Timaeus' description but also of the *kallipolis*.[31]

Seen in the light of Socrates' and Critias' statements, Timaeus' introductory remarks, and two of them in particular, might obtain a new meaning. Timaeus twice underlines that the likeliness of his account will lie in its logical coherence (27c7–d1; 29c5–6). As an aspiring composer of a verbally conveyed world, Timaeus expresses the view prevalent in modern theories of fiction that a fictional world is possible when it has certain rules, which are respected by every-

---

[29] Racionero 1998; Burnyeat 2005; McBride 2005; Betegh 2010; Regali 2012, 118–121; Hoenig 2013; Mourelatos 2010 and 2014, 180–190.
[30] See, most importantly, Burnyeat 2005, discussed by Betegh 2010 and Mourelatos 2010.
[31] Johansen 2004, 9 and *passim*, but mainly 48–116; Desclos 2006, 176–177.

thing that is explicitly stated or inferred in it. In the second passage in which Timaeus expresses this view (29c5–6), he seems to refer exclusively to the internal logical organisation of the myth. However, in the first passage (27c7–d1), he might imply that what he will say should fit in well with the principles of the *kallipolis* and the Atlantic myth. This direction of thought is followed by those scholars who look for logical and conceptual linkages between, on the one hand, Timaeus' account and, on the other, the Socratic state and the myth of Atlantis.[32] At any rate, independently of whether or not in 27c7–d1 Plato also draws our attention to intertextual connections between the myth, the *Republic* and *Critias*, my point here is that Timaeus' wish to base the likeliness of his world on the logical connections of this world's parts does not stand alone but participates in a wider program stated from the outset by Socrates and Critias: the composite world which is to emerge from the *kallipolis*, the cosmological myth and the Atlantis story should be structured by shared logical axes.

2.2 Fictional worlds are incomplete and indeterminate constructs

While possible worlds of modal logic are maximal and complete logical structures, fictional worlds are marked by what Doležel defines as "empty domains".[33] No one can know, as Lewis comments, how many sisters, cousins and aunts Joseph Porter has.[34] A fictional world can infer the existence of a great number of characters, but only a handful of them appear in the plot. Also, the objects of a fictional world cannot be fully described and many of their properties are impossible to reveal. As far as the characters of a plot are concerned, their historical background (their lives before the period in which they are described to act) but also their future after the end of the story are not explicitly stated but are rather inferred or, sometimes, are totally omitted. Nor do we learn all the thoughts of the characters in the same depth. Last but not least, fictional worlds are also geographically incomplete. As Ronen notes, "dramatic texts as well as lyrical poetry and narrative prose all construct worlds or fragments of worlds."[35]

---

[32] Cornford 1937, 6; Hadot 1983, 115; Brisson 1992; Pradeau 1997; Johansen 2004; Broadie 2012; Johansen 2013.
[33] Doležel 1988, 486–487.
[34] Lewis 1978, 37.
[35] Ronen 1994, 13.

The incompleteness and indeterminacy of fictional worlds are repeatedly addressed by Socrates, Timaeus and Critias in their programmatic statements both before the cosmological myth in the *Timaeus* and the account of Atlantis in the *Critias*. Most importantly, some of the reasons for the incompleteness of fictional worlds are addressed both in the Platonic dialogues and by modern critics. To begin with, the partial conception of an imaginary world stems from the deficiency of the imagination of both the author and the audience. According to Ryan, fictional worlds are incomplete because our apprehension of objects is incomplete.[36] Other critics attribute the inefficacy of the human imagination both to the inherent features of the human mind and to social factors. First, both authors and audiences are more prone to imagine things that concern them. An author includes elements which (s)he believes are closely related to the narrative goal of the plot and the messages (s)he wishes to convey, while (s)he passes over or even omits whatever (s)he finds irrelevant to his narrative.[37] On the other hand, readers may be capable of imagining whatever they do not read in a text by reaching conclusions and projecting them onto the objects of a story, but they activate their imagination mainly for whatever they are interested in, while they occasionally cannot understand the deeper meanings of a story and the secret aspects of a fictional world. The cultural background of both the author and the audience also confine the capacity of their imagination. It would be very difficult for a reader of our era to fully capture the pieces of the religious world which are not explicitly stated but merely denoted in a Purgatory work of the 12th century.[38]

The finite potential of human imagination is also recognised by Socrates as one of the reasons for the incompleteness of the world of *kallipolis*. In asking himself how the ideal city would interact with other cities at war (19b3–c8), Socrates essentially admits that the city he constructed is incomplete, given that it lacks descriptions of its foreign policy. Socrates not only recognises this "empty domain" of his imaginary *kallipolis* but also admits that this gap partly emerges from the incapability of the *kallipolis*' creator, namely himself, to imagine its possible military feats (19c8–d2). Although he avoids explaining the reasons for his own conceptual barrenness in this respect (19d2–3), he does so for two certain social groups. In particular, he claims that neither poets nor sophists

---

36 Ryan 1991.
37 Pavel 1975, 69, 94–95; Lewis 1978, 39; Pavel 1986, 66–70; Ryan 1991, 20–21; Doležel 1998, 169–184.
38 Pavel 1986, 98–99; cf. Pavel 1975, 170–171; Lewis 1978, 39–44; Ryan 1991; Ronen 1994; Doležel 1998.

would ever be in a position to conceive of such a polity's military activity and convey it well in discourse, and attributes the inadequacy of these groups to their social backgrounds. For neither poets nor sophists are familiar with citizens who possess public offices and simultaneously engage in philosophy (19d3–e8). The role played by the social environment of a literary work in determining which fictional world of this work is captured and rendered by its author and the audience will be further analysed in Section 2.4. At this point, it suffices to note the similarity between modern narrative theory and Socrates in terms of the attention that both sides pay to lack of imagination as a cause of fictional worlds' indeterminacy.

The incompleteness of textual worlds is also attributed to the limited epistemological capacity of the human mind. Pavel, when assuming the existence of a world H, maintains that there are countless propositions that refer to this world and that no reader is able to know all of them. He also adopts a similar stance towards authors of fictional worlds, by claiming that books are nothing more than summaries of what could be written about a world, summaries which owe their concise nature to the inefficacy of the authors' minds.[39] In a similar line of thought, Eco refers to the naivety of those readers who cannot conceive of all those they are invited by the author to see.[40] The limited epistemological and cognitive potential of the human mind is also the reason why fictional worlds will never reach not only their descriptive perfection but also what Ryan describes as their "logical completeness".[41] In a similar vein, Pavel notes that fictional worlds are marked by a certain degree of heterogeneity in terms of the logical rules they convey the one moment and the other, which is why texts cannot "faithfully depict worlds".[42] Ryan comments on this issue that only a "divine mind" could gather all possible features of an object and convey it in its logical completeness.[43]

Similarly, in the *Timaeus* the eponymous character and composer of the cosmological myth repeatedly interrupts his description to express his scepticism about the capacity of human nature to capture a world and convey it perfectly, or even to receive it in the form of discourse.[44] We have already seen that

---

39 Pavel 1975, 167; Pavel 1986, 64–65, 69, 73–113.
40 Eco 1978.
41 Ryan 1991, 20–21.
42 Pavel 1986, 73.
43 Ryan 1991, 21.
44 Cf. Hadot 1983, 113 and for this passage 123–124. Cf. 124 on 69b–c. On Plato's speculations on the degree of completeness in verisimilar accounts such as that in the *Timaeus*, see Ashbaugh 1988, 77–89 and *passim* on Plato's effort in the *Timaeus* to answer the question of how

Timaeus prefaces his myth with the statement that the description of the world he will offer will not be a truthful but rather a likely one. Timaeus explains to Socrates that he contents himself merely with a plausible account because he is fully aware of the limited potential of human nature (29c4–d3):

> ἐὰν οὖν, ὦ Σώκρατες, πολλὰ πολλῶν πέρι, θεῶν καὶ τῆς τοῦ παντὸς γενέσεως, μὴ δυνατοὶ γιγνώμεθα πάντῃ πάντως αὐτοὺς ἑαυτοῖς ὁμολογουμένους λόγους καὶ ἀπηκριβωμένους ἀποδοῦναι, μὴ θαυμάσῃς· ἀλλ' ἐὰν ἄρα μηδενὸς ἧττον παρεχώμεθα εἰκότας, ἀγαπᾶν χρή, μεμνημένους ὡς ὁ λέγων ἐγὼ ὑμεῖς τε οἱ κριταὶ φύσιν ἀνθρωπίνην ἔχομεν, ὥστε περὶ τούτων τὸν εἰκότα μῦθον ἀποδεχομένους πρέπει τούτου μηδὲν ἔτι πέρα ζητεῖν.

> Don't therefore be surprised, Socrates, if on many matters concerning the gods and the whole world of change we are unable in every respect and on every occasion to render consistent and accurate account. You must be satisfied if our account is as likely as any, remembering that both I and you who are sitting in judgement on it are merely human, and should not look for anything more than a likely story in such matters.

Timaeus foregrounds here the two *desiderata* which, according to modern theorists, human descriptions of worlds fail to generate: precision (29c6: ἀπηκριβωμένους)[45] and logical cohesion (29c5–6: πάντῃ πάντως αὐτοὺς ἑαυτοῖς ὁμολογουμένους). Comments which express this pessimistic view about the limited capacity of a work of discourse — either written or oral — to describe a world and to convey its logical completeness are one of the recurring motifs and thus distinctive features of the myth. More importantly, Timaeus attributes narration's limited descriptive capacity not only to the finite abilities of the human mind but also to the bounded representational potential of discourse. Such a distinction between the conception and the verbal rendering of a world is discernible in Timaeus' words that "to discover the maker and father of this universe is indeed a hard task, and, having found him, it would be impossible to tell everyone about him" (28c3–5).[46] Also, when discussing the movements of the earth, moon and sun, he notes that only a few people have knowledge of

---

the human soul can grasp the structure and essence of the world. Skemp (1989) approaches the issue of what is presented as truth in the *Timaeus* from the perspective of the world's reception by the human soul and concludes that καταληπτικὴ φαντασία ('apprehending perception') is feasible in the wise man's soul; Brisson 2001⁵, 14–15, 48–53, and 70.

45 On the challenge of offering a precise account, cf. *Phaed.* 58d8–9.
46 Humans' inability to conceive of the nature of the gods is a recurring idea in the Platonic dialogues. See, e.g., the discussion in the *Euthyphro*; *Cratyl.* 400d6–401a6. On the difficulty of both conceiving of something and teaching it to someone else, cf. *Parm.* 135a7–b2 which emphasises the incompleteness of such teachings (135b2: ταῦτα πάντα ἱκανῶς διευκρινησάμενον); *Lach.* 178b3–4.

other celestial bodies' movements and rotations. For this reason, given that science has no models of these movements at its disposal, any attempt to describe them is futile (40c3–d5). Elsewhere, he repeats that it is impossible for him to depict the genesis of the universe through his narrative, which, as a means of expression, is again presented as insufficient (48c2–e1).[47] Also, when treating the form of the natural elements (56b–c), he creates an antithesis similar to the one expressed by Ryan between the divine *nous* which knows everything and human mind which does not. In particular, Timaeus maintains that god defined the movements, size and structure of the smallest particles of each natural element, the form of which humans cannot perceive due to their smallness (cf. *Cr.* 106b5–6).[48]

One of the most significant reasons why we cannot discover fictional worlds in their entirety is believed to lie in the fact that not only the actual world but also every imaginable possible world is of an inconceivable size. Pavel elegantly highlights this fact in his extensive allegory about the so-called *Magna Opera* that can describe a world. In his effort to help the reader grasp the unfathomable vastness of the universe, Pavel weaves the following story together: for every universe there can be written countless works, which, all together, are named *Magna Opera*. All these *Magna Opera* constitute the *Total Image* of the universe they refer to. Of course, the universe consists of innumerable worlds, each of which can also be described by countless *Magna Opera*. For Pavel, human books constitute "imperfect imitations", as they are mere summaries of the enormous, inconceivable universe. At the same time, even those texts which have been composed by the strongest minds could never fully depict the infinite universe because texts are finite, have specific scopes and create only limited narrative goals. Pavel notes that this is a truth which all authors over time have in mind, which is why, in his opinion, authors very rarely aspire to offer through their texts complete universes or maximal worlds. In the history of literature, only science-fiction writers are sometimes lured by the impossible task of describing entire universes.[49]

Timaeus' very first words about his account betray a similar line of thought. After his interlocutors have completed their preliminary discussion and it is time for him to open his narrative, he is encouraged by Socrates to begin by invoking the gods to help him in his attempt, as usually happens in the prologues

---

47 Cf. Hadot 1983, 120 on 69a–b.
48 On this kind of antithesis, cf. *Apol.* 42a3–5; in terms of naming objects, see *Cratyl.* 391d2–392b7; *Parm.* 134e7–8; *Phaedr.* 246a3–6.
49 Pavel 1986, 52–72.

of narratives (27b7–9). Timaeus answers that, given that anyone who endeavours to discuss something asks the gods to help him, he is naturally entitled to do so, since he will try to describe the entire universe (27c1–d1). Here he creates a sharp contrast between those who elaborate on small issues (27c3: σμικροῦ καὶ μεγάλου πράγματος) and himself who will examine the whole universe (27c4: ἡμᾶς δὲ τοὺς περὶ τοῦ παντός). With this introductory remark, Timaeus prepares his interlocutors and us for all these points of the myth at which he will admit that he cannot include all the elements of the universe in his description, which is also finite due to the pressure of time.

Literary theorists recognise that fictional worlds are also incomplete due to the authors' selectivity.[50] In the previous chapter, it was demonstrated that Plato was particularly interested in the selection procedure through which a narrator arranges the material at his disposal in the plot he constructs. It was also maintained that in the *Statesman* the Visitor approaches this theme from a rather formalist perspective, as he stresses the way in which selectivity defines not only the pre-compositional stage in which the material is selected, but also the very structuring of the data in the process of the composition and formation of the plot. The Visitor repeatedly informs us that the transitions from the one stage to the next of the narrative route '*cosmos* → human nature → politics' were realised through the omission of certain data and the inclusion of information more relevant to the storyline.[51]

Similarly, in the cosmological myth of the *Timaeus* the narrator repeatedly interrupts his narration in order to remind his interlocutors and the reader of the fact that he is choosing what to describe in length, what to offer in a concise way and what to omit. However, differently from the Visitor of the *Statesman*, Timaeus proceeds with these comments by laying emphasis on the impact of this selection procedure upon the descriptive capacity of his account. Let us see the passages which make this point.

In 38b3–5, Timaeus explains that he will avoid penetrating into the proper semiotics about the three temporal levels (past, present, future) and comments that "this is perhaps not a suitable occasion to go into the question in detail" (περὶ μὲν οὖν τούτων τάχ' ἂν οὐκ εἴη καιρὸς πρέπων ἐν τῷ παρόντι διακριβολογεῖσθαι). Timaeus not only states that he will omit certain themes, as the Visitor does in the *Statesman*; he also lays emphasis on the fact that his omission deprives his description of a precise analysis of the omitted elements. He uses the verb διακριβολογεῖσθαι, which does not merely mean "to expose with precision"

---

50 See above, n. 37.
51 See Chapter 1.

but, due to the preposition διά, "to expose with the uppermost precision". This verb constitutes an echo of Timaeus' words μὴ πάντῃ πάντως ...λόγους ... ἀπηκριβωμένους λόγους in the prologue to his account (29c5-6) and thus serves as a deliberate reminder to the reader of the view expressed in the prologue that the myth lacks precision. As we saw, in the prologue Timaeus attributed the inadequacy of his treatise to the vastness of the object of inquiry. Here, he adds one further reason for the incompleteness of his fictional world, the narrator's selectivity.

After a few lines, Timaeus states, as we saw, that he will skip the movements of celestial bodies, saying that, if one tries to describe them all, one will spend more time than needed for the completion of his goal setting in narrating the myth (38d6-e1). He concludes his comment with the words "the topic is one with which we might deal as it deserves at some later time when we have leisure (38e2-3: ταῦτα μὲν οὖν ἴσως τάχ' ἂν κατὰ σχολὴν ὕστερον τῆς ἀξίας τύχοι διηγήσεως). Once again, Timaeus does not content himself with saying that he will omit something; he rather feels the need to apologise by saying that on a certain occasion in the future he will perhaps discuss this issue *as it deserves*, inferring that the present account is incomplete and therefore does not do justice to some issues.

In 51c5-d2, Plato dramatises the effort of a narrator to reach a compromise between his wish to pass over some facets of the world he describes and his need to limit the ramifications of such omissions for the completeness of his description. We have reached the point at which Timaeus poses the rhetorical question of whether or not there are, apart from the sensible objects, things which are perceptible only through the mind. Timaeus notes that he should not argue for the existence of such entities without proving it. Still, he also clarifies that he does not find it necessary either to dedicate a great deal of his exposition to this matter. He thus decides to offer a general and brief argumentation. We are faced here with Timaeus' intention to confine as much as possible the indeterminacy and logical ungroundedness of his account but also to keep up with the rules he himself adopts in this selection procedure.

The incompleteness of fictional worlds lies at the focal point of Plato's interest not only in the *Timaeus* but also in the *Critias*. The myth of Atlantis is also introduced by the narrator's apologetic statements on the difficulty of composing a narrative that will be taken by the audience as reliable, complete and sufficiently descriptive. In the opening paragraphs of the *Critias*, the eponymous character expresses the following thoughts: although Timaeus is indeed entitled to ask for his audience's lenience in case he fails to depict the universe faithfully, he himself deserves the audience's tolerance even more. In his opinion, people, who are ignorant of the gods' and universe's natures, content themselves with less faithful theological treatises such as that of Timaeus. On the other hand, when someone, like himself, narrates human affairs, people who are familiar with human nature thoroughly scrutinise the details of such stories and judge imprecisions much more strictly. In a similar vein, paintings depicting nature enjoy people's tolerance to a higher degree than paintings representing the human body (106b8–107e3).[52]

Differently from Timaeus, Critias pays less attention to a narrator's dexterity to conceive of and verbally convey a world, and shifts his interest to the audience's ability to catch the degree of incompleteness (107d3: τὸ παραλειπόμενον) and indeterminacy (107d1: ἀσαφεῖ) in the verbal depiction of a world. His point is that it is easier for someone not so much to offer a sufficient description of the gods rather than men but instead to convey the impression that she or he does so (107a8–b1: δοκεῖν ἱκανῶς λέγειν). Similarly, in paintings Critias does not examine the easiness or the difficulty one faces in creating sufficient imitations of reality but in convincing the audience that she or he does so (107c1–2: πρὸς τὸ τοῖς ὁρῶσιν δοκεῖν ἀποχρώντως μεμιμῆσθαι). The emphasis is laid upon the receivers: when we are acquainted with the object of imitation, we are pedantic judges, but when we are not, we are satisfied with incomplete representations.

Critias' statements imply how descriptive and faithful Timaeus' εἰκὼς λόγος may seem to its audience. When comparing narrative representation with painting, Critias claims that, whenever one aspires to describe the divine affairs and celestial bodies through discourse, it is as if one wishes to depict in her or his paintings the earth, mountains, rivers, sky and all the bodies found in it. Within the framework of this parallelism, he connects the two cases through a verbal cross-reference. With regard to paintings depicting nature, he states that "we are satisfied if the artist can produce quite an elementary likeness of earth", etc. (107c4–6: ἀγαπῶμεν ἄν τίς τι καὶ βραχὺ πρὸς ὁμοιότητα αὐτῶν ἀπομιμεῖσθαι δυνατὸς ᾖ), and deems such an inadequate painting "an imprecise and deceptive[53] sketch" (107d1: σκιαγραφίᾳ δὲ ἀσαφεῖ καὶ ἀπατηλῷ). Similarly, with regard to verbal descriptions of gods and the heaven "we are content with faint likeness" (107d6–7: τὰ μὲν οὐράνια καὶ θεῖα ἀγαπῶμεν καὶ σμικρῶς εἰκότα λεγόμενα). Through this comparison, Critias invites the reader to think that the εἰκὼς λόγος Timaeus was reservedly satisfied with may be treated by other literati

---

52 Schalcher (1997, 158) notes that a key subject in the opening discussion of the *Timaeus*, both in the words of Socrates as well as in those of Critias, is the memory of the audience, i.e. how well one remembers a story one has been told.
53 I replaced Lee's "inaccurate" with "deceptive".

as "an imprecise and deceptive sketch", i.e. as a representation which does not reach the absolute correspondence between what represents and what is represented. What is taken by Timaeus as the maximum we can reach, given our finite epistemological capacity, is seen by Critias as the minimum we reach in terms of correspondence between discourse and reality. This message resembles Thomas Pavel's words that, "construed as linguistic conformity between worlds and their texts, realism is a remarkably courageous project".[54]

Whether or not we should take Critias' roundabout underestimation of Timaeus' account literally is insignificant. In his effort to predispose his friends favourably towards his account, Critias may be exaggerating and possibly does not really believe Timaeus' cosmological treatise to be that inefficient. After all, he begins his prologue with a warm praise of his friend's description (107a4–6).[55] However, independently of how we are invited to interpret the meaning of Critias' words, we are also left to vacillate, with regard to the incompleteness of verbal representations of worlds, between different perspectives such as those of Timaeus and Critias.

At this point, it is worth drawing one further parallel between Plato and modern theorists of fictional worlds. It is a *communis opinio* among modern critics that incompleteness constitutes a feature not only of literary fictional worlds but also of those which emerge from deliberate representations of the actual world, such as those of historical accounts and treatises of physics. Pavel contends that readers find it equally difficult to interpret historical literature in comparison with poetry and novel.[56] Ryan discerns three categories of fictional worlds depending on the degree of their incompleteness and takes as less incomplete more realistically conveyed worlds such as those of historical books.[57] Doležel embraces Ryan's schematisation and, already in 1988, admits that even realistic worlds are incomplete. What is more, in 2010 he wrote his monograph *Possible Worlds of Fiction and History*, in which he discusses at length the incompleteness and indeterminacy of worlds depicted in historical narratives and concludes that the latter are no less imperfect than imaginary worlds.[58] Last, Ronen, although opposing any attempt to classify literary genres on the basis of a world's incompleteness, notes that there are no gradations of fictionality and that, whatever world, be it imaginary or historical, is depicted in a text, that

---

54 Pavel 1986, 73.
55 On the competitive spirit in which Critias treats Timaeus, see Desclos 2006, 181–188.
56 Pavel 1986, 81.
57 Ryan 1991, 31–47.
58 Doležel 1988, 487; Doležel 2010.

world is fictional and thus incomplete.[59] In a similar vein, in the *Timaeus* and *Critias* Plato presents descriptive imperfection as being the distinctive feature of both Socrates' purely fictional world and the worlds of Timaeus' cosmology and Critias' historical account, both of which are claimed to refer to reality.

One further prevalent theme in the theory of fictional worlds which is also discernible in the *Timaeus* concerns the audience's ability to overcome the empty domains of a fictional world and to cover them by imagining what is inferred in the narration. Vaina, in her distinction between the main textual world and those which emerge from the characters' thoughts about it, notes that some of these sub-worlds are not explicitly stated but inferred, adding that the text itself encourages speculations on how the textual world could have been, had one character not participated in the plot (counterfactual thoughts).[60] In the same spirit, Lewis notes that some propositions about a fictional world should not be deemed true or false exclusively on the basis of what is stated but on the basis of what the readers conclude by reading the text through the filter of their beliefs and experiences in the actual world.[61] Furthermore, one of the cornerstones of Doležel's approach to fiction is the thesis that an inherent feature of the text is that the world it depicts is divided into two worlds, the explicitly stated one and an implicit one.[62] In this line of thought, Pavel focuses on the question of up to what point readers are entitled to infer untold elements from a text, and favours a balanced "inference procedure" which respects the diversity of fictional worlds from logical maximal structures.[63] Last, Ryan shapes her theory on the principle of minimal departure through which readers overcome the impediments emerging from the fictional worlds' incompleteness and restore with their imagination the missing parts of fictional states of affairs.[64]

It is exactly this reconstructive ability of his friends that Socrates invokes in the *Timaeus*. In essence, he may admit, as demonstrated, that his fictional utopia remains incomplete in many respects, but he also recognises that it contains enough explicitly stated data from which to assume how the *kallipolis* would behave in war. As we saw, Socrates does not merely ask his friends to imagine his city's potential military achievements independently of the description he offered on the previous day. He asks them to base their assumptions

---

[59] Ronen 1994, mainly 76–107.
[60] Vaina 1977, 356–361.
[61] Lewis 1978, 45.
[62] Doležel 1979, 207–210; 1988, 486–487; 1998, 169–184.
[63] Pavel 1986, 21, 97, 105–113.
[64] Ryan 1991, 48–60.

exactly on this portrait. As a result, the reader is led to the conclusion that the incompleteness of Socrates' delineation of the *kallipolis* is not totally insurmountable but can be outdone by the audience's ability to imagine the untold.

As far as Timaeus and Critias are concerned, Plato presents two composers of textual worlds as being concerned with the limits of their narratives' descriptive and semiotic potential. He brings to life the anxiety of authors of his age, which I believe he strongly identifies with, on the possibilities they have to convey verbally the worlds they conceive as faithfully as possible.[65] This theme draws one further connection between Plato and modern theorists of fictional worlds. Pavel lays special emphasis on authors' concern about their inability to offer maximal worlds, and urges them not to struggle to maximise the incompleteness of their writings for any reason (aesthetic, ideological etc.) or minimise it for the sake of more realistic results.[66] In a similar vein, Ryan's effort to categorise the various genres of literature on the basis of the degree of their (in)completeness essentially mirrors her treatment of literary genres as emerging from different modes of maximising and minimising the incompleteness of textual worlds.

What also matters for our comparison between Plato and Pavel is that, for the latter, highly descriptive depictions of worlds are traditionally taken as the most realistic ones and are pursued by authors who are confident that the inability of a text to include something so immense as a universe can be mitigated by the minimisation of a fictional world's gaps. This optimism, Pavel adds, often increases in periods in which the scientific circles of a society feel confident that they have a clearer picture of the world. On the other hand, in periods of intense discordance and confusion about nature's and society's essence, authors produce works of a deliberate vagueness, such as the works of Modernism.[67] In any case, Pavel notes, "such thematised, one could say *enacted*, incompleteness can be construed as a reflection on both the nature of fiction and the nature of the world."[68]

The prologues to the *Timaeus* and *Critias*, as a pair of announcements, diffuse in the two dialogues a key idea which serves for us as the main filter through which to read both myths.[69] As is the case with Pavel's and Ryan's

---

65 Cf. Racionero's (1997) approach.
66 Pavel 1986, 105–109.
67 Pavel 1986, 109.
68 Pavel 1986, 108.
69 On the function of prologues in Plato, see the papers gathered in Kaklamanou/Pavlou/Tsakmakis 2021.

analyses, this key idea is the authors' concern of their and their audiences' limited epistemological and conceptual potential and the representational and semiotic weaknesses of discourse, which doom fictional worlds to ambiguity. It is worth noting that, among the plethora of Plato's cosmological and historical accounts, these two myths are the only ones to be prefaced by their composers with apologetic explanations of their content. Similarly, Socrates' statements on the empty domains of his fictional utopia in terms of military operations retrospectively assess the *Republic* through the same prism, i.e. the incompleteness of fictional worlds. Timaeus' and Critias' words reflect Plato's meta-compositional speculation on issues of texts' referentiality and their relationship with the worlds, imaginary or historical, which they aim to convey.

By extension, the present analysis may add to modern scholarship one further basis on which some main compositional features of the *Timaeus*' cosmological account and the *Critias*' myth of Atlantis may be explained. In particular, Pavel's view that the deliberate informational density of an account occasionally reflects its author's concern about the incompleteness of the account's fictional world may help us explain the distinct descriptiveness of the cosmological myth and of some segments from the Atlantis story. It has repeatedly been noticed by classicists that both accounts have a special place among other Platonic myths of similar content in that they are marked by an unprecedented eagerness, on Plato' part, to lead us to immerse ourselves into the details of both descriptions.[70] In the *Timaeus*, the description of the soul's formation, the inner structure of the natural elements and the form of the universe itself are not found in other cosmological myths of Plato, such as those we read in the *Statesman*, the *Laws* and the *Phaedrus*. This is also the case with the thorough delineation of Atlantis' geomorphology and urban design, which may resemble Herodotus' detailed descriptions of Babylon but reminds us of no other Platonic account.[71] Many explanations have been proposed for the distinct descriptiveness of both dialogues.[72] However, through the prism of Timaeus' and Critias'

---

[70] See, e.g., Broadie 2013, 249.
[71] Rosenmeyer 1956, 166. On Herodotus' descriptions of Ecbatana and Babylon as a source of inspiration for Plato, see Bidez 1945, 33 ff.; Friedländer 1954 I, 214 ff. and 330 ff.; Vidal-Naquet 1964, 427–429; Dušanić 1982, 27. On Atlantis as Carthage see Dušanić 1982, 27–28 with exhaustive bibliography. Rousseaux (1970, 338–339) draws a parallel between Persian imperialism and Atlantis.
[72] Vidal-Naquet (1964, 430–434) finds that the topography of Athens creates links with the actual past of the city. Golding (1975) draws parallels between the *Timaeus* and *Laws* in terms of the way that Plato experiments in designing the urban plan of a city. On the discourse and structure of Timaeus' account, see Hadot 1983; Brague 1985; Brisson 1987; Osborne 1996.

externalisation of their wish to depict so far as possible the worlds they are invited to imagine, the elaborate descriptiveness of the two myths can be understood to mirror the narrators' effort to achieve this very goal.[73] Had Timaeus' and Critias' introductory apologies on their narratives' incompleteness not been supplemented by detailed accounts, we could assume that the two apologetic prologues merely exemplify the usual rhetorical programmatic statements we find in historiographical and rhetorical works, statements which target the audience's favour. However, in the *Timaeus* and *Critias* we are faced with two narrators who from the outset explain to their audience what motivated them in offering such descriptive accounts. Plato's message in both cases is not different from Pavel's: the special descriptiveness of texts often reflects their authors' aspiration to convey the worlds they conceive as faithfully as possible.

In this respect, Timaeus and Critias, as narrators, resemble the authors who, according to Pavel, intend to minimise the incompleteness of their descriptions and to offer a realistic picture of the world. Timaeus may be presented as being sceptical about whether or not he will succeed in doing so, but simultaneously his social environment, represented by his friend Timaeus, believes that his expertise and knowledge make him the most promising candidate for such a challenge (27a3–6).

2.3 The author's and audience's immersion in the fictional worlds

Critics believe that a naively realistic assessment of fiction does not correspond to the intuitive fashion in which the audience receives the fictional world of a work. Pavel recognises that literary works, especially when composed in the form of a myth, a mimesis, or a novel, force us to disclaim the world we live in and thereby to change our "ontological perspective". This shift entails that, while following the narration, we assess the degree of reliability, truth and possibility of what we are told by the narrator from the ontological perspective of the fictional world. Pavel defines this transference of our gaze from the angle of the actual world to that of fiction as the "uprooting of the reader".[74] Accordingly, Ryan describes this process as "recentering".[75] Ronen traces the reasons of

---

[73] Cf. Lee 1965, 150–153, who discerns in the richness of details in the Atlantis story Plato's experiments in writing science fiction. Also, see Morales Caturla 2013.
[74] Pavel 1975, 174 and *passim*.
[75] Ryan 1991, 77–95.

this psychological phenomenon in our intuitive tendency to take it for granted that fictional worlds are marked by "closedness".[76]

Theorists of fictional worlds do not traditionally connect Plato with their theories on this make-believe game. If we were to describe how modern literary and narrative theorists relate their views on this issue with Platonic thought, we would have to say that Platonic philosophy and the tradition it has created are treated over time not as something to identify with but as a distraction from the issue of the audience's immersion in fiction. As demonstrated in the Introduction and Section 2.1, critics recognise Plato as the founder of the realist view that a representation is true only if it depicts reality. We also saw that, for these critics, this thesis becomes irrelevant once we discuss the possibility and truthfulness of fictional worlds.

Indeed, no one can deny the fact that certain views expressed in the Platonic corpus about *mimesis* prevent us from apprehending the peculiar way in which the laws of logic are abolished once we immerse ourselves in imaginary realms. Nonetheless, with regard to exactly this phenomenon, we may also discern many similarities between modern theories of fictional worlds and Platonic thought. This is so, because the absorption of audiences, as well as that of poets and performers, by the world of a fictional work is discussed in length in the *Ion* and in the dialogue we are mainly interested in here, the *Timaeus*. Let us present and analyse the passages from the *Timaeus* which attest to this view.

The first passage is the one in which Socrates expresses his wish to listen to someone praising the military feats of his *kallipolis*. The psychological state in which Socrates' curiosity is elicited about the way in which his ideal city would act in war resembles the state of the audience's immersion in a fictional world as presented by modern theorists, with the only difference being that Socrates is not the receiver but the composer of the fictional world in which he imaginarily enters. Socrates confesses that he feels like someone who is observing some beings, either painted or living, standing still and is occupied by the desire to see them being in motion and employing their qualities in competition with other beings. In a similar vein, he would like to see the *kallipolis* interacting with other cities according to the portrait he has sketched for it (19b3–d2).

Socrates emphasises the mental experience of his situation (19b4: οἷόν τι πρὸς αὐτὴν πεπονθὼς τυγχάνω; 19b5: τὸ πάθος; 19b7: εἰς ἐπιθυμίαν ἀφίκοιτο)[77] and presents himself as being affected by his imaginary utopia in the same way that audiences are described by modern theorists as being absorbed by fictional

---

76 Ronen 1994, 29, 33, 47 n. 1, 96.
77 Regali 2011, 80; Reydams–Schils 2011, 349.

worlds. For with these words, he is essentially presented as taking for granted that people are capable of activating their imagination about the possible expansions of artefacts to the same degree that people feel curious about how an actual being could act (19b6–7: εἴτε ὑπὸ γραφῆς εἰργασμένα εἴτε καὶ ζῶντα ἀληθινῶς). Socrates seems to forget for a moment that his *kallipolis* is imaginary, and enters the fictional world he himself has created by treating it as being the actual world. His curiosity is triggered about something non-existent. In essence, Socrates presents himself as transferring his "ontological perspective" which Pavel talks about from the actual world he belongs to towards the newly-established world of his ideal city. The *kallipolis* world for a moment serves for Socrates as the sphere around which all alternative possible worlds are re-centered. One from among these worlds is the one in which the *kallipolis* interacts with other cities.

The parallelism between the worlds that emerge from discourse and those who are brought to life in the works of visual arts opens one further channel of comparison between Platonic thought and modern literary theory, and in particular recalls Pavel's statement that "to read a text or to look at a painting means already to inhabit their worlds".[78] Of course, it is worth noting that there is a marked difference between the receptions of a story and a painting in terms of the way that we receive the stimulus which will activate our brains to restructure the artificial world in each case. Through paintings, as well as through the works of any other visual art, we receive the message of the artist by our sight, which is also the case with how we sense actual objects and beings. On the other hand, a verbally conveyed fictional world emerges from the thoughts we make while reading or listening to a narrative. However, no matter the way in which each world is reconstructed by its audience, the actual world, the worlds of visual arts and those of discourse are all treated by Socrates mainly in terms of the possibilities inherent in them. His clarification that the audience's thoughts on the possible motion of a being are enhanced regardless of whether the being is actual or fictional reveals that for Plato fictional worlds, whether visual or verbal, have a capacity equal to that of the actual world to serve as the source of speculation on what possible worlds can be inferred by their semiotic spectrums.

The state of immersion is also addressed in the *Ion*, where we read that the performer and his audience immerse themselves in the world created by the poet (*Io.* 533c9–536d7). However, in the *Ion* emphasis is laid mainly on the affective

---

[78] Pavel 1986, 74. On this passage of the *Timaeus*, see Reydams–Schils' (2011, 352–353) fine analysis.

impact of this mental state upon people's psychology.⁷⁹ In the *Timaeus*, Socrates transfers our focal point of interest from the emotions elicited by verbal worlds towards the way in which immersion contributes to the reconstruction of a fictional world and the mental processes through which the composer or the audience endeavour to conjecture and unlock its hidden possible dimensions.

Furthermore, the distinction we just addressed between the mechanisms of a visual or an actual world's reception (sight) and those of the reception of a narrative world (thinking) is also hinted at by Socrates through specific verbal choices. As transpires from what he says, we enter the world of painting and the actual world after seeing them (19b6: θεασάμενος). Differently, Socrates claims that he immersed himself in his fictional utopia not after seeing it but through its oral description (19c2: πρὸς τὴν πόλιν ἣν διήλθομεν). What is verbally described is indeed equated to what is painted and what is actual, but it is perceived through hearing (19c2–3: ἂν ... ἀκούσαιμ᾽).

Last, in all three cases, the audience is presented as wishing to 'see' something in action. The meaning of the infinitive θεάσασθαι (19b7–8) should better be analysed separately for each of the three cases. First, in case someone observes an actual living being, her or his desire to see it moving should be taken at face value. Second, in the case that someone observes a painted creature, her or his wish to see it should not be identified with an illusionary state of mind because we never *really* forget the world we belong to and what is real or not. As will be demonstrated below, this is also what Socrates reasonably believes. So, one plausible reading of this text is as follows: Plato could be taken as meaning here that, whenever we observe a painted creature, we wish to see it moving but, being cognisant of its artificial nature, are aware of the fact that we will never do so and we merely imagine it moving. On this logic, the infinitive θεάσασθαι could mean in this case "to imagine", which fits well with the fact that another verb suggestive of sight (ὁρᾶν) often has this meaning in Plato.⁸⁰

However, an equally reasonable, in my view, interpretation is that, whenever we observe a painted object, for a moment we wish not to imagine it but to see it, exactly because we are swayed by the world of the visual artefact and momentarily feel that what we are observing is alive. On this logic, with regard to the third case, Socrates may mean that, while listening to his own description of the *kallipolis*, he wished to see it fighting other cities as if the *kallipolis* truly existed. However, given that he did not totally immerse himself in the *kallipolis*'

---

79 Liveley 2019, 13–15.
80 See, e.g., *Rep.* 514a–515a.

fictional world, he knows that this is impossible and is content to listen to his friends' description.

While up to this point Socrates has addressed the immersion in the imaginary *kallipolis* he undertook as a narrator, from now on he will share with his companions his wish to experience the same state as a listener, while he is listening to the delineation of the fictional world being created by them. After explaining the reasons why he considers them to be capable of imagining and composing the military *encomium* of his ideal city, he reassures them that he is ready to receive their "hospitality" (20c1–3: ξένια ... ἐπ' αὐτὰ καὶ πάντων ἑτοιμότατος ὢν δέχεσθαι). Both here and elsewhere throughout the dialogue, his friends' "hospitality" figuratively denotes the composition of the laudatory description of the *kallipolis*' military achievements.[81] Through the infinitive δέχεσθαι Socrates thus refers to his reception of this *laus*. However, nowhere in the *Timaeus/Critias* is Socrates presented as experiencing a state of immersion in Timaeus' and Critias' fictional worlds, which is why we are not allowed to take his words at this point as foreshadowing the way Socrates will later be presented as receiving what he will listen to. Nonetheless, taken together with his preceding statement examined above that he wishes to 'see' his *kallipolis* 'in motion' through his friends' recitations, his promise to 'accept' his friends' 'hospitality' can be taken as Plato's invitation to us to read the *Timaeus*, and especially the *Critias*, as fictional worlds alternative to the world of the *Republic*, in which the virtues of the *kallipolis*' inner political organisation manifest their positive effect on its foreign policy.

The second passage in which Plato draws our attention to the make-believe game through which narrators and audiences conceive of a fictional world is the one in which Critias suggests that he and his friends pretend that Socrates' ideal city is not a fictional creation but was in fact the Athens of the remote past. After completing his narration of the Egyptians' story on the war between Athens and Atlantis (20d7–25d6), Critias makes the following suggestion (26c7–d3):

> τοὺς δὲ πολίτας καὶ τὴν πόλιν ἣν χθὲς ἡμῖν ὡς ἐν μύθῳ διῄεισθα σύ, νῦν μετενεγκόντες ἐπὶ τἀληθὲς δεῦρο θήσομεν ὡς ἐκείνην τήνδε οὖσαν, καὶ τοὺς πολίτας οὓς διενοοῦ φήσομεν ἐκείνους τοὺς ἀληθινοὺς εἶναι προγόνους ἡμῶν, οὓς ἔλεγεν ὁ ἱερεύς.

> We will transfer the imaginary citizens and city which you described yesterday to the real world, and say that your city is the city of my story and your citizens those historical ancestors of ours whom the priest described.

---

81 Broadie 2013, 254 with n. 14. Cf. *Phaedr.* 227b6–7.

Critias proposes a make-believe state different from the one described by Socrates about himself. While Socrates seems to mean that he had *unwittingly* immersed himself in the possible scenarios generated by the fictional world of his *kallipolis*, Critias propounds the idea of a deliberate immersion, a predetermined effort to pretend that the world imagined by Socrates is the actual world of the Athenian remote past. This proposition is addressed both to the aspiring composer of the imminent narration, Critias, as well as to his audience, i.e. Socrates, Timaeus and Hermocrates.

Furthermore, besides the difference between Socrates' instinctive immersion and the deliberate and conscious one proposed by Critias, we may also discern one further difference between the two cases. As already demonstrated in Section 2.1, while Socrates proposed to his friends to use the fictional world of the *kallipolis* as the main point of reference for other, alternative possible worlds (a point of reference independent of the actual world), Critias suggests that they confirm the validity of Socrates' description by proving that it corresponds to what happened in the actual world of the past. With regard to the issue of immersion of an audience in a fictional world, these two divergent propositions may reflect Plato's aim to draw our attention to two levels of immersion: a more intense one introduced by Socrates and a milder one proposed by Critias.

Critias proceeds with a similar proposition just before letting Timaeus begin his cosmological account (27a2–b6). A detailed presentation and analysis of this passage will be offered in Section 2.5. For now, let us discuss its content and wording that pertain to the issue of immersion. Once again, Critias suggests that he narrate the account on the Athenians' war against Atlantis as if these events were parts of the human history to be delineated by Timaeus and as if the Athenians had the educational system and moral code sketched by Socrates in his description of the *kallipolis*. Plato's intention to underline the make-believe origins of the proposed connections between the three worlds of Socrates, Timaeus and Critias is evident in the use of participles escorted by ὡς (27a7–b6: ἐμὲ δὲ ... ὡς ... δεδεγμένον ... ὡς εἰς δικαστάς ... ὡς ὄντας τοὺς τότε Ἀθηναίους ... ὡς περὶ πολιτῶν καὶ Ἀθηναίων ὄντων).[82]

As transpires from our analysis so far, one further affinity between the *Timaeus* and modern literary theory lies in the fact that both Plato and modern critics recognise that an unwitting immersion into fiction and similar deliberate make-believe games are not only experienced by the receiver but also by the narrator of a story. In his seminal monograph *Mimesis as Make-Believe. On the Foundations of the Representational Arts*, Kendall Walton focuses mainly on the

---

[82] On the accumulation of ὡς in this passage, cf. Johansen 2004, 37–38.

audience's experience of the representational arts and argues that the receiver of a narrative or a theatrical play adopts a fictional ego which enters the fictional world of a literary work. It is the receiver's *alter ego*, Walton maintains, that participates in the storyline by reconstructing the field of action and by observing the events that take place in it.[83] Ryan enriches Walton's theory by arguing that, apart from the audience, the narrator too impersonates a fictional narrator who belongs to the fictional world she or he exposes.[84] Influenced both by Walton and Ryan, Pavel develops his own theory about the way in which we enter fictional worlds, approaching the matter from both the perspectives of the sender and the receiver of a narrative.[85]

Socrates says that he, as a world composer, was absorbed by his own description of the *kallipolis* and believed that, although he did not present the city as fighting other cities, it is like a real animal which can "move".[86] We may assume that Socrates was swayed by his hypotheses on the potential military *aristeia* of his city either while describing it or after completing his exposition. Socrates, of course, clarifies that, already before starting his description of the *kallipolis*, he had decided to confine his account to the *kallipolis*' inner organisation and to let his friends fill in the empty domains of his account with a presentation of its military activities. This means that Socrates did not ask himself about the potential military conduct of the *kallipolis* in the process of describing it but before doing so. However, as transpires from what he says, he also wondered which military feats would fit well with the features he attributed to the ideal city, and this question can only have emerged in his mind while being absorbed by these features, i.e. either while delineating them or after doing so, and not before.[87] So Socrates is presented as having immersed himself in the world he created as a narrator.[88] On the other hand, Socrates also promises to willingly enter the world which will be delineated by his friends, i.e. as a listener. Similarly, Critias explicitly states that he noticed the linkages between Socrates' fictional world and that of Solon's story while listening to Socrates, i.e. as a

---

83 Walton 1990.
84 Ryan 1991, 23–24.
85 Pavel 1986, 85–89.
86 This statement echoes Socrates' similar thoughts in *Rep.* 472d4–e5. Cf. Johansen 2004, 26; Morgan 2010, 269–270; Reydams-Schils 2011, 351.
87 Osborne (1996, 181–182) lays emphasis on Socrates' reflections on the lifelessness of his *kallipolis* when he talks about this with Timaeus and Critias. Differently, I take his statements as denoting the reflections he had on this issue shortly after completing his account.
88 On the emotional or intellectual engagement of a narrator with his narrative, cf. *Phaed.* 58d4–6.

receiver of the fictional world. Further, when he urges his own audience to immerse in the connections he proposes between the worlds of Socrates, Timaeus and his own, he also promises that he too will follow this make-believe game as a narrator.

In contrast to what we read in the *Ion*, the characters of the *Timaeus*, similarly to modern critics, describe an immersion of limited range. Ion confesses that, while reciting parts from the Homeric epics, he believes that he is where the narrated events take place, and that he cries whenever he relates sad states of affairs, or is frightened whenever he talks about frightening situations. Ion and Socrates also agree that the performer does not only enter the world he narrates but also invites his listeners to travel with him in the worlds of the *Iliad* and *Odyssey*. However, neither Socrates nor Ion proceed with any clarification on the limits of this communal immersion. They only describe this psychological state as madness or, at least in the *aoidos*' case, as some kind of absorption by the divine. In Socrates' mind, no sane individual would ever actually believe that she or he is placed in Troy of the *Iliad* or in Ithaca of the *Odyssey* (*Io.* 533c9–536d7).

Differently, in the *Timaeus* Plato invites us to infer from the discussion the restricted range of the make-believe game of narrators and audiences. While describing the ideal city, Socrates thought that, as soon as he would complete his presentation, his friends would answer his questions about the possible military feats of the city with their own narrations. In essence, Plato presents Socrates as being fully aware of the world he belongs to, given that, in contrast to Ion, he expects individuals from his own world to describe the possible world in which the *kallipolis* is at war. So, the immersions described in the *Timaeus* are different from those in the *Ion*. In the *Ion*, the performer and the audience believe that they are in the fictional world, which means that they take it as their ontological base. Differently, in the *Timaeus* Socrates does not use the *kallipolis* world as an ontological base, since he is fully aware of where he is, but as an ontological perspective from which he assesses what is possible or impossible. In a similar vein, Critias, in suggesting to his friends to pretend that the fictional world of the *kallipolis* is identified with the world in which Athens defeated Atlantis, essentially proposes, as we saw, a deliberate make-believe game and not an instinctive immersion in a non-existent world.

Modern theorists address the issues of immersion and make-believe games using a similar line of thought. Pavel, although recognising that fictional worlds have their own core around which alternative possible worlds revolve, notes that fictional worlds merely serve for us as an ontological perspective without making us lose contact with the actual world. For Pavel, while reading a book or watching a movie, we are fully aware of the world we ontologically belong to.[89] For Ryan too, the audience never forgets that fictional worlds are fake.[90] Last, Ronen, although recognising the usefulness of the possible–worlds theory for literary semantics, notes that critics should also cautiously avoid the extremist view that the audience's sense of what is possible or true in fictional worlds also defines what is *really* true.[91]

2.4 Fictional worlds as products of our sociocultural background

One of the points at which literary theorists of fictional worlds distance themselves from formalist approaches to literature concerns how they examine the messages of a text in close relation with its cultural context. There are many ways in which the historical era of a fictional work defines the way it is received. First, our sociocultural environment affects our view of what is true, possible or necessary in a fictional world. For Pavel, as we saw, to deem what elements of a fictional world are possible according to the degree to which the elements resemble states of affairs or objects of the actual world stands in conflict with the intuitive way in which audiences digest fiction. Nonetheless, Pavel also recognises that such a realist approach to literature is diachronically adopted by people and takes different shapes in different periods of time and societies. For Pavel, to convince others that what we say is true does not require us to commit ourselves to the reliability of our propositions, but rather to adapt our style of expression to the epistemological base of the language of the community we address.[92]

Lewis too lays special emphasis upon the value of communal beliefs as a criterion of a fictional world's reliability and possibility. Let us consider one of his analyses of truth in propositions: "A sentence of the form "In the fiction f, φ" is non-vacuously true iff, whenever w is one of the collective belief worlds of the community of origin of f, then some world where f is told as known fact and φ is true differs less from the world w, on balance, than does any world where f is told as known fact and φ is not true. It is vacuously true iff there are no possible worlds where f is told as known fact." Lewis clearly recognises that speakers

---

[89] Pavel 1975, 175 and 1986, 85–89.
[90] Ryan 1991, 23–24.
[91] Ronen 1994, 11.
[92] Pavel 1986, 17 and 22.

should first reassure us about the truthfulness of their words in order for them to be deemed as true. Nonetheless, as Pavel does, he also recognises the significance of the cultural framework in this kind of assessments. Furthermore, he defines as collective beliefs of a community those which enjoy general approval in the community which generated a fiction, namely the beliefs of the author and his audience.[93] Consequently, a cultural decision is ultimately not only to judge what is true, possible or their opposites in fiction, but also to distinguish fiction from nonfiction. According to Pavel, the corpus of our 'reliable' sources fluctuates depending on the period and society we are parts of or even on our moods. There are texts which were once composed by their authors and received by their audiences as truthful accounts but are today taken as fictional.

The ramifications of such an approach are also evident in the way that modern critics of fictional worlds treat the issue we examined in the previous section, the audience's immersion in fictional worlds. According to Doležel, although it is pointless to assess the reliability of propositions of fiction according to the degree to which they correspond to the laws of the actual world, still we cannot deny that the actual world participates in the formation of fictional worlds by offering structural models which emerge from the author's and audience's experiences or from historical events. In this respect, the more that a fictional world temporally and culturally deviates from the receivers' actual world, the less the receivers find it easy to impersonate their fictional *alter ego* and subsequently fail to immerse themselves in the fictional world.[94]

The influence of the sociocultural environment of a work on the way its composer conceives it and creates its fictional world and on the way in which this world is received by the audience is placed at the focal point of interest in the introductory chapters of the *Timaeus*. Plato foregrounds this issue through the following technique: first, Socrates introduces the reader to this subject through the thoughts he expresses about what groups of people can imagine and verbally convey the fictional world in which the *kallipolis* wages a war. Socrates argues that, due to their education and socio-political experience, Timaeus, Critias and Hermocrates are the most qualified to successfully deliver this task. These introductory remarks of Socrates serve as the interpretive prism through which we are invited by Plato to read the passages that shape the portraits of Socrates' friends but also those of the other narrators of the dialogue (the Egyptians, Solon and Critias the elder).[95] In this way, we are led to assess all

---

[93] Lewis 1978, 43–45.
[94] Doležel 1988, 484; cf. Pavel 1986, 89–93.
[95] Cf. Schalcher 1997, 159–161.

these characters not only on a moral level but also, and in particular, by the criterion offered by Socrates: how do the social origins and cultural environment of narrators affect their ability to faithfully convey the fictional worlds of their narratives?[96] As will be demonstrated in what follows, most information which constitutes the images of the dialogue's characters is closely related to this question.

Let us begin with Socrates' comments on the matter (19c8–20b7):

> ταῦτ' οὖν, ὦ Κριτία καὶ Ἑρμόκρατες, ἐμαυτοῦ μὲν αὐτὸς κατέγνωκα μή ποτ' ἂν δυνατὸς γενέσθαι τοὺς ἄνδρας καὶ τὴν πόλιν ἱκανῶς ἐγκωμιάσαι. καὶ τὸ μὲν ἐμὸν οὐδὲν θαυμαστόν· ἀλλὰ τὴν αὐτὴν δόξαν εἴληφα καὶ περὶ τῶν πάλαι γεγονότων καὶ περὶ τῶν νῦν ὄντων ποιητῶν, οὔτι τὸ ποιητικὸν ἀτιμάζων γένος, ἀλλὰ παντὶ δῆλον ὡς τὸ μιμητικὸν ἔθνος, οἷς ἂν ἐντραφῇ, ταῦτα μιμήσεται ῥᾷστα καὶ ἄριστα, τὸ δ' ἐκτὸς τῆς τροφῆς ἑκάστοις γιγνόμενον χαλεπὸν μὲν ἔργοις, ἔτι δὲ χαλεπώτερον λόγοις εὖ μιμεῖσθαι. τὸ δὲ τῶν σοφιστῶν γένος αὖ πολλῶν μὲν λόγων καὶ καλῶν ἄλλων μάλ' ἔμπειρον ἥγημαι, φοβοῦμαι δὲ μή πως, ἅτε πλανητὸν ὂν κατὰ πόλεις οἰκήσεις τε ἰδίας οὐδαμῇ διῳκηκός, ἄστοχον ἅμα φιλοσόφων ἀνδρῶν ᾖ καὶ πολιτικῶν, ὅσ' ἂν οἷά τε ἐν πολέμῳ καὶ μάχαις πράττοντες ἔργῳ καὶ λόγῳ προσομιλοῦντες ἑκάστοις πράττοιεν καὶ λέγοιεν. καταλέλειπται δὴ τὸ τῆς ὑμετέρας ἕξεως γένος, ἅμα ἀμφοτέρων φύσει καὶ τροφῇ μετέχον. Τίμαιός τε γὰρ ὅδε, εὐνομωτάτης ὢν πόλεως τῆς ἐν Ἰταλίᾳ Λοκρίδος, οὐσίᾳ καὶ γένει οὐδενὸς ὕστερος ὢν τῶν ἐκεῖ, τὰς μεγίστας μὲν ἀρχάς τε καὶ τιμὰς τῶν ἐν τῇ πόλει μετακεχείρισται, φιλοσοφίας δ' αὖ κατ' ἐμὴν δόξαν ἐπ' ἄκρον ἁπάσης ἐλήλυθεν· Κριτίαν δέ που πάντες οἱ τῇδε ἴσμεν οὐδενὸς ἰδιώτην ὄντα ὧν λέγομεν. τῆς δὲ Ἑρμοκράτους αὖ περὶ φύσεως καὶ τροφῆς, πρὸς ἅπαντα ταῦτ' εἶναι ἱκανὴν πολλῶν μαρτυρούντων πιστευτέον. διὸ καὶ χθὲς ἐγὼ διανοούμενος, ὑμῶν δεομένων τὰ περὶ τῆς πολιτείας διελθεῖν, προθύμως ἐχαριζόμην, εἰδὼς ὅτι τὸν ἑξῆς λόγον οὐδένες ἂν ὑμῶν ἐθελόντων ἱκανώτερον ἀποδοῖεν – εἰς γὰρ πόλεμον πρέποντα καταστήσαντες τὴν πόλιν ἅπαντ' αὐτῇ τὰ προσήκοντα ἀποδοῖτ' ἂν μόνοι τῶν νῦν – εἰπὼν δὴ τἀπιταχθέντα ἀντεπέταξα ὑμῖν ἃ καὶ νῦν λέγω.

Now, my dear Critias and Hermocrates, I know that I am myself incapable of giving any adequate account of this kind of our city and its citizens. This, as far as I am concerned, is not surprising; but in my opinion the same is true of the poets, past and present. Not that I have a low opinion of poets in general, but it is clear that in all kinds of representation one represents best and most easily what lies within one's experience, while what lies outside that experience is difficult to represent in action and even more difficult in words. The sophists, again, I have always thought to be very ready with glowing descriptions of every kind, but I am afraid that, because they have travelled so much and never had a home of their own, they may fail to grasp the true qualities which those who are philosophers and statesmen would show in action and in negotiation in the conduct of peace and war. There remain people of your kind, who are by nature and education imbued with philosophy and statesmanship. For Timaeus here comes from the Italian Locris, a very well-run city,

---

[96] On the Egyptians, see McEvoy 1993, 247–250. On the poets, see Schalcher 1997, 159–160, who also reads Socrates' characterisation of poets in light of the *Republic*.

where he is second to none in wealth and birth: there he has enjoyed the highest office and distinction the city can offer, and has also in my opinion reached the highest eminence in philosophy. Critias, of course, all of us here know to be no amateur in these matters, while there are many witnesses to assure us that Hermocrates is well qualified in them also, both by his natural gifts and by his education. I had this in mind yesterday when I agreed so readily to your request for an account of my ideal society: I knew that there was no one more fitted to provide the sequel to it than you — you are the only living people who could adequately describe my city fighting a war worthy of her. So when I had done what was asked of me, I set you the task I have just described.

In Socrates' words we may recognise modern theorists' *communis opinio* that authors' and audiences' sociocultural background, as well as the experiences they shape in it, define the way they structure or receive a fictional world. Socrates' view is clear: poets can hardly conceive of a world that does not correspond to the reality of the actual world in which they have been moulded. As already demonstrated, when Socrates asks his friends to describe how a fictional state would wage war, he is obviously aware of the fact that he is asking them to build a fiction on the basis of another. Consequently, the fictional world which Socrates is looking for is compossible not to the actual world but to the fictional protoworld of the *Republic*. Socrates should be taken to mean about poets that their lack of experience in the social states of affairs of the world he delineated in the *Republic* renders them incapable of imagining a world compossible to that of the *Republic*, in which the *kallipolis* is at war. Hence, Socrates' claim is not that the poets cannot imagine a world from scratch but that they, as the audience of a fictional world that lies beyond their cultural territory, cannot imagine the compossible worlds which emerge from the logical rules imposed by this fictional world. For Socrates, as it seems, to observe and understand the rationale of a fictional world is not enough; one should also identify this rationale with that of her or his world. Otherwise, one cannot apprehend a fictional world to such a degree that she or he can discern the realm of possibilities which emerges from these fictional rules.

The divergence between, on the one hand, the receivers' experiences and cultural identity and, on the other, the states of affairs of a fictional world prevents them from realising the set of possibilities latent in this world and therefore from acting as composers of a fictional world which serves as a sequel to the first. The negative impact of incompletely grasping an imaginary world on the quality of its narrativisation is addressed in Socrates' statement that "in all kinds of representation one represents best and most easily what lies within one's experience, while what lies outside that experience is difficult to represent in action and even more difficult in words" (19d5–e2: ἀλλὰ παντὶ δῆλον ὡς τὸ μιμητικὸν ἔθνος, οἷς ἂν ἐντραφῇ, ταῦτα μιμήσεται ῥᾷστα καὶ ἄριστα, τὸ δ' ἐκτὸς τῆς τροφῆς ἑκάστοις γιγνόμενον χαλεπὸν μὲν ἔργοις, ἔτι δὲ χαλεπώτερον λόγοις εὖ μιμεῖσθαι). By saying that one can represent a fictional world "most easily", Socrates probably refers to the easiness with which one imagines and organises in her or his mind a state of affairs. The poets' weakness does not lie in some kind of inadequate competence in the use of discourse. They, similarly to the sophists, are taken by Socrates to be keen connoisseurs of language. However, what prevents them from verbally conveying a state of affairs is the fact that they have not fully conceived of it and have therefore not reached in their minds a total correspondence between words and meaning. Given that they cannot grasp the meaning, they are incapable of conveying it through words, no matter how artful users of language they are. A similar approach is found in the *Laws*, where the Athenian Visitor claims that poets should be virtuous and have practically applied their virtues during their lives, so that they will be able to faithfully represent through their mimetic art characters which they are both theoretically and practically acquainted with (*Leg.* 829c6–d4). So, if one manages to imagine a fictional world, one may then verbally convey it easily and such a representation will be the best (ἄριστα).[97]

In what sense Socrates speaks of a representation's excellence can be better approached in relation to the meanings of this concept in the Platonic corpus. Εὖ μιμεῖσθαι may either mean (a) the representation of morally approvable characters and behaviours, or (b) a faithful representation of an object. In this case, a "best representation" should be taken as having the latter meaning. In the *Laws*, the Athenian Visitor argues that one cannot assess the quality of a representation if one is not familiar with the object of representation. For example, we can never say whether or not a painting which represents a man is good or bad unless we have knowledge of this man's appearance (668b9–669b3). Accordingly, Socrates means here that the most faithful representation of the *kallipolis*' military feats would emerge from the poets' acquaintance with the philosophers-statesmen's way of life.

But again, the reliability of such a representation is not meant to lie in the way that the fictional world would faithfully represent the actual world but in the degree to which it would depict in a plausible way what might happen in the fictional protoworld where the *kallipolis* belongs. This view is evident in what Socrates says about the sophists. The latter, Socrates claims, being unfamiliar with engaging with both politics and philosophy, would probably fail in faithfully representing not what a philosopher-statesman is but how he would act at war. When an author wishes to write a sequel to a fictional protoworld, she or

---

[97] Cf. Desclos 2006, 177–178.

he is invited to be or become culturally familiar with this protoworld. Now, her or his familiarity with the protoworld is expected by Socrates to help her or him not so much to faithfully represent reality but to plausibly depict the possible worlds that logically emerge from the proto-fiction, which they are expansions of.

Let us now see why for Socrates the poets' and sophists' sociocultural background deviates from that of the *kallipolis* and, conversely, why his friends' upbringing fits well with it. Socrates begins by saying that neither he nor the poets and the sophists would be in a position to depict the *kallipolis*' military feats. However, he does not offer an in-depth explanation of this view. The vague certainty with which he says that he is unable to praise the ideal state surprises the reader who has seen him in the *Republic* as shaping, step by step and with extraordinary meticulousness and imagination, his political construction. How is it possible, one wonders, that he who conceived the state in all its details cannot come up with its military activity too, especially given the fact that he defined many of the inner functions of the city which help its defence against external enemies? An easy and admittedly plausible choice for us would be to assume that Socrates' self-depreciation carries no deeper meanings and merely serves for Plato as a dramatic trick through which to pass the baton from Socrates to Timaeus and Critias.[98]

Equally enigmatic is the way in which Socrates questions the potential of the poets' imagination. He does not doubt only the poets but everyone who tries to represent a situation which is foreign to her or his lifestyle. However, he never explains why the two groups of poets he mentions, those from an older age and his contemporaries, have been raised in a way that conflicts with the *kallipolis*' socio-political program. Since he does not refer here to any specific poet, his statement is an overgeneralisation on poets' ethics and place in society, an overstatement which no doubt fits well with Plato's proneness to criticise this art and its practitioners. Also, we are not in a position to say exactly what aspects of the Socratic state do not come under the poets' upbringing. However, on this specific point, some conclusions can be reached from what Socrates says immediately afterwards about the sophists. He argues that they, although engaged with philosophy, do not participate in the political life of any polity because they travel from place to place. Judging from this statement, one could assume that Plato builds here a climax from the most unsuitable group (poets) towards the less unsuitable one (sophists), in the sense that the poets participate neither in politics nor in philosophy, while the sophists are at least engaged

---

98 Cf. Gill 2017, 5–6. Taylor (1928, 13) claims that Socrates means that he has not "the art of putting life into the figures", because he is a philosopher but not a politician.

with one of them. However, nowhere does Socrates express this view. If this is the meaning of Socrates' words, one could object that at times there have been poets who significantly contributed to their homeland's political life and were also famous because of their wisdom, such as Solon, who is later on mentioned by Critias.

Another interpretation may be that certain features of the poets oppose the ethico-political rationale of the *kallipolis*. Indeed, if we read this passage through the prism of other statements on poets in the Platonic corpus, we find some striking antitheses between the poets' activity and views and certain key principles of the ideal state. In the *Ion*, poets are presented as believing that they can conceive of and represent situations and activities pertaining to arts which they are totally unfamiliar with (*Io.* 536d8–542b4). This strikes the *kallipolis*' authorities as a scandalous viewpoint, as it opposes the principle that any individual confine their activity exclusively to what they are specialised in. In essence, both in the *Ion* and *Timaeus*, Socrates expresses the same view, i.e. that no one can faithfully represent something that she or he is unaware of.[99] Also, he elsewhere questions the validity of poetic descriptions, such as in the *Republic* those narratives which present the gods as adopting behaviours that are, in Socrates' view, inconsistent with their true nature (377b11–392c5). Furthermore, elsewhere Platonic characters criticise the moral content of the messages disseminated by poets through their art.[100] Given all the aforementioned cases, it may be assumed that Socrates, in referring to the poets' upbringing, denotes their moral principles and implies that the latter do not satisfy the *kallipolis*' ethical code. Socrates' fleeting statement leaves us wavering somewhere between all these interpretations. In any case, the sole merit of the poets which is useful in their effort to depict a fictional world is their competence in discourse, although the latter, as we saw, is a far more challenging means of representation than drama.

As far as the sophists are concerned, Socrates is slightly more enlightening as to why he doubts their ability to aptly grasp the philosophers-kings' military and diplomatic activities. The sophists, although being excellent practitioners of rhetoric and engaging with philosophy, do not participate actively in the

---

[99] On the poets' ignorance of the themes they touch upon in their poems, cf. *Apol.* 22a8–c8. See Reydams-Schils 2011, 349–350.

[100] The bibliography is vast. See, most recently, the discussions in Destrée's (2011) volume.

political life of their homelands, nor do they administer domestic affairs.[101] For this reason, they cannot imagine the way in which philosophical inquiry and political service are combined and the materialisation of this blend on a level of military choices and diplomatic negotiations. Socrates treats the sophists partly favourably, as he recognises their expertise in the art of discourse and does not deny the fact that they have a certain kind of relationship with philosophy. Given that from the dipole philosophy–politics he doubts their experience in the latter, it may be inferred that he reasonably recognises their relationship with the former.

However, simultaneously and in an implicit way, he undervalues at least two ways in which the sophists were said to benefit the political life of the states they visited and their citizens: the rhetorical education they offered to the youth and the political usefulness of this education for those who received it. Protagoras boasted about his ability to teach young men political virtue, meaning the dexterity in speaking and decision-making in both private and public affairs (*Prot.* 318e5–319a7). However, although these skills were especially popular in the circles of young citizens of the Greek democratic cities, they are of no help for those who wish to imagine parts of the Socratic utopia's foreign policy. The governors of the *kallipolis* engage with philosophy and apply the knowledge they obtain from this practice to the way they rule the state. Differently, the sophists' involvement in the political life of a state does not lie in their application of philosophical knowledge to the way they govern but in the fact that they train orators. Similarly to the poets' verbal competence, their art of rhetoric is for Socrates a resource that allows them to verbally convey what they think, but it does not help them to apprehend the logic of the *kallipolis* because they do not have a social background akin to it.

Let us now examine those characters who, according to Socrates, are the ideal potential composers of the *kallipolis*' military portrait. Most elements of Timaeus' portrait are immediately connected to his ability to fulfil the challenge posed by Socrates to come up with a fictional world which complies with the *kallipolis*' rules, or to his ability to conceive of the world he eventually decides to sketch. Timaeus is first presented to us long before Socrates mentions his exemplary involvement in both politics and philosophy, through his short responses to Socrates in the introductory discussion of 17a1–19b2. His first words are those with which he reassures Socrates that he and his friends will honour

---

101 On the sophists' travelling from city to city, cf. *Apol.* 19e1–20a4. In the *Symposium* (177b5–c3) too Eryximachus repeats Phaedrus' view that Eros was not praised through discourse either by poets or by sophists.

the agreement they made with him and that they will describe to him what he asked on the previous day. According to Timaeus, this is the right thing to do (17b1–4).

He expresses these friendly words in a way that foreshadows the spirit in which he will narrate the cosmological myth, a spirit of full awareness of human nature's limited capacity to offer an accurate representation of the universe: "Yes; we'll certainly do our best" (17b1–2: πάνυ μὲν οὖν, καὶ κατὰ δύναμίν γε οὐδὲν ἐλλείψομεν). It is worth noting that Plato from the very beginning presents Timaeus as touching upon the issue of the incompleteness of fictional descriptions and as implying that it is impossible to minimise this element altogether. This is one further piece of evidence in support of the view that this subject lies at the focal point of Plato's interest in the *Timaeus* and *Critias*. Timaeus' next statement contains his words that whatever was said by Socrates on the previous day seems to him and the others reasonable (17c4–5). These words serve as a prelude to Socrates' statement that Timaeus' experience in philosophy and politics render him one of the most suitable persons for the task of accepting everything he heard from Socrates and of enriching the *kallipolis*' fictional world by composing the encomium of its military feats.

Socrates also offers some information about Timaeus which, at first sight, seems irrelevant to the question whether or not the latter is capable of imagining the philosophers-statesmen's activity: Timaeus is of high birth and possesses great wealth (20a2–3). Both elements can be taken as differentiating him from the poor leaders of the *kallipolis*. However, in a context where Socrates argues for the affinities of Timaeus' sociocultural background with the combination of philosophy and politics, Socrates' interest in Timaeus' fortune and origins should better be interpreted as explaining the latter's venerable place in the political life of his homeland. Also, Timaeus' engagement with the Locrian political arena is not an involvement in a corrupt system of domestic politics but an energetic contribution to a city which, similarly to the *kallipolis*, is virtuously governed (20a1–2). Last, he is a master of astronomy (27a3–5), information which highlights his suitability for the task of verbally describing the universe.

Critias' portraiture too is offered throughout the *Timaeus* from the same perspective, namely in terms of the degree to which he is, as Socrates claims, capable of imagining the military feats of men who practice both philosophy and statesmanship. Socrates' laudatory comments are short and vague: "Critias, of course, all of us here know to be no amateur in these matters" (20a6–7). It has been argued that Socrates' indifference in offering further details on Critias' sociocultural background betrays Plato's underestimation of the latter.[102] However, later in the dialogue, while narrating the events and revealing the way in which he received the Egyptian story, Critias offers us several personal details about his family, education and social activities, details which lead us to think that Socrates reasonably chooses him as an aspiring composer of his *kallipolis'* military feats.[103] First, by establishing intercourse with wise men such as Solon, his family offered him the stimuli to turn his interest towards knowledge and philosophy.[104] When he explains to Socrates that he knows a story of Solon about the remote past of Athens, he informs us that Solon was a close friend to his ancestor Dropides and that Solon repeatedly commemorates in his oeuvre his friendship with him (20e1–3). This information indicates Solon's high appreciation of Dropides and that the latter, enjoying the appreciation of wise men of that period, was himself a wise man. Similarly, Critias the elder, this Critias' grandfather, is presented as admiring Solon as a poet, which means that he had similar intellectual interests (21c4–d3). These men (Solon, Dropides and Critias the elder) served as models for Critias which encouraged him to engage with philosophy.

What is more, what Critias heard about Solon shaped his mentality in a way that his soul is now a fertile ground for creating the picture of the philosophers-statesmen's activity. First, Solon in a way resembles the philosophers-kings in that he is a virtuous statesman, wise lawgiver, and simultaneously an intellectual and, as a poet, an avid user of language (20d7–21d8).[105] Due to his social environment which brought him closer to Solon, Critias is familiar with this combination of wisdom and statesmanship and can therefore more easily imagine the *kallipolis*' statesmen and take them as plausible figures. Second, as a narrator he builds a world in which wise men govern and have a political organisation similar to that of Socrates' fiction. Last, his family has brought him close to poetry and the art of discourse (21a7–d8), the basic instrument through which

---

102 Welliver 1977 (followed by Dušanić 1982, 32–33) finds that Socrates favours Timaeus over Critias and Hermocrates.
103 Cf. Morgan 2010, 272–273; Broadie 2013, 250.
104 On the emphasis laid on the family line of Critias, see Pender 2007, 21–25.
105 On Solon see Arrighetti 1991, 20–34. Osborne (1996, 183–185) argues that Solon, as a poet, dissatisfies Socrates' wish to avoid listening to a poet's military encomium of his *kallipolis*. I disagree. I follow Johansen's (1998, 200–201) view that Solon demonstrates both a talent in poetry and political experience, which is exactly what Socrates expects an imitator to have. Johansen (1998) sees the stories of Timaeus and Critias as satisfying Socrates' view of proper past narratives in *Rep.* Books 3 and 10. For the relation between Critias' family and Solon, see also *Charm.* 155a2–3 and 157e5–158a1.

he now, as a composer, will convey the world he has been told about.[106] Consequently, Critias is an ideal figure both as a receiver as well as a narrator of fictional worlds similar to the one composed by Socrates, because he possesses three key elements: experience in philosophy, political career and linguistic competence.[107]

Solon's story not only teaches Critias that fictions such as that of Socrates depict possible worlds but also that what we take as possible or impossible, what we treat as fiction or historical accounts, is defined to a high degree by our social environment. The Egyptians believe stories such as the one about Atlantis because the geographical place of their homeland and the resultant preservation of written sources create, in comparison with Athens, radically different circumstances, under which people determine what is fiction and what is truth. According to Critias, the Egyptians explained to Solon that their city's proximity to the Nile's banks protected them from natural catastrophes. While mountaineer settlements, lying closer to the sun, are more vulnerable to phenomena such as the overheating of the atmosphere, cities founded close to riverbeds and marine coasts, like Athens, have continuously been destroyed by cataclysms. However, independently of why a city is destroyed, the result is always the same, i.e. the literate population, who preserve the written stories, die and with them these stories are lost. On the contrary, the inhabitants of Sais, living on the banks of the Nile, have always been protected from all natural phenomena and therefore preserved both their reading skills and their written tradition (21e1–23e6). For this reason, stories which have either been forgotten by other peoples or are mentioned only in a fragmentary way and covered by mythical symbolism constitute for the Egyptians a clear, well-known and written historical material, which shapes their historical consciousness and, most importantly, is taken as true.[108]

The Egyptians, Solon, Timaeus and Critias are not only narrators of stories; all of them first act as receivers of stories. The Egyptians are told tales which lie in their written sources and then disseminate them as history. Solon is equipped with his experience and wisdom, which allow him to be open-minded and to trust the Egyptian priests without being afraid of the diversity of the sociocultural

---

106 On Timaeus' and Critias' myths as poetic works, see Nagy 2000, followed by Desclos 2006.
107 Taylor (1928, 24) assumes that Critias is not to be identified with Critias of the Thirty but with his grandfather, who was a poet of elegies. If this is true, Socrates trusts him as a potential fictional world-maker also because of his acquaintance with the art of discourse; cf. Zeyl 2000, xxv. See, *contra*, Vidal-Naquet 1964, 420; Dušanić 2002, 63 and n. 1 with further bibliography.
108 Johansen 2004, 39–41.

environment in which what is forgotten by his fellow citizens or is taken as myth is treated as history. With this mentality he has no qualms about adopting the Egyptians' point of view, treating the Atlantis myth as history and transporting it as such to his compatriots. Lastly, Critias, as a member of a family which encourages trust towards Solon, receives the myth and reproduces it as if it was a true story. Plato leads the reader to a conclusion which is nothing less than modern theorists' view that what is taken as fiction or truth, what is possible or impossible is determined by the society in which stories are created and preserved.

2.5 Fictional worlds and intertextuality

It is commonly recognised that Plato wrote the *Timaeus* and *Critias* to be read along with the *Republic*.[109] In the opening chapters of the *Timaeus* (17a2; 17b2; 19a7; 20b1; 20c6; 25e2; 26a4; 26b4; 26c4), the interlocutors say that they meet one day after Socrates had described the ideal polity which we read of in the *Republic*. Specifically, in the *Timaeus* Socrates says that this city distinguishes the *demiourgoi* from its defenders. Now these guardians' souls are both gentle in the way they serve justice and tough in the way they defend the city from its enemies, and are also both spirited and philosophical. Also, their education resembles the one we read of in the *Republic*, as it comprises both mental and bodily training. The defenders of the city are here too called 'guardians' and 'assistants' of the society and possess no gold or silver but only the payment which they receive for their service. They live together, separately from the rest of the society, and, having no other occupation, devote their lives mainly to the possession and understanding of virtue. Furthermore, both in this summary and the *Republic* the main principle on the basis of which the city is organised and its classes are distinguished from each other is that each individual, and by extension each class, serves only a single occupation. Also, women are of a nature similar to that of men and share with them the same occupations during periods of both peace and war. Even the suggestion that parents do not recognise their children and vice versa is here too characterised as unusual.

It is immaterial whether or not Socrates refers to the very conversation which is described in the *Republic*.[110] Although there has been some controversy

---

[109] Hadot 1983, 114–116.
[110] For this view see Taylor 1928, 13, 27, who argues that in the *Republic* Socrates narrates his conversation at Cephalus' house to Critias, Timaeus and Hermocrates (cf. Proclus *Timaeus* 3d–e [I 8.30–9.13 D.]). According to this logic, the conversations in the *Timaeus* and *Critias* are treated by Taylor as taking place two days after the conversation at Cephalus' place. For other

on this issue, even those critics who maintain that in the *Timaeus* the characters refer to a discussion different than the one of the *Republic* agree that Socrates, when he is invited by Timaeus to remind the interlocutors of the main features of his ideal *kallipolis*, offers a summary of the main parts of the *Republic*.[111] Even if in this summary Plato implies that Socrates had repeatedly discussed the imaginary state on other occasions as well except at the night of the Bendidia,[112] it is only in the *Republic* that we, the readers, can retrace an extensive and detailed exposition of what is described by Socrates at the beginning of the *Timaeus*.

Indeed, the three dialogues have repeatedly been co-examined as a trilogy. For some scholars, the three works, alongside with the *Laws*, suggest that Plato was fully aware of the theoretical and technical intricacies inherent in the designing of a state.[113] To others, the three works are worth co-examining in terms of the way Plato combines the art of dialectic and the use of history and utilisation of mythical narratives.[114] Occasionally, in the *Timaeus* and *Critias* critics discern Plato's aspiration to compose a prose hymn for Athens and Athena in order to fulfil the wish he expresses in the *Republic* to create myths through which to lead the people of a city (in this case the Athenians) to reconsider the past of their country.[115] In light of all these considerations, given that Plato invites us to read the three dialogues as a trilogy and given our keenness to accept this challenge, it is also worth weighing the contingency that Plato also reflected on the potential usefulness of intertextual connections in the literary creation of a fictional world.

For theorists of fiction, intertextual readings may be of great help also in cases in which a fictional world is sketched by more than one work, as is the case with the world which collectively emerges as a whole from the *Republic*, *Timaeus* and *Critias*. With regard specifically to this kind of intertextual creation of a fictional world, we are in a position to discern certain affinities between the observations of modern theorists of fiction and the way Plato seems to have approached the matter. First, the way in which Plato uses all three worlds as

---

scholars who have followed this view between the 18th and the 20th centuries, see Ausland 2000, 196 n. 45.
111 Cornford 1937, 1 n. 1, 3–5; Vidal-Naquet 1964, 421; Lee 1965, 146; Hadot 1983, 116; Osborne 1996, 181 n. 4; Rowe 1997, 51–52; Ausland 2000, 195–196; Morgan 2000, 262; Zeyl 2000, xxvi–xxvii; Johansen 2004, 7–8; Morgan 2010, 268–269; Johansen 2013, 90; Broadie 2013, 254; Tulli 2013, 274; Gill 2017, 2 and 9.
112 For earlier instances of this view, see Ausland 2000, 196 n. 48.
113 See, e.g., Golding 1975.
114 Rowe 1999.
115 Hadot 1983, 117–118; Johansen 2004, 24–47; Garvey 2008; Haddad 2013.

parts of one and the same world can be analysed from the perspective of modern theories about sequels and prequels. Second, the views expressed by Socrates, Timaeus and Critias carry seeds of two specific narratological schemes about the intertextual construction of a fictional world. In particular, we may discern some similarities between certain statements in the *Timaeus* and *Critias* and Thomas Pavel's thoughts about what he defines as the *Magnum Opus* of a fictional world. Further affinities can be traced between the views of the Platonic characters and Doležel's theory about the three ways in which a fictional world can be intertextually constructed and about the four levels on which it can be delineated.

With regard to the first aforementioned modern theory, even if we do not penetrate the details of views about sequels and prequels, it is obvious, as already argued, that the three dialogues function in an interdependent way with one another. However, at this point a crucial clarification should be made. There are two kinds of worlds delineated in these three works. First, there is the actual world of Athens, in which Socrates shapes his *kallipolis* at Cephalus' place, Timaeus develops his cosmological account, and Critias narrates the Atlantis tale. However, there are also the three worlds delineated by each character, namely the world of Socrates' *kallipolis*, the universe delineated by Timaeus, and the world of the Athenian distant past when Athens defeated Atlantis. It is the relationship of the latter three worlds that concerns me in this section and the intertextual linkages through which they unite into a single world.

The critic who elaborated in a more systematic way on the role of sequels and prequels in the construction of fictional worlds is Doležel. He discerns three types of relationship between different but intertextually linked fictional worlds: (a) "transposition", through which the plot of a story is located in a period of time or geographical area different than those of the initial fictional world (in Doležel's terms, the "protoword"); (b) "expansion", through which one broadens the perspective of the protoworld of a literary work by either creating its prehistory or posthistory. Doležel brings as an example the way in which Jean Rhys presents in *Wide Sargasso Sea* a world which constitutes an expansion of the world delineated in Charlotte Brontë's *Jane Eyre*. In *Wide Sargasso Sea* we read of the prehistory of a woman who has a secondary role in *Jane Eyre*; (c) the third type of transfictional relationships is defined by Doležel as "displacement", through which a work draws the setting, characters and plot of another work but with significant changes. As an example of displacement

Doležel takes J.M. Coetzee's *Foe*, in which Robinson Crusoé is presented as not interacting with the civilised world and as not writing any diary.[116]

Plato seems to play with the usefulness of these three levels of transfictional relationships and to put into effect some of their principles in the way in which he expands the hypothetical protoworld of the *Republic* in the *Timaeus* and *Critias*. However, before analysing this view further, it is worth noting that, although the protoworlds discussed by Doležel are presented by their creators as having once existed and as comprising events that did take place, the protoworld of the *kallipolis* is claimed by Socrates to be hypothetical and therefore impossible to define in terms of its temporal and geographical settings. This peculiarity of the fictional world of the *kallipolis* deprives us of the opportunity to identify its exact temporal and spatial relationship with the worlds of the *Timaeus* and *Critias*. On a temporal level, the latter two worlds may be at best taken as prequels of the world of the *kallipolis*, as they refer to the past and present, while the world built by Socrates in the *Republic* can possibly exist only in a hypothetical future. On a spatial level, as will be argued, we can discern more clearly in the *Timaeus* and *Critias* an expansion of the world of the *kallipolis*.

To begin with the *Timaeus*, the world delineated by the eponymous character constitutes an expansion of the hypothetical field of action of the *kallipolis*. This is so because, although hypothetical, the world delineated by Socrates in the *Republic* owes a great deal of its plausibility to the fact that it draws elements from the actual world on a spatial level. The professions described in the *Republic* are the same as those of the actual societies of the interlocutors' age. Also, the various fields of action in which the three classes are presented to act resemble those in which similar activities take place in the actual world of that period. The biological nature of the people is human nature as it is known to Socrates and his friends on both a physical and mental level. Although the principles that govern the interrelation between the authorities and the citizens fundamentally differ from the actual socio-political structures of that period, the primary elements that compose these interrelations (people, objects, nature, cities) match their counterparts of the actual world. It can therefore be assumed that, in Plato's mind, if there was any chance for the *kallipolis* to exist, it would do so in the actual world. It is exactly this world that the universe sketched by Timaeus is an expansion of: an expansion of the hypothetical field of action in which Socrates' political plan could be realised.

The *Critias*, for its part, supplements the two worlds of the *Republic* and *Timaeus* in two different ways. First, it may be taken as an extreme version of

---

116 Doležel 1998, 206–207.

Doležel's transposition, as it not only locates the political plot of the *Republic* in a new temporal and spatial setting but offers for the first time to the *kallipolis* its temporal and spatial substance. In this location of the *kallipolis* in Athens of a remote past, we may also discern Doležel's third type of tranfictional relations, i.e. displacement, according to which a literary work creates a world similar to the protoworld of a preceding work by changing the end of the story. In the case of the relation between the *kallipolis* and Athens of the Atlantis story, Critias is not merely invited to offer to an initial plot an alternative end but to invent one *ex nihilo*. This is so because the world of the *kallipolis* does not emerge from a plot but from a static description (see below). With regard to the world delineated by Timaeus, the world of the Atlantis story serves as a sequel, as it refers to a period of time that follows that of the creation of the universe and men.[117]

Let us read the passage in which we may see Plato's reflections on this matter. Critias says to Socrates (27a2–b6):

> Σκόπει δὴ τὴν τῶν ξενίων σοι διάθεσιν, ὦ Σώκρατες, ᾗ διέθεμεν. ἔδοξεν γὰρ ἡμῖν Τίμαιον μέν, ἅτε ὄντα ἀστρονομικώτατον ἡμῶν καὶ περὶ φύσεως τοῦ παντὸς εἰδέναι μάλιστα ἔργον πεποιημένον, πρῶτον λέγειν ἀρχόμενον ἀπὸ τῆς τοῦ κόσμου γενέσεως, τελευτᾶν δὲ εἰς ἀνθρώπων φύσιν· ἐμὲ δὲ μετὰ τοῦτον, ὡς παρὰ μὲν τούτου δεδεγμένον ἀνθρώπους τῷ λόγῳ γεγονότας, παρὰ σοῦ δὲ πεπαιδευμένους διαφερόντως αὐτῶν τινας, κατὰ δὲ τὸν Σόλωνος λόγον τε καὶ νόμον εἰσαγαγόντα αὐτοὺς ὡς εἰς δικαστὰς ἡμᾶς ποιῆσαι πολίτας τῆς πόλεως τῆσδε ὡς ὄντας τοὺς τότε Ἀθηναίους, οὓς ἐμήνυσεν ἀφανεῖς ὄντας ἡ τῶν ἱερῶν γραμμάτων φήμη, τὰ λοιπὰ δὲ ὡς περὶ πολιτῶν καὶ Ἀθηναίων ὄντων ἤδη ποιεῖσθαι τοὺς λόγους.

> Here then, Socrates, is the plan we have made to entertain you. We thought that Timaeus, who knows more about astronomy than the rest of us and who has devoted himself particularly to studying the nature of the universe, should speak first, and starting with the origin of the cosmic system bring the story down to man. I will follow him, assuming that human beings have come into existence as he has described and that some of them have had your excellent education; these I will bring to judgement before us here by making them citizens of Athens governed as she was in the days of Solon's story — an Athens whose disappearance is accounted for in the priestly writings, and about whose citizens I shall in the rest of what I have to say assume I am speaking.[118]

Through Critias' words Plato invites us to read the world shaped in the Atlantis story of the *Critias* as the last part of the trilogy, which supplements the worlds created by Socrates and Timaeus. Plato evidently takes the three dialogues as jointly shaping a united, composite world. The *Timaeus* builds the overall, uni-

---

117 Cf. Broadie 2013, 249.
118 The *Timaeus* aims at providing the great canvas for the war between Athens and Atlantis, as it gives a similar conflict between reason and necessity (Hadot 1983, 118).

versal canvas, the *Republic* offers the details of the political education and organisation of the men whose creation was described in the *Timaeus*, and the *Critias* will offer a historical example of how such a state acts at war. If in the *Statesman* Plato is concerned with the narrativisation of the scheme '*cosmos* → human nature → politics' in one and the same account (see Chapter 1), in the trilogy *Republic/Timaeus/Critias* he experiments on this technique within a wider framework of intertextual linkages.

The reading of the three dialogues as narratives which represent different facets of one and the same world resembles Pavel's theory that each world can be described by a plethora of works, which are named the *Magnum Opus* of this world:[119]

> The true sentences about the entire universe are collected in the set of books about each of its worlds. We may give this set the name of *Magnum Opus* on U, and reserve its First Book for the true sentences in the base or actual world of the universe. Another volume, which could be called the Book of Rules, would include higher-order considerations about the universe, its worlds and their books, explanations of the ways in which the relation R links the worlds of the universe U, or hints concerning the nature of the language used in the *Magnum Opus*.

Pavel's theory can help us interpret Critias' words. Each work of the trilogy offers a different part of the universe U, which includes all possible worlds. The *Republic* offers the fictional protoworld of the *kallipolis*, which serves as a source of inspiration for Timaeus to write his own Book of Rules, in which he offers exactly what Pavel says: he explains the rules on the basis of which the different worlds of the trilogy are connected to each other. The world of the gods follows specific rules in order to create the world of the natural environment. One further possible world, that of the *kallipolis* described in the *Republic*, can be taken to exist in the universe created by Timaeus' description only if it is considered to follow the rules of this universe. Last, in the *Critias*, Plato offers us one further possible world, in which the state described in the *Republic* interacts with other cities.

On the other hand, the share attributed by Critias to each work in the creation of this universe resembles Doležel's theory about the four levels on which a fictional world can be shaped. According to Doležel, there are four types of fictional worlds: (a) static worlds, which consist of static objects of unchangeable natural qualities and consolidated relationships. Doležel draws a parallel between this kind of world and Parmenides' theory about immobility and silence,

---

[119] Pavel 1986, 52.

according to which nothing changes and nothing new emerges. This is the world of the eternal ideas; (b) the second type of world is the one in which a new entity, the power of nature, appears. This power, which Doležel identifies with the rules of the universe, causes changes in the state of the world, which are defined as natural events. This dynamic world is the object of inquiry in physics as well as in poetry, art and music which describe nature; (c) on the third level of its creation, a fictional world is enriched and broadened by the emergence of a new category, the person, which, apart from its biological features, is also depicted as an individual of intellectual qualities. The person has certain intentions, which lead to actions that change the world; (d) on the fourth and last level of its delineation, a fictional world is marked by the presence of more than one person and their interaction. This world, which is taken by Doležel as the most complicated of all, demonstrates the various modes of interaction between persons, such as communication and interchange of information. According to Doležel, only a world of persons, either of one or more than one, can be a narrative world because it is a person's actions and coexistence that generate stories and plots.[120]

Critias seems to identify each work of the trilogy with certain world types of Doležel's scheme. It is worth noting that he encourages Socrates and the reader to observe the trilogy's composite world by beginning not from the *Republic* but from the *Timaeus*. Critias says that he will first consider the world and its creation as will be described by Timaeus. He will then use Timaeus' placement of human nature into the world and only at the end he will offer an account on the persons' interaction. Plato seems here to discern three stages of verbally conveying a world. The first Platonic stage combines Doležel's first two levels of a world's delineation. For Timaeus does not only describe the static objects of the world and their relations but also the god, who can be paralleled to the natural power of Doležel's second level, since by setting certain rules the god generates the natural events, such as the motion of the stars, the interaction of the natural elements and the activity of humans in this world.

The *Republic* coincides with the third level of Doležel's typology. The *kallipolis* is the 'person', which is added to the world sketched by Timaeus. As Doležel's third level of a world's delineation differs from the previous two ones in that it also describes a person's intellectual activity, the reader is similarly invited by Critias to focus on the intellectual qualities, the motives and the actions of the *kallipolis*' citizens in the way they have all been described by Socrates (i.e. in the *Republic*). Critias clearly leads us to the conclusion that what the *Republic* adds

---

[120] Doležel 1998, 32 ff.

to the world of Timaeus' myth lies in how the *Republic* transcends the theme of humans' creation and biology and enriches Timaeus' world by conveying the intellectual life of the ideal state. In the *Republic*, Socrates repeatedly explains that the three classes of the *kallipolis* are identified with the three parts of the soul, which means that Plato in a sense invites us to treat this state as a person.[121] This city-person is identifiable with the person of Doležel's third type of a world's delineation. It is a person of intellectual qualities, motives and activity which is governed by them, but still a person which does not interact.

This person's interaction with other ones (Doležel's fourth level) comes at the last Platonic stage of a world's depiction, the Atlantis myth in the *Critias*. Socrates characteristically asks Critias and the others exactly this: to describe to him how such a state could interact with other cities. What is more, Plato also touches upon the issue of the static nature of world descriptions which lack any interaction between distinct persons. For, as demonstrated above, Socrates comments that the way he has described the *kallipolis* as not being in touch with other states resembles depictions of motionless animals. From a narrative point of view, the metaphorical mention of immobility which emerges from the absence of any kind of interaction denotes descriptions of states cut off from others. Critias will satisfy Socrates' desire and will enrich the composite world of Timaeus and Socrates by incorporating into it Atlantis, which serves as the person which the *kallipolis*/Athens will interrelate with. Doležel seems to recognise the difference, which is also discerned by a number of narratologists, between description and narration. Specifically, he states:[122]

> World-without-person can provide the initial or the end state of some elementary stories (the genesis of the human race or its apocalyptic extinction) but by itself is below the threshold of narrativity. It is worlds with persons or, better, persons within worlds that generate stories.

We may trace seeds of this narratological distinction between description and narration in Socrates' distinction between his static description of the *kallipolis* and the account he expects his friends to narrate about this state's interaction with other polities.

---

121 See, e.g., *Rep.* 368e2–369a4.
122 Doležel 1998, 33. For an overview of the narratological theories on this distinction and of its pitfalls, see Koopman's (2018, 1–39) fine introduction to his book on ancient Greek *ekphrasis* as a technique which lies somewhere between description and narration.

2.6 Conclusion

Plato is traditionally mentioned by modern critics merely as the forefather of a naively realist approach to fiction which assesses the truthfulness or plausibility of what is described in fiction, or of what is stated about it, by the criterion of whether or not fiction represents reality. According to this view, we are justified to deem as true or possible only the content of those fictional worlds that depict states of affairs similar or identical to those we find in the actual world. Such an approach, narratologists and theorists of narrative object, overlooks the fact that in the audiences' minds fiction is ontologically and logically independent of the world we live, and has its own system of rules which define the degree of possibility or impossibility of all the states of affairs it contains. Plato's view of narratives as representations of reality is thus inevitably banished by such a theory that focuses not so much of what is actually true or possible in a story but rather on what is intuitively taken as such by the audience.

In this chapter, it was argued that, although modern theorists of fiction have traditionally been indifferent to, or even sceptical about, tracing points of congruence between their views and those we find in the Platonic oeuvre, the *Timaeus* and *Critias* have much to say about the emergence of a 'proto-theory' of fictional worlds. It is a common knowledge among classicists that in these two dialogues Plato pays less attention to the truthfulness of narrative representations of reality and transfers his focal point of interest towards what is taken by narrators and audiences as likely. In other words, Plato does exactly what modern theorists do: without overlooking that fiction is at the end of the day nothing but an unreliable depiction of reality, he is rather interested in examining what is convincing in the receivers' minds. In this line of thought, he touches upon issues that constitute the cornerstones of modern theory of fictional worlds.

3 The *Laws*: Formalism and Reception Theory Intermingled

In the first chapter, I argued that in the *Statesman* the arrangement of the cosmological account and the Visitor's statements on the act of composing it have much to say about Plato's formalist approach of narratives. I based my analysis on the *communis opinio* that the myth serves, at least to a certain degree, as a therapeutic junction between the initial false definition of statesmanship and the more fruitful investigation of the matter in the last part of the dialogue. Developing further this popular reading of the myth, I argued that, from a structural point of view, the Visitor's numerous meta-methodological statements reveal to the reader his reflections upon the contribution of specific facets of narrativity to this educational function of the act of narrating. The principal goal of a dialogue, i.e. the improvement of the interlocutors in dialectic and in defining categories, is served by the following concepts that also concern classical narratology: the procedures through which the transformation of a raw material into a coherent narrative whole is achieved (the selection and distribution of data and the (re)construction of causality and temporal relations), and the narrating/listening time of a story.

In the second chapter, I maintained that in the *Timaeus* and *Critias* Plato's concern is more focused on the reception of narratives in a similar way to the way in which modern theorists of fiction approach the reception of fictional worlds. As it has hopefully transpired from my comparative analysis, in these two dialogues Plato draws our attention to the fact that both narrators and audiences speculate on the nature of fictional worlds with regard to the following issues which are also very popular in modern theory of fictional worlds: (a) the degree to which a fictional world is taken as possible; (b) the incompleteness of fictional worlds; (c) the impact of the sociocultural background of narrators and audiences on the way(s) a fictional world is both conceived and interpreted; (d) the immersion of narrators and audiences into the world of a narrative; and (e) the way in which a fictional world emerges from intertextual linkages. I also argued that Plato's reflections on these matters go hand in hand with his aspiration to expand in the *Timaeus* and *Critias* the fictional world of the *kallipolis* described in the *Republic* in a way that would make the imaginary state a scenario possible in the audience's minds. While in the *Timaeus* the cosmological myth shapes the very universe in which a political world like the *kallipolis* makes sense, the Atlantis tale in the *Critias* offers a historical example which proves that Socrates' political world of the *Republic* is feasible since it already existed once in the past.

In this chapter, it is argued that these two distinctive but closely interrelated directions of theoretical speculation addressed in Chapters 1 and 2 meet each other in the *Laws*. In particular, I will endeavour to demonstrate that in the *Laws* Plato invites us to reflect on the way in which certain concepts of narrativity which are also touched upon in the *Statesman* (selection and distribution of the material into a plot and the creation of causal and temporal relations between the events of a story) aim to shape our view about the plausibility of a fictional world.

While in the *Statesman*, *Timaeus* and *Critias* we find a single main narrative in each context, in the *Laws* we read a group of accounts which are narrated consecutively in Book 3 and cover again a vast amount of time. The similarities with the *Statesman*, *Timaeus* and *Critias* are many and, at least in terms of content, have been well analysed in previous scholarship.[1] However, it is also worth noting in advance some similarities in terms of narrative structuring and theoretical reflection on it. First, as in the *Statesman*, in the *Laws* the accounts of Book 3 serve as a connecting link between a preliminary stage of investigating the issue in question (Books 1–2) and the main part of the dialogue, which is the composition of a hypothetical city's laws (Books 4–12). The three interlocutors (the anonymous Athenian Visitor, the Cretan Clinias and the Spartan Megillus) explore what is the proper kind of legislation and what goals a legislator should set in his effort to secure the virtue and happiness in a city. From the twelve books of the *Laws* the first three serve, the interlocutors claim, as a prelude to the constitution to be composed in the last nine books (722c6–d2). In Books 1–2, the companions express a number of theses about the proper, in their opinion, goal setting of a legislator. These views constitute the cornerstones of the logic in the legislation of Books 4–12.[2] However, between Books 1–2 and the laws of Books 4–12 Plato strikingly places Book 3, which essentially comprises a series of accounts on the development of human politics and legislation from the very beginning of human society up to the interlocutors' time. These stories often serve as the transmission line of the views we find in Books 1–2 into the institution of Books 4–12.[3] It goes without saying that the latter draw ideas from Books 1–2 in

---

[1] See the discussions in this chapter.
[2] England 1921, 1–2; Des Places 1951, V; Gauss 1961, 208–264; Stalley 1983, 5, 37.
[3] Des Places 1951, V; Schaerer 1953, 392; Weil 1959, 57; Stalley 1983, 8; Lisi 2000, 12; On reading Book 4 through the prism of Book 3, see Zuckert 2013, who unconvincingly sees the Athenian's account of Book 3 as an effort to win over Clinias' and Megillus' trust by praising the Dorian institution and by accusing the Athenian.

an immediate fashion as well, borrowing precisely from the way that these views were expressed in the first two books. However, as will be argued in Section 3.1.3, the legislation of Books 4–12 also occasionally echoes these views in the enriched form in which they occur exclusively in the accounts of Book 3.

One further affinity between the myth of the *Statesman* and the narratives of the *Laws* lies in the fact that the latter too are presented by Plato as an alternative educational method. In this case, it is not a philosopher who educates a boy but a legislator who explains to the population of a city the reasons why they should obey the laws. Narration again does not emerge as the principal mode of argumentation but as an auxiliary tool to the main method of persuasion, which is the prelude to a law. What is a prelude to a law will be discussed in Section 3.1.2. At this point it suffices to say that Plato strengthens the arguments we read in the preludes of Books 4–12 through the accounts of Book 3. In this way, as will be argued, the narratives share with the preludes a plethora of features and functions and thereby become an integral part of the legislator's art of persuasion.[4]

Last, similarly to what we read in the *Statesman*, *Timaeus* and *Critias*, in the *Laws* too we are faced with an abundance of statements about the structuring, function and reception of narratives. The Athenian Visitor addresses some elements of narrativity which we discussed in the first chapter, such as selectivity, the creation of causality and the structuring of temporal sequences between the events. However, while in the *Statesman* the focal point of Plato's interest lies in the procedure of the emplotment (the transformation of a raw material into a coherent narrative whole) and in the length of the narrating time, in the *Laws* the lion's share of the meta-methodological comments belongs to the ways in which narration participates in the legislator's rhetoric of persuasion, a theme closely related with the receiver's intellectual and affective responses elicited by an account.

In this respect, the main point of argument in this last part of the book, which is also denoted by the title of the chapter, is that in the *Laws* certain issues of structuring a narrative we examined in the first chapter are now approached by Plato from the perspective of the narrative's reception by its audience. I will endeavour to show that the aspects of selectivity, causality and temporality, and some others as well, are not addressed *per se* but in close association with their contribution to the way the narrative outcome will affect the emotional and intellectual world of its receivers. Plato not only underscores the choices that composers of stories make in the process of shaping them; he also intends

---

4 Cf. *Apol.* 40e4–41c7 on Socrates' use of myths concerning the benefits of an afterlife; *Phaed.* 107c1–115a3.

to share with us his view that these compositional choices serve the way in which the composers want their stories to influence the audience's intellect and emotions. Since the main purpose of the narratives in Book 3 is to persuade the citizens of Magnesia and the reader of the plausibility of the legislators' political program, the *Laws* may be read in relation with the views expressed in the *Timaeus* and *Critias* about the audience's sense of what is possible or not in fictional worlds.

The chapter is divided into three main sections. In the first section (3.1), I will gather and analyse those passages which betray Plato's interest in the affective and intellectual responses a story may elicit in its audience. Passages will be taken from all the books of the dialogue. First, I will analyse the parts of Books 1–2 in which the interlocutors touch upon the effectiveness of stories upon the population of a state (3.1.1). It will be argued that these passages from Books 1–2 serve for the reader as short teasers of the narratives in Book 3 and of their intense impact on the inner world of both the dialogue's characters and the reader. Second, I will focus on the cross-references between the accounts of Book 3 and the rest of the work (Books 1–2 in Section 3.1.2 and Books 4–12 in Section 3.1.3). It will be argued that through these cross-references the stories of Book 3 promote the legislators' moral doctrines and enhance their argumentation, with which they aspire to entchant the psychology of their imaginary citizens and therefore to persuade them to adopt a virtuous life.

In shaping the history of legislation and politics on the basis of the moral doctrines he wishes to impose on the imaginary Magnesia, the Athenian essentially creates for his hypothetical people his own 'intentional history'. More specifically, he filters the past through the ideology he aspires to impose in the present. In order to do so, the Athenian adapts the already existing material about the events he narrates (parts of a raw material drawn from poetry, oral tradition or other literary works) to the logic of his narrative under construction. In Section 3.2, I will analyse the narrative arrangement of the accounts in Book 3 and the metanarrative comments of these accounts and conclude that, as transpires from the analysis of the passages in question, Plato invites the reader to reflect on three special ways in which a narrator can base his narration of the past on his own moral code: (a) the narrator ideologically 'coats' material drawn from literature with aspects of the proposed communal moral code; (b) he poses questions about the past and then uses the proposed communal moral code as a tool through which to answer these questions; and (c) the proposed moral code offers the structural backbone of a past narrative. Through these techniques, Plato creates strong linkages between the fictional world of Magnesia and the fictional world of the Mediterranean political past. In essence, he leads us to the conclusion that both societies of the past and the hypothetical Magnesia are defined by the same, diachronic, principles. The interlocutors' assumptions about how Magnesia will politically thrive are thereby presented as plausible, given that they are confirmed by what took place in the past. It is exactly at this point, it will be argued, that the *Laws* is conceptually associated with the *Timaeus* and *Critias*, as in both cases Plato leads the reader to speculate on how fictional worlds emerge as possible structures in the audience's minds.

3.1 Narration as a means of persuasion and the audience's psychology

It would be no exaggeration to say that in the *Laws* Plato places the psychology and intellectual world of the citizens at the focal point of his interest.[5] The interlocutors' goal is not merely to compose a set of ideal laws but also to find the ways in which to convince the citizens to obey these laws. What is at stake is thus not only a legislator's insight and moral virtues but also his persuasion skills.[6] Even more importantly, the Athenian Visitor believes that the current, established mode of formulating a law, which was marked by a limited focus on precepts and penalties, did not suffice to persuade the citizens to conform to the legislator's will. The latter, the Athenian repeatedly argues, should constantly look for alternative means of argumentation and support of the law's content. These means are songs and dances, which explain and promote the moral values a city should have, the advantages for the citizens who adopt the proposed moral code, and the disadvantages for those who do not. One of these means, according to the Athenian, is the narration of accounts.

The main weapon of the legislator and one of Plato's most striking novelties in the *Laws* are the so-called preludes, through which the lawgiver is invited to convince the citizens to follow his orders.[7] As is the case with songs and dances,

---

[5] England 1921, 5–6; Bury 1937, 306–311 on the psychological value of education; Morrow 1953, 237 on the way that the legislator's rhetoric targets the people's psychology, just as Aristotle instructs aspiring rhetoricians on how to manipulate their audiences; Rankin 1958; Mouracade 2005; Meyer 2015, 116–117.

[6] Bury 1937, 312; Morrow 1953; Fuks 1979, 34–35; Nightingale 1993, 285; Powell 1994; Stalley 1994; Clark 2003; Lisi 2017, 118–121.

[7] On the preludes in Plato's *Laws*, see England 1921, 1–3; Post 1929; Müller 1951, 171–172; Morrow 1953; Görgemanns 1960, 30–49; Stalley 1983, 42–44;. The views expressed in these studies are discussed throughout this chapter; Vickers (1988) focuses on the preludes as a form of deceit. See, *contra*, Yunis 1990; Bobonich 1991; Nightingale 1993; Stalley 1994, 269–277; Clark 2003;

in the preludes too the lawgiver should highlight the benefits which emerge from virtue and the subsequent obedience to the law, and the drawbacks which stem from malice and disobedience. In this respect, a law's prelude is described as a means of persuasion which is aimed at luring the citizens' utilitarian expediencies and manipulating them towards a mode of life which champions their city's legislation.[8]

Plato composes the preludes of the laws on a level of both macro-structure and micro-structure. As already said, in terms of macro-structure, the first three books of the work serve as preludes to the laws composed in the last nine books. In Books 1–2 the interlocutors, although they from the outset announce their purpose to discuss legislation and constitutions, address some topics which at first sight seem quite irrelevant to legal issues, such as dance, music, banquets and wine drinking. However, through the speculations they express on the proper manifestations of these phenomena, they essentially establish, step by step, the moral basis whereupon they will later on set the laws of Books 4–12.[9] In Book 3, the Athenian narrates the history of legislation from the very first stages of human civilisation up to his age. And after completing these three first books, in their concluding remarks on them, the three companions repeatedly explain to the reader that what has been said so far will serve as a prelude to the rest of the work, as a reservoir of ideas, wherefrom they will draw the main principles for the composition of the laws and for the argumentation through which they will endeavour to convince the citizens and the reader that the proposed laws are worth preserving (702b4–e2; 722c6–d2). It is of particular importance to stress the fact that the function of the first three books and of the narratives we find in them is not confined to the fact that they substantiate the three aspiring legislators' choices in Books 4–12; their function also lies in how they serve as a means of persuasion, which aims at tugging at the citizens' heartstrings, at 'entchanting' them, as the Athenian puts it, and at motivating them to choose by themselves to follow the laws.[10]

On a level of micro-structure, many categories of laws are introduced by individual preludes, by means of which the Athenian legislator tries to convince the citizens that they should follow each category of laws. In these preludes too,

---

Laks 2007. Most recently, Mayhew (2007) questions Bobonich's view of "rational persuasion"; Baima 2016; Zichi 2018.
8 Stalley 1983, 41.
9 Post (1929) believes that Books 1–2 are the preludes of the laws composed in Books 4–12 and, on the basis of *Ep.* 3.316a and *Leg.* 722c, concludes that the first two books were written much earlier than the rest of the work, and makes further assumptions about the date of the work.
10 On philosophical discussions and doctrines as chants, cf. *Charm.* 155e5–157d8.

just as in Books 1–3, the legislator acts, we could say, as a rhetorician who tries to expose his arguments. As we will see, the Athenian repeatedly touches upon the luring nature of these preludes, which aim at eliciting a number of the citizens' emotions. These caresses often target the young members of the city but also address the rest of the citizens too. Hence, for the Athenian Visitor and so Plato, all citizens, independently of their age, should be treated as children to be educated.[11] The means of persuasion, such as preludes, narratives, dance and music, target the psychology of all citizens and not only of the young ones.

Much has been said about the ways in which the preludes mould the psychological state of the audience, elicit specific emotions, and activate the desired cognitive reactions of the citizens.[12] Nonetheless, we do not possess a systematic treatise on the way that the accounts of Book 3 emerge as pivotal and integral parts of this rhetoric of persuasion. However, as just explained, in Plato's mind these narratives constitute both a part of the great prelude shaped by the first three books and, as will hopefully be demonstrated in this chapter, one of the main arrows in the Athenian's quiver, a tool which repeatedly and very actively participates in the manipulation of the audience on a level of microstructure as well, i.e. by creating numerous cross-references with the individual preludes of Books 4–12. It is therefore worth collecting and analysing the passages which strengthen this view, and it is also worth categorising the various kinds of affective and intellectual interaction of the laws with the citizens, which emerge from the Athenian's use of narratives both outside and within the preludes.

The already existing categorisations of the ways in which the preludes influence the audience will serve as a source of inspiration for the present analysis. However, simultaneously and conversely, I also aim at enriching the outcomes of previous studies, sometimes by clarifying how already noticed functions of the preludes are reinforced by the use of narratives of Book 3 or, in other occasions, by shedding light on unnoticed functions of the preludes, functions which can be more easily apprehended through the analysis of these narratives which are related to these preludes. All this is analysed in Sections 3.1.2 and 3.1.3.

---

11 Cf. Morrow 1953, 239.
12 See n. 7 above.

3.1.1 The 'teaser' reflections in Books 1–2

Here, I will present and analyse certain comments made by the three interlocutors in Books 1–2 which pertain to the contribution of narratives to the stabilisation of laws in a state. The main point of argument in this section is that these comments serve as short 'teasers' of the energetic role the narratives of Book 3 will have in the three legislators' effort to promote the moral code they wish to impose in Magnesia. Differently from what we saw in the *Statesman* and the *Timaeus/Critias*, in this case the metanarrative reflections (the short teasers of Books 1–2) prepare us for the narrative paradigms (the accounts of Book 3) on a level of macro-structure, i.e. from the one book to the other.

Let us open our analysis with a summary of Books 1–2. The dialogue begins in a quite abrupt manner, as if in the middle of a conversation between the three interlocutors. The field of action is Crete and the three men walk down the road from Cnossos towards the cave of Zeus in which Minos was said to have taken from the god the laws of Cnossos. The Athenian Visitor straightforwardly proposes the subject of the dialogue, which, as we are later informed, begins at dawn and ends in the night of the same day (722c7–8). The Athenian suggests to his companions that they discuss the issue of the proper legislation. Clinias explains to him that both the lawgiver of the Cretans and that of the Spartans have written their laws with their main goal being that their cities prevail in war, given that war constantly takes place between cities even in seemingly peaceful periods of time (624a1–626c5). The Athenian disagrees and leads the conversation to the following conclusion: each man, *oikos*, village or city is conducting an internal war between their good and bad elements. In this respect, a virtuous entity is to be considered the one in which the good elements prevail over the evil ones. Thus, in a city the goal of an ideal legislator is to secure the balance between the citizens without causing the death of the non-virtuous ones but by means of laws which will bring about a peaceful compromise between all sides. For the legislator's goal is not war but concord between the people of a city (626c6–628e5). Besides, the Athenian argues, civil war is a much more demanding situation than the war against other cities, as it invites each man to retain the quality of his soul by demonstrating all virtues (moderation, prudence, justice and bravery), while external war requires only bravery. In this respect, given that a legislator aims at preserving concord during a civil war, he targets at something far superior than mere bravery, i.e. virtue in its entirety (629a1–631b2). In what follows, the three men examine what bravery is and the nature of laws which teach people to be brave. The Athenian observes that the Cretan and Spartan laws, while defining the ways in which the citizens will learn how to resist their fear for sorrow and pain, have not defined the activities through which young men should learn how to resist pleasure. He then expresses the view, which is met sceptically by his companions, that inebriation and banquets help people to practise controlling themselves in situations in which they become fearless and devoid of shame (631b3–650b10).

In Book 2, the interlocutors continue exploring the way in which the proper conduct of banquets contributes to the proper education of the youth. The Athenian offers a second definition of education: it trains young people to love and hate what they should. Children should be led to the proper pleasures and sorrows through habituation without initially using their reason. Later on, when they will grow up, they will use their logic to think of what they should be happy or unhappy for. If they realise that what reason shows them as proper pleasures and sorrows coincides with the way of life they were taught in young age, this means that they had been offered a proper education (653a5–c4). However, exactly because people always tend to change their views about what is right or wrong in these matters, the gods offered humans festivities, in which people have the opportunity to be reminded of these subjects by getting in touch with Apollo, the Muses and Dionysus. This is so, the Athenian claims, because the very first form of education people are offered are dance and music. The educated man is the one who is acquainted with dancing and singing. Now, the proper education for someone is to dance and sing in the proper fashion. Given that the quality of music and dance is commonly assessed by the criterion of pleasure (how many people a performance satisfies and to what degree it does so), they should be assessed on the basis of the educated elders' pleasure. In this way, the city will secure for its people a proper education, as proper performances will lead young people to pleasures and emotions which comply with the law's logic, which in turn complies with the logic of the elders (657c3–660d10). As happens in Crete and in Sparta, legislators should force poets to tell to people through their works that a virtuous life is a happy life, while a non-virtuous life is painful and ugly. The elders should also take over the supervision of wine drinking in order to teach young people how to cope with situations of shamelessness and fearlessness.

Already from the opening lines of the *Laws*, narratives emerge as a hallmark of both the legislator's authority and the quality of a city's laws. The dialogue begins with the Athenian asking Clinias and Megillus if, according to local traditions, the laws of Crete and Sparta are attributed to a god. Clinias answers affirmatively and tells the Athenian that the laws of Cnossos are attributed to Zeus, while those of Sparta are attributed to Apollo. The Athenian then penetrates even further the details of these stories; he asks Clinias if he refers to the tale we find in Homer, in which Minos, after living with Zeus for nine years, wrote the laws for the Cretan cities in compliance with his father's admonitions (*Od.* 19.178–181). Clinias answers that this is exactly the story he refers to, while he adds one further tale about Minos' brother, Rhadamanthys. According to the Cretan narrative tradition, Rhadamanthys offered so just verdicts in trials that he reasonably gained the fame of the most just man and is still praised for his virtue ever since (624a1–625a3).[13]

Although Plato could have opened the dialogue by merely praising the laws of Crete and Sparta, he seems not to be content with a mere *laus* and transfers the focal point of our interest to the local stories circulating in Crete and Laconia, with which the authorities and the peoples themselves exalted the legal systems of their countries. The Athenian, after listening to these tales, offers a striking answer: "Now since you and our friend here have been raised under such distinguished laws, I expect you would not find it unpleasant if we whiled away our journey today in a conversation about law codes and legislation" (625a5–b1).[14] The Athenian seems, at first sight, to recognise such stories on the divine origins of a city's legislation as a piece of evidence for the qualities of the laws. It is as if he says to his friends "Come on, since the stories about Minos, Rhadamanthys and Apollo prove the virtue of your countries' legislations, let us talk about laws". Of course, his words are marked by a latent playfulness, if not irony,[15] since he is well aware of the fact that such stories, although helpful in the legislator's effort to convince the citizens to obey the laws, can and should be put to the test (634d7–635b1). Nonetheless, one cannot but notice Plato's intention to open the *Laws* by laying emphasis on the contribution of local narrative traditions to the blazoning of a community's laws both to its natives and

---

13 Cf. Ephorus *FGrHist* 70 F 147; Arist. *Cretan Constitution* f 611.14 Rose.
14 For the text of the *Laws* I use Burnet's (1907) OCT edition. For Books 1–2 I use Meyer's (2015) translation, while for the rest of the work I use the translation by Bury 2001^8.
15 Cf. Gigon 1954, 202–209, who, despite recognising that Plato was aware of the fictive nature of these stories, argues that the mention of Minos encourages the reader to draw a parallel between the walk of the three elders to the altar of Zeus and the regular visits of Minos to the place where Zeus resided (that is, the place where his altar where the three men walk to). Cf. Morrow 1960, 27–28 and Nightingale 1993, 282–283. Stalley (1983, 4) also identifies the two spots. On this issue, cf. Sallis 2013, 77; Meyer 2015, 78 with further bibliography. Stalley (1983, 4–5) also finds that the Athenian's scepticism towards the stories on the divine origins of the Cretan and Spartan laws is latent in the criticisms he expresses on the two legislations in the ensuing chapters of the work. Schöpsdau (1994, 155) notes that the Athenian's irony on the Cretan tradition about Minos is expressed by the μῶν οὖν of 624a7. Meyer (2015, 79) seems to find no irony in the Athenian's words. Cf. England 1921, 198.

to foreigners.[16] These opening paragraphs foreshadow the discussants' special interest in the usefulness of narratives in a legislator's effort to convince the citizens to respect the laws of their city.[17]

The main method through which, according to the Athenian, a lawgiver should employ narratives as a means of persuasion and control of a people is to render them an organic part of the preludes with which he will affect the citizens' psychology. These two aspects, (a) the manipulative role of the preludes and (b) the contribution of narratives to the legislator's endeavour to assert himself, will be presented as two elements of a common method only from Book 2 onwards. However, two further passages in Book 1 prepare the reader for the fact that in the Athenian's mind these two aspects are inextricably related to each other.

Let us begin with the first aspect, the manipulative role of the preludes. The first time the Athenian expresses his wish that the laws be accompanied by an introduction of moral deontology is found in 631b3–632d1. He has just registered his arguments against Clinias' view that a legislator should write laws which render his city competent at war (625c9–631b2). After convincing Clinias that a lawgiver's goal should be instead to secure peace, the Athenian confesses to him his wish that they have started their conversation in a different manner than they had done. He had expected Clinias to offer the following prelude to laws: Clinias should have said that the laws of Crete are famous because they make citizens happy by offering them superior goods, such as wisdom, moderation, justice and bravery. For, whenever the laws of a city lead people to these virtues, they also help them to obtain some lesser goods, such as health, strength, wealth and power. The Athenian explains that these thoughts should have first been expressed by Clinias as a prelude to the laws he would then decree about the following subjects, which pertain to all the phases of human life: marriages, the making and upbringing of children, the ways in which citizens are expected to earn and spend their money, their interpersonal relationships and their burial customs (631d1–632d1).[18] The Athenian offers here a thematic and structural miniature of Books 4–12. In essence, he proposes the following structure: an introductory, didactic prelude to the ensuing legislation. In a similar

---

[16] Reverdin 1945; Pangle 1974; Stalley 1983, 24; Nightingale 1993, 282–285; 1999, 309–310; Whitaker 2004; de la Fuente 2010, 108–111.

[17] See also Gigon 1954, 204, who recognises that 624–625 and 663d ff. carry the same message. For the connection between the two cases, see below.

[18] Although the Athenian here does not describe this introductory scheme as προοίμιον, I take this passage as his first reference to the preludes of the laws. See, *contra*, Des Places 1951, 69 n. 2; Nightingale 1993, 286.

vein, in Book 4 the Athenian opens the legislation for Magnesia with a prelude of content similar to that of 631b3–632d1 and then proceeds with the different categories of laws and, what is more, in roughly the same order as the one he offers here.[19]

The Athenian clearly pays particular attention to the effectiveness of such introductory remarks upon the citizens' psychology, given that, in his view, the distinctive feature of the Cretan laws carries an enticing promise which elicits the people's hope for a happy life.[20] This promise is generated by the classification of the two kinds of goods, as the Cretan laws are claimed to lead the people to happiness exactly because they lead them to the superior goods and thereby teach them to ship the inferior goods to the minors.[21] What is more, this is the first time we read of one of the Athenian's main theses about how laws and their preludes should persuade the citizens to obey the legislator's commands: through the laws the latter should praise and castigate the citizens.[22]

Narratives are soon included by the Athenian in the legislator's weaponry of persuasion. The interlocutors discuss about communal meals and athletic training, which were very popular in both Crete and Sparta. Megillus claims that these institutions are to be praised as they assist young men reach both bravery and moderation (633a1–636a3). The Athenian, however, is sceptical about this view, countering that communal meals and athletic training create certain communicational circumstances which foster the emergence of homosexual affairs (636a4–c7). He also adds that this is definitely a black spot in the image of both Sparta and Crete and, at this point, says (636c7–d4):

> πάντες δὲ δὴ Κρητῶν τὸν περὶ Γανυμήδη μῦθον κατηγοροῦμεν ὡς λογοποιησάντων τούτων· ἐπειδὴ παρὰ Διὸς αὐτοῖς οἱ νόμοι πεπιστευμένοι ἦσαν γεγονέναι, τοῦτον τὸν μῦθον προστεθηκέναι κατὰ τοῦ Διός, ἵνα ἑπόμενοι δὴ τῷ θεῷ καρπῶνται καὶ ταύτην τὴν ἡδονήν.
>
> Indeed, we all fault the Cretans for coming up with the story of Ganymede. Convinced as they are that their laws come from Zeus, they saddle him with this tale so that they can be following the god even when reaping this particular pleasure.

The Athenian's wording mirrors his interest not only in the content of the Ganymede tale (636c7: μῦθον) but also in the procedure of its composition (636d1: λογοποιησάντων). This myth circulated with or without the part about Zeus'

---

19 On the prelude of this case as foreshadowing later preludes in the dialogue, see Ritter 1985², II 3–4 Cf. England 1921, 214–219; Des Places 1951, n. 1 on 631d6 ff.; Schöpsdau 1994, 186–187.
20 Schöpsdau 1994, 179–180; Welton 1996, 216–218.
21 Schöpsdau 1994, 179–190; Clark 2003; Meyer 2015, 114–122.
22 On the laudatory character of the preambles, see Morrow 1953, 240–242.

relationship with the boy. The participle λογοποιησάντων therefore involves the Cretans' incorporating the element of the sexual relationship into a pre-existing myth.[23] In this example, Plato draws the reader's attention to the way in which a mythical narrative helps one's effort to impose, or at least to legitimise, certain types of behaviours and customs, even those of questionable moral value.[24] As we saw, the Cretans used the myth that their laws originated from Zeus through the wisdom of his sons Minos and Rhadamanthys. Now, borrowing the *topos* that whatever Zeus does is righteous and therefore worth imitating, the Cretans fabricated a story in which they presented Zeus as having a homosexual affair. With this anthropomorphic portraiture of Zeus they shaped for themselves a model to follow, a model which is simultaneously aimed at validating in a foreigner's mind a controversial distinctive feature of their societal identity. In essence, what legitimises homosexual affairs in the Cretan society is the fact that they are embraced by the divine lawgiver. After all, it would be an oxymoron on the Cretans' part to obey the god's laws but to consider his choices unacceptable. This appeal to authority is based on the view, which is common both in the Platonic oeuvre and in ancient Greek literature, that gods are flawless and totally virtuous in whatever they do.[25] As we will see in Sections 3.1.2 and 3.1.3, the accounts of Book 3 similarly offer to the citizens of Magnesia an example to follow.

The Cretan tales about Zeus' love for Ganymede introduce one further permanent characteristic of the narratives in the *Laws*, not only of those we read in Book 3 but also in the entire dialogue: this narrative embodies the Cretans' effort to create for their country what Hans-Joachim Gehrke defines as "intentional history".[26] Gehrke recognises that communities very often give certain meanings to the events related to their past. And this kind of signification of history is sometimes a guided, inventive and manipulative act. According to the theory of intentional history, the main goal of the intentional exploitation of the past is

---

[23] England 1921, 231; Schöpsdau (1994, 204) provides ancient sources on Ganymede; Meyer 2015, 143.
[24] Schöpsdau 1994, 204. In the *Phaedrus* too (255c) Plato touches upon the abuse of the Ganymede myth in the praise of homoerotic affairs. Plato recognises the persuasiveness of religion and stories of religious content in people's minds (738b–c). Cf. Powell 1994, 287–292; Salem 2013, 54.
[25] *Apol.* 21b5–6; *Cratyl.* 391d3–e1; *Symp.* 202c6–d6 and 204a1–2.
[26] Gehrke 2001; Foxhall/Gehrke/Luraghi 2010, 9–14; Möller 2019; Gehrke 2019; Gehrke's studies on this subject are gathered in Trampedach/Mann 2019.

the consolidation and preservation of a national identity and the legitimisation of those distinctive features which form this differential identity in the present.[27]

In this case, the Cretans distinguish a certain feature of their current society (homosexuality) and seek ways to absolve this feature from moral censure. The fabrication of stories which present a prestigious figure of their past as exhibiting this attribute is a way for them to create their own intentional history. Through such accounts, the Cretans create tight linkages between themselves and their forefathers, or the gods who protected their forefathers. This 'rhetoric of narrative tradition' transforms the element of homosexuality from a disgraceful communal flaw into a trait which secures currency for those who embrace it, as it constitutes a linkage of their society's present with its ancestors.[28] In this way, homosexuality, as a characteristic of Zeus, who is not only a god but also the father of and brain behind the lawgiver of the Cretans, becomes something to be followed. For, first, embracing this feature is an expression of respect towards the god and constitutes a carrier of national identity of the Cretans, as it is a common feature of their society since its infancy. As will be later demonstrated, throughout the *Laws* the three discussants are repeatedly presented as using narratives as pieces of intentional history or as admonishing other to do so, pieces of intentional history through which they will secure, in their opinion, the citizens' permanent obedience to law.

Let us return to the view expressed above that the structural miniature of the *Laws* in 631b3–632d1 and the Athenian's mention of the Ganymede story reveal to us two basic aspects of Plato's theory about the impact of narratives on the affective and intellectual world of their recipients and, by extension, about the usefulness of narratives in a society. Up to this point the Athenian, the central legislator of the imaginary Magnesia, has offered the reader a preliminary idea of his view that the body of a city should be guided by lures such as introductory ethical guidance and past narratives. As a result, the reader on her part is not caught by surprise when she reads in the ensuing chapters of the *Laws* that in the Athenian's mind these two means of persuasion may be employed in combination to one another: the legislator can enrich the content of a prelude with a narrative and thereby enhance the prelude's logical and psychological imprint upon the receivers' inner world.

This realisation on the reader's part comes in the chapters in which the Athenian discusses the legislation pertaining to music and dance in Book 2. The Athenian maintains that the laws on these issues (as on any other subject)

---

27 Gehrke 2001.
28 Gehrke 2001; 2019.

should be permanent and unalterable (653c7–657c2) and, second, should convey the optimistic message we saw in the structural miniature of the *Laws* that a virtuous life secures happiness (660d11–664d4). Both the chapters on the desired stability of the laws as well as those on the legislator's optimist identification of virtue and happiness culminate each time in the Athenian's statement that the lawgiver should endeavour to reach his goal through the use of narratives. It would thus be no exaggeration to say that in 653c7–664d4 the composition and narration of stories emerges as an exceptionally effective means of persuasion with a multi-layered impact on the citizens' minds.

Let us begin with the Athenian's view that the laws should remain unchanged. At this point, the discussants decide to investigate what is a good song, dancing move and rhythm. The Athenian says that, given that all these are different types of imitation, one should therefore take as good dancing moves, songs and rhythms those which imitate and enact the character and deeds of a virtuous man. By contrast, bad moves, melodies and songs are those which simulate the morality and behaviour of a non-virtuous man. Consequently, men should get used not to getting satisfaction from — or become indifferent towards — attending bad imitating activities, in order to avoid being assimilated with bad characters. For this purpose, in a law-abiding state laws should not allow poets to compose whatever songs, poems or dances they wish but only those which are consistent with what the law defines as virtuous (654e9–656c7).

Exactly at this point, the Athenian complains that all states, except Egypt, offer poets the freedom of creating whatever they want. When Clinias asks him what is the case in Egypt, he finds the opportunity to narrate a story about the way the Egyptians established a steady legal framework for the issue in question and about how they succeeded in preserving those laws through time. In Egypt, the story goes, a long time ago the authorities decided that only good songs and dances be performed by young people and, after defining what good songs and dances are, they exposed their laws in their temples and prohibited the artistic production of pictures and generally of works incongruent with the standards of the law. As a result, artists have ever since proceeded with no innovations in this respect for over ten thousand years (656d1–657a2).

The comments with which the Athenian ends this short story reveal to us two ways in which a narrative may help legislators convince the citizens to obey the laws: first, the narrative offers a historical *exemplum* which proves that what one proposes is possible, since it has also been realised in the past.[29] Second, as was the case with the Ganymede tale, here too we are faced with a similar mention of a

---

[29] England 1921, 286; Domanksi 2007.

narrative on the goddess Isis, a narrative which validates mentalities and laws promoted by a legislator by underlining their divine origins.

Let us begin with the narrative as a proof of the feasibility of a proposed law. According to the Athenian, the Egyptian *logos* proves that "it is possible (δυνατὸν ἄρ' ἦν) to provide enduring stability to songs that have a natural correctness, provided the legislator is bold enough" (657a5–8). He also adds that the story does not only suggest what *is* possible but also what *is not*. For the Egyptians' example shows that proneness to innovations in music and dance, under such circumstances, cannot harm the already enacted laws, because "in Egypt at any rate it has turned out to have no such power — indeed, quite the opposite" (657b7–8: τὴν γοῦν ἐκεῖ οὐδαμῶς ἔοικε δυνατὴ γεγονέναι διαφθεῖραι, πᾶν δὲ τοὐναντίον).

The significance of the realisation that one can consolidate a law lies in the fact that it offers one the courage to enact the law. The Athenian three times repeats that the story is aimed at eliciting the aspiring legislators' courage to decree what they deem right in music and dance. First, as we just saw, he claims that it is possible for someone to impose the songs that are deemed to be proper, provided that he has the mettle needed for such a decision. Shortly afterwards, he concludes that, given that a lawgiver can succeed in securing legal stability, the only thing which remains for him is to find the courage to do so (657b3: θαρροῦντα χρὴ εἰς νόμον ἄγειν καὶ τάξιν αὐτά, "he should be bold enough to regiment them into law"). Then, after completing his short narrative and his comments on it, he urges his interlocutors to investigate the correctness of music and dance with courage (657c3: ἆρ' οὖν θαρροῦντες λέγομεν ...). The legislator who listens to this story, as well as the reader, are thus invited to follow a syllogistic route, which in turn will affect their emotions and lead them one step closer to the enactment of laws. This syllogism is as follows: first, the legislator realises that he can possibly secure the stability of his laws, as this has already been happening in Egypt. This rational realisation should enhance the emotions, namely his optimism and hope that his efforts will be successful. What is more, in order to fulfil his hopes he must experience one further emotion, courage.[30]

---

[30] The presence of the verb θαρρεῖν at three points (a7, b3, c3) has troubled critics, some of whom have endeavoured to exclude the θαρροῦντα at a7 as a sloppy interpolation. However, Schöpsdau (1994, 278–279), followed by Meyer (2015, 240), aptly notes that the recurrence of the verb reflects the Athenian's effort to enhance his interlocutors' and our confidence that the installation of laws on music is feasible. Cf. Morrow's (1953, 242) view that preambles too influence the emotions of the citizens in a rational way. Bobonich (1991) also introduces the concept of "rational persuasion", while Stalley (1994) develops this idea by claiming that persuasion is

Apart from the emotions of hope and courage, the Egyptian narrative also exerts its influence on the receiver in a similar way to the Ganymede story. This is so because the Athenian presents the Egyptian authorities as using a story about a god in order to convince their people to follow the laws about music. At the end of his narration he says that to discern what is proper and to impose it on a permanent base through laws is the work of either a god or a divine man, and he adds that "in Egypt, they say it is Isis who composed the songs that have lasted this great expanse of time" (657a9–b1). As the Cretans fabricated the story about Zeus' love for Ganymede, the Egyptians similarly claim their established songs to be the creations of Isis. This is one further example which shows that the invocation of a god's authority is occasionally used as a means to convince a people about the correctness of law.[31] The Athenian does not clarify whether he gives credit to the Egyptians' story about the divine origins of the songs they imposed.[32] Nonetheless, he presents the Egyptian case as a paradigm case of the successful imposition of laws and thereby implies that all the means the Egyptians used had an important, if not equal, share in their success. Besides, the Athenian himself seems to take advantage of the religious connotations of the Isis story, when he admits, perhaps rhetorically, that the inception and imposition of such laws must be indeed the result of a god's or a divine man's activity (657a8–9).[33]

Narratives are also presented as enhancing the legislator's promise that a virtuous life leads people to happiness. Immediately after the discussants agree that a state should have a stable legislation about the proper dances, songs and melodies, the Athenian begins examining which of these mimetic performances are to be taken as ideal. He first develops the following reasoning: melodies, dances and generally all kinds of mimetic entertainment are usually assessed by people according to the criteria of how many people they offer pleasure and of the degree to which they do so. Now, each category of people finds joy in different imitating acts. For example, small children are impressed by puppeteers, while older children would choose the composers of comedies. Adolescents and educated women, and perhaps the majority of the population, prefer attending a tragedy. Last, old men, like the three discussants, get pleasure from listening

---

the effort of reason to control necessity, as this process is described in the *Republic* and *Timaeus*. See also Mouracade 2005, 78ff; Buccioni 2007.

31 Joly 1982, 263–264.
32 Cf. Lefka 1994, 166; Sallis 2013, 77.
33 Cf. the Athenian's opening words with which he foreshadows what he will argue in Book 10 on the divine nature of virtuous human legislation. On this technique, see Sallis 2013, 76–78.

to a reciter who performs beautifully parts from the *Iliad*, the *Odyssey* or some passages from Hesiod's works (657c3–658d9). From among all these kinds of pleasure, the old men should choose the correct and proper one. The old men will instruct the young men how to get used to feeling pleasure and sorrow for those things the law defines as fitting to each emotion. The law in its turn is the embodiment of true reason, which coincides with the judgment of the old educated men. Now, the means by which the latter should lead the youth to the proper pleasures and sorrows are songs, music and dance, because children do not like being taught through seriousness. For this reason, the old men use songs and dances as chants through which they instruct children.[34] Hence, given that songs and dances have such a special place in the education of children and young men, the legislator should obligate poets to identify through their works the virtuous life with happiness and, vice versa, the non-virtuous life with misery. In this way, the citizens will be convinced to pursue virtue in the belief that only this way they will reach happiness (658e6–663d5).

We saw that the Athenian, already in his structural miniature of the *Laws* in 631b3–632d7, argued that a legislator should offer some kind of assurance to the citizens that obedience to law and a virtuous life will lead them to happiness. In this part of the work, the Athenian reveals to the reader the levels on which such a promise is persuasive and the way in which it affects the emotional world of the citizens. The pledge that virtue leads to happiness is now approached from a psychological perspective. The young citizens' souls are bridled (a) due to the persuasiveness of the message as well as (b) by the captivating nature of the means whereby the message is disseminated, and (c) by the idealised self-presentation of the sender.

As far as the means of dissemination of the message is concerned, dance, music and singing are chosen exactly because they are more pleasant to young people in comparison with a dry and therefore unpleasant, serious lecture (659d4–e5). Children thereby learn their lesson in the most pleasant fashion possible. The Athenian strengthens this thesis through a parallelism between the children who are lured through songs and dances, and patients who are cajoled through tasty drinks, in which physicians infuse medicine (659e5–660a3).

Apart from the means of its dissemination, the message itself, by serving as a guarantee for a happy life, motivates children and all citizens in general to live virtuously. Similarly to the structural miniature of the *Laws* (631b3–632d7), here too justice and virtue in general are presented as leading to happiness, a message

---

[34] On the meaning of ἐπῳδή and its appearance throughout the *Laws*, see Morrow 1953, 238–239 with n. 10.

which creates the hope for a smooth life, while material goods are debunked (660d11–663c5).[35]

Last, the Athenian maintains that the legislator, as the sender of the message, should earn the trust of his people. If the legislator urges the citizens to live a virtuous life but at the same time allows others to declare that happiness does not emerge from virtue but from pleasure, in this case the citizens will probably conclude that his promise is inconsequential, and will therefore not follow his admonitions. For this reason, the Athenian continues, the authorities of a city must always insist that a virtuous life leads to happiness, so that the citizens will hope that, if they obey the laws, they will profit, and will fear that, if they adopt an unjust way of living, neither money nor beauty nor power and health will save them from misery and disgrace. As a result, the people, thinking that the legislator leads them to virtue in order to secure their prosperity, will trust him with regard both to his reason and his motives (663a9–d5). All these emotions, the hope elicited by the message, the joy for the means of the message's dissemination, and the trust to the sender of the message, constitute the ideal psychological state in which a desire is born in the citizens' souls to pursue the virtuous life.

The Athenian adds that the legislator should constantly search for the proper methods of persuasion, and strikingly places narration at the top of this quest (663d6–664b2):

ΑΘ. Νομοθέτης δὲ οὔ τι καὶ σμικρὸν ὄφελος, εἰ καὶ μὴ τοῦτο ἦν οὕτως ἔχον, ὡς καὶ νῦν αὐτὸ ᾕρηχ' ὁ λόγος ἔχειν, εἴπερ τι καὶ ἄλλο ἐτόλμησεν ἂν ἐπ' ἀγαθῷ ψεύδεσθαι πρὸς τοὺς νέους, ἔστιν ὅτι τούτου ψεῦδος λυσιτελέστερον ἂν ἐψεύσατό ποτε καὶ δυνάμενον μᾶλλον ποιεῖν μὴ βίᾳ ἀλλ' ἑκόντας πάντας πάντα τὰ δίκαια;
ΚΛ. Καλὸν μὲν ἡ ἀλήθεια, ὦ ξένε, καὶ μόνιμον· ἔοικε μὴν οὐ ῥᾴδιον εἶναι πείθειν.
ΑΘ. Εἶεν· τὸ μὲν τοῦ Σιδωνίου μυθολόγημα ῥᾴδιον ἐγένετο πείθειν, οὕτως ἀπίθανον ὄν, καὶ ἄλλα μυρία;
ΚΛ. Ποῖα;
ΑΘ. Τὸ σπαρέντων ποτὲ ὀδόντων ὁπλίτας ἐξ αὐτῶν φῦναι. καίτοι μέγα γ' ἐστὶ νομοθέτῃ παράδειγμα τοῦ πείσειν ὅτι ἂν ἐπιχειρῇ τις πείθειν τὰς τῶν νέων ψυχάς, ὥστε οὐδὲν ἄλλο αὐτὸν δεῖ σκοποῦντα ἀνευρίσκειν ἢ τί πείσας μέγιστον ἀγαθὸν ἐργάσαιτο ἂν πόλιν, τούτου δὲ πέρι πᾶσαν μηχανὴν εὑρίσκειν ὄντινά ποτε τρόπον ἡ τοιαύτη συνοικία πᾶσα περὶ τούτων ἓν καὶ ταὐτὸν ὅτι μάλιστα φθέγγοιτ' ἀεὶ διὰ βίου παντὸς ἔν τε ᾠδαῖς καὶ μύθοις καὶ λόγοις. Εἰ δ' οὖν ἄλλῃ πῃ δοκεῖ ἢ ταύτῃ, πρὸς ταῦτα οὐδεὶς φθόνος ἀμφισβητῆσαι τῷ λόγῳ.
ΚΛ. Ἀλλ' οὔ μοι φαίνεται πρός γε ταῦτα δύνασθαι ἡμῶν ἀμφισβητῆσαί ποτ' ἂν οὐδέτερος.

---

35 On the connection between the two passages in terms of this theme, see Meyer 2015, 104–116.

ATH: But even if matters were not as the present argument maintains, could any halfway decent legislator, if he dared to lie to the youth for the sake of the good, tell a lie more beneficial than this? Is there any lie with greater potential to make everyone always act justly — not because they are forced, but willingly?
CL: Truth is a beautiful thing, Stranger, and an enduring one. But persuasion, it seems, is not an easy matter.
ATH: Well, haven't people been easily persuaded of the Sidonian's tale, implausible though it is, and of many others as well?
CL: What kind of tales?
ATH: About armed warriors growing from teeth sown in the earth — a perfect example to show the legislator that if he tries he can persuade the souls of the young of whatever he wants. All he needs to figure out is what doctrine will deliver the greatest good to the city should he convince them of it. Then he must use every means at his disposal to ensure that the whole community, all their lives long, are of one voice on this topic — in their songs, in their stories, and in their judgements. Of course if you think at all differently, no one will begrudge you the chance to dispute the argument.
CL: I don't see either of us as capable of disputing these points.

With these words the Athenian lays emphasis on how effectively with narration works as a means of persuasion. His view that the story of the Sidonian Cadmus is very hard to believe (663e6) is not to be taken as an expression of scepticism towards the effectiveness of narration in the education of young people. On the contrary, the implausibility of the myth's content is foregrounded as the strongest piece of evidence for the persuasiveness of narrating. Narration has such a great effect on the souls of the young that it convinces them about the most improbable stories, such as those about the earth-born men.[36] Of course, one further reason why the receivers of this story are more prone to believe its content lies in the fact that, similarly to Ganymede's tale, this myth too contributes to their endeavour to shape their national identity. If the myth on Ganymede's homosexuality serves for the Cretans as an embellishing alibi, on the basis of which they legitimate in their minds and in those of others a controversial feature of their society, the myth on the hoplites who germinate from the dragon's teeth satisfies the Thebans' need to believe that they are natives and therefore the rightful possessors of the Cadmean land. This flattering function of such narratives renders them in the Athenian's mind one from among the useful tools at a legislator's disposal in his effort to secure the national and legislative coherence of a polity's population.

These thoughts of the Athenian prepare the reader for the view he expresses immediately afterwards on the necessity of narration in the legislators' and

---

[36] On this story as the *Laws*' "noble lie", see Baima 2016, 120–121 and 131–132 with nn. 11–12 with further bibliography.

politicians' struggle of persuasion. His argumentation in favour of the association between virtue and happiness culminates with a comment on the usefulness of narration. Immediately after explaining his reasoning of the usefulness of stories such as those of Cadmus and the earth-born hoplites of Thebes, he reaches the following conclusion: all three choruses of the city should charm young people, while they are still soft and malleable, by declaring all the admonitions the Athenian and his interlocutors have proposed so far and by showing that it is the gods who say that the virtuous life is the most joyful. In this way, the choruses will be both sincere and convincing. In particular, the first chorus, the one consisting of children, should disseminate these doctrines through songs. The second chorus, the one made of adults up to thirty years old, should invoke the authority of the god Paean in support of the truthfulness of their messages and thereby make young people happy by means of persuasion. This is also the duty of the third chorus, that of people of age between thirty and sixty years (664b3–d2). However, at the end of his exposition the Athenian lists one further group of people, namely those who are older than sixty years (664d2–4):

> τοὺς δὲ μετὰ ταῦτα – οὐ γὰρ ἔτι δυνατοὶ φέρειν ᾠδάς – μυθολόγους περὶ τῶν αὐτῶν ἠθῶν διὰ θείας φήμης καταλελεῖφθαι.

> Those who are beyond all that and no longer up to the challenge of singing will be allotted the role of storytellers. They will recount divinely inspired stories about these same characters.

All critics, as far as I know, take the word μυθολόγους as "storytellers", i.e. as narrators.[37] The Athenian, by referring to these elderly narrators, not only specifies who must take over the duty of composing and disseminating stories throughout the city, but also prepares us about what he and his friends will do in Book 3, where they will narrate the history of legislation and politics. Both he and his interlocutors can justifiably be identified with those elderly storytellers. The Athenian, Clinias and Megillus repeatedly inform the reader that they are very old.[38] Of course, Plato never enlightens us about exactly how old they are. For this reason, it is hard for us to decide whether we should include them in the third chorus of those between thirty and sixty years old or in that of the

---

37 Des Places 1951 ("pour raconter des fables"); Schöpsdau 1994, 50 ("Geschichten ... zu erzählen"); Bury 2001[8], 129 ("shall handle the same moral themes in stories"); Meyer 2015, 62 ("storytellers").
38 See, e.g., 625b1–7; 634d1–2; 635a3–5; 657d1–6; 658d6–7; 892d2–5.

storytellers in ripe old age.³⁹ However, in the dialogue these three figures, and especially the Athenian, are presented as not singing and, more importantly, as shaping stories in support of their view that a virtuous life leads to happiness. In other words, they are presented as doing exactly what the Athenian asks the elderly narrators to do in 664d2–4. For, as we will see, in Book 3 the three friends narrate tales through which they strengthen the message of both the first two books as well as of the preludes of Books 4–12 that, for the citizens of the hypothetical city, happiness lies in the obedience of law. In this respect, 664d3–4 serves as a metanarrative, self-referential instruction to the reader, as it foreshadows the spirit, goal setting and function of the narrative paradigms of Book 3.

Even more importantly, by presenting narratives as an alternative means of persuasion to songs, the Athenian highlights the strong influence of narratives upon the citizens' psychology. Through this connection, narration is presented as eliciting affective and intellectual responses in the young and in the entire population's souls in general. While referring to the songs of the choruses about the equation between a virtuous and happy life, the Athenian repeats what he has already said in 659e1–2 (ἐπῳδαὶ ταῖς ψυχαῖς), i.e. that these songs will serve as weapons through which to charm the young's souls (664b4–5: ἐπᾴδειν ... νέαις οὔσαις ταῖς ψυχαῖς ... τῶν νέων). Hence, narratives, as a method alternative to songs, are treated as an expressional means of dissemination of moral admonitions, which targets the malleable souls (664b5: ἁπαλαῖς).

It is worth noting that the impact of narration upon the audience's psychology is approached here from the same three perspectives from which the effectiveness of songs and dances were approached in 658–663. We noted earlier that songs and dances were deemed by the Athenian as effective on three levels: first, as a means of dissemination of a message, they are more pleasant to young people and thus more persuasive. Second, the very message they carry, namely the promise that virtue leads to happiness, is charming since it elicits the citizens' hope. Last, the sender of this message, the legislator, is trustworthy.

Stories are presented as carrying all those features of the songs which affect children's emotions. First, their message brings hope for a pleasant way of living because their heroes are virtuous like the types of character promoted by the songs (664d3–4: μυθολόγους περὶ τῶν αὐτῶν ἠθῶν). Second, the *exempla* of the institutionalised stories which have been mentioned so far touch young souls in

---

39 Perhaps an exception is 770a6, where the Athenian says that he and his partners are not merely old but are approaching the end of their lives. We also learn that Megillus is older than Clinias (712c8–9).

a similar way to that of the songs of the second chorus. The Athenian urges the members of this group to defend the validity of their messages by invoking Apollo, the god of medicine (664c7–d1). Similarly, the stories on Zeus' love for Ganymede and Isis' songs speak for the value of homosexual love and of the songs proposed by the Egyptian authorities. Besides, the elderly narrators themselves of the city under construction are claimed to compose their tales in the aid of divine inspiration (664d4: διὰ θείας φήμης). Third, the reader is offered one further piece of evidence in support of the reliability of the stories to be narrated: their narrators will not be randomly distinguished among their co-citizens but are those who up to this point have been delineated as the most virtuous and reasonable of all, namely the elders.[40]

As a result, narratives, as a vessel of communication, are promoted by Plato as the ideal means of manipulation of the young on all levels (composition, recitation and reception of a narrative). As far as it is a source of inspiration of the narrative composition, divine aid seals the validity of its content. The favourable self-fashioning of the narrator functions in a similar way. Last but not least, with regard to the receivers of the stories, the audience which is targeted by these narratives is marked by a frame of mind which constitutes the most fertile ground to receive the graces of the expressional procedure of narration. For young people prefer to listen to songs and stories rather than to admonitions in the form of a strict exposition of ideas.

The Athenian's comments on the Egyptian stories, the myths about the foundation of Thebes, and the elderly narrators serve as metanarrative reflections which prepare the reader for the very function of the narrative paradigms in Book 3. In essence, these comments serve as short teasers of a technique which will unfold in almost forty pages of OCT. They may therefore be taken as metanarrative pre-notifications of the manipulative nature of the narratives in Book 3. The latter will not be, of course, stories about the exploits of gods and mythical heroes; they will deal instead with historical events and actual polities. However, as will be demonstrated in the ensuing two sections, the stories of Book 3 aim at affecting the inner world of their receivers in a similar way to the way the tales examined so far do.

Second, these mentions of narratives of Books 1–2 prepare us for the auxiliary role of the stories of Book 3. In all three cases, the issue of narration is addressed at the end of each discussion. In the first case, the Athenian initially narrates how the Egyptians established their laws about music and dance and

---

[40] On the favourable portrait of the elders in the *Laws*, see Powell 1994, 274–284 with further bibliography.

only at the end of his story does he present the account about Isis' songs as a reinforcing element at the Egyptian authorities' disposal in their effort to convince their citizens to respect their laws. In a similar vein, when he argues that a legislator should disseminate the message that a virtuous life is a happy life while a dissolute one leads to misery, again only at the end of his argumentation does he add that a lawgiver should also use, *inter alia*, myths such as the one about Cadmus. Last, in his exposition about the three choruses, the stories of the elderly narrators come again at the very end as an additional element to the songs. Each time, the Athenian conveys the impression that narration is intended to have an auxiliary but useful contribution to an effort already described. These three examples foreshadow the auxiliary function of the narratives of Book 3 for what has already been argued in Books 1–2. The Athenian first details his main argumentation on the superiority of virtue over material goods (Books 1–2) and then uses the narratives (Book 3) as one further means through which he reinforces his claims.

At this point, it is worth noting a similarity between the Eleatic Visitor of the *Statesman* and the Athenian Visitor of the *Laws* in terms of the way they use their accounts in order to reach their goals. As demonstrated in Chapter 1, the Eleatic Visitor uses his cosmological account as a supplementary digression through which he endeavours to remedy the flaws of his own definition of statesmanship in the first chapters of the dialogue. It is also commonly accepted that this myth offers some key ideas on the basis of which the Eleatic Visitor, in the last part of the work, builds a new approach of the matter. However, despite the usefulness of the myth in the investigation of statesmanship, the Eleatic Visitor undoubtedly leads the reader to the conclusion that narration is not the main method of investigation but has an additional, auxiliary function and, most importantly, a number of disadvantages: its length may be taken by many as a deviating interruption, while the myth itself offers only a general view of statesmanship and not the details of its nature. In the *Statesman*, dialogue remains the main method of investigation. Similarly, in the *Laws* the Athenian Visitor bases his argumentation on the views expressed in Books 1–2 and in the laws and their preludes of Books 4–12. The short mentions of narratives examined so far, the accounts of Book 3, and those mentioned in the preludes of Books 4–12 only strengthen, enrich and validate views already expressed.

3.1.2 The connections between Books 1–2 and the accounts of Book 3

Let us now analyse the way in which the narratives of Book 3 supplement, enrich and validate the views expressed in Books 1–2. Here is a summary of Book 3. The Athenian, after completing his exposition in favour of wine drinking, banquets and intoxication, now urges his companions to explore the history of regimes and legislation. He suggests that they begin their survey from a remote stage of the past, a period immediately following one of those cataclysms which usually cause the annihilation of the human population. In this period, the only surviving humans are reasonably those who lived in highlands and therefore managed to survive the cataclysm. These people were not acquainted with arts or with political manoeuvres popular in urban environments. Each settlement was cut off from others, since the people of those times did not have the technology with which to construct means of transportation and also because, remembering the cataclysm, they were afraid of visiting the lowlands. Nor had they developed any kind of official, written legislative system and political regime. Nonetheless, despite — or rather because of — their isolation and technological and political primitivism, these pre-political communities of shepherds are described by the Athenian as living a happy and serene life, which was marked by concord, blind respect for ancestral rules and customs, and lack of greed (676a1–680e5).

The highlanders' clans gradually began joining in larger settlements. At the beginning of this phase, each family kept its own rules, but they eventually decided to form a common legal system, which would consist of the best rules of each family. For this reason, the clans choose some members of each clan and assign them with the duty of selecting the best, in their opinion, rules of each tribe and of uniting these rules into a common constitution. These men will be named "legislators" and will give the chiefs of each clan the right to rule. In this way, they will produce an aristocracy or even a monarchy. This is what the Athenian defines as the second form of constitution (680e6–681d6).

As for the third stage of human politics, the Athenian argues that this should be placed in a period of time that is far remote from the second, and relates the events of this period in a short account of the Trojan War and its aftermath in the political life of the Greek cities. In this phase, men start founding cities in lowlands, with the most characteristic example being Troy, which, according to Homer, was built close to rivers at the plains. It is this period in which the Greeks attacked Troy and waged the ten-year war against it. In the meantime, during these ten years, the domestic political life of the Greek cities was marked by the young citizens' efforts to take control of their cities by exterminating their compatriots who were returning from Troy. As a result, many from among the latter were executed or exiled, while others managed to return to their cities and were now named "Dorians", as it was Dorieus who gathered and organised them (681d7–682e6). The last three stories pertain to (a) the creation and fall of the Dorian confederation between Argos, Messene and Sparta (683c8–693c5); (b) how the Persian kingdom was twice led to political decadence due to the governances of Cambyses and Xerxes (694a3–698a8); and (c) the events that brought about the degeneration of the Athenian constitution after the Persian Wars (698a9–701c4). These three stories will be discussed in detail in Sections 3.2.3 and 3.2.4. Although it has been repeatedly noted that the views expressed in Books 1–2 are either confirmed or reinforced by the accounts of Book 3, there has been no systematic treatise on the matter.[41] The ensuing analysis aspires to fill this gap.

The story on the shepherds serves in many respects as a supplement to the ideas previously developed by the Athenian. To begin with, we have already seen that the Athenian has disagreed with Clinias' view that legislators should aim at rendering a city competent at war (626c6–631b2). The story of the mountaineers refutes Clinias' thesis and strengthens the Athenian's objections. Let us look at Clinias' view in detail and clarify with which part of it the myth is in opposition. Clinias believes that legislators should write laws which will help a city prevail over other cities in battles because war will always take place between cities and that even peace is nothing less than a camouflaged form of hostility (625c9–626b4). The account of the shepherds' peaceful life is aimed at refuting this view, as it shows that there are — or at least there must have been — periods in human history when societies can develop without waging any war, either external or civil. Of course, Clinias' point is centrally that war is waged between cities which interact and have developed channels of communication between each other. In this respect, the myth of the shepherds strikes no significant blow against Clinias' thesis because the cities of the shepherds are claimed to have lived peacefully not because they have reached a high level of moral code in the way they interact, but merely because they are not in a position to communicate each other due to their ignorance of metallurgy and woodworking (677b5–6; 677c4–7; 678c6–d6; 678e2–4; 680d7–8). After all, we may deduce from the story that, even if there have been cities at lowlands and close to the sea, the highlanders, remembering the cataclysm which they survived, would not dare meet them because they would be afraid to come close to the riverbeds and the sea (678c2–3).

---

41 Stalley 1983, 6.

This segment of the past narrative also belies Clinias' view that war is a diachronic phenomenon and an unavoidable distinctive feature of human nature. Clinias essentially seems to use the diachronic presence of war in human history as a strong piece of evidence for the view that hostilities are inherent in human behaviour. In particular, we read his words "in fact every city is by nature always in an undeclared war against every other" (626a3–5: τῷ δ' ἔργῳ πάσαις πρὸς πάσας τὰς πόλεις ἀεὶ πόλεμον ἀκήρυκτον κατὰ φύσιν εἶναι). The two adverbs ἀεί and κατὰ φύσιν may be taken in a paratactic way, but Clinias seems to suggest that war should be included in the permanent elements of human nature exactly *because* it is a diachronic phenomenon. In this respect, the myth, in conveying the message that human societies do not *always* wage war, proves that war is not to be taken as a perpetual and therefore natural phenomenon.

The story of the shepherds also serves as a historical example in support of the Athenian's view that there are two kinds of goods for people, the divine goods (wisdom, reason, moderation, courage and justice) and lesser goods (health, beauty, bodily strength and wealth), and that a city prospers only when lawgivers lead the citizens to the divine goods. Although the Athenian has already proceeded with this classification of goods (631b3–d1; 643e3–644a5; 660d11–662a3), he has not explained how a society can reach the desired compromise between the two kinds of qualities. As we saw, the Athenian argues that it is harder for people to adopt a morally virtuous attitude during a civil war than in a war against enemies from outside the city. His main point of argument is that in civil war one should demonstrate all kinds of virtue (justice, moderation, wisdom and bravery), while in a war with external enemies one is only invited to have courage. In his effort to support this view, he distinguishes the goods in the two aforementioned categories (631b3–d1) and the only connection he draws between them is found in his comment that "a city that receives the greater ones acquires the lesser as well; otherwise, it is bereft of both" (631b8–c1). However, these words by no means explain why the lesser goods do not suffice for someone to obtain the divine goods.[42] The Athenian speaks equally vaguely when he adds that the laws of a prosperous state should teach people to pursue moderation and justice and not wealth and honours (643e3–644a5). Once again, we are faced with an antithetical relationship between moral qualities and material benefits, but we are deprived of any explanation of why we should prefer the former to the latter.

---

[42] Nor are we told how the human goods depend on the divine ones. Carone (2002 and 2003) tries to fill this gap and penetrate the relationship between virtue and the "externals", which is her term for the human goods; cf. Meyer 2015, 108.

This explanation comes only at the narratives of Book 3, beginning with the story of the shepherds. Those men were free from any kind of concern about how to find food, although they were not excessively rich either (678e9–679a4). Bucolic economy is presented as offering people a balanced way of living, which holds them away from both excessive wealth and poverty, elements which generate, according to the narrator, envy and hubris, and thus civil war (679b3–c2). Protected from these elements and naïve as they were due to their inexperience in many respects, they obeyed the laws they had inherited from their forefathers (679c2–8). Independently of its validity, this is the first explanation we are offered in the *Laws* of how wealth can harm justice.

This account also supplements the Athenian's view about the relation between expertise and virtue. In his first definition of education, the Athenian maintained that proper education elicits men's desire to be virtuous citizens and to know how to rule and to be ruled showing the due respect to justice. On the contrary, one should not take as proper education the one which leads men to pursue wealth and power or any kind of expertise without reason and justice (643d6–644a5). So, apart from the aforementioned antithetical pair 'wealth *vs.* justice', the Athenian offers one further dipole, the one between reason-free expertise and justice.

This relationship is also addressed in the account of the shepherds in a converse fashion. While in his definition of education the Athenian speaks of expertise without reason and justice (644a3–4), in his account he describes a way of living which is marked by justice without expertise or, to put it more precisely, a life in which justice is achieved exactly because expertise is absent. As mentioned above, the highlanders' absolute virtue emerges from their lack of expertise in certain arts; they do not engage in external wars because they do not possess the arts of metallurgy and woodworking, which would allow them to communicate each other (678c8–d3). Nor do they possess any other kind of knowledge which could lead them to question the regulations of their fathers (679c3–7). Last, they do not know how to construct weaponry or juristic tricks with which to manage civil rivalries (679d4–e2). As a result, the Athenian concludes, those men were braver and more moderate than the men of his age (679e2–3). In this respect too, this part of the past narrative offers clarifications on how expertise can harm reason and virtue, a theme which is only fleetingly mentioned in Books 1–2.[43]

---

[43] Cf. Schöpsdau 1994, 227 and Meyer 2015, 112, who read 644a4 alongside 677c, but not the passages we examine here, and alongside 696c2 (Schöpsdau), 701a and 732a (Meyer).

These first societies are also linked with the Athenian's views of Books 1–2 from one further perspective. In essence, the highlanders exemplify exactly what the Athenian has already described in an allegorical way as a body which never needed any medicine because it never fell ill. In his effort to refute Clinias' view that one of the lawgiver's priorities should be the laws which reconcile citizens in times of civil war, the Athenian expresses the following view: neither external nor civil war are ideal choices for a city because states should only pursue concord and peace. Therefore, victory in both kinds of war should not be a *desideratum* for a city; it is rather a necessity. For we may feel joy whenever a sick man is cured after receiving a treatment, but the ideal for this and any man is not to fall ill. This is also the case with states (628d2–e1). Statesmen and legislators should not aim at offering laws which will secure victory in external or civil conflicts but to secure peace (628c10–11: εἰρήνη δέ ... καὶ φιλοφροσύνη). This figurative delineation of an ideal legal system of a state as a political 'body' which is not sick meets its historical counterpart in the first polities of the shepherds. According to the account, these communities satisfy the Athenian's demand for concord, as those people coexisted in a peaceful manner (678e9: ἐφιλοφρονοῦντο ἀλλήλους). They also did not need any kind of cure – written laws – because they were not 'ill', i.e. corrupt (680a3: οὔτ' ἐδέοντο νομοθετῶν). They did not possess the art of writing and obeyed the unwritten but time-honoured regulations (680a5–7).

As mentioned above, the story about these first post-cataclysmic communities by no means proves that the cities which can communicate each other are also in a position to coexist harmoniously and thereby obtain the desired virtues. On the contrary, those remote states reached a virtuous way of living 'from a safe distance'. What is more, the Athenian comments that those first citizens had reached an absolute state of both virtue and malice (678b1–3). However, it is also evident that the Athenian's intention in this account is to lay emphasis upon the ethical merits of such an isolated and primitive life. As transpires from the narrative, this mode of living leads to prosperity and virtue rather than to moral and political decadence. The usefulness of the myth of the shepherds lies in the fact that, while it logically fails in refuting Clinias' belief in the cyclical nature of war, it introduces the reader to the principles that allow a state to safely reach its constitutional and legal stability. These principles will repeatedly be promoted as the proper ones in the preludes of the laws as well as in the laws themselves from Book 5 onwards until the very end of the dialogue.

The ensuing stage of the account, on the period of the Trojan War, confirms in turn some further principles put forward in the two preceding books. Similarly to the story of the shepherds, this too enriches the Athenian's views by introducing new ideas and by creating new associations, from which the central theses of the preludes will be formulated in Books 4–12.

One of the major views in these books has to do with the connection between a state's geographical place and the resilience of its laws. Plato is not interested in the exact character of the Trojan legislation and regime. He uses it instead as an example of a state which could have any kind of government (681d8–9). However, he foreshadows that such a city, being exposed to threats due to its spatial affinity with the sea, is vulnerable to all different kinds of misfortunes (681d8). The term παθήματα (681d8) is occasionally translated as "varieties" or "changes" of constitutions.[44] To change an institution is typically treated by the interlocutors in the *Laws* as something avoidable.[45] In this respect, the Athenian's choice of a term with negative connotations (suffering, distortion)[46] is pivotal; it marks that we have now departed from the idyllic stage of the isolated and thus politically stable societies of the shepherds. We are entering a period when the cities can no longer protect themselves from those factors which bring about the fall of their constitutional and legal systems.[47] One of these corroding factors is the very geographical place of a state.[48] The Athenian is very careful in clarifying that Troy was founded in a lower land than the shepherds' cities, close to lowlands and rivers (682b2–5). What is more, he explains that it was attacked by the Greeks only when Troy and other cities as well had already started communicating with each other on land and by the sea (682c6–10). The message of this part of the myth is that, in cases in which a city is not protected by its geographical place, it can be the victim of attacks and be defeated. The three men have already expressed their interest in the relationship between geography and politics in Books 1–2 (625c10–d7). However, this specific kind of association is made for the first time only here and will serve as

---

44 Bury 2001⁸, 183 ("varieties"); Saunders 1970, 126 ("modifications"); Schöpsdau 1994, 67 ("Veränderungen") and 355.
45 This message is first conveyed in the Egyptian story of 656d1–657c2. The interlocutors' aim in composing the stories of Book 3 is also to reveal which factors lead to the destruction of legislations and institutions (676a1–6; 683e3–684a2; 686b8–c3).
46 Cf. England 1921, 355; Des Places' (1951) translation "vicissitudes"; Weil 1959, 76; Schöpsdau 1994, 372.
47 Given the Athenian's clarification that the narrative on human politics and laws is aimed at shedding light on the causes of institutional and legal developments and changes (676a1–c4), I cannot accept England's (1921, 355) view that the παθήματα refer only to the πόλεων and not to the πολιτειῶν.
48 Cf. England 1921, 356, who also assumes that the παθήματα have an ominous meaning and foreshadow the episodes of civil strife (στάσεις) of 682d7.

the main thesis on which the interlocutors will found their hypothetical city in Books 4–12.

The Mycenaean narrative also strengthens the Athenian's view that a city's victories in external wars do not necessarily mean that this city also possesses the virtues required for normality in its domestic politics (630a1–b8). Through the technique of the narration of simultaneous events, the Athenian transfers the focal point of interest from Troy to Greece.[49] During the Trojan War, the story goes, certain factions of young citizens emerged in the Greek cities and overturned the political *status quo* of their countries. As soon as their co-citizens returned from Troy, they treated them unjustly and removed them from the political life of their cities either through banishments or executions (682d5–e6). This development in the plot is aimed at confirming the view of Book 1 that a city's success in external wars does not entail that this city has the desired internal political system (630a1–b8). This function of the Mycenaean account resembles the historical examples of 638b1–3. At that point, the Athenian argues that history has proved that normality in internal politics does not necessarily secure success in external wars (638a3–7). In support of this view, the Athenian offers two historical examples: Locri and Cea, two cities of a virtuous political system, have been defeated by the Syracosians and Athenians respectively.

Plato essentially invites the reader to assess the durability of the legislation of cities, such as those of the period of the Trojan War, through the prism of the division we have read in Book 1 between external and civil wars. The story reinforces the view that, on a moral level, civil war is a more demanding phenomenon than external war. In Book 1, the Athenian has maintained that only a few are in a position to demonstrate justice, reliability and moderation during civil strife. Conversely, there are many, such as mercenaries, who during an external war are highly brave but lack the aforementioned virtues and therefore perpetrate hubristic and arrogant deeds, especially in the case that they prevail in battle (630a1–b8). The civil strife which goes on in the cities, whose armies conquered Troy, serve as pieces of evidence in support of the view that polities, however brave their citizens may be, fail to secure the preservation of their institutions if they lack justice, moderation and reason.

That Plato treats this legislative and constitutional evolution of the Greek cities as a failure to the same degree as he does in Book 1 is also evident in the derogatory words with which he describes the activities of the subversive mem-

---

[49] On this technique in ancient past narratives, especially in Homer and Greek historiography, see Rengakos 2006b, 188–190 and 189 n. 12 with further bibliography. See also Rengakos 2006a, 288–291.

bers of the Greek cities. First, these men are presented as not acting "fittingly and justly" (682d9: οὐ καλῶς οὐδ' ἐν δίκῃ) and as causing misfortunes (682d7: κακὰ πολλά) to their cities. Second, they are young (682d7–8). The central role of young citizens in the overthrow of the established constitutional *status quo* in this case is a historical example in support of the Athenian's thesis that young men are typically prone to searching for new institutions and replacing old ones with them in 643b4–644b4 and 653a5–c4. At these points, the Athenian has argued that a legislator's concern is to withhold the tendency of young people towards innovation and not to allow them to overturn the legislative and constitutional achievements of a city. The failure of the Greek cities to avoid the overthrow of their constitutions is markedly presented as being in full accordance with what we have read in Book 2, namely as emerging from their inability to restrain the innovative nature of their young members.

The account of the young rebels thus reflects the Athenian's two definitions of proper education (643b4–644b4 and 653a5–c4). As already demonstrated, he has initially argued that the proper education lies in the harmony between all that which one has been taught in young age to hate and love and his reason, which follows the reason of the elders (643b4–d4).[50] The Athenian later on enriches this definition by connecting it more closely with the issue of legislation. He adds that in a city the harmony between the youth's desires and true reason entails that their desires do not come against the law (643d6–644b4).[51] In the Greek cities of the narrative, the young citizens are presented as coveting, contrary to the aforementioned definition of education, things which overturn the law. Through this connection, the Athenian essentially fulfils his promise that he will narrate these stories in order to discover the causes of the laws' evolution and the constitutional changes (676c6–8). These changes seem to emerge whenever the young members of a society have not received the proper education, as this has been defined in Books 1–2.

Up to this point, the Athenian does not explicitly state that his narrative creates echoes of the views expressed in Books 1–2. He merely leads us to this conclusion through the way he weaves the plot development of his story. However, in the last part of his narration the Athenian explicitly connects his account with the ideas he has already developed, by repeatedly sharing with his interlocutors and with us his wish to interpret the events pertaining to Sparta,

---

50 For an analysis of this passage, see Meyer 2015, 164–166.
51 As Bury (1937, 305) puts it, the education proposed by the Athenian in the *Laws* aims at producing virtuous men as citizens and not as individuals isolated from their communities.

Argos and Messene on the basis of what he has already said.⁵² He offers the first reminder of what he has said in his introductory remarks to the story of the three Peloponnesian cities. When he invites his interlocutors to travel through their imagination to the time of the foundation of this tripartite confederation (683c8–d4), he foreshadows that its end will coincide with the distortion of these cities' institutions. At this point he says that, in most cases when a city's legislation is led to decadence, the blame should be placed on its governors and he reminds his friends that this view has already been expressed at a preceding stage of the discussion (683e3–6).⁵³ The Athenian refers to the calamities caused by civil strife and especially to the view already expressed by Clinias that the gravest defeat of individuals or polities is the one they suffer from themselves, which occurs whenever their passions prevail over their reason (626d1–627d7).⁵⁴ The Athenian explicitly states that he will use this part of his account as support for the already expressed view that cities are destroyed by domestic conflicts (683e7–684a1).⁵⁵

Echoes of the views expressed in the first two books, mainly those of the Athenian, are also found in the two narratives on the Persians (694a3–698a8) and the Athenians (698a9–701c4). Let us begin with the account on the corruption of the Persian political system. The Athenian's main thesis is that the Persians gradually ceased to have a moderate monarchy which respected its citizens' freedom on various levels, and ended up to a despotic reign which led people to a state of slavery. One of the qualities that reflected the modesty of the initial Persian monarchy, before it was corrupted by governances such as those of Cambyses and Xerxes, lay in the fact that the king allowed the citizens to participate in the decision making in cases where they demonstrated prudence and a dexterity in conferring and in making the proper political decisions. It was this kind of freedom which, according to the Athenian, led the Persians to prosperity, as they lived in concord and had their share in political reason (694b1–7).

The same principle, expressed with similar wording, is also found in Book 1. We have reached the point where the Athenian explains to Clinias how one should speak about a legislator's goal. Almost at the end of his thesis, the Athenian argues that a lawgiver, after examining what laws should be decreed for

---

52 Ritter 1985²; Schöpsdau 1994.
53 On the reminders of 682e and 702a, see Müller 1951, 19–20, n. 1. Müller (1951, 20) also argues that the Dorian account proves the view of Books 1–2 that a state needs all virtues and that only power is not sufficient.
54 Stalley 1983, 73.
55 See Zuckert 2013, 88 on the Dorian story as an argument in support of the view that wealth and power are of no use without moderation and self-control.

different facets of the citizens' daily lives, should assign guardians, some of whom will act with prudence and others will be marked by the aptness of their views. This is the way, the Athenian maintains, in which mind will harmonise the divergent elements of human life into a harmonious whole (632c4–d1). In both cases, a political leading figure, a king in the Persian account and a legislator in the Athenian's argumentation of Book 1, offers mentally qualified members of the society the opportunity to participate in the political life of a state. These members are each time marked by shrewdness (632c5: φρονήσεως; cf. 694b2: φρόνιμος and 694b5: φρονεῖν). Also, in both cases the *nous* brings harmony to the state which practices this principle (632c6: νοῦς; cf. 694b6: νοῦ).

Similarly to the story of the dissolution of the Peloponnesian confederation, so too in the narrative of the Persian monarchy the Athenian invites his interlocutors to speculate on the way in which this story may contribute to the investigation of proper legislation. Specifically, he argues that one of the conclusions the story invites them to reach is that to be brave, powerful and rich carries no value in the absence of self-control because, within the hierarchy of goods, the qualities of the soul come first, then follow those of the body, and the least significant of all is fortune. The Athenian's invitation to his interlocutors to examine the usefulness of the narrative for the issue of legislation can be taken as Plato's overt expression of his wish to employ the narratives of the *Laws* as functional and thus integral parts of the overall syllogistic development of the dialogue. In practice, the association of the narrative with the rest of the work emerges from the very content of the conclusion to which, according to the Athenian, the Persian account leads us. For, as we have seen, the view that elements such as wealth, power, health and strength are useless if not followed by virtue has already served as the cornerstone of the Athenian's argumentation in Books 1–2 and of his effort to explore the reasons of the Peloponnesian confederation to preserve itself. This is also the case with the priority of the soul over the body and material goods. Both in the account of the Peloponnesian alliance as well as in that of the Persian Empire, the Athenian weaves the plot with the ultimate goal to interpret the events he narrates through the prism of the principles found in the first two books. This thesis will be analysed in detail in Section 3.2.3.

As soon as he completes his accounts on the degeneration of the Persian and Athenian institutions, he notes that the reason why he narrated all these stories and he introduced the issue of intoxication and music was because he wanted to shed some light on how a city may function in the best possible way and on terms in which individuals can live their lives in the best possible way. The Athenian proceeds with a concise retrospection of what has been said in the first three books by means of a long-scale polysyndeton. It is characteristic that in this scheme the lion's share belongs to the narratives of Book 3, while what has been discussed in the first three books is mentioned in a noticeably compendious fashion. Plato wishes to give special emphasis to the contribution of these narratives for the investigation of the topic under discussion.

The Athenian completes his comment by posing the question of whether or not he and his partners could possibly scrutinise any degree of usefulness of the discussion up to this point, including the accounts. At this point, Clinias responds that he thinks there is a way to answer this question. The Cretans intend to found a colony and have assigned the organisation of this project to his homeland Cnossos. What is more, the Cnosseans, for their part, delegated to Clinias and nine others the task of composing the legislation of the colony. Clinias ends his statement with the following words (702c8–d5):

> νῦν οὖν ἐμοί τε καὶ ὑμῖν ταύτην δῶμεν χάριν· ἐκ τῶν εἰρημένων ἐκλέξαντες, τῷ λόγῳ συστησώμεθα πόλιν, οἷον ἐξ ἀρχῆς κατοικίζοντες, καὶ ἅμα μὲν ἡμῖν οὗ ζητοῦμεν ἐπίσκεψις γενήσεται, ἅμα δὲ ἐγὼ τάχ' ἂν χρησαίμην εἰς τὴν μέλλουσαν πόλιν ταύτῃ τῇ συστάσει.

> Let us, then, grant this favour to me, and yourselves also; let us select from the statements we have made, and build up by arguments the framework of a State, as though we were erecting it from foundation. In this way we shall be at once investigating our theme, and possibly I may also make use of our framework for the State that is to be formed.

Clinias' prompt to select certain parts of what they have said in the first three books and to use them as a basis on which to compose the regiment of Books 4–12 is one further metanarrative instruction to the reader about the way in which the narratives of Book 3 will be used in the rest of the work.[56] In this respect, these closing paragraphs of the book serve as both an epilogue to it and also as a prologue to the rest of the work.[57]

---

56 England (1921, 414) believes that, although the phrase ἐκ τῶν εἰρημένων should better be taken as referring to everything said in Books 1–3, the participle ἐκλέξαντες indicates that they will choose only those parts of the earlier conversation that are relevant to what they are to discuss from now on. Weil (1959, 158) does not discuss this issue.

57 England (1921, 414) compares this passage with *Tim.* 19c, noting that "the advantage to the three speculators would be — ultimately perhaps — the opportunity of putting their views to the test of experience".

3.1.3 The connections between the accounts of Book 3 and the preludes of the laws of Books 4–12

In the opening remarks to this chapter, it was explained that the accounts of Book 3 contribute to the argumentation of the preludes on both the levels of macro- and microstructure. In terms of macrostructure, we have demonstrated so far that the narratives of Book 3 enrich and validate the views expressed in Books 1–2 and constitute, along with the first two books, an extensive prelude to the entire legislation of Books 4–12. What remains is to examine the ways in which the stories of Book 3 participate, on a level of micro-structure, in the logic of individual preludes of Books 4–12.

In Book 4, Plato offers the reader the opportunity to penetrate further into the affective responses and the intellectual processes which a narrative elicits in the audience's minds and through which it convinces them to follow the legislator's doctrines (718b5–724b5). The thoughts we are invited to make on this issue do not emerge from the characters' explicit statements about the art of narration but from the Athenian's lengthy analysis of the preludes' effectiveness upon the citizens' psychology. However, the Athenian repeatedly clarifies that narratives constitute an integral part of the preludes. For these reasons, the views expressed about the psychological effect of the preludes on people can reasonably be taken to pertain to the narratives of Book 3 as well.

What is more, certain preludes of Books 5–12 are reinforced by tales. In her monograph on the preludes of the *Laws*, Claudia Zichi has brilliantly underscored the variety of ways in which the argumentation of the preludes is enhanced by short stories, and essentially finds that such preludes which contain tales should be distinguished from the rest as a special category.[58] However, Zichi focuses on the connections between these preludes and the individual tales they contain, while she does not expand her analysis in similar linkages between the preludes and the narratives of Book 3. In this section, I aim to supplement Zichi's theory by arguing that the relations she notes between the preludes she analyses and the tales these preludes include are also discernible between some other preludes of Books 4–12 and the accounts of Book 3. So far, we have read the short mentions of stories in Books 1–2 as 'teasers' of the contribution of the narratives of Book 3 to the views expressed in Books 1–2. In a similar vein, I take the preludes that include supplementary tales as Plato's metanarrative instructions to the reader that the accounts of Book 3 too have an equally supplementary role in the argumentation of the preludes.

---

[58] See the last section of her book "Myth as a Form of Poetic Rationale" (Zichi 2018, 162–239).

This section is organised as follows. First I will analyse the Athenian's thesis about the impact of the preludes upon the psychology and intellectual world of the hypothetical Magnesians. Second, I will present some of the preludes which include tales and reflect on what they can tell us about the function of narratives in a legislator's rhetoric of persuasion. Last, I will use the conclusions drawn from 718b5–724b5 and the preludes with tales as a prism through which we read certain cross-references between the narratives of Book 3 and the preludes of Books 4–12.

Here is a summary of Book 4, with special emphasis being given to the chapters about the effectiveness of the preludes and narratives. The three interlocutors begin by setting up the delineation of Magnesia's portrait. It will be inhabited by people coming from all over Crete but also from the rest of Greece, mainly from the Peloponnese. It will be built fourteen kilometres from the sea and its citizens are expected to be able to produce some goods and import others (704a1–709d9). After expressing some thoughts about the regime the polity should adopt (709d10–715e2), the Athenian suggests that the authorities of the hypothetical city gather the citizens and deliver to them a public speech, through which they should urge them to live a law abiding and virtuous life (715e3–5). After presenting this public speech (715e7–718a6), the Athenian begins by expressing his views on the necessity of the preludes as an alternative means by which to disseminate the spirit of the laws. In particular, the Athenian notes that the legislator cannot explain certain ideas to the people through the typical mode in which laws are formulated. For this reason, a lawgiver should always search for alternative ways to lead people to virtue. These modes of expression should make citizens more docile. The legislator should not only mention what citizens should do and the penalties for those who disobey the laws; he should also soothe men's souls with persuasion and consolation. So, the Athenian concludes, each law should be introduced by a prelude, in which the lawgiver should develop his argumentation about the reasons why the citizens must obey his orders, as physicians do with their patients. In this respect, he concludes, what has been said in the first three books may be taken as a prelude to the laws to be decreed from now on (718a6–724b5).

Let us present and analyse the Athenian's views in detail. He believes that the admonitions delivered to the Magnesians are of great use for the lawgiver, as they soften the people's souls (718d3–4: μὴ παντάπασιν ὠμῆς ψυχῆς λαβόμενα), placate them (718d4: ἡμερώτερόν) and thereby render them more submissive (718d4: εὐμενέστερον). As a result, the citizens, being in this way friendlier to the lawgiver, become more docile. In this case, the legislator has much to gain, given that most people are unwilling to follow a virtuous life and by nature have an inclination towards malice and disobedience. In this respect, docility will secure the citizens' willingness to obey the law (718c7–719a3).

Plato presents here the emotional part of our soul and our learning skills as being inextricably interconnected and interdependent upon one another. The logical argumentation of the lawgiver in favour of the advantages of a virtuous life calms our souls, a procedure which should be thought of as referring to our emotions.[59] It is reasonable to assume that the words ἡμερώτερόν and εὐμενέστερον (718d4) denote a mental state in which emotions we experience such as anger, scepticism or even antipathy to legal instructions are assuaged and replaced by serenity, goodwill and rapport.[60] This alleviation of our emotions is taken by Plato to secure the ideal conditions under which we can put into effect and thus take full advantage of our learning potential (718d5–6: τὸν ἀκούοντα ὅπερ φησὶν εὐμενέστερον γιγνόμενον εὐμαθέστερον ἀπεργάσεται). Docility (εὐμαθέστερον) is equally approached from a psychological as well as an intellectual point of view. In other words, docile is meant here to refer to the one who is not only able to learn something but also *willing* to do so, an approach which we also find in other cases too throughout the Platonic oeuvre.[61] Mental serenity is treated here as a factor which allows us to take advantage of our intellectual capacities to a higher degree, as we also read elsewhere in the Platonic dialogues.[62]

Such a combinatory interpretation seems to be the most proper, which also agrees with what the Athenian says in 719e7–720e5 about the similarities between the physicians' admonitions and those he proposes for legislators. The Athenian explains that there are two kinds of doctors: free men and slaves. The slave who works as a physician takes care of other slaves and, in order to spare some time for both himself and the doctor he works for, orders his patients, as a tyrant, to follow the treatment he proposes to them without explaining to them the benefits of the treatment. He essentially tries to impose his verdict. On the other hand, a physician who is also a free man, exactly because he deals with other free men, does not content himself to suggest a therapy but also explains to his patients and their associates the nature of their diseases and thereby learns through discussion about their needs, while he also finds the opportunity to explain to them how they will recover. In this way, he tranquilises them by means of persuasion and leads them to those choices which will help them

---

[59] For this view in modern literature, see n. 31 above.
[60] Schöpsdau 1994, 229; Zichi 2018, 19.
[61] England 1921, 458; Schöpsdau 2003, 229.
[62] See, most recently, Price 2011; Warren 2014; Scott 2020.

restore their health. This is also the way in which a legislator must interact with the people of his polity.

The legislator's art of persuasion seems to go hand in hand with the preludes' impact on the people's emotions, as is evident in the Athenian's words παραμυθίας δὲ καὶ πειθοῦς (720a1).[63] Plato also offers some information about how the lawgiver will manage to placate the citizens. The latter will become more serene because the very way in which the lawgiver will impose the laws will be as mild as possible (720a5: πρᾳότατον). The roots of this serenity are not to be sought in our emotional world but in our reason. The legislator is invited, like the democratic doctors, to avoid being opinionated in order not to provoke the citizens' sense of pride. On the contrary, he should explain to them (720d6: διδάσκει) and learn from them their needs. This liberal mode of interaction between legislator and people is based on dialogue and the logical explanation of the reasons why obedience to law benefits men's mental health. In this respect, Plato's view that the citizens will become more docile is to be read as such: clarifications about the profits gained from obedience will offer the citizens the opportunity to use their reason in order to be convinced.

Although narration is not explicitly mentioned in these chapters, two passages signal Plato's view that it belongs to the legislator's weaponry of persuasion. In 718b5–c10, the Athenian makes it clear that a lawgiver should present his argumentation about the usefulness of laws not only in admonitory lectures but also in a plethora of other ways:

ἃ δὲ χρὴ μὲν αὖ καὶ ἀναγκαῖον εἰπεῖν νομοθέτην ὅστις ἅπερ ἐγὼ διανοεῖται, ἐν δὲ σχήματι νόμου ἀναρμοστεῖ λεγόμενα, τούτων πέρι δοκεῖ μοι δεῖγμα προενεγκόντα αὐτῷ τε καὶ ἐκείνοις οἷς νομοθετήσει, τὰ λοιπὰ πάντα εἰς δύναμιν διεξελθόντα, τὸ μετὰ τοῦτο ἄρχεσθαι τῆς θέσεως τῶν νόμων. ἔστιν δὲ δὴ τὰ τοιαῦτα ἐν τίνι μάλιστα σχήματι κείμενα; οὐ πάνυ ῥᾴδιον ἐν ἑνὶ περιλαβόντα εἰπεῖν αὐτὰ οἷόν τινι τύπῳ, ἀλλ' οὑτωσί τινα τρόπον λάβωμεν, ἄν τι δυνώμεθα περὶ αὐτῶν βεβαιώσασθαι.

There are also matters which a lawgiver, if he shares my view, must necessarily regulate, though they are ill-suited for statement in the form of a law; in dealing with these he ought, in my opinion, to produce a sample for his own use and that of those for whom he is legislating, and, after expounding all other matters as best he can, pass on next to commencing the task of legislation. What is the special form in which such matters are laid down? It is by no means easy to embrace them all in a single model of statement (so to

---

[63] Morrow 1953; Görgemanns 1960, 30–49; Stalley 1983, 42–44; Vickers 1988; Yunis 1990; Bobonich 1991; Nightingale 1993; Stalley 1994, 269–277; Clark 2003; Laks 2007; Mayhew 2007; Baima 2016; Zichi 2018, 23 and 26.

speak); but let us conceive of them in some such way as this, in case we may succeed in affirming something definite about them.

Although the Athenian does not clarify what are the forms in which such matters are addressed and whether narration should be included in these forms of expression, the next passage encourages us to believe that tales are one of the means of persuasion at the legislator's disposal and that they serve as preludes to a law (722c6–d2):

> Ἐξ αὐτῶν ὧν νυν<δὴ> διειλέγμεθα ἡμεῖς κατὰ θεόν τινα γεγονός. σχεδὸν γὰρ ἐξ ὅσου περὶ τῶν νόμων ἤργμεθα λέγειν, ἐξ ἑωθινοῦ μεσημβρία τε γέγονε καὶ ἐν ταύτῃ παγκάλῃ ἀναπαύλῃ τινὶ γεγόναμεν, οὐδὲν ἀλλ' ἢ περὶ νόμων διαλεγόμενοι, νόμους δὲ ἄρτι μοι δοκοῦμεν λέγειν ἄρχεσθαι, τὰ δ' ἔμπροσθεν ἦν πάντα ἡμῖν προοίμια νόμων.

> A matter which, by a kind of divine direction, has sprung out of the subjects we have now been discussing. It was little more than dawn when we began talking about laws, and now it is high noon, and here we are in this entrancing resting-place; all the time we have been talking of nothing but laws, yet it is only recently that we have begun, as it seems, to utter laws, and what went before was all simply preludes to laws.

The phrase τὰ δ' ἔμπροσθεν ... πάντα constitutes an explicit explanation on the Athenian's part that the accounts of Book 3 should be included in what is claimed to be the great prelude to the ensuing composition of the Magnesian laws.[64] For this reason, the thoughts the Athenian expresses about the intellectual and affective impact of the preludes on the citizens' souls should be taken to pertain to the accounts of Book 3 as well.

The Athenian's appreciation of narration as part of the prelude's persuasive potential is also signalled by his view that accounts are of great help in the legislator's struggle of persuasion, especially in cases where the laws to be decreed are expected to be strongly opposed by the people. Let us begin with the Athenian's mention of the stories about the Sauromatidae women's military dexterities (804e4–805a3). While discussing the city's venues of gymnastics and military training, he adds that women too must participate in training and war. As a counterargument to the hypothetical objection that women are incapable of fighting, he invokes not only his personal experience but also stories he has heard of about fighting skills of the women called Sauromatidae. According to these stories, countless such female warriors live somewhere in the Black Sea and are trained, along with men, in equestrian art and in the use of bows and other weapons. Such stories, the Athenian argues, lead us to the conclusion

---

64 Cf. England 1921, 466; Schöpsdau 2003, 245.

(λογισμόν) that, since military laws have already been imposed in other nations, they should also be decreed for the women of Magnesia as well. The Athenian's phrasing echoes his thoughts about the usefulness of the Egyptian stories (657a6: ἄξιον ἐννοίας, ὅτι δυνατὸν ἄρ' ἦν; cf. 805a3–5: λογισμόν ... ἔχω ... εἴπερ ταῦτα οὕτω συμβαίνειν ἐστὶν δυνατά) and the Dorian tale (684a1) and speak for the feasibility of his legal program.

The value of narration as a means of persuasion in cases where laws seem difficult to impose is also addressed in 839–840, where the Athenian suggests that the Magnesians write a law which will prohibit any other kind of sexual intercourse except the one which aims at procreation. Once again, the Athenian admits that this law will face people's opposition, especially of the young members of the society. Similarly to 722c6–d2 and 804e4–805a3, we easily sense the Athenian's concern to find means of persuasion in support of this law. In this spirit, he suggests to his interlocutors to invoke examples to follow, in particular celebrated athletes who, according to a short narrative, demonstrated admirable self-control in sexual affairs in order to keep in shape and fulfil their goal, i.e. victory in athletic games.[65] The Athenian concludes that they should disseminate the message that this kind of abstinence is the noblest victory with the words that they "shall tell them from their childhood's days, charming them into belief, we hope, by tales and sentences and songs (840c1–3: ἐν μύθοις τε καὶ ἐν ῥήμασιν καὶ ἐν μέλεσιν ᾄδοντες, ὡς εἰκός, κηλήσομεν). These words echo his concluding words ἔν τε ᾠδαῖς καὶ μύθοις καὶ λόγοις in 664a6–7. The stories about the athletes aim to convince the citizens of Magnesia that to abstain from sex is possible, since athletes have succeeded in doing so.[66]

Especially interesting are the Athenian's comments on tales about the posthumous judgment of the souls in 870–871, as this is perhaps the only case throughout the *Laws* in which we find an explicit formulation of the view that narratives must accompany preludes. As soon as he completes his prelude to the laws about murders, the Athenian says that "concerning all these matters, the preludes mentioned shall be announced, and, in addition to them, that story which is believed by many when they hear it from the lips of those who seriously relate such things at their mystic rites" (870d4–7: τούτων δὴ πάντων πέρι προοίμια μὲν εἰρημένα ταῦτ' ἔστω, καὶ πρὸς τούτοις, ὃν ... λόγον ...). These stories are aimed at intimidating people and thereby serve as deterrents to crime. Similar stories of supernatural content are also presented as a means of charming (ἐπῳδαί) in 887c5–d5, where the Athenian complains against those who do not

---

65 Zichi 2018, 163–165.
66 Gonzáles 2013, 159–160.

believe in gods and refers to "their disbelief in those stories which they used to hear, while infants and sucklings, from the lips of their nurses and mothers — stories chanted to them, as it were, in lullabies, whether in jest or in earnest; and the same stories they heard repeated also in prayers and sacrifices". In these last two cases, Plato focuses on the circumstances under which a story is recited and highlights two different modes of performance: (a) the stories should be narrated as pleasant fairy tales to children and as parts of solemn hymns during rites. The divine will must also be disseminated through tales about tragic heroes. While arguing that young people should respect their parents to the same degree that they respect the gods (930e2–931b4), the Athenian claims that a legislator can use as a means of persuasion the stories of Oedipus, Amyntor and Theseus, who cursed their children. The fact that in these stories the gods responded to those fathers' curses proves, according to the Athenian, the gods' view that whoever does not respect their parents must be punished (931b5–c2).[67]

In 736c5–d4, Plato invites the reader to conclude that the narratives of Book 3 should contribute to the argumentation of the preludes in a similar way to the aforementioned stories. The Athenian argues that the story of the Heracleidae offers a historical example with which the aspiring lawgivers can identify and thereby enhance their hopes that their legislative program will not cause social turbulence. In the Dorian narrative, he had argued that one of the merits of the Dorian League lay in the fact that, at the time the legislation was being set, the citizens had no debts to each other or to the state and that they managed to distribute the land to the people without being questioned. The Dorian lawgivers thereby avoided facing the pressure usually exercised upon a legislator who, in his effort to secure equality among the members of a city, is forced to proceed with land redistribution and to change the financial status of the citizens (684d4–e5, see Section 3.2.3). In a similar vein, when the Athenian begins exploring how they could distribute the land in Magnesia, he reassures his interlocutors that they are equally fortunate, as they will not be invited to redistribute the land, given that this is the first time this land is distributed. He is so optimistic that he believes that, if the Magnesian state experiences social tensions, such a development would be both implausible and incongruent with human nature. The Athenian opens his thoughts about this by reminding his friends of the fact that this merit of the Magnesian state resembles that of the Dorian confederation. Plato foregrounds this link between the two states through strong verbal cross-references (684d7: γῆς τε κτῆσιν κινεῖν καὶ χρεῶν διάλυσιν,

---

[67] Zichi 2018, 186–187, 210–213 and 202–205.

684d9–e2: ἐπιχειροῦντι κινεῖν … μὴ κινεῖν τὰ ἀκίνητα … γῆς τε ἀναδασμοὺς … καὶ χρεῶν ἀποκοπάς; cf. 736c7–d1: γῆς καὶ χρεῶν ἀποκοπῆς καὶ νομῆς πέρι … ἀκίνητον … κινεῖν). In this case, the Dorian story contributes to the Athenian's argumentation in a similar way to that of the Egyptian account in Book 2. It offers a historical example, which proves that what the legislator embarks on is feasible, as under similar circumstances some other legislators succeeded in the same thing in the past. This message animates the aspiring legislators of Magnesia and enhances their optimism about the future of their state.

If 736c5–d4 indicates that Plato wants the Dorian account to play a key role in the argumentation of the preludes of Books 4–12, in another passage we are led to the conclusion that this is also the case with the story about the shepherds. In 780–783, the Athenian explains that the legislators must decree laws not only about the conduct of those who possess public offices but also with regard to the citizens' private life. In particular, the Athenian focuses on the daily life of married couples, admitting that it will be difficult for the lawgiver to convince the citizens to let their lives be restricted by laws pertaining to the way they will satisfy their basic needs (food, drinking and sexual intercourse). Nonetheless, the Athenian encourages his companions by saying that such laws, although initially causing the citizens' reactions, can be gradually imposed. In support of this view, he brings as a piece of evidence the laws pertaining to the communal meals in Sparta and Crete. In particular, the Athenian narrates that the law which imposed the institution of communal meals was decreed for the people's protection in an emergency situation, either during a war or in some other equally dangerous occasion. Although the citizens doubted that such an institution will survive, especially during peace, everyone now finds it quite natural that these states have communal meals. This story, as well as the ensuing one, prove, in the Athenian's mind, that laws which are to change men's daily lives *can* be established, given that men across time have been proven to be susceptible to changes of this kind.[68]

The Athenian finds further support for his view in a dialogic narrative about the mutability of men's mentality in terms of their dietary habits. In this story, the Athenian argues that through time men have repeatedly changed their dietary habits, as is evident in myths about the emergence of new vegetables which were eventually dedicated to Demeter, or in the fact that different people have adopted different modes of sacrifice.

This narrative resembles in many respects the opening paragraphs of the story about the highlanders. The dramatic time starts at the very beginning of

---

[68] Zichi 2018, 164 and 183.

human civilisation, in essence even earlier than the starting point of the shepherds' story, i.e. since the genesis of humanity. The Athenian also touches upon the difficulty of men in apprehending the extent of human history since its beginning. Last, he once again refers to the natural catastrophes and changes which occasionally generate shifts in our way of life. Although critics have previously addressed these cross-references, their significance for our understanding of Plato's view about the place of Book 3 in the overall logic of the dialogue has been overlooked. Through these similarities between the dialogic narrative of 780–783 and that about the introductory paragraphs of the account in Book 3, Plato implicitly offers one further piece of evidence for the view that accounts about the prehistory of human civilisation such as the one we find in Book 3 can be of great help in the legislator's effort to convince the citizens that what he proposes is feasible.

Let us now focus on the cross-references between the accounts of Book 3 and the preludes of Books 4–12. From the very beginning of the composition of the laws, in the first and pivotal prelude we find echoes of the narratives of Book 3. This first prelude is the lengthiest of all and provides all the ensuing preludes with moral principles, offering in this way the ethical basis upon which the laws of Books 4–12 will be decreed.[69] Let us begin with its content and its relation with Books 1–3 including the narratives in question. The Athenian asks his partners to imagine that they gather the citizens of the city under construction and that they admonish them with the following words: god controls and leads the world having justice by his side. Modest and humble men follow the suggestions of justice, while conceited and arrogant men, swayed by the belief that they are destined not to be ruled but to rule, disturb the normality of their country's political life. However, the honours to gods, heroes and parents are of some value only if they are offered by virtuous men, whose mentality lies in close affinity with that of the god. For this reason, modest and just citizens should honour the gods, their heroes and their parents showing due respect to the traditional morals, so that they will reach happiness. At this point, the Athenian interrupts the prelude in order to share with his friends his thoughts on why it is useful for a legislator to introduce a law with a prelude, through which he will render the citizens of his city more obeisant (715e7–718a6).

After arguing for the usefulness of preludes (718a6–724b5), the Athenian resumes this first prelude in the first ten pages (OCT) of Book 5 (726a1–734e2). In

---

69 Morrow 1953; Görgemanns 1960, 30–49; Stalley 1983, 42–44; Vickers 1988; Yunis 1990; Bobonich 1991; Nightingale 1993; Stalley 1994, 269–277; Clark 2003; Laks 2007; Mayhew 2007; Baima 2016; Zichi 2018.

his opinion, the citizens should keep in mind that after the gods the most divine good for an individual is her or his soul. And, just as the gods rule the world, the soul governs the inferior elements of human nature. Each citizen should therefore take care of this powerful quality and not the weak ones. (S)he should not spoil her/his soul by allowing it to do whatever it wants, nor should (s)he wheedle it with money, honours and presents. Otherwise, (s)he will suffer the worst of all punishments, as a result of which (s)he will become the same as immoral men. Having in mind that the soul is more important than the body and wealth which is obtained in the service of the body, each individual should search for ways to reach the measure in focusing on her/his body and fortune. (S)he should take care of her/his parents and relatives and should set as her/his goal to serve her/his friends and to protect guests and suppliants. In what follows, the Athenian commends those who are not only just, modest and prudent but also contribute to the dissemination of these virtues in society. Also, individuals should not love themselves more than justice and should experience both joy and sadness with measure. The Athenian ends this prelude by presenting four virtuous types of life (modest, prudent, brave and healthy) and their opposites (libertine, coward, morbid).

The views expressed in Books 1–2 reverberate at many points of this prelude. To begin with the first part of the prelude, here too justice emerges at being positioned at the top of all virtues. The prelude begins with the god being accompanied by *dike* (716a2–3), which is touched upon repeatedly later on (716d3; 717d3–6; 728c3; 730d2–7; 731b5–c8; 731e6; 732a3–4). This logic echoes the Athenian's view in 631c7–8 that justice encompasses all the other virtues (moderation, prudence, bravery).[70] Furthermore, justice, as well as moderation, is juxtaposed with honours, money, physical strength and beauty (631b6–d1 and 660e6–662a4; cf. 726a1–6).[71] The Athenian, as we saw, believes that the citizens of a city should not overthrow their country's political *status quo* swayed by the beauty of their bodies, the honours they pursue and money (716a2–7). He also adds that the human soul should not be spoiled by honours and money (727a4–7). These views constitute reiterations of the Athenian's thoughts at 631b6–d1 and 660e6–662a4.[72] Last, the thesis expressed in Book 2 that people should respect and preserve the traditional laws and institutions (656c1–660c1) is also reflected in

---

[70] Schöpsdau 2003, 257, 264, 269.
[71] For connections of 726a1–6 with further passages from the *Laws*, see Schöpsdau 2003, 251–254.
[72] Schöpsdau 2003, 254–255.

the Athenian's view that people should bury their parents in full accordance with their ancestral morals (717d7–e3).

Some of these themes are touched upon in a way which corresponds to the way they appeared in the narratives of Book 3. Specifically, we find again the association of money and honours with hubris and the corrosive effects of young citizens upon domestic politics. To begin with the first of these, in the prelude the Athenian preaches the Magnesians that love for honours and glory (716a5–6: χρήμασιν ἐπαιρόμενος ἢ τιμαῖς) leads people to hubris (716a7: μεθ' ὕβρεως) and by extension to political impunity. Although money and honours are repeatedly presented in a pejorative fashion in Books 1–2, they are not causally connected there with hubris. Only in 661d6–662a2 do we read that a powerful, rich and healthy man, if unjust, is led to hubris, but in this case it is not wealth but injustice that causes one's hubristic behaviour.[73] The sole occasion before the prelude where money and honours are presented as generating arrogance and hubris is found in the stories about the mountaineers and the Peloponnesian confederation. In the account of the mountaineers, the Athenian describes the economy of those first communities and explains, as we saw, that they were shepherds and that they possessed such a quantity of goods that they were neither starving nor rich (678e9–679b5). In this way, according to the Athenian, they secured happiness for their societies, given that poverty leads to envy and immense wealth brings about hubris and injustice (679b8–c1: οὔτε γὰρ ὕβρις οὔτ' ἀδικία). In the prelude too, people are presented as adopting hubristic behaviour because of money they have or they pursue. What is more, both in the account of the shepherds and in the prelude, hubris is associated with injustice (cf. Book 2, 661e2: ἀδικίαν δὲ καὶ ὕβριν).[74]

In the account about the dissolution of the Peloponnesian League, the Athenian concludes that the legislators of the confederation would have been more successful if they had acquainted themselves with the following principle: "if one neglects the rule of due measure, and gives things too great in power to things too small – sails to ships, food to bodies, offices of rule to souls – then everything is upset [...]" (691c1–3). This thesis presumes that no human soul could ever take over the ultimate degree of power without being infected by

---

[73] See, contra, Moore 2007, 127. Cf. 637a3 ἡδοναῖς καὶ ὕβρεσι καὶ ἀνοίᾳ πάσῃ which echoes 716a6–7 ἀνοίᾳ ... μεθ' ὕβρεως but does not delineate any causal links between hubris and money or honours. In 641c3–5 hubris emerges from military feats (πολλοὶ γὰρ ὑβριστότεροι διὰ πολέμων νίκας γενόμενοι μυρίων ἄλλων κακῶν δι' ὕβριν ἐνεπλήσθησαν; in 649d5–6 hubris is paratactically – but not causally – connected with money (θυμός, ἔρως, ὕβρις, ἀμαθία, φιλοκέρδεια, δειλία, καὶ ἔτι τοιάδε, πλοῦτος, κάλλος, ἰσχύς.

[74] Cf. Fuks 1979, 49 nn. 76 and 82, and 53.

thoughtlessness and arrogance, or in other words without becoming corrupted and destroyed (691c5–d6). This view, the Athenian adds, holds true especially for the souls of young individuals (691c7–d1: νέα καὶ ἀνυπεύθυνος). The same view is expressed in the prelude and, what is more, with similar wording. Young citizens (716a6: νεότητι; cf. 691c7: νέα), being proud of their body, honours and money corrupt their souls and disturb the political life of their city (691d3–4: ὃ γενόμενον ταχὺ διέφθειρεν αὐτὴν καὶ πᾶσαν τὴν δύναμιν ἠφάνισεν αὐτῆς; cf. 716b4–5: ἑαυτόν τε καὶ οἶκον καὶ πόλιν ἄρδην ἀνάστατον ἐποίησεν) and are eventually led to their doom. In both cases, this kind of behaviour is taken as thoughtlessness (691d1: ἀνοίας; cf. 716a6: ἀνοίᾳ), which leads to hubris (691c3–4: ἐξυβρίζοντα ... ὕβρεως; cf. 716a7: μεθ' ὕβρεως).

In essence, the narrative of Book 3 offers a developmental model, which includes historical examples for the citizens of the hypothetical city and the reader both to follow (the mountaineers) and to avoid (the Peloponnesian League). The same principle is used as an assessment criterion for both the shepherds' happiness and the Peloponnesians' failure. These two historical examples serve as evidence in support of the correctness of the Athenian's admonitions in the first prelude. As will be demonstrated in what follows, this is also the case with many other points in the rest of the preludes.

The second theme of this prelude which points to the account of Book 3 is the distortive effect of young individuals upon political tranquillity (716b1–5). Such an overt reference is only found in the story about the Trojan War. As noted above, according to the Athenian, while the soldiers of the Greek cities were at Troy, the young members of these cities found the opportunity to organise political fractions (682d5–e2). This situation exemplifies the Athenian's view of the prelude that young individuals, after being excited, gather others as well. Both in the account of the Trojan War and the prelude, the young citizens join political parties in order to overthrow the institution of their city.

Also closely connected with the first three books, including the narratives of Book 3, is the second part of this prelude. As far as its connections with Books 1–2 are concerned, here too we read the view found in 631b6–d1 and 660d11–662a3 that the soul is a divine entity (726a1–727a2) superior to human goods, such as bodily strength, beauty and money (727d6–728a5; 728c9–729b2).[75] Also, we find here the view that one's goal should not be to do whatever she or he wishes (727b1–2; cf. 661b1–2 and 662a1)[76] and that one's pleasures

---

[75] Schöpsdau 2003, 271–272; Metcalf 2013, 119–120.
[76] Schöpsdau 2003, 255.

should not ignore the legislator's logic (659c9–660a8).[77] Furthermore, special emphasis is paid to the view that reliability is a moral prerequisite for the political harmony in a city (730c1–d2; cf. 630a5–d1).[78] Last, here too we find the triptych prudence-moderation-bravery (733d7–734e2) about which we have already read in 631b3–d1.

In this part of the prelude, some of these issues are also addressed in such a way that they constitute echoes of the narratives of Book 3. These themes are money and the pampering of one's soul. With regard to the first issue, we read in the prelude that excessive wealth and the extravagant possession of one's fortune leads both states and individuals to hostilities (728e5–729a2). The Athenian does not explain here why wealth has negative ramifications upon men's interstate or private relationships. However, his account on the post-cataclysmic societies serves as an explanatory supplement to 728e5–729a2. In that account the Athenian had claimed that the shepherds' serene and virtuous way of life partly lay in the fact that they had reached a balanced compromise between wealth and poverty. They were neither rich nor exceedingly poor, which was a special advantage of their political life, as both wealth and poverty cause "the growth of insolence and injustice, of rivalries and jealousies" (679b8–c2). In both the account and the prelude, the Athenian does not merely discuss the negative effects of wealth upon social structures but also compares the destructive impact of wealth to that of poverty. Furthermore, the account of the shepherds not only offers to the reader a historical example that proves the view developed in the prelude but also enlightens the reader about the reasoning of this view.

In this prelude, we also find a distant echo of the Persian queens' spoiling their children, which we first read of in the Persian account of Book 3. In this story, the Athenian maintains that the decadence of the Persian constitution emerged from the Persian queens' wish not to allow anyone to oppose their children's will. In particular, we read that "they brought them up from earliest childhood as though they had already attained to Heaven's favour and felicity, and were lacking in no celestial gift; and so by treating them as the special favourites of Heaven, and forbidding anyone to oppose them in anything, and compelling everyone to praise (694d6: ἐπαινεῖν) their every word and deed, they reared them up into what they were" (694d2–7). This upbringing is described by the Athenian as "a rearing that 'spared the rod'" (695b2: τροφῇ ἀνεπιπλήκτῳ; cf. 695b4: ἀνεπιπληξίας). In a similar vein, in the prelude the Athenian argues that most people believe that by spoiling their souls from young age they will

---

[77] Schöpsdau 2003, 255.
[78] Schöpsdau 2003, 262.

honour them in the best possible way while they essentially harm themselves (726a1–727c8). As in the Persian account, the Athenian says that one spoils his soul whenever he "deems himself capable of learning all things, and supposes that by lauding (727b1: ἐπαινῶν) his soul he honours it, and by eagerly permitting it to do whatsoever it pleases" (727a7–b2).

Let us return to the issue of this prelude's pivotal place and try to explain the meaning of the fact that the Athenian links the narratives of Book 3 with such a focal prelude. If anything, the accounts, by offering ideas to a central part of the work which exercises a great ideological influence over all the laws, obtains a principal role in the construction of the dialogue's logic. First, this introductory prelude pertains to all the laws which will be composed in the ensuing books. The Athenian makes it clear that this prelude is a speech which the legislators should deliver in front of all the citizens (715e3–5) in order to convince them to obey not only a single category of laws but anything to be announced to them in the rest of the work (734e2). Second, the moral values and the elements of the worldview which emerge from this prelude recur in the preludes of individual categories of laws.[79] And, as we saw, some of these elements are drawn from the accounts of Book 3. In this way, this prelude serves as a channel of diffusion of the narratives' messages into the rest of the work, thus betraying Plato's intention in the *Laws* to organise the logic of the dialogue on the basis of these narratives.

Messages of the narratives are also traceable in the two preludes to the laws against enrichment. In the first one (741a6–e6), the Athenian admonishes the citizens to preserve the agreed number and size of the fortunes defined by the legislator and to set as their goal to respect the values of equality and similarity — the distribution of the fortunes is actually aimed at securing these two elements among the population — as well as whatever has been agreed upon. In what follows, the Athenian announces the law which defines proper and improper transactions (741e7–742c6), and then proceeds with one further admonishing speech (742c6–743c4). In essence, the first prelude propounds the idea to the citizens that the preservation of the number and size of the land lots secures equality and uniformity among the members of a society, while the second prelude explains why an immensely rich individual cannot be virtuous.

The very idea that money is of small value for those who do not possess virtue has already been expressed in 631c4–5. However, there are certain points, both in the first and the second prelude about enrichment, where we find close echoes of the narratives of Book 3. First, in the first prelude the Athenian advises

---

[79] Stalley 1983, 66–70.

that officers write on plates made of cypress wood the cases of the violators of the law, as a reminder to the next generations (741c6–d4). The Athenian essentially advises the citizens to act as the Egyptian priests were said to have acted in the account of 656d5–657b8. The principle expressed in that account, i.e. that written discourse can serve as a preserver of communal memory and thus of the value of the laws through time, appears again in this case. This idea is also found in the narrative about the mountaineer shepherds (680a5–7).

In the second prelude about enrichment (742c6–743c4), the Athenian claims that a legislator's goal should not be to make his city as powerful and rich as possible but rather as virtuous and happy as possible (742d2–e1). In Book 1, the Athenian has already argued that a city should not aim at being effective in war but to secure for itself not only bravery but also virtue in its entirety, namely prudence, moderation, justice and bravery (630a7–d1). However, at that point the contrast was created between military effectiveness and inner politics with no discussion of the elements of wealth and geopolitical supremacy. On the other hand, the Athenian has also juxtaposed the elements of wealth and power with virtue in his division between divine and human goods (631b2–d1; 660d11–662a3), but he did so without laying any emphasis on the ramifications of this scheme for the foreign policy of a state. This contrast between power, wealth and control over others, on the one hand, and virtue, on the other, is for the first time related to a state and not to an individual in the account on the dissolution of the Peloponnesian League. When the Athenian poses the question of why Argos and Messene, despite their power, did not manage to preserve their legislations, he proceeds with the following correction: one should not assess the success of a city by judging its wealth and power but on the basis of the degree to which this city's will complies with true reason (687a2–688d5). This principle is identical with that of 742d2–e1 in the second prelude on enrichment.

Both in the Peloponnesian account and the prelude, this view is also expressed in a quite similar way. In both cases, the Athenian juxtaposes his own view with that of the many, which, although being established and more commonplace, is to be questioned. In the narrative, the expectation that the Peloponnesian confederation would be preserved in time because it enjoyed the advantages of wealth and honours is presented as being shared by all the Greeks and non-Greeks (685b7–e4; 686e4; 687c1–3). Similarly, in the prelude the Athenian twice (742d3; 742e7) stresses that what he says amounts to a sharp contrast with common beliefs of his age.

To continue with one further prelude, the way in which the Athenian introduces the legislation about the limitation of poverty (744d2–8) points to the account on the mountaineer shepherds. The issue of poverty, which is not only addressed in this minute prelude but in many others as well,[80] is first touched upon in the shepherds' story. The Athenian maintains there that one should avoid not being poor but extremely poor (679b3–4: πένητες ... σφόδρα οὐκ ἦσαν) because it is excessive poverty and immense wealth that infuse, as we saw, injustice, hubris and envy into society (679b8–c2). In the Athenian's mind, the demarcation of poverty is inextricably associated with political and legislative normality. We read exactly the same reasoning in this short prelude (744d5–7: μήτε πενίαν τὴν χαλεπὴν ἐνεῖναι παρά τισιν τῶν πολιτῶν μήτε αὖ πλοῦτον, ὡς ἀμφοτέρων τικτόντων ταῦτα ἀμφότερα).[81] The Athenian's choice to shape the dipole 'poverty-wealth' at a point where a mere reference to poverty without one to wealth would suffice reflects Plato's intention, as in many other points of the preludes, to create at every opportunity linkages between the stories of Book 3 and his legislative construction of Books 4–12.

It is also worth examining one further prelude due to its connections with the accounts on the mountaineers and the Trojan War on the dangers lurking in the communication of cities by land and sea. The Athenian distinguishes the legitimate ways of hunting from the illicit ones (823d3–824a9). People should hunt by exploiting their physical strength, in the aid of horses and dogs, and by hitting their prey by themselves. On the other hand, one should not hunt animals in an idle fashion, either on land or in sea, by using nets and traps. Within this framework, almost in the middle of the prelude, the Athenian offers the following advice: "and may no longing for man-hunting by sea and piracy overtake you, and render you cruel and lawless hunters; and may the thought of committing robbery in country or city not so much as cross your minds" (823e2–5).

The Athenian is obviously looking for a law which could mitigate the negative consequences of communicating with men. He strikingly emphasises the double form of human interaction in the sea (823e3: κατὰ θάλατταν) and by land (823e4: ἐν χώρᾳ). The hostile relationships of men and the degree to which these relationships are facilitated by the land and maritime interaction of cities and the very pair 'sea-land' are for the first time addressed in the account of the mountaineers' settlements. In this story, the Athenian attributes the prevalence of peace among the cities of that remote era to the fact that, *inter alia*, men had not yet developed the technology which would help them travel far away from their homelands (678c5–e5 and in terms of the 'sea-land' *topos* see 678c7: κατὰ

---

[80] On the centrality of this issue in the *Laws* and a detailed analysis of the passages related to this issue, see Fuks 1979, 41–78. See also Skultéty 2006, 189, who connects 919b with 679b–c.
[81] Cf. Des Places 1951, 103 n. 1.

γῆν ἢ κατὰ θάλατταν). Afterwards, when he narrates the expedition of the Greeks against Troy, the Athenian clarifies that the enterprise was realised in a period of time in which many cities had already started fearlessly engaging with overseas travels (682c9–10: κατὰ θάλατταν … τῇ θαλάττῃ). This clarification reflects the Athenian's intention to create a contrast between the age of the mountaineers, who, by not traveling, were absolved from the contingency of an external war, and the era of the Trojan War, in which the price of the maritime journeys is war and the destruction of cities.

Furthermore, in the prelude of 869e10–871a1 on the legislation on premeditated murders, the issue of immense wealth is addressed in such a way that evokes the accounts of the shepherds and the Peloponnesian confederation. In this prelude, the Athenian lists the most common reasons why people knowingly perpetrate planned murders. Two from among these reasons, which are mentioned first and are thereby marked as the most crucial of all, are one's desire to obtain extravagant wealth and the aspiration to be honoured by society. Both these elements are also presented as the causes of political turbulences in the accounts of the shepherds and the Peloponnesian League. In the story of the shepherds, as in the prelude, limitless wealth emerges as the fountain of all evils for humanity, while in the account about the Peloponnesian cities the Athenian underlines that the criterion by which to assess the success of an individual or a community is not to be sought in extraordinary enrichment but in virtue and happiness. This prelude too echoes the Athenian's view of Book 2 that the overestimation of wealth is a common practice among men. The underestimation of the desire for offices and honours is also found in the account of the Peloponnesian League, in which the leaders of Messene and Argos violated the stipulations of their agreement with Sparta motivated by their desire to amplify the power and glory they had been enjoying up to that point. This choice brought about disastrous consequences for their cities, just as in the prelude pernicious ramifications, i.e. murders, are claimed to emerge from ambition.

3.2 The poetics of intentional history

The narratives mentioned so far are presented by Plato as pieces of intentional history. In other words, they are stories of the past which promote, reflect and legitimise the current moral code of the people who use them. The tales about Minos and Isis ascribe the quality of the Cretan and Egyptian laws respectively to their divine origins and thereby inculcate the citizens' respect to the institutions of their countries. The story of Zeus and Ganymede valorises a certain feature of social behaviour and thereby inspires people to endorse this feature.

Myths about a people's autochthony, such as the one on the earth-born Thebans, also assist a nation to develop bonds of love for their country and to claim their rights on the area where it is placed. Last, the stories of Book 3 offer examples of polities or individuals, some of which apply the rules proposed in the present, while others do not. In this way, these tales educate the citizens by providing them with examples to follow or to avoid. Not only these cases but also numerous others from the rest of the Platonic oeuvre reveal Plato's concern for the way he could encourage us to speculate on the usefulness of this approach to the past in legislators' efforts to establish a legal system in a state.[82]

At this point, from the perspective of those who, like us, investigate Plato's possible reflections on the shaping of narratives, the following question naturally emerges: did Plato ever reflect on the compositional choices that a fabricator of such stories is invited to make in her or his effort to render them pieces of intentional history? The passages from Books 1–2 and Books 4–12 analysed so far cannot help us to answer this question because we find in them nothing more than concise mentions of such tales with no detailed presentation of or/and discussion about their arrangements. The Athenian merely touches upon the affective impact of these stories on the receivers' inner world but is not interested in the circumstances in which these stories were composed. In some cases, we only read terms which superficially denote their structuring. For example, when addressing the necessity of the preludes in the dissemination of laws, the Athenian seems to be concerned about issues of composition. He argues that the preludes should be artfully crafted similarly to proems in songs (722d2–e1). He also seems to distinguish the more elaborate procedure of structuring some preludes from the spontaneous and improvisational creation of others, as is evident in his statement that Books 1–3 serve as preludes that "provide a kind of artistic preparation" (722d5: ἔχουσαί τινα ἔντεχνον ἐπιχείρησιν; cf. 722d7–e1: θαυμαστῶς ἐσπουδασμένα about the poetic proems with which he compares his own preludes). However, first, these passages do not refer to narratives — at least not in an immediate fashion — but to preludes and, second, they do not penetrate the details of the elaboration of the material to be used for the composition of a prelude. Therefore, these passages can hardly enlighten us about Plato's views on the 'poetics of intentional history'.

However, in the *Laws* Plato seems to be fully aware of the fact that the narration of the past, as a means to promote the moral values of the present, presupposes greater elaboration or even the radical amendment of the material to

---

[82] On this issue, see Farrar's (2013, esp. 33–35 and *passim*) fine analysis and discussion of previous literature.

be narrated. When the Athenian Visitor emphasises the negative corollaries of Athens' naval acme for its political life (705c7–707d6), Clinias objects that it was their navy by which the Athenians saved both themselves and the Greeks in their victory at Salamis (707b4–6). Clinias' objection typifies the laudatory spirit of narratives articulated in oral conversations, panegyric speeches or in works such as that of Herodotus about the naval feats of Athens.[83] Plato skilfully presents Clinias as reacting in this specific way in order to show us that the way that the Athenian reproduces and assesses the past affects how he changes the popular logic of the stories from which he draws his material.[84]

Plato's interest in the modification of the past in constructing intentional history is also evident in the narrative of the Dorians. When the Athenian comments that the Dorian alliance, with all its merits, failed to preserve itself, it is the Dorian Megillus who now reacts by saying "What do you mean? What fault have you to find with it?" (685a1). Although elsewhere agreeing with the Athenian about certain constitutional defects of the Dorians, Megillus seems here to believe that the Athenian's attitude contradicts the Dorians' propensity to treat this alliance as part of their glorious past and not as an example to avoid.[85] Last, one cannot but notice the fact that, although the shepherds resemble the Cyclopes in many respects, their primitivism is here not attributed by the Athenian to their savagery, a fact also noted by Megillus (680d1–3).

So, by means of what techniques does a narrator, according to Plato, change the material to be narrated in order to adapt it to the needs and goal setting of her or his account? As demonstrated in Chapter 1, Plato is concerned with this issue in terms of the composition of cosmological narratives. It was also argued that, both in the introductory remarks to the myth and through the way he shapes its plot, Plato invites the reader to reflect on these techniques of modification of the material. In this section, I will argue that Plato encourages speculation on similar issues in Book 3 of the *Laws*. In contrast to the brief mentions of stories we find in the rest of the dialogue, the extensive narratives of Book 3 have a clear-cut structure and are enriched by a significant number of meta-compositional statements, so that the entire book is turned, we could say, into a handbook for the reader on the 'poetics of intentional history'. What is more, the Athenian draws special attention to the elaboration of the material drawn from tradition, its amendment and incorporation into a new plot. In par-

---

83 Atack 2019.
84 This is defined by Burnyeat (1992 in Fine 1999, 306–307) as an "alienating description" (I draw the quotation from Farrar 2013, 33). Cf. Schofield 2006 and Farrar 2013, 33–34, 37–38.
85 Cf. Farrar 2013, 41–42; Zuckert 2013, 88.

ticular, it will be argued that Plato underlines three main ways in which a narrator revises the data to be narrated on the basis of the ideological and ethical code she or he belongs to: (a) the narrator ideologically 'coats' material drawn from literature with aspects of the proposed communal moral code; (b) she or he poses questions about the past and then uses the proposed communal moral code as a tool through which to answer these questions; and (c) the proposed moral code offers the backbone of a past narrative.

3.2.1 Selectivity and temporality

The Athenian opens his narration with some preliminary remarks similar to those expressed by the Visitor before the cosmological myth in the *Statesman*. Let us see the Athenian's introduction (676a1–c10):

> ΑΘ. Ταῦτα μὲν οὖν δὴ ταύτῃ· πολιτείας δὲ ἀρχήν τίνα ποτὲ φῶμεν γεγονέναι; μῶν οὐκ ἐνθένδε τις ἂν αὐτὴν ῥᾷστά τε καὶ κάλλιστα κατίδοι;
> ΚΛ. Πόθεν;
> ΑΘ. Ὅθενπερ καὶ τὴν τῶν πόλεων ἐπίδοσιν εἰς ἀρετὴν μεταβαίνουσαν ἅμα καὶ κακίαν ἑκάστοτε θεατέον.
> ΚΛ. Λέγεις δὲ πόθεν;
> ΑΘ. Οἶμαι μὲν ἀπὸ χρόνου μήκους τε καὶ ἀπειρίας καὶ τῶν μεταβολῶν ἐν τῷ τοιούτῳ.
> ΚΛ. Πῶς λέγεις;
> ΑΘ. Φέρε, ἀφ' οὗ πόλεις τ' εἰσὶν καὶ ἄνθρωποι πολιτευόμενοι, δοκεῖς ἄν ποτε κατανοῆσαι χρόνου πλῆθος ὅσον γέγονεν;
> ΚΛ. Οὔκουν ῥᾴδιόν γε οὐδαμῶς.
> ΑΘ. Τὸ δέ γε ὡς ἄπλετόν τι καὶ ἀμήχανον ἂν εἴη;
> ΚΛ. Πάνυ μὲν οὖν τοῦτό γε.
> ΑΘ. Μῶν οὖν οὐ μυρίαι μὲν ἐπὶ μυρίαις ἡμῖν γεγόνασι πόλεις ἐν τούτῳ τῷ χρόνῳ, κατὰ τὸν αὐτὸν δὲ τοῦ πλήθους λόγον οὐκ ἐλάττους ἐφθαρμέναι; πεπολιτευμέναι δ' αὖ πάσας πολιτείας πολλάκις ἑκασταχοῦ; καὶ τοτὲ μὲν ἐξ ἐλαττόνων μείζους, τοτὲ δ' ἐκ μειζόνων ἐλάττους, καὶ χείρους ἐκ βελτιόνων γεγόνασι καὶ βελτίους ἐκ χειρόνων;
> ΚΛ. Ἀναγκαῖον.
> ΑΘ. Ταύτης δὴ πέρι λάβωμεν, εἰ δυναίμεθα, τῆς μεταβολῆς τὴν αἰτίαν· τάχα γὰρ ἂν ἴσως δείξειεν ἡμῖν τὴν πρώτην τῶν πολιτειῶν γένεσιν καὶ μετάβασιν.
> ΚΛ. Εὖ λέγεις, καὶ προθυμεῖσθαι δεῖ, σὲ μὲν ὃ διανοῇ περὶ αὐτῶν ἀποφαινόμενον, ἡμᾶς δὲ συνεπομένους.

> ATH: So much for that, then! Now, what are we to say about the origin of government? Would not the best and easiest way of discerning it be from this standpoint?
> CL: What standpoint?
> ATH: That from which one should always observe the progress of states as they move towards either goodness or badness.
> CL: What point is that?

ATH: The observation, I suppose, of an infinitely long period of time and of the variations therein occurring.
CL: Explain your meaning.
ATH: Tell me now: do you think you could ever ascertain the space of time that has passed since cities came into existence and men lived under civic rule?
CL: Certainly it would be no easy task.
ATH: But you can easily see that it is vast and immeasurable?
CL: That I most certainly can do.
ATH: During this time, have not thousands upon thousands of states come into existence, and, on a similar computation, just as many perished? And have they not in each case exhibited all kinds of constitutions over and over again? And have they not changed at one time from small to great, at another from great to small, and changed also from good to bad and from bad to good?
CL: Necessarily.
ATH: Of this process of change let us discover, if we can, the cause; for this, perhaps, would show us what is the primary origin of constitutions, as well as their transformation.
CL: You are right; and we must all exert ourselves — you to expound your view about them, and we to keep pace with you.

These paragraphs introduce, apart from the account about the mountaineers, the rest of the narratives in Book 3 as well. They also show several notable similarities with the introduction to the myth in the *Statesman*. In both cases, it is announced that the starting point in the dramatic time of the ensuing narrative will be a time that is significantly remote from the interlocutors' present. In the *Statesman*, the Eleatic Visitor announces that he will examine the issue of statesmanship, taking as a point of departure the time when men lived in the Age of Cronus (269a7–8). In the *Laws*, the Athenian similarly urges his interlocutors to investigate legislation and political organisation from the very beginning of men's political life (676a–c).[86] Also, in both cases the narrators pay particular attention to the element of selectivity (see below). Furthermore, both the Eleatic Visitor and the Athenian state that the accounts they will compose will shed light on each subject in question by restoring the causative relations between the events to be narrated. As demonstrated in the previous chapter, the Eleatic Visitor concluded his preface with the promise that he will search for the common cause of three stories (those on the change of the sun's route, the Age of Cronus and the earth born men) and that he will thereby elaborate on the nature of statesmanship (269b5–c2). Similarly, the Athenian says about the internal change of human politics "of this process of change let us discover, if

---

[86] Des Places 1951, XIII; Weil 1959, 57.

we can, the cause" (676c6–7).⁸⁷ Furthermore, in both cases the subject pertains to some kind of alteration. In the preface to the myth of the *Statesman*, the Eleatic Visitor explores the cause of certain natural changes (269a1–5: περὶ τῆς μεταβολῆς δύσεώς τε καὶ ἀνατολῆς ἡλίου καὶ τῶν ἄλλων ἄστρων ... μετέβαλεν), while the Athenian investigates the cause of an alteration in men's political life, namely of the constitutional and legislative changes that cities diachronically suffer (676a6: μεταβαίνουσαν; 676b1: τῶν μεταβολῶν; 676c6–8: ταύτης ... τῆς μεταβολῆς ... μετάβασιν).⁸⁸ Both narrators also choose to outline the various temporal phases of human civilisation by referring to periods of great annihilation in the human population (270b10–d1; 677a1–b4).⁸⁹ Last, in both cases the basic elements of the *fabula* on the basis of which the plot of the *sujet* is structured are old stories (268e8 and 269b4: τῶν πάλαι λεχθέντων; cf. 677a1: οἱ παλαιοὶ λόγοι).

In this case too, as in the *Statesman*, Plato underlines a basic element of the configuration of the narrative plot, namely selectivity.⁹⁰ If in the *Statesman* the Eleatic Visitor wished to select certain pieces from an abundance of stories, here the emphasis is laid upon the choice of the proper period to be used as the starting point for the story under construction. The Athenian from the outset states that his goal is not only to find the cause but also the origins of human constitutions (676a1: πολιτείας δὲ ἀρχὴν τίνα). Clinias twice asks him where this starting point should be sought (676a4 and 676a7), and the Athenian reveals to him his aspiration to look back at a great depth of time (676a8–b1). The definition of the beginning of the narrative thread is a particularly difficult task because, as the Athenian claims, he and his partners are not in a position to apprehend the greatness of the interval between their own age and the beginning of men's political organisation.⁹¹ The vastness of time is stressed by the words ἀπὸ χρόνου μήκους τε καὶ ἀπειρίας (676a8), χρόνου πλῆθος (676b4), ἄπλετόν τι (676b7), while the inability of the human mind to appreciate this vastness is indicated by the words δοκεῖς ἄν ποτε κατανοῆσαι (676b4) and ἀμήχανον ἂν εἴη (676b7).⁹² Plato draws our attention to this methodological as well as compositional issue and thereby shares with us his intention to shed light on the choices

---

87 The cause of political and institutional changes through time is stressed throughout Book 3. See Schöpsdau 1994, 354.
88 Weil 1959, 57.
89 Des Places 1951, XIII.
90 Cf. Nightingale's (1999, 301) short comment on this aspect.
91 Weil 1959, 59, who compares this passage with the *Timaeus*.
92 Weil (1959, 57) compares this passage and *St.* 302a and *Ti.* 22b ff. Se also Nightingale 1999, 303; Sallis 2013, 78–79.

that narrators are invited to make in their effort to solve this problem, and on the narrative techniques through which they can realise their choices in the delineation of dramatic time.

The element of selectivity is approached in direct connection with the construction of narrative time, but is also linked with further issues. The Athenian comments that, within such a great amount of time, countless cities must have been founded (676b9–c1: μυρίαι μὲν ἐπὶ μυρίαις ... πόλεις ... οὐκ ἐλάττους), which must have adopted countless regimes (676c1–2: πεπολιτευμέναι δ' αὖ πάσας πολιτείας πολλάκις ἑκασταχοῦ). In this respect, the Athenian narrator is invited not only to define the temporal boundaries of his plot but also to do the same on a spatial level and with regard to various kinds of constitutions. The reader reasonably wonders what city from among all those the Athenian will choose in order to begin his narrative. However, although on a temporal level the Athenian will manage to choose a starting point for his story, he does not make a definite choice on a spatial level; the first account, the one about the mountaineers, does not focus on a specific city. Although we are offered the designation that at this phase settlements are found on the top of the mountains, we are not informed about what part of the world the Athenian refers to.[93] The emphasis is laid on the narrator's effort to define the time and not the field of action in this period of human history. The words πολλὰς ἀνθρώπων φθορὰς γεγονέναι κατακλυσμοῖς τε καὶ νόσοις καὶ ἄλλοις πολλοῖς (677a4–5) denote the abundance of the information of the *fabula*, from which the narrator should select certain data for the starting point of his account.

Even the Athenian's statement that he intends to search for the cause of political mutability reflects his ulterior goal, which is the temporal definition of the very first constitutional change. Finally, the Athenian then chooses his starting point: a period which typically follows a natural destruction, namely when human species has been decimated, with the mountaineers being the sole inhabitants of the earth (677a8–b4). This period too emerges as only one from among a plethora of other destructions (677a8–9: φέρε δή, νοήσωμεν μίαν τῶν πολλῶν ταύτην τὴν τῷ κατακλυσμῷ ποτε γενομένην). Furthermore, we are not faced with a specific point in human history but one which always follows great disasters.[94]

Through this choice the Athenian reveals to the reader that he will, in a sense, begin his story *in medias res*. The point he chooses as the beginning of

---

93 Cf. Nightingale's (1999, 302) view that the narrative of the mountaineers implies that different stories of other civilisations were taking place at the same time.
94 Weil 1959, 59; Nightingale 1999, 302.

dramatic time in his account is not identified with the period which followed the first cataclysm of all times, but with the period which followed one from among many cataclysms. Nor do we learn exactly what cataclysm the Athenian refers to. Also, we do not read of the first attempt of humanity to enter a state of political organisation; the Athenian takes it for granted that before the cataclysm cities had developed political life and civilisation (677b5–c9).[95]

Furthermore, in Book 4 the Athenian clarifies that only the Age of Cronus, in which the gods ruled living beings including humans, should be taken as the ultimate beginning of his account about the creation of human political life. In this short account, the Athenian offers the following comment: "long ages before those cities existed whose formation we have described above, there existed in the time of Cronus, it is said, a most prosperous government and settlement" (713a9–b3). He shortly afterwards explains that he deliberately had not started his account from the Age of Cronus because he intended to mention it in a flashback exactly at this point (713b6–7: διὸ καὶ παρήγαγον αὐτὴν εἰς τὸ μέσον τοῖς λόγοις). Through the Athenian's prompt to his interlocutors to begin their story in a period which typically follows a natural disaster (677a8–9) and with this delayed metanarrative statement that he had intentionally began *in medias res* (713b6–7), Plato leads the reader to think that the selection of the proper starting point of a narrative constitutes a difficult procedure whenever the origins of a phenomenon in time are so remote and thus hard to conceive.[96]

In the myth of the *Statesman* the delineation of the causal relations and temporal sequences, as well as the selection of the proper material, are treated from a clearly structural point of view. The main criterion for the selection of the information is its content, while Plato is not interested in stressing that the transformation of the *fabula* into the *sujet* is influenced by social factors, such as the narrator's ideological and intellectual background.[97] Differently, in the *Laws* the procedure of composing a narrative is foregrounded as a phenomenon

---

95 Des Places 1951, XIII; Schöpsdau 1994, 354.
96 Weil 1959, 59.
97 Of course, in both the *Sophist* and the *Statesman* Plato offers us some information mainly about the intellectual background of the Eleatic Visitor: he is a philosopher of Parmenides' school, which is why the reader is not surprised by the fact that in the *Sophist* the Visitor enjoys exploring the issue of being and non-being and that in the *Statesman* he chooses to compose a cosmological account, in which distinctive features of the Parmenidean doctrines on the creation and structure of the universe are discernible. However, in the process of narrating the account, the Visitor does not draw readerly attention to his socio-cultural background. Nor do we find any stichomythia between him and Young Socrates which underlines these elements, such as those between the Athenian, Clinias and Megillus in the *Laws* examined below.

which can be defined by socio-political factors, specifically the narrators' age and nationality.⁹⁸

The technique through which Plato leads the reader to reflect on this issue is as follows: first, he repeatedly presents Clinias and Megillus as choosing what to say or as favouring what they listen to on the basis of their nationality. However, Plato simultaneously presents them as not letting their love for their countries affect the way they select the material to be narrated and how they shape the temporal backbone of a story.⁹⁹ They are instead presented as reflecting on such compositional issues, being guided by the wisdom and tastes they have been offered by a long-life experience. In this way, seen through the prism of their general sympathy and respect for their homelands, the cases in which Clinias and Megillus resist approaching the Athenian's account from a nationalist point of view are emphasised even further in the reader's mind.

In what follows, we first present the passages in which Clinias and Megillus display their ethnic identity within their discourse with the Athenian. We then analyse the cases in which they are presented as remaining unaffected by local partialities in the way they make their decisions about the creation of temporal relationships in the plot. When the Athenian quotes some verses of Tyrtaeus, he notes that the poet hailed from Athens but was a citizen of Sparta (629a4–5). Also, after reciting the verses, he makes the assumption that Clinias might have heard of them, while he is positive that Megillus is certainly familiar with them, a certainty confirmed by the Spartan (629b3–5).¹⁰⁰ Elsewhere, when the Athenian hesitates to expatiate about intoxication, considering that the rest of the Greeks accuse the Athenians of chatter (641e2–642b1), the other two men encourage him to speak as much as he wishes, each of them mentioning the connections they have with Athens. Megillus reveals that he is a public friend of Athens (642b2–d2), while Clinias refers to Epimenides. Cnossos demonstrates certain bonds with Athens because Epimenides once visited the Athenians and saved them from the Persians through his prophecies (642d3–643a1).

Both Clinias and Megillus put aside their ethnic identity when it comes to issues related to the selection of the data to be narrated and the delineation of temporal sequences in an account. When the Athenian assumes that the post-

---

98 On Plato's emphasis on the virtue of old men, see Stalley 1983, 3.
99 Weil 1959, 39–42 finds that nationality is the element which colours most strongly the two characters and differentiates them from each other, rendering them in this way something much more than the passive figures of other dialogues.
100 On Plato's intention to emphasise the Spartan perspective from which Tyrtaeus is treated in this passage, see Powell 1994, 302.

cataclysmic shepherds were not acquainted with the arts and the political manoeuvres which were developed before the cataclysm, Clinias interrupts him and proceeds with a prolepsis, the range of which he attempts to define on the basis of some historical figures. It is obvious, Clinias says, that it has only been one or two thousand years from his and his partners' age that these arts were rediscovered, as is evident from technological and artistic inventions such as those of Daedalus, Orpheus, Palamedes, Marsyas, Olympus and Amphion. What is of great interest is the stichomythia which follows (677d7–e5):

> ΑΘ. Ἄριστ', ὦ Κλεινία, τὸν φίλον ὅτι παρέλιπες, τὸν ἀτεχνῶς χθὲς γενόμενον.
> ΚΛ. Μῶν φράζεις Ἐπιμενίδην;
> ΑΘ. Ναί, τοῦτον· πολὺ γὰρ ὑμῖν ὑπερεπήδησε τῷ μηχανήματι τοὺς σύμπαντας, ὦ φίλε, ὃ λόγῳ μὲν Ἡσίοδος ἐμαντεύετο πάλαι, τῷ δὲ ἔργῳ ἐκεῖνος ἀπετέλεσεν, ὡς ὑμεῖς φατε.
> ΚΛ. Φαμὲν γὰρ οὖν.

> ATH: You have brilliantly, Clinias, left out your friend who was literally a man of yesterday.
> CL: Is it Epimenides you mean?
> ATH: Yes, I mean him. For he far outstripped everybody you had, my friend, by that invention of his of which he was the actual producer, as you Cretans say, although Hesiod had divined it and spoken of it long before.
> CL: We do say so.

Plato addresses here one of the principles which should govern the selection of the material of a plot, including the elements which shape dramatic time: a narrator should leave aside his origin and the prejudices and partialities imposed to him by his love for his country. In light of his respect to Epimenides (642d3–643a1), in this stichomythia Clinias is thus presented as not being swayed by his appreciation of his glorious ancestor and as not making the mistake of falsely using him as a marker of the temporal relations between the dramatic time of the story narrated by the Athenian and the present of the interlocutors.[101]

Instead, the Athenian and Clinias are presented as selecting their material on the basis of their reasoning and their preference to Homer and Hesiod. In Book 2, while arguing that music and dance should be assessed in agreement with the educated elders' predilections, the Athenian explains that people's tastes are influenced by factors such as genre, education and age. Small children prefer puppeteer shows, while older children choose comedies. Differently, educated women, adolescent boys and, perhaps, the majority of the population

---

[101] For de la Fuente (2010, 118), Plato underlines in this passage the symbolic nature of Epimenides as a mythical figure, a nature which prevents one from safely using him as the basis for chronology.

are more satisfied by tragedies (658c10–d5). At the top of this list of different audiences the Athenian places old men, namely himself and his partners, in saying that they would prefer someone who would beautifully perform a rhapsody from the *Iliad* or the *Odyssey* or of some part from Hesiod's works (658d6–9). The Athenian and Clinias agree that the elders' judgment on the most proper kind of artistic imitation should prevail in a city.[102]

In the converse passage of 677d7–e5, Plato raises some readerly speculations on the social and cultural dimensions of selecting the material which is to be used in the construction of a narrative. Plato's goal here is to demonstrate how the narrator will compose a narrative which will promote his moral and political doctrines. Clinias' choice to omit Epimenides from the elements with which the temporal backbone of the story is shaped,[103] as well as the stichomythia to be analysed in what follows, mirror Plato's interest in the intense effectiveness of the narrator's personality on his choices in transforming his material into an organised narrative whole.

One further, and equally illuminating, passage in this respect is found at the end of the account about the shepherds (680b1–d6):

ΑΘ. Δοκοῦσί μοι πάντες τὴν ἐν τούτῳ τῷ χρόνῳ πολιτείαν δυναστείαν καλεῖν, ἣ καὶ νῦν ἔτι πολλαχοῦ καὶ ἐν Ἕλλησι καὶ κατὰ βαρβάρους ἐστίν· λέγει δ' αὐτήν που καὶ Ὅμηρος γεγονέναι περὶ τὴν τῶν Κυκλώπων οἴκησιν, εἰπών —

τοῖσιν δ' οὔτ' ἀγοραὶ βουληφόροι οὔτε θέμιστες,
ἀλλ' οἵ γ' ὑψηλῶν ὀρέων ναίουσι κάρηνα
ἐν σπέσσι γλαφυροῖσι, θεμιστεύει δὲ ἕκαστος
παίδων ἠδ' ἀλόχων, οὐδ' ἀλλήλων ἀλέγουσιν.

ΚΛ. Ἔοικέν γε ὁ ποιητὴς ὑμῖν οὗτος γεγονέναι χαρίεις. καὶ γὰρ δὴ καὶ ἄλλα αὐτοῦ διεληλύθαμεν μάλ' ἀστεῖα, οὐ μὴν πολλά γε· οὐ γὰρ σφόδρα χρώμεθα οἱ Κρῆτες τοῖς ξενικοῖς ποιήμασιν.
ΜΕ. Ἡμεῖς δ' αὖ χρώμεθα μέν, καὶ ἔοικέν γε κρατεῖν τῶν τοιούτων ποιητῶν, οὐ μέντοι Λακωνικόν γε ἀλλά τινα μᾶλλον Ἰωνικὸν βίον διεξέρχεται ἑκάστοτε. νῦν μὴν εὖ τῷ σῷ λόγῳ ἔοικε μαρτυρεῖν, τὸ ἀρχαῖον αὐτῶν ἐπὶ τὴν ἀγριότητα διὰ μυθολογίας ἐπανενεγκών.
ΑΘ. Ναί· συμμαρτυρεῖ γάρ, καὶ λάβωμέν γε αὐτὸν μηνυτὴν ὅτι τοιαῦται πολιτεῖαι γίγνονταί ποτε.
ΚΛ. Καλῶς.

---

[102] Cf. 624a7–625a4, where the Athenian draws on Homer to say that Minos was the first legislator of the Cretans. On the reasoning behind the Athenian's support to the elders' aesthetic judgment, see Bartels 2012.
[103] On Clinias' use of these mythical figures as an effort to shape the temporal frame of the Athenian's story, see Sallis 2013, 79–80.

ATH: Everybody, I believe, gives the name of "headship" to the government which then existed, — and it still continues to exist to-day among both Greeks and barbarians in many quarters. And, of course, Homer mentions its existence in connection with the household system of the Cyclopes, where he says —

"No halls of council and no laws are theirs,
but within hollow caves on mountain heights
aloft they dwell, each making his own law
for wife and child; of others reck they naught."

CL: This poet of yours seems to have been a man of genius. We have also read other verses of his, and they were extremely fine; though in truth we have not read much of him, since the Cretans do not indulge much in foreign poetry.
MEG: But we Spartans do, and we regard Homer as the best of them; all the same, the mode of life he describes is always Ionian rather than Laconian. And now he appears to be confirming your statement admirably, when in his legendary account he ascribes the primitive habits of the Cyclopes to their savagery.

As will be argued in the next section, the quotation of these verses from the *Odyssey* serves as a metanarrative instruction to the reader that the account of the first societies was composed on the basis of Book 9 of the *Odyssey*. It is worth noting that once again in this passage Plato lays emphasis on the influence exercised by the narrator's socio-political identity upon the composition of the plot. By delineating Clinias' and Megillus' reactions to the Athenian's use of these verses, Plato reminds us of the issues of age and origin both for the narrator and the receivers of the story. When he hears the lines on the Cyclopes, Clinias spontaneously praises Homer for his cleverness and admits that he has studied some parts of the Homeric epics, although not many because the Cretans do not use foreign poets.[104] As in the case in which he ignored Epimenides, Clinias is again presented as disregarding the current stances of his countrymen, this time towards a poet, and treats Homer with an eye free from regional prejudices. This passage too should be read through the prism of 658d6–9, in which the three partners admit that their old age, virtue and education make them love the Homeric epics. Of course, in that case the Athenian referred to his contemporaries' admiration for a bard's performance of a rhapsody. At this point, we are informed of one further facet of their appreciation for Homer: their recognition of his value as a source of historical and ethnographical material to be used for

---

[104] Müller (1951, 68 n. 2) finds that in this case Clinias praises the content and not the form of Homeric poetry. Cf. Weil 1959, 70.

the composition of a narrative which offers a dependable representation of the past.[105]

The audience's age is also highlighted in Megillus' reaction. He admits that in Sparta, differently from on Crete, people include Homeric epics among their most popular readings and, what is more, consider him the central representative of epic poetry. It is worth noting that, although the Spartan recognises that Homer does not describe the Laconic but the Ionic way of living, he is willing to admit that the Homeric verses can be taken as a valid piece of evidence in support of the Athenian's view that there were once societies with no official legislative system. Megillus' comment on the Ionic character of the Homeric world exemplifies the Spartans' celebrated — and therefore known to ancient readerships — protectiveness towards their institutions and way of living. His admission that a literary work, although not in keeping with the Spartan code of conduct, can be harnessed in the composition of an account conveys again the same message: the choice of the material's sources should remain insusceptible to preconceptions which may emerge from the nationality of the aspiring composer of a story. We should keep in mind that Megillus is here acting not only as the receiver of the Athenian's story but also as a co-narrator, given that it is all three partners who decide jointly what material to choose and how to organise it both temporally and causally. Selectivity, as an element of the transformation of the *fabula* into the *sujet*, is presented by Plato as governed by the wisdom which results from the old age and education of the narrator.[106]

3.2.2 The ideological 'coating' of the material

Let us now return to our observation that the quotation of these verses can be taken as a self-referential statement of the narrator that he based his account not only on these four verses but rather on a significant part of Book 9 of the *Odyssey*. In particular, the account echoes the verses which pertain to Odysseus' visit at the island of the Cyclopes (9.105–566). In what follows, we will present the Homeric allusions of the account of the first societies, allusions which some-

---

105 On Megillus' appreciation of Homer as a historical source, see Weil 1959, 70 and Schöpsdau 1994, 368.
106 See Weil 1959, 70–71 on Plato's intention to show through Megillus' statement the difference between Homer's scope and that of the Athenian.

times emerge only in terms of content but in other instances are also accentuated through verbal affinities.[107]

The members of these first societies demonstrate a plethora of similarities with the Cyclopes of the *Odyssey*. At the beginning of the Athenian's account, we read that these populations did not merely inhabit mountains but lived at the top of mountains (677b1–2: ὄρειοί τινες ἂν εἶεν νομῆς, ἐν κορυφαῖς). This is also what we read about the Cyclopes in *Od*. 9.113 quoted by the Athenian (ἀλλ' οἵ γ' ὑψηλῶν ὀρέων ναίουσι κάρηνα). Furthermore, the epithet ὑψηλῶν of the Homeric verse recurs in the Platonic account in 678c2 (ἐκ γὰρ τῶν ὑψηλῶν) and twice in 682b2–3 (ἐκ τῶν ὑψηλῶν and οὐχ ὑψηλόν). The people of the Athenian's account are also inexperienced in arts, as they are not acquainted with metallurgy, while woodworking still remains at an initial stage of substandard development. As a result, they do not possess those means of transportation which could help them travel by land and sea and meet people of distant areas (678c6–d3). This information resembles the description of the Cyclopes in *Od*. 9.125–129. These verses belong to the unit of narrative on the island close to that of the Cyclopes (*Od*. 9.116–129), in which the epic poet introduces Odysseus' adventure in Polyphemus' cave. This island is uninhabited and its vegetation is wild because its land has never been cultivated.[108] One can find there packs of wild goats, which live free and are not organised by any shepherd. Furthermore, although no one has ever hunted in this island, there is an abundance of prey.

The Cyclopes, although living in proximity to this island, leave its wealth unexploited because they do not possess the art of shipbuilding, through which they could construct ships and visit it. Nor do they have any craftsmen in their workforce, who could build the ships for them. These elements, the presence of this island so close to the Cyclopes and their inability to approach it, highlight the isolation of the Cyclopes from the rest of the world, a fact which is attributed to the primitivism of their technological development. The poet obviously wishes

---

107 Cf. *Phaed*. 61b3–7, where Socrates states that he based his poetic stories on the plots of Aesop in the belief that the work of a poet is to come up with plots.
108 On this primitive period in Thucydides' *Archaeology*, see Weil 1959, 63–65. In general, Weil compares this part of the Platonic account mainly with Aristotle and Thucydides. Schöpsdau (1994, 356 ff.) believes that the Athenian's account owes much to Protagoras' and Democritus' theories, as they are expressed in the *Protagoras*. Castelnérac (2008) argues that the account of the shepherds demonstrates a great number of similarities with views expressed in the *Republic*, *Timaeus* and the *Statesman*.

to juxtapose the Cyclopes' introversion with the cosmopolitanism of Odysseus and his companions.[109]

The similarities between *Od.* 9.116–129 and the Platonic account are the following. First, both the Cyclopes and the shepherds do not possess ships, which would allow them to travel by the sea. Although the absence of naval expertise of that period was a popular theme in classical Greek literature, Plato wishes here to orientate us specifically towards the Homeric Cyclopes through the verbal echo of the Homeric ἐπ' ἀλλήλους νηυσὶν περόωσι θάλασσαν (*Od.* 9.129) in the Athenian's words on the shepherds πορεῖα δέ, ὥστ' ἐπ' ἀλλήλους τότε πορεύεσθαι κατὰ γῆν ἢ κατὰ θάλατταν (678c6–7). The inaccessible island and the Cyclopes' isolation match with the information from the Platonic account that the mountaineers did not dare to visit lowland areas (678c2–3). In both cases, the reason why the isolated population contacts other civilisations lies in the lack of technology. For the Cyclopes we read οὐδ' ἄνδρες νηῶν ἔνι τέκτονες (*Od.* 9.126), while in the Platonic narrative we find the word τέχνῃ, which comes from the same root as τέκτονες in the Athenian's words ἀπείρους εἶναι τεχνῶν (677b6) and σὺν ταῖς τέχναις (678c7–8).

As the narrative unfolds, Plato moves beyond the popular theme of naval primitivism and zooms in on some particular details of the Homeric Cyclopes' civilisation. Apart from their deficient technological training and subsequent isolation, Plato's shepherds also resemble the Cyclopes with regard to certain aspects of their daily life, namely diet, wealth, household utensils and the arts by means of which they shape them. As for their diet, the mountaineers are presented as mainly eating milk and meat (679a2–3: γάλακτος γὰρ καὶ κρεῶν οὐδαμῶς ἐνδεεῖς ἦσαν). Similarly, engagement with the extraction of milk and dairy production constitutes one of the recurring motifs in Polyphemus' portraiture (*Od.* 9.219; 222–223; 225; 232; 244–249; 297; 308–309; 340–341. The Cyclops is presented as exclusively eating meat and drinking milk and as frequently milking his animals. Furthermore, the Athenian's comment on the abundance of meat and dairy products echoes *Od.* 9.184–185 and 219–223, where we read that Polyphemus' animals were so numerous that they were crowded in the kraal, while equally plenty was the milk, which was distributed both for drinking and the production of cheese and other goods.

With regard to household utensils and the arts which produce them, Plato says that the shepherds had clothes, mattresses and houses, and that they used articles in fire for cooking and others which could not be used in fire (679a5–6:

---

[109] Of course, Plato is also inspired by current accounts of a peaceful and virtuous life as found in other sources of the Classical era. See Weil 1959, 60.

καὶ σκευῶν ἐμπύρων τε καὶ ἀπύρων ηὐπόρουν). Immediately after this description, the Athenian clarifies that the highlanders had such equipment because they were acquainted with the arts of moulding and weaving, whose application does not presuppose the use of iron (679a6-7: αἱ πλαστικαὶ γὰρ καὶ ὅσαι πλεκτικαὶ τῶν τεχνῶν οὐδὲ ἓν προσδέονται σιδήρου). The use of these arts explains (γάρ) not only the shepherds' utensils but also their clothing and the mattresses. However, with regard to the utensils in particular, the art of moulding makes us think of vessels made of clay, while the art of weaving is associated with baskets. Furthermore, the clarification that the shepherds use these vessels is offered immediately after the detail that they ate meat. In this way, the narrator conveys the impression that they used these vessels in order to stock or cook meat and milk. This information echoes the scene from Book 9 of the *Odyssey*, in which Polyphemus is presented to distribute the milk by putting half of it in weaved wicker baskets (*Od.* 9.247: πλεκτοῖς ἐν ταλάροισιν; cf. *Leg.* 679a5-7: σκευῶν ... ἀπύρων ... αἱ πλεκτικαί) and the other half in pails (*Od.* 9.248: ἐν ἄγγεσιν; cf. 679a5-6: σκευῶν ἐμπύρων ... αἱ πλαστικαὶ γάρ ...).

However, despite the unquestionable similarities between the Cyclopes and the Platonic shepherds, the latter represent an ethically inverted reflection of the former. The main similarity between the two societies, which Plato stresses more than any other point, lies in the fact that neither of them has written laws, with each family living separately from other families and following the rules imposed by the father. As for the shepherds, the Athenian says that they "had no need of lawgivers, and that in those days it was not as yet usual to have such a thing [...], but [they] lived by following custom and what is called "patriarchal" law" (680a3-7). With regard to the Cyclopes he cites *Od.* 9.112: τοῖσιν δ' οὔτ' ἀγοραὶ βουληφόροι οὔτε θέμιστες and *Od.* 9.115: παίδων ἠδ' ἀλόχων, οὐδ' ἀλλήλων ἀλέγουσι. The words πατρίοις νόμοις (680a6-7) could mean "traditional" and not necessarily patriarchal, namely those who are inherited by a father. However, in this specific context the characterisation πάτριος is to be taken as meaning paternal and therefore to echo the reference to the Cyclopes' fathers who administer their children and wives. This is so because, after a few lines, although referring to a power which is exercised both by fathers and mothers (680e1-2: τὴν ἀρχήν ... ἐκ πατρὸς καὶ μητρὸς γεγονέναι, οἷς ἑπόμενοι καθάπερ ὄρνιθες), the Athenian describes the bucolic society as patriarchal (680e3: πατρονομούμενοι). At this specific point, the Homeric flavour is further underlined by the phrase καθάπερ ὄρνιθες (680e2), equivalents of which are frequently found in both the *Iliad* and the *Odyssey*.[110]

---

110 *Il.* 5.778; *Il.* 7.59; *Il.* 9.323; *Il.* 14.290; *Od.* 5.51; *Od.* 22.302 (Weil 1959, 72).

However, although the absence of a common legislative framework is presented for the Cyclopes as a flaw which is synonymous with their savagery and injustice, for the shepherds it emerges as the fruit of a harmonious and in all respects just life. In the Cyclopes' case, the absence of laws stems from their arrogance and savagery, as the very first characterisation offered by the poet for them is that they are "arrogant" and "lawless" (*Od.* 9.106: ὑπερφιάλων ἀθεμίστων). By contrast, the shepherds of the Platonic account lack an official legislative system not because they condemn the institutions of justice and legislation but because they are absolutely obedient to their ancestral rules and because they lack writing skills. Also, in the *Odyssey* lawlessness is associated with the antisocial temperament of Polyphemus, who is presented as disdaining the company of others and as having unjust thoughts in his isolation. We read the same association in Odysseus' words that he decided to visit a man who "was wild, with no knowledge of justice or civil rights" (*Od.* 9.215: ἄγριον, οὔτε δίκας εὖ εἰδότα οὔτε θέμιστας). This characterisation of Polyphemus is also offered by Odysseus' companions, who try to dissuade him from irritating with his words as a "savage" (*Od.* 9.494: ἄγριον ἄνδρα). On the other hand, the Platonic shepherds are presented by the Athenian as enjoying living with one another and as doing so in concord and friendship (678c5; 678e9–679c8).

Another difference between the Cyclopes and the shepherds emerges from a strong verbal echo. Odysseus says to his comrades that he wishes to explore the Cyclopes' island in order to discover whether its inhabitants are "cruel, wild, and unjust, or whether they love strangers and fear the gods in their thoughts" (*Od.* 9.175–176).[111] The words offered by the poet in this case are ὑβρισταί τε …οὐδὲ δίκαιοι, which essentially represent what the Cyclopes will be proved to be. By contrast, as we saw in the previous section, the shepherds, who are neither excessively rich nor poor, were neither insolent nor unjust (679b8–9: οὔτε γὰρ ὕβρις οὔτ' ἀδικία; cf. 662a2: εἴπερ ἄδικος εἴη καὶ ὑβριστής). This verbal echo, like others too, are instances of Plato's effort to demonstrate to a careful reader the way in which the composer of a narrative can change the details of the material she or he draws from another story in order to realise the goal setting of her or his own account. In this way, the Athenian narrator conveys the message that the features of societies such as those of the shepherds and the Cyclopes should be treated as virtues and not flaws.

The story of the highlanders inverts the ethical core of the Homeric episode not only by idealising what is presented by the poet as the Cyclopes' defects but also by demonising what was commonly taken as Odysseus' virtues. This tech-

---

111 I follow Murray's (1919) translation of the *Odyssey*.

nique is discernible in the contrast that Plato shapes between Odysseus' counterfactual thoughts about the island close to the land of the Cyclopes and the mountaineers. When Odysseus describes the island, he shares with the Phaeacians his thoughts about how this island would be, had it been exploited by a population of developed material arts and culture. The Cyclopes could have had a beautifully built island. The epithet Odysseus uses here is ἐυκτιμένην (*Od.* 9.130), which is used in Homer seventeen times for cities and islands when they are mentioned as cities.[112] This epithet therefore denotes the existence of a developed political life and urban infrastructure. In this respect, the poet, by saying that the Cyclopes do not have a well-built island, implies that they are not organised within the framework of an urban design. Odysseus also believes that the Cyclopes could have profited from the fertile earth of the island had they developed agriculture. Last, the island could be exploited in terms of fishery and shipping, as it is surrounded by waters rich in marine life and because at many points its coastline shapes natural ports. Odysseus' thoughts about how the Cyclopes could have taken advantage of the island had they developed shipping, agriculture and technology mirror his disdain towards the Cyclopes' primitivism.

On the other hand, in the Platonic account the absence of advanced material culture is nowhere treated as a blemish of the first societies but is instead foregrounded as the source of their ethical and political merits. The fact that they have not built cities and are not in a position to visit others offers them the opportunity to remain unstained from the deceits and guiles by means of which citizens try to harm each other. The two main *desiderata* in Odysseus' mind (familiarisation with other cities through sea travelling and the development of urban political life) are thus presented by the Athenian as choices to avoid, choices which generate more negative than positive effects. Second, although the shepherds are presented as having not developed agriculture, they live a prosperous life rich in animal-based foods. In all respects, the mentality of Odysseus' counterfactual speculations in *Od.* 9.130–141 is juxtaposed with the idyllic picture delineated by Plato in the account of the highlanders.

One further antithesis emerges between Odysseus' insight and the shepherds' naivety. In the scene of Odysseus' encounter with Polyphemus, the two characters are juxtaposed with each other mainly on an intellectual level. To present here all the facets of this contrast transcends the scope of our analysis.[113]

---

[112] *Il.* 2.570; *Il.* 2.712; *Il.* 5.543; *Il.* 6.13; *Il.* 6.391; *Il.* 9.129; *Il.* 9.271; *Il.* 17.611; *Il.* 20.496; *Il.* 21.40; *Il.* 21.77; *Od.* 4.342; *Od.* 9.130; *Od.* 17.133; *Od.* 22.52; *Od.* 24.226; *Od.* 24.336.
[113] See Schein 1970; Bremmer 2002.

However, it is worth noting one specific antithesis that is particularly illuminating of the way that Book 9 of the *Odyssey* is associated with the Athenian's account in the *Laws*. Odysseus and Polyphemus differ in terms of the degree to which each of them realises that someone lies to them or tries to deceive them. In *Od*. 9.279–280, Polyphemus endeavours to fish Odysseus out on where his ship is anchored, obviously in order to find and destroy it. Odysseus senses the trap and lies to him that his ship has already been destroyed by Poseidon. Referring to his ability to apprehend such efforts of deceit, Odysseus says "so he spoke, tempting me; but I knew too much to be tricked / and when I replied it was with guile of my own" (*Od*. 9.281–282: ὣς φάτο πειράζων, ἐμὲ δ' οὐ λάθεν εἰδότα πολλά, / ἀλλά μιν ἄψορρον προσέφην δολίοις ἐπέεσσι). On the other hand, Polyphemus fails to take notice of Odysseus' lies. He believes that Odysseus' ship is destroyed, gets intoxicated by the wine cunningly offered to him, and never doubts that Odysseus is named "No one".

What serves in the *Odyssey* as the cornerstone of Polyphemus' caricature is promoted by the Athenian as an ethical merit of the shepherds. The latter, "being simple-minded, when they heard things called bad or good, they took what was said for gospel-truth and believed it. For none of them had the shrewdness of the modern man to suspect a falsehood" (note the contrast between Odysseus' cunning in *Od*. 9.281: ἐμὲ δ' οὐ λάθεν εἰδότα πολλά and the shepherds' lack of knowledge in *Leg*. 679c4–5: ψεῦδος γὰρ ὑπονοεῖν οὐδεὶς ἠπίστατο διὰ σοφίαν).[114] In the Platonic account, to distinguish truth from lies, which is Odysseus' virtue, appears to be unwelcome in a community where ignorance breeds serenity and obedience to the ancestral rules. What is more, ignorance is also the reason why the shepherds differ from the Cyclopes too, as the highlanders believed in gods while the Cyclopes did not.

One last antithesis between Odysseus and the highlanders pertains to issues of artistic expertise. The shepherds' ignorance of metallurgy and their elementary knowledge of woodworking are contrasted with the two similes through which Odysseus describes how he blinded Polyphemus. In the first simile, Odysseus compares the way that he and his comrades revolved the stake in Polyphemus' eye with the rotation of a carpenter's gimlet (*Od*. 9.384–388). It is worth noting that Odysseus refers to woodworking tools, while the Athenian repeatedly states that in the age of the shepherds all tools were lost due to the cataclysm (677c4–9). In the second simile, Odysseus compares the sound com-

---

114 Fagan (2013, 110) discerns the antithesis between Odysseus' knowledge, which stems from his cosmopolitanism and the shepherds' isolation and naivety, but she compares Homer with *Laws*' Book 4.

ing out from Polyphemus' burning eye with the sound that an incandescent metal makes when it is put out by the blacksmith (*Od.* 9.391–394). The words χαλκεύς (*Od.* 9.391) and σιδήρου (*Od.* 9.393) are echoed by the words of the Athenian about the shepherds' ignorance of metallurgy (678c9–d1: σίδηρος γὰρ καὶ χαλκός ... ἠφάνιστο).

In essence, the Athenian extracts the main feature of the Homeric delineation of the Cyclopes' image, their primitivism,[115] and disengages this element from the Homeric interpretation that this stems from the Cyclopes' savagery. He furthermore replaces this interpretation with his own, which emerges from his own narrative. The absence of technology, the elementary development in terms of arts and reading and writing, and the lack of agriculture are no longer signs of the savagery of a people, but, on the contrary, can occasionally secure the ideal circumstances under which this people may reach absolute virtue and harmony.[116] This alternative delineation of primitivism as a model of a virtuous life serves the goal of the three aspiring legislators: to shape through the representation of the past a national identity for the Magnesians, an identity which is marked by simplicity, contempt for wealth, respect for the traditional customs, aversion to sea travelling and indifference to foreign institutions.

It is of particular importance for our analysis that Plato is not only concerned with the use of narratives as a means of configuring a national identity for a people under construction; he also draws our attention to the question of what are the compositional procedures through which to construct stories which serve the creation of intentional history. He invites us to confront questions such as "How should we structure these stories?", "On what material should we base their content?", and "How are we to incorporate this material into the plot of the stories?" That Plato is not only interested in the sources of the material (in this case, Homer) but also in how a narrator should elaborate on it in support of the goal setting of the *sujet* under construction is also evident from Megillus' reaction to the Athenian's quotation of the epic verses. For, after recognising Homer as the most significant epic poet (see above), he closes his statement with the following words (680d1–3):

> νῦν μὴν εὖ τῷ σῷ λόγῳ ἔοικε μαρτυρεῖν, τὸ ἀρχαῖον αὐτῶν ἐπὶ τὴν ἀγριότητα διὰ μυθολογίας ἐπανενεγκών.

---

115 England 1921; Weil 1959, 71; Prauscello 2017.
116 In this way, Plato also questions the progressivist accounts of his age, which presented humanity as advancing from an uncivilised state into a civilised stage, such as are evident from Protagoras' myth in the *Protagoras* (Piette 1985 followed by Nightingale 1999, 304–305).

> And now he appears to be confirming your statement admirably, when in his legendary account he ascribes the primitive habits of the Cyclopes to their savagery.

In this passage, Plato touches upon the act of modulating the material, which is to be used for the synthesis of a plot, from a similar perspective to that from which he examines the same subject in the *Statesman*. In Chapter 1, we saw that the Eleatic Visitor, instead of merely narrating his cosmological account, introduced it with some comments, through which he allowed us to enter his compositional laboratory. He revealed us what tales he would use (the quarrel of Atreus and Thyestes, the one on the Age of Cronus, and tales on earth-born men) and encouraged us to realise that, by elaborating on this material, he would endeavour to denude the selected data of the role it had in the plot, and to colour it with a new role, which will serve a new plot and the specific goals of its narrator.

The Athenian's quotation of the Homeric verses and the Spartan's aforementioned comment play a similar role in the account of the shepherds to the introduction of the myth in the *Statesman*. Here too, Plato opens for us a window into the compositional laboratory of the Athenian Visitor and lets us tail after him in his effort to transform the material drawn from the *Odyssey* into a fully incorporated and integral part of the plot he is composing. Similarly to the Eleatic Visitor, the Athenian could have merely described the life of the highlanders without informing his interlocutors and the readers that he was inspired by Book 9 of the *Odyssey*. However, as was the case in the *Statesman*, here too Plato wishes to lay emphasis on the very procedure of the material's extraction from a source and its incorporation into a new plot. Megillus addresses exactly the same issue posed by the Eleatic Visitor: the composer of a narrative occasionally uses his material in a completely different fashion to the way this material is used to contribute to the logic of the plot from which it was drawn.

Plato's keen interest in sharing the ways in which material from the epics is incorporated into new plots is also shown by the fact that the Athenian proceeds with a second metanarrative clarification that he bases his account on Homeric material, this time from the *Iliad*. After completing his story of the shepherds, he turns, as we have already seen, to the second phase of human political society and legislation. The several families join each other and construct bigger cities, while people move from the highlands to the foot of the mountains and start engaging with agricultural activities. These families join forces on a legal level too, as certain individuals are elected by them to distinguish the best rules, in their opinion, from among the unwritten laws of each fraction. The third phase of human history then follows: people now found cities in the lowlands and begin to conduct maritime enterprises. Ilium is one from among these cities. The Athenian introduces this part of his narrative by explaining that both for the second and the third phase he has drawn on *Il.* 20.216–218 (681e1–5):

ΑΘ. "Ὁ μετὰ τὸ δεύτερον καὶ "Ομηρος ἐπεσημήνατο, λέγων τὸ τρίτον οὕτω γεγονέναι. "κτίσσε δὲ Δαρδανίην" γάρ πού φησιν, "ἐπεὶ οὔπω "Ιλιος ἰρὴ

ἐν πεδίῳ πεπόλιστο, πόλις μερόπων ἀνθρώπων,
ἀλλ' ἔθ' ὑπωρείας ᾤκουν πολυπιδάκου "Ιδης."

The same that Homer himself mentioned next to the second, when he said that the third form arose in this way. His verses run thus "Dardania he founded when as yet the holy keep of Ilium

was not built upon the plain, a town for mortal folk,
but still they dwelt upon the highland slopes of many-fountained Ida."

Similarly to the previous quotation of the verses on the Cyclopes, this one too is followed by a brief praise of Homer. The Athenian confirms Megillus' opinion that Homer can offer testimonies about the past, by saying that he refers to the foundation of Dardania and Troy as well as to the Cyclopes inspired by the gods and occasionally telling the truth about actual events (682a1–5). Once again, Plato does not miss the opportunity to remind us of the interlocutors' love and admiration of the Homeric epics. In this way, he underlines how age and education play an important role in the narrator's choice of the material on the basis of which the *sujet* will be arranged.

These verses constitute the groundwork for both the events themselves of the plot and their temporal arrangement. In particular, the verses offer two periods of time which follow the age of the highlanders. The first period is when people inhabit semi-mountainous places and develop agriculture. The Athenian places this Iliadic information at the narrative juncture between the bucolic period and the next one by saying that "next [...] they turn to farming on the hill-sides" (680e6 – 681a1: μετὰ δὲ ταῦτά [...] ἐπὶ γεωργίας τὰς ἐν ταῖς ὑπωρείαις τρέπονται πρώτας), which echoes *Il.* 20.218 ἔθ' ὑπωρείας ᾤκεον. In the ensuing transition from the second period to the third one, the Athenian rephrases the epic "Ιλιος ἰρὴ ἐν πεδίῳ πεπόλιστο (*Il.* 20.216–217) at the beginning of his short story about Troy (682b2–3: κατῳκίσθη δή, φαμέν, ἐκ τῶν ὑψηλῶν εἰς μέγα τε καὶ καλὸν πεδίον "Ιλιον). He also takes advantage of the details that the mountain Ida is crossed by many rivers (*Il.* 20.218: πολυπιδάκου "Ιδης) when he adds that the hill where Troy was founded had many rivers flowing down from Ida (682b4–5: ποταμοὺς πολλοὺς ἄνωθεν ἐκ τῆς "Ιδης ὡρμημένους).

3.2.3 Creating questions and answering them

In the narratives about the Doric confederation (683c8–693c5) and the decadence of the Persian institutions (694a3–698a8), Plato demonstrates one further way in which a narrator can filter the material to be narrated through the moral code he proposes for a society. This scheme can be synoptically described as follows: the narrator initially relates the events in such a way that certain questions are raised in the readers' minds about the ensuing plot development. Suddenly, the narrator interrupts the unfolding of the story and reveals, in an ethico-didactic excursus, some views, on the basis of which the questions which emerged from the preceding account can be answered. Finally, the narrator resumes his narration, interpreting the events and thereby answering these questions on the basis of the views he expressed in the excursus.

Let us see how this scheme is first employed in the account on the Doric alliance. The Athenian opens his narrative with the comment that everything he has related so far, but also all those he will narrate about Sparta in what follows, will be of great help for the three conversation-partners in their effort to apprehend what choices of the polities in the past have contributed to the preservation of laws and what other choices led to their attrition (683b1–6). This programmatic statement prepares the readers that what they will read in the ensuing account might pertain to the eventual corruption of the Doric institutions.[117] The Athenian urges his interlocutors to follow him in their imagination to the period when Argos, Messene and Sparta, as well as all their Greek allies, had reached the pick of their prime (683c8–d4). The three cities agreed that they divide their army into three parts, and then appointed Temenus as a king of Argos, Cresphontes of Messene, and Procles and Eurysthenes as kings of Sparta. The three cities then exchanged mutual oaths to help each other in case someone would attempt to overthrow their governments or those of any city-member of the confederation (683c8–e2).

Exactly at this point, the Athenian interrupts the plot development in order to remind his friends of the fact that kingship and all kinds of government are periodically overthrown by the governors' own mistakes, before expressing his confidence that what is to be narrated will confirm this view (683e3–684a2). In this way, through the opening remarks of 683b1–6 and this comment, this first part of the Doric narrative unfolds within the framework of a ring composition, which prepares us to witness a story of corruption and fall of a kingship. This

---

[117] For this kind of hint that creates readerly suspense, see Liotsakis 2021, 5–6.

segment of the story thereby elicits its audience's interest in the way that the Doric alliance was led to its doom.[118]

However, our expectation that we will read about the Doric kings' decisive mistakes is for a while held in suspense, as the narrator declines to reveal the revelation of these mistakes. For in the immediately ensuing account the Athenian shifts his interest towards the political merits of the Doric confederation. The first advantage of the Dorians lies in the fact that they shared common laws on how rulers will exercise their power and on how the peoples will obey their kings' will. Also, as we saw, the kings swore not to succumb to the temptation of gradually adapting authoritarian modes of kingship, while the citizens swore not to allow anyone to overthrow their kings. Each king and each people were asked to offer their assistance to anyone who needed it. This agreement, the Athenian argues, had two significant, positive ramifications for the three cities: first, each of them enjoyed the assistance of the other two and, second, they had also secured what has been presented in Book 1 as a legislator's major goal, namely a people's willingness to obey the laws (684a2–c10). The Athenian describes this advantage as "the most important" (684b5: τό γε μέγιστον). In this way, he enhances our wonder about how a kingship which had secured such a crucial merit was led to fall. Furthermore, the Athenian maintains that the Dorians' willingness to obey to their laws is an element which everyone would advise a legislator to secure for his country (684c1–6). In this way, Plato invites the reader to identify with the interlocutors' view that this was indeed one of the advantages of the Dorians. As a result, when Megillus is later surprised by the Athenian's statement that these cities would eventually decline (685a1), the reader is already predisposed to sympathise with the Spartan's wonder.[119]

This retarding section of the account unfolds with one further merit of the Doric confederation. According to the Athenian, a legislator sometimes realises that he cannot secure equality among the citizens of a city unless he proceeds with the action of land redistribution and the prescription of debts. However, in these cases, the Athenian notes, the lawgiver faces the reactions of those citizens whose interests are harmed by such changes. The Dorians, the Athenian adds, were absolved of such turbulence when they decreed their laws, because they shared their land without disagreements and there were no debts owed from the past (684d1–e6). This positive element too is presented by the Athenian

---

[118] This is the so-called 'harm anticipation phenomenon' in suspense. See Liotsakis 2021, 5–6.
[119] On the techniques through which a narrator leads the reader's horizon of knowledge to identify with that of the characters in a story and thereby creates suspense, see Liotsakis 2021, 10–15.

as significant (684d1: οὐ σμικρόν), as the Dorians avoided social uneasiness, which is one of the greatest calamities for a polity (684d4: ἡ μεγίστη τῶν μέμψεων). This new and positive aspect of the Dorian confederation increases even more our curiosity about how the Dorians ended up destroying the harmonious social life which they once used to enjoy. And exactly at this point, the Athenian emphatically repeats this question in the minds even of those readers who have forgotten it (684e7–8): "How was it then, my good sirs, that their settlement and legislation turned out so badly?"

At the beginning of the narrative, the Athenian had warned that the Dorian account would be a story of political fall. However, at that point he had not clarified whether this fall would pertain to the Dorians or the preceding political formations. By means of the technique of piece-meal revelation, the Athenian here removes all doubts we have had up to this point, and reveals that he is referring to the fall of the Dorians.[120] The additional information we receive here is that, from among the three cities, only Sparta succeeded in retaining its legal and political system. Nonetheless, no details are offered about the way in which this unpleasant development came about. We are thus forced to speculate on these unspecified circumstances, while our suspense about whether or not the ensuing narrative will answer our question is further enhanced by Megillus' comment "the question is no easy one" (685a5). Our fear that our question will remain unanswered coexists with the hope that the ensuing account can enlighten us in the best possible way, as the Athenian says to Megillus (685a6–b1): "yet surely in our consideration and enquiry into this subject, indulging in an old man's sober play with laws, we ought to proceed on our journey painlessly, as we said when we first started out".[121]

However, the Athenian once again frustrates our expectations and, instead of exposing the Dorians' mistakes, offers us a second retarding section on two further merits of the Dorian confederation. The basic technique through which he elicits our suspense on why the regimes of Messene and Argos declined equates our horizon of knowledge with that of the protagonists of the story.[122] For in the ensuing account, he does not merely relate what he himself takes to be the Dorians' strength, as he did with the previous two advantages, but instead he presents the picture that both Greeks and non-Greeks (including the

---

120 On piece-meal revelation as a means by which to create suspense, see Rengakos 1999, 321–323.
121 The coexistence of fear and hope is a major prerequisite for creating suspense in narratives. See Liotsakis 2021, 5–6.
122 Liotsakis 2021, 10–15.

Dorians themselves) had for the Dorians. First, we read of the Greeks' hope that, if necessary, the alliance would come for help not only of the cities of the Peloponnese but also of the entire Greece, as the enemies of Troy once dared to attack it counting on the power of Ninus' Assyrians (685b7–c5). We then read of the fears of the Dorians' enemies, who were afraid of them out of the belief that the Greek power which conquered Troy was only a part of the current Dorian League. Besides, the army was now organised by three cities and under the rule of kings, all of whom were descendants of Heracles. The kinship of the kings, the Athenian narrates, was taken by many people of that period to guarantee concord among the three leading members of the alliance. Third, the Heracleidae were even more powerful than the Pelopidae, given that the latter may have conquered the Trojans but were defeated by the Heracleidae. Last, everyone's optimism of that period about the future of the Dorians is enhanced by the fact that the latter have received the reassurances of the oracles (685c5–686a6).

We as readers thus have to keep asking ourselves how such a robust political and military power could possibly have declined. And, as in 684e7–8, here too even those readers who have not retained this question as the prism through which to read about all the aforementioned merits of the Dorians, are reminded by the Athenian of this very question (686a7–b7):

ΑΘ. Ταῦτα δὴ τὰ μεγάλα οὕτως προσδοκώμενα διέπτατο, ὡς ἔοικε, τότε ταχύ, πλὴν ὅπερ εἴπομεν νυνδὴ σμικροῦ μέρους τοῦ περὶ τὸν ὑμέτερον τόπον, καὶ τοῦτο δὴ πρὸς τὰ δύο μέρη πολεμοῦν οὐ πώποτε πέπαυται μέχρι τὰ νῦν· ἐπεὶ γενομένη γε ἡ τότε διάνοια καὶ συμφωνήσασα εἰς ἕν, ἀνυπόστατον ἄν τινα δύναμιν ἔσχε κατὰ πόλεμον.
ΜΕ. Πῶς γὰρ οὔ;
ΑΘ. Πῶς οὖν καὶ πῇ διώλετο; ἆρ' οὐκ ἄξιον ἐπισκοπεῖν τηλικοῦτον καὶ τοιοῦτον σύστημα ἥτις ποτὲ τύχη διέφθειρε;

ATH. But it seems that these great expectations speedily vanished, except only, as we said, in regard to that small fraction, your State of Laconia; and ever since, up to the present day, this fraction has never ceased warring against the other two. For if the original intention had been realised, and if they had been in accord about their policy, it would have created a power invincible in war.
MEG. It certainly would.
ATH. How then, and by what means, was it destroyed? Is it not worth while to enquire by what stroke of fortune so grand a confederacy was wrecked?

So, up to this point the Athenian has elicited readerly suspense about why the Dorian alliance failed to retain its laws and regimes unharmed. Through the short introduction of the account, we were informed that we were reading a story which would reveal to us, as the preceding narratives did, not only what choices contribute to the preservation of a polity's laws and regime, but also what other decisions lead to their destruction. In this way, the Athenian foreshadowed that the Dorian account will be a story of political decline. This message is indeed confirmed by the ensuing plot development. However, as we saw, in the meantime the narrator chooses not to answer how the Dorians were led to their decline, but prefers instead to leave readerly curiosity unsatiated through the repetition of the same retarding scheme: he twice presents the merits of the Dorian legislation and regime and each time ends his exposition by posing the question of how the laws of such strong and well-promising polities were destroyed. The reader is thereby forced not only to ask why the Dorians corrupted their laws but also to experience uneasiness because the narrative cannot offer her the answer so far. Consequently, the Athenian conveys the impression in the reader's mind that the narrative up to this point is insufficient and that the reader needs something more in order to find the answers to her questions. This "something more", as the Athenian will presently reveal, will offer an interpretive filter of the events which stems from the views expressed in Books 1 and 2.

This interpretive filter is offered in the extensive digression of 686c7–690c9, where the Athenian interrupts his narration and introduces three criteria for assessing political systems. The first criterion contends that the degree of a polity's success should not be deemed according to the polity's power, wealth, honours and the freedom to do whatever it wishes. In particular, the Athenian complains that he and his companions have not chosen the proper method to assess the Dorians. As many other people usually do on sundry subjects, they too assume that the Dorian confederation could have achieved significant feats had its leaders known how to take advantage of it. Usually, the Athenian continues, such counterfactual thoughts commonly take as political feats the ability of a city to impose its free will on others, or its exceptional wealth, the honours it receives from other cities, and the aristocratic origins of its leaders. Still, the Athenian objects, all these should not be used to judge the quality of a polity (686c7–e8). The Athenian reminds us of what a careful reader would anyway remember: this thesis, namely the underestimation of wealth, honours and the ability to do whatever one wishes, has already been expressed in 631b3–632b1.[123] In particular, he reminds us of the disagreement he had with his partners about what goal a legislator should have. Although Clinias and Megillus had argued that all lawgivers should pursue the military power of the cities they decree laws for, the Athenian had argued that a lawgiver should endeavour to secure not only the bravery of the citizens but also all other virtues. It is in this spirit, the

---

[123] On the connection between 631–632 and 688a–b, see Stalley 1983, 38.

Athenian says, that he believes that the Dorians also did not fail in preserving their laws because of their cowardice but due to their ignorance (688a1–e2).

The second principle of political assessment emerges from the definition of ignorance offered by the Athenian immediately afterwards. Ignorance is defined here as the mental state in which (a) we find unpleasant what our reason, opinion and knowledge recognise as virtuous, and/or conversely (b) in which we find pleasure in things which our reason, opinion and knowledge recognise as unethical. In other words, ignorance is the mental state in which our pleasures and dissatisfactions do not co-operate with what is prescribed to us as ethical or unethical according to our opinion emerging from our reason (689a1–c5). This definition of ignorance echoes the definition of education of Book 2. So, according to the Athenian, on a collective level a city is marked by ignorance when its citizens disobey its governors and laws. In this respect, political power should not be offered to disobedient citizens, no matter how intelligent and skilful they are in other arts, but to the obedient ones even if they are utterly inefficient even in the most basic affairs (689c6–e3). This thesis is one further echo of the views expressed in Books 1 and 2, specifically of the view that any kind of expertise which lacks reason is of no value.[124]

The third principle of political evaluation, which has not been previously expressed, states that there are numerous different kinds of power: parents control their children; the noble lead the ignoble; the elders impose their will to the younger ones; masters rule their slaves; the powerful master the weak; most importantly, the ignorant should follow the connoisseurs; and, lastly, offices should be assigned by lot (690a1–e6).

These three principles constitute the key which unlocks the answer to the question about both the decadence of the Argive and Messenian polities and the preservation of the Spartan laws. The Athenian offers his interpretation of these events by imparting advice to a lawgiver to reconsider the reasons why the kings of Argos and Messene destroyed their own powers and those of their cities. Plato helps us realise that the ensuing account will interpret the past on the basis of the ethical principles and views of the interlocutors' present. The first explanation of the Doric decline is based on the second principle of political assessment, namely the definition of ignorance as the incompatibility between one's reason and one's pleasures and dissatisfactions. For, according to the Athenian, the kings of the two Doric cities, from a certain point onwards, found pleasure in endeavouring to preponderate over the laws of their countries, although their reason had once led them to swear not to do so (691a3–9). This

---

[124] Brisson 2012, 288–289.

incompatibility is taken by the Athenian as "the height of ignorance" (691a6). For this reason, the lawgivers should not have bestowed such a great power on these kings, given that human nature is inescapably corrupted by great power (691b1–d6).

After this explanation, the only question left to be answered pertains to why Sparta managed to avoid the corruption of its power and institutions. The Athenian answers this question through the prism of his third principle of the digression, namely the classification of different modes of rule. According to the Athenian, the Spartans, contrary to the decision taken by the Argives and the Messeneans, did not offer excessive power to their kings. First, the god helped them by administering the royal power to two kings. Later on, a certain lawgiver, escorted by divine assistance (i.e. Lycurgus), as he was seeing the two kings becoming arrogant, intermingled the audacious youth of the kings with the prudence of the elders, by rendering the votes of the twenty elders equal to those of the kings. The Athenian seems here to mean that this political change satisfied two kinds of power: the supremacy of the noble ones over the ignoble and the young ones' respect to the elders. Afterwards, another lawgiver introduced the institution of the ephors, an office which was assigned to citizens by lot, which exemplifies the seventh mode of political rule of the digression. The narrative ends with the Athenian's counterfactual comment that, had the three cities managed to remain united, the alliance would have survived and they would not have brought shame upon Greece in the way in which they, divided as they were, faced the Persians (691d5–693c5).

This tripartite scheme — the narration of the events, digression with political views, and the interpretation of the events on the basis of these views — is also used, in a slightly different form, in the account on the decadence of the Persian institutions (694a3–698a8). As in the Doric account, here too the Athenian programmatically explains that the ensuing narrative will be a story of a gradual political corruption. After completing his account on the Dorians, the Athenian concludes that every polity should preserve concord, freedom and friendship (693b1–c5). When Clinias encourages him to develop his thoughts on this matter (693c6–d1), the Athenian explains that monarchy and democracy constitute the two principal regimes, from which all cities should draw elements in order to prosper and secure love, freedom and concord for their citizens. He also adds that the two polities which represent monarchy and democracy, namely Persia and Athens, were led to the extremes of each regime respectively, the Persians by strengthening the king's power more than was needed and the Athenians by offering excessive freedom to the people (693d2–694a2). With these words, the Athenian foreshadows that the two stories to follow will pertain the fall of the Persian and the Athenian institutions.

Similarly to the Doric account, in his narrative on the Persians, although preparing the reader that through his story he will explain the reasons of their political corruption, the Athenian begins with the period in which the Persian kings ruled their country properly. During Cyrus' reign, the Persians had found the 'golden ratio' between slavery and freedom. The authorities offered much freedom to the citizens, who were therefore satisfied with their leaders and followed them to war willingly. Furthermore, citizens who demonstrated a special degree of cleverness were allowed by the authorities to participate in the process of decision-making (694a3–b7). However, as in the Doric narrative, this favourable delineation of the Persian politics ends with the following question (694c1–3): "How came it, then, that they were ruined in Cambyses' reign, and nearly restored again under Darius? Shall I use a kind of divination to picture this?"

In our analysis of the Doric account, we have demonstrated that the Athenian, each time he asks the reasons of Argos' and Messene's political decadence, delays answering this question by offering further merits of the Doric confederation. Yet in this case, he offers his answer immediately by continuing his weaving of the plot development. The explanation he offers for the Persians' corruption stems from the views expressed in Books 1 and 2. The Athenian attributes the decadence of the Persian institutions to the fact that Cyrus was constantly engaged with military expeditions and therefore neglected his children's education. The mothers of the princes educated and overindulged them by allowing no one to oppose their will. As a result, the spoiled children never learned to deign any kind of power upon them, which is why they had no qualms to assassinate each other, a situation which culminated in Cambyses' despotism (694c5–695c2).

This interpretation is based on certain views of Books 1 and 2. One echo of them pertains to the obfuscation of proper reason by factors such as anger, power, etc. What is more, this connection too is not only realised on a semantic but also on a verbal level as well. In Book 1, the Athenian develops his argumentation in favour of the usefulness of inebriation in human life. His first argument is as follows: inebriation assists people to develop their shame and self-control. This is so because, when one enters a state of intoxication, her or his emotions, such as anger, love, hubris, cowardice and lust for money, become more intense and in such cases one boasts more about her or his beauty, wealth and power (649c8–d7). Furthermore, the Athenian exaggerates by claiming that all these elements, due to the pleasure which accompanies them, can even drive an inebriate individual mad (649d6–7). It is worth noting that the Athenian associates anger and lack of knowledge with madness when these two elements are followed by inebriation.

In a similar vein, while touching upon the Persian queens who spoil their children, the Athenian proceeds with the following comment on Cambyses (695b3–6): "over-pampered and undisciplined as they were, first, the one killed the other, through annoyance at his being put on an equality with himself, and presently, being mad with drink and debauchery, he lost his own thrown at the hands of the Medes". Needless to say, in this case the element of intoxication is used in a metaphorical fashion. Nonetheless, here too we are faced with a phenomenon similar to the one the Athenian described in 649c8–d7. Whenever an individual possesses power but has not received the proper education, she or he may be intoxicated by arrogance and anger to the point of insanity. The verbal echoes between the two passages accentuate the similarity of content even further (649d5–7: ἀμαθία ... ἰσχύς ... μεθύσκοντα παράφρονας ποιεῖ; cf. 695b5–6: μαινόμενος ὑπὸ μέθης τε καὶ ἀπαιδευσίας; compare the metaphorical use of inebriation in 639b7: ὑπὸ μέθης τοῦ φόβου ναυτιᾷ).[125]

A similar explanation is also offered by the Athenian for the second fall of the Persian institutions, the one from Darius' reign to that of Xerxes. Here, the Athenian, as in the Dorian account, proceeds with an ethico-didactic digression (695d5–697c4), in which he reiterates some views already developed in Books 1–2. He will use these views as interpretive filters of the Persian history. Differently from the excursus of the Dorian narrative, this one does not offer *all* the filters of interpretation of history because the Athenian has already offered his explanation of the Persian corruption. The digression this time enriches the Athenian's interpretation with further views, so that he eventually offers a fuller interpretation.

Let us now examine the content of the digression. The Athenian begins by praising the Cretans and Spartans for holding as little worth excessive power, wealth or other material goods, and claims that this should be the goal of all legislators. What is more, the hierarchy of honours offered by a state to different kinds of goods is based on the degree to which each good, if accompanied by moderation, benefits humanity. Now, the most useful goods, provided that they are followed by moderation, are those of the soul. Second come those of the body, while last come those pertaining to wealth. Of course, the Athenian uses here as a filter to interpret history views which have already been expressed by

---

[125] On the connection between 631–632 and the didactic excursus in the Persian account, see Stalley 1983, 38.

him about the division of human goods in Book 2. In this way, when he finally offers his recapitulative estimation of the Persian history, he once again mentions the hate of the conquered people to the arrogant Persian monarchs but enriches his interpretation in accordance with the principle he held up in the digression and completes his thoughts with the following words: "And besides all this, they inevitably display their ignorance, inasmuch as by their acts they declare that the things reputed to be honourable and noble in a state are never anything but dross compared to silver and gold" (697e4–698a3).

3.2.4 The narrator's political views as the backbone of the plot

In the accounts of the shepherds, the Dorian League and the Persians, the views already expressed in Books 1–2 do not offer the narrator events to incorporate into the plot. In these cases, the preceding conversation merely offers types of behaviour and mentality, which are exemplified by what takes place in these stories. However, in none of these narratives is the sequence of events, either as a whole or in part, based on situations and stories that have already been revealed. For example, the shepherds' lifestyle may represent the mentality of underestimating wealth, but, as a chain of actions, it does not draw from the conversation of Books 1–2. As demonstrated, such details are drawn by the Athenian from Book 9 of the *Odyssey*. Similarly, in the Dorian account the information that the three city-states convinced their citizens to obey their laws and the subsequent arrogance of the Messenian and Argive kings reflect the Athenian's views that (a) it is necessary for a lawgiver to persuade the people to follow his legislation and (b) that governments and cities are typically destroyed by the statesmen themselves. However, these two events and their temporal and causal linkages constitute the Athenian's original fabrication.

Differently, in the last account of Book 3, the one about the decadence of the Athenian political system, the plot borrows sequences of activities, fields of action and characters from Books 1–2. In particular, the Athenian draws from the views he has expressed in Book 2 to discuss the right kind of music and the way it should be assessed.[126] Let us see how the two parts of the *Laws* are connected, following step by step the plot of the Athenian story.

The narrative follows the logic of the Dorian and Persian stories, in that the Athenian narrates first the period of the Athenians' acme (698a9–700d2) and

---

[126] Cf. Folch 2013, who sees the Athenian account as re-examining the views expressed in Book 2.

then the fall of their constitution (700d2–701d4). The technique which we are interested in is employed only in the second half of the tale, as in the first half the plot does not draw actions already described, but, as in the preceding accounts, the sequence of the events merely exemplifies mentalities exposed in Books 1–2. In this first part of the story, the Athenian narrates the history of Athens down to the Persian Wars and presents his compatriots as obeying the laws of their country. He explains that, at that period of time, the Athenians blindly followed their laws out of shame (αἰδώς) and because they feared the Persians' imminent invasion. In the period of Darius' attack and faced with Xerxes' expedition against them, the Athenians, out of fear of the immense power of the enemy, remained united and, although hoping that they were also aided by other Greeks, eventually managed to oppose the Persians themselves. As in the Dorian story, the Athenian concludes this part of his account with a counterfactual syllogism: had the Athenians not been controlled by their αἰδώς towards their laws, they would not have stayed to defend their country but would have retreated, each of them pursuing his personal survival (699c6–d2).

This story echoes in many respects the views expressed in the previous two books. First, the view that the Athenians defended their city out of shame is a reminder of the Athenian's thesis about the two kinds of fear. In 647a4–b7 he has argued that people can experience fear about their enemies and fear for the opinion of their friends about them. This is also the case with the Athenians of Book 3. Except hope (699b6–7), these are the only two emotions they are presented to feel – the fear for their enemy and their αἰδώς for their laws. What is more, although the Athenian could have merely mentioned his compatriots' shame without describing it as one kind of fear, at the end of this part of his account he reminds his interlocutors that αἰδώς is the type of fear they have already discussed (699c1–6).[127]

However, besides its ideological linkages with the preceding discussion, this first unit of the Athenian account does not draw the backbone of its plot from it. This is what happens in the second unit. In its first stage (700a3–c1), the Athenian narrates that, until the Persian Wars, the Athenians willingly followed the law and particularly those about music. The latter was divided into genres and styles (hymns, dithyrambs, *nomoi* and paeans) and no artist was allowed to combine elements from different styles in a single song. The Athenians, as a people who respect the traditional laws about music, resemble the Egyptians of 656d5–657b8. Also, the three kinds of songs (hymns, paeans of Apollo and

---

127 On the two types of fear in the *Laws*, see Pfefferkorn 2020.

dithyrambs of Dionysus) have already been mentioned when the interlocutors discussed the three different choruses of cities (653d3 ff.).

In the second stage (700c1-d2), the Athenian describes the rules according to which the Athenians used to assess musical pieces in competitions. The duty of knowing these rules and of judging songs on the basis of this knowledge was assigned to literati and not to the noisy and uneducated crowd. These wise men used to listen the songs silently and until the end and made their decisions about what songs were of a higher quality and which of them not, while they also had the authority to punish those who did not comply with their verdicts. As a result, the quality of the songs was not assessed through the whistles, bawling or laudatory clapping of the many. On the contrary, the crowd, including children and their teachers, were superintended by armed guardians and were thereby familiarised with being ruled and not judging songs through noise.

The components of this story, i.e. the field of action, the characters and their actions, and the way they interact, are all drawn from the views expressed by the Athenian in 658e6-659c7 about the proper procedure of musical assessment. In these chapters, the Athenian maintains that music should be assessed according to the pleasure a song offers not to anyone but to the educated and moral exemplars of a society. Both in 658e6-659c7 and in the account about the Athenians, the character is the same: educated men who should take over the assessment of music, a similarity which is further stressed by verbal echoes (658e9-659a1: τοὺς βελτίστους καὶ ἱκανῶς πεπαιδευμένους ... τὸν ἀρετῇ τε καὶ παιδείᾳ διαφέροντα; cf. 700c5: τοῖς μὲν γεγονόσι περὶ παίδευσιν δεδογμένον ἀκούειν).

In 659a1-b2 the Athenian argues that their education provides the judges with two desired features: (a) wisdom, which helps them make the right decisions (γιγνώσκοντα) and (b) courage, which enables them to base their verdicts on their wisdom without fearing the crowd's noisy hoots. This twofold need for the judges to properly assess music but also to base their decisions on their assessments is the very first thing the Athenian mentions in his account about his compatriots (700c2: γνῶναί τε καὶ ἅμα γνόντα δικάσαι). Also, one further character in both cases, which comes in a sharp contrast with the literati, is the uneducated mob. In 659a5-6 we read that a judge should not be afraid of the noise made by the crowds (ὑπὸ θορύβου τῶν πολλῶν) during musical performances. In a similar vein, in the narrative we read that the Athenian crowd was familiar with obeying and not making noise, while they had no part in the determining of the verdicts (700c3-d2: οὐ σῦριγξ ἦν οὐδέ τινες ἄμουσοι βοαὶ πλήθους ... οὐδ' αὖ κρότοι ... μὴ τολμᾶν κρίνειν διὰ θορύβου).

One further facet of interaction between the narrative's literati and the crowd is drawn from 659a4–b3, where the Athenian claims that an educated judge should not act as the mob's student but as their instructor (οὔτε γὰρ παρὰ θεάτρου δεῖ ... μανθάνοντα; οὐ γὰρ μαθητὴς ἀλλὰ διδάσκαλος ... θεατῶν μᾶλλον ὁ κριτής). Similarly, in the account the Athenian does not vaguely refer to the people but specifically mentions children and their teachers. The latter, the Athenian says, were taught to conform to the literati's will and judgment by force (700c6: παισὶ δὲ καὶ παιδαγωγοῖς). The reference to the teachers is not a coincidence. Although serving as instructors to the children, they are not entitled to teach the judges but, on the contrary, act as their students. The view of 659a4–b3 that the judges should act as teachers of the audience is here underlined by the instructors' presence: in musical performances the literati serve as instructors, even to those who in daily life act as teachers.

In the next stage (700d2–701b3), the Athenian narrates how, after the Persian Wars, the poets of Athens gradually contributed to the abolition of these rules of musical assessment. The transition from the preceding ideal situation towards this picture of decadence is achieved by a phrase of temporal compression (700d2–3: μετὰ δὲ ταῦτα, προϊόντος τοῦ χρόνου). As the time passed by, the poets adopted a more hedonistic attitude in terms of the ways in which they composed their works. Being acquainted with the arts of poetry and music but ignorant of what is just and legal in music, they were swayed by creative pleasure and proceeded with generic and stylistic combinations by composing works that gathered elements of both, say, hymns and laments, while they also mingled paeans with dithyrambs and works of wind and stringed instruments. They did all this in the belief that there is no point in defining what is just in music and that the quality of a work should rather be assessed according to the pleasure it causes, without examining whether a work satisfies the morally best citizens or the worst.

The poets are presented as acting in a similar way in the conversation of Book 2, in which the interlocutors discuss the criteria by which musical propriety should be sought. In his narrative, the Athenian characterises these kinds of poetic and musical innovations as illegal because they emerge not from what is proper but from the degree to which they satisfy the poets and their audiences. Similarly, Clinias argues that in most Greek cities of his age the poets proceed with novelties that do not comply with musical laws but with the pleasure of the uneducated (660b6–7: οὐχ ὑπὸ νόμων μεταβαλλόμενα ἀλλ' ὑπό τινων ἀτάκτων ἡδονῶν; cf. 700d3–6: ἀμούσου παρανομίας ... νόμιμον ... ὑφ' ἡδονῆς). The contrast between the poets' knowledge of music and their ignorance of what is good in music, which we read of in the narrative, has already been delineated in

670e4–5 (τὸ γὰρ τρίτον οὐδεμία ἀνάγκη ποιητῇ γιγνώσκειν, εἴτε καλὸν εἴτε μὴ καλὸν τὸ μίμημα), where the Athenian notes that, besides their expertise in music and poetry, the poets are not expected to know what is the good or bad representation. In this context, a good act of representation is the one which enacts morally approvable characters or behaviours. In this respect, in 660b6–7 the poets, by not knowing what is good or bad, are also taken not to know what is just and legal in music.

One further element of the Athenian account that is drawn from Book 2 is the poets' hedonistic attitude towards poetry and music. We saw that in the narrative the poets are presented as being swayed by the pleasure they experience for their works (700d6: μᾶλλον τοῦ δέοντος κατεχόμενοι ὑφ' ἡδονῆς). This information echoes 656c3–4, where the Athenian underlines that poets should not be allowed to do whatever pleases them (ὅτιπερ ἂν αὐτὸν τὸν ποιητὴν ἐν τῇ ποιήσει τέρπῃ).

What matters is the fact that Plato invites us to apprehend the ways in which a narrator incorporates his ideology, as it is delineated in Books 1–2, into the historical accounts of Book 3. In the account of the shepherds the Athenian could have narrated the shepherds' way of life without clarifying that he draws from Book 9 of the *Odyssey*. However, through the citation of the Homeric verses Plato clearly draws our attention to the way the Homeric material is restructured in the new plot. In a similar vein, in the Dorian and Persian accounts, Plato repeats the suspenseful scheme in order to highlight it as a method of structuring the ideological imprint of Books 1–2 into the plots of these accounts. Last, in the story of the Athenian decadence the striking verbal and thematic echoes of Book 2 serve as metanarrative instructions for the reader, which reveal one further way in which ethical principles promoted in the present can define the backbone of the plot of a narrative piece of intentional history. In all three cases, Plato evidently orientates our interest towards narrative structuring.

The question is why, and the answer emerges more easily through a comparative reading of the *Laws* alongside the *Statesman* and the *Timaeus/Critias*. In Chapter 1, we demonstrated that in the *Statesman* Plato underlines the ways in which a narrator reshapes the material he draws from the narrative tradition in order to incorporate it into the overall logic of his narrative's plot. The Visitor's interest is not to compose a piece of intentional history with which to promote an ideology to the citizens of a city. His goal is rather to instruct his student how to compose accounts in which humanity can be set within a wider cosmological narrative canvas. Now, in Chapter 2 we saw that in the *Timaeus/Critias* Plato's interest lies in the ways in which a narrator can compose a past narrative which will strike its audience as likely and valid. For this purpose, a narrator is invited to be especially descriptive and, above all, to base the logic of his account on the natural and ethical rules already set by him. In the *Laws*, these two concerns, the one about the structuring of the material (*Statesman*) and the other about the logical coherence of a narrative (*Timaeus/Critias*) meet each other. Similarly to the *Timaeus/Critias*, in the *Laws* we are taught by Plato how to compose stories of the past that base their logical coherence on their congruence with the moral system of the narrator, as this system has been revealed from the outset. If in the *Timaeus/Critias* the ethical and political physiognomy of the prehistoric Athens has already been delineated in the *Republic*, in the *Laws* the accounts of Book 3 follow the moral system which has already been developed in Books 1–2. However, although in the *Timaeus/Critias* Plato eventually abandoned the challenge of composing a story which ideologically follows the *Republic* (i.e. he never completed the Atlantis story), in the *Laws* he did so and with an intensely formalistic eye on how the past narrative's congruence with the narrator's ideology is narrativised through specific modes of plot structuring.

3.3 Conclusion

In the *Laws*, the combination of metanarrative reflections and narrative paradigms defines the whole structure of the dialogue. In the *Statesman*, the metanarrative framework of the cosmological myth is found only in its prologue and the digression on the two kinds of measuring. Similarly in the *Timaeus/Critias*, the cosmological myth and the Atlantis story are framed by the two introductory discussions of the two dialogues. Differently in the *Laws*, the narratives of Book 3 interact with metanarrative statements which are spread throughout the work. Books 1–2 offer a series of references to local stories which promote a city's ideology, while they also provide the narrator of the accounts in Book 3 with the ethico-political foundations on which they are structured. It is only because these accounts are shaped by this moral agenda that they become plausible in our minds and consequently offer historical examples to follow or to avoid which are able to trigger our fears about an unethical life and our hope that a law-abiding conduct will lead us to happiness. These accounts of Book 3 constitute the legislators' pieces of intentional history with which they enhance the persuasive potential of the preludes of their laws. Through his metanarrative instructions Plato draws our attention to the methods of plot structuring through which the legislator/narrator's moral code is dispersed into the past narratives with which he endeavours to entchant the citizenship of his country.

4 General Conclusions

As explained in the Introduction, my goals in this book were three. First, I endeavoured to show that in the *Statesman*, *Timaeus/Critias* and the *Laws* Plato employs a specific scheme through which he foregrounds speculation on narrative issues. This scheme can be summarised in the following way: Plato expresses, through the characters of his dialogues, certain reflections on the procedure of composing narratives and on aspects of narrativity. At the same time, he composes one or more than one account, which, in the way they are shaped and through the narratorial comments they contain, serve as narrative paradigms of the way in which the metanarrative speculations expressed by the characters define the compositional choices of the narrator, the structure of the narrative and its reception by the audience. My second goal was to recognise the narrative issues addressed by Plato in these works and to analyse the views expressed about them. Last, my third goal was to trace connections between, on the one hand, the views that emerge from the interaction of the metanarrative reflections with the narrative paradigms and, on the other hand, facets of modern theories of narrative and narratology.

Since this scheme is used not once but three times, in a similar way and in all three cases in works of a political orientation, in this last part of the book I would like to address what I believe the conclusions of the present analysis can offer to our efforts to answer the following two questions. First, are we justified in claiming that Plato conceptualised a scheme for expressing views on narrative, like the one that marks modern narratological studies? Second, in what ways did Plato's concern about socio-political matters influence his interest in the nature of narratives? In my view, the answers which the present study offers to these two questions lead to the conclusion that we should radically reconsider our view of Plato's place in ancient Greek theories of narrative and his relationship with modern narratologies.

4.1 The emergence of a proto-narratology: the typicality of the interaction between metanarrative reflections and narrative paradigms

Despite its diverse and multidimensional nature, the interaction between metanarrative reflections and narrative paradigms demonstrates some features which are common in all three cases in question. First, the scheme always develops on the basis of what may be described as *dispersive statements*. These are statements which are asserted outside the narrative and the content of which is echoed in the narrative through authorial comments. The technique manifests itself in the following way: the characters proceed, either before or after the narrative, by uttering a statement on an aspect of narrativity. Then, in the process of relating his story, the narrator repeatedly interrupts the unfolding of the plot with comments which return to the issue of narrativity that is addressed in the dispersive statement. Plato essentially weaves a net of cross-references between the statement outside the narrative and those made within it. He thereby leads the reader to the conclusion that the narrator, in relating his story, is constantly concerned with the narrative aspect in question and, in the final analysis, defines the texture of his account on the basis of his views about this aspect.

As we saw, in the *Statesman* Plato orientates readerly interest towards four factors of narrative composition: selectivity, causality, temporality and narrating/listening time. It is worth noting that all of these factors are highlighted through the technique of dispersive statements. With regard to selectivity, we saw that the Visitor introduces the myth by stating that he will narrate a story which constitutes only a part of another, larger myth. Then, he and Young Socrates constantly remind us that each of the stories which will be temporally and causally connected by the myth has been selected among many others. The emphasis on the element of selectivity is dispersed, as we saw, within the myth through the comments made by the Visitor at the most pivotal points of the account, i.e. in the transitions from the one stage to the other of the scheme '*cosmos* → human biology → politics'. This is also the way in which Plato disperses in the myth the core message of the Visitor's introductory remarks on the creation of causal and temporal connections between the events which will be narrated. The Visitor persistently reminds us that the myth is exactly what he programmatically claimed it to be, namely an effort to causally and temporally connect stories which were at that time narrated in a scattered way. Similarly, the view that narrating/listening time needs to be controlled and not increased for pleasure's sake is dispersed in the myth when the Visitor decides not to ramble on about whether or not men were engaged with philosophy in the Age of Cronus, and when he explains that he will omit certain information about animals because this would need more time.

The technique is also employed in the *Timaeus* and *Critias*. We saw that Timaeus introduces the myth with two statements. First, he recognises that man cannot conceive of the universe and god in a wholly accurate and consistent way. This view leads him to the second statement, i.e. that he cannot offer a true but only a likely description of the universe's creation and function. The core of the meaning in these two statements recurs at points where Timaeus interrupts his exposition. What is more, this net of cross-references belongs to a wider framework of speculation on the relation of fiction between truth and possibility, which is shaped by Socrates' and Critias' statements. Plato also disperses in the myth Critias' and Timaeus' concern for the incompleteness of fictional worlds in the cosmological myth.

In the *Laws*, Plato employs dispersive statements in order to touch upon the impact of the narrator's social background on his selection of the narrated material and his construction of temporal and causal linkages. We saw that one of the main motifs not only in Books 1–2 but also in the whole work is the intellectual and ethical superiority of the elders over the younger members of a society. We also saw that one of the features of the elders in the way they interact with literature lies in their love for Homer and Hesiod. This is the dispersive statement we read before the accounts of Book 3, the content of which is spread throughout the first accounts on the shepherds and the Trojan War, at points where the interlocutors express their admiration for the two epic poets and draw material from their poems for the plot of their story. In a similar way, the introductory metanarrative statement of the Athenian at the beginning of Book 3 that his account will unveil the cause of the mutable nature of legislation and constitutions recurs at central points of the narrative.

The second typical technique through which metanarrative reflections interact with narrative paradigms can be defined as *component-endowing statements*. These are passages in which the characters, and in particular the narrator himself, reveal to the reader the material to be used for the plot of a story. The narrator reveals the source of the main parts of his plot by means of a list of elements, a citation of a work or by developing his personal view on a matter. Whatever the form of such passages, they always endow the narrative with a 'primordial' material, which, by being modified in a more or less radical way, constitutes the backbone of the narrative's plot.

In the *Statesman*, the component-endowing statement is the point at which the Visitor, in his opening remarks to the myth, arrays the three stories on the change of the west and east, the Age of Cronus, and the earth-born men. As explained, the Visitor allows Young Socrates and the external readers to enter his compositional laboratory and to discover the fountain of the material he uses for his myth. Afterwards, in the main body of the cosmological narrative, Plato repeatedly has the Visitor and the boy remind the reader that the account is based on these three stories.

The same result is also achieved by Socrates' summary of the *Republic* in the opening remarks of the *Timaeus*. The concise presentation of the *kallipolis* constitutes the basis on which Socrates expects the plot of the *kallipolis*' military encomium to be built. We also saw that Critias indeed describes the three classes of the Atlantic Athens in agreement with Socrates' sketch. At this point, it could be objected that Critias is not presented as basing his account on what he has been told by Socrates but merely mentioning a state which he has been acquainted with long before listening to Socrates describe his *kallipolis*. However, as demonstrated in Chapter 2, this issue can be better examined through the prism of the tripartite distinction between (a) what Socrates asks his friend to do, (b) what Critias does, and (c) what Plato does. Although presenting Critias as narrating the Atlantic story on the basis of the Egyptians' story and not of Socrates' summary of the *Republic*, at the end of the day Plato himself does fabricate a fiction, Critias' Athens, on the basis of another fiction, that of Socrates. In this way, Socrates' concise presentation of his *kallipolis* does serve as a component-endowing statement to Critias' description of the three Athenian classes.

We are not in a position to say how Socrates' summary would actually function as a component-endowing statement for the myth of Atlantis, because Plato never completed the myth. Many views have been expressed about the reasons why Plato abandoned the composition of the *Critias*' remaining parts. From the perspective of the role the *Republic* would have had as a component-endowing source for the structure of the myth, especially for those parts of it which would perhaps elaborate on the ethical and ideological background of the Athenians' institutions and political decision-making, it can be conjectured that Plato was eventually discouraged by the laborious duty of reading afresh the *Republic* and drawing from it the material with which he would endow the plot of the Atlantic story. In other words, Plato was perhaps not unwilling to write the myth itself but rather to scan its component-endowing source, the *Republic*.

Although this is no more than a conjecture, it is true that, in comparison with the *Statesman* and the *Timaeus* and *Critias*, in the *Laws* Plato is more clearly engaged with displaying the technique of component-endowing statements. The first kind of such statements are the citations of Homeric verses and, in particular, the citation of the verses from the *Odyssey*. As demonstrated in Chapter 3, these verses serve as a teaser of the entirety of Book 9. Plato's message to the reader is that the Athenian does not draw material exclusively from these three verses but from the entire book. In contrast with the immediate way in which the Visitor's list of the three stories in the *Statesman* instruct us how these tales are the foundational ingredients of the myth, the citation of the verses of the *Odyssey* refers to the source of the shepherds' story in a more implicit way, as we are expected to have been equipped with the literary competence which will allow us not to confine ourselves to these three verses but to read the entire book of the *Odyssey*. The second statement which endows the narrative with its components should be traced in the Athenian's thoughts on who decides the awards of the poets in the Greek cities of that period. As we saw, these chapters provide the story of the Athenian institutions' decadence with the backbone of its plot. In all three cases, Plato underscores the fact that the narrator draws from the component-endowing statement through striking verbal and thematic cross-references between the source of the material and the narrative in which this material is incorporated.

Furthermore, in two out of the three cases, Plato reveals the source of the narrative material in order to emphasise the difference between the way this data is used in the primary source and the way in which it is absorbed into the new account. The Visitor initially mentions the three stories about the Age of Cronus, the change of west and east and the earth-born men separately from one another exactly in order to stress the difference with the way in which they become one in the cosmological myth. Similarly, Plato draws our attention to the way in which the shift of the celestial bodies' direction is transformed from a sign of divine favour into the main cause for the changes of human nature. Accordingly, in the *Laws* the Athenian cites the verses from the *Odyssey* in order to mark the inverted way in which Polyphemus' savagery is used as a merit of the shepherds and Odysseus' cleverness as an example to avoid. Plato thereby elicits readerly interest in the fact that the extraction of data from its source and its adoption to a newly composed narrative often entails the defamiliarisation of the data from the established way it is used.

In all three cases, the narrative itself occasionally serves as a mirror of metanarrative speculation. This is the case with the technique of *recurring narrative schemes*, which develops as follows: the characters, through metanarrative statements, invite the reader to wonder how the narrator will handle a certain issue of narrative composition. Then, the narrator underlines the way in which he decides to deal with this issue by repeating a narrative scheme. By recurring, this narrative scheme is foregrounded as the ideal solution to the handling of the compositional issue in question.

With regard to the myth in the *Statesman*, we demonstrated that already in Socrates' digression in the *Theaetetus* the reader has become familiar with the scheme '*cosmos* → human biology → politics'. The repetition of this form in the Visitor's account enhances the message in the reader's mind that this is a convenient scheme through which to contextualise politics against the broader canvas of the universe's inner world. What is more, this scheme is not practiced only once, but twice: once in the account of the Age of Cronus and for a second time in the story of the Age of Zeus. One further recurring narrative scheme in the myth of the *Statesman* is the alternation of a focus on all three temporal levels and a shift of interest only in the two of them (past and present). As demonstrated, in his introductory remarks the Visitor complains that the three stories are usually narrated in a scattered way. It was also noted that, although by the term "disconnected" the Visitor does not make it plain whether or not he refers, apart from the absence of causal links, to temporal connections, the structure of the myth itself indicates that Plato transfers the focal point of our interest towards this issue. The recurrence of the transition from present tenses to past tenses, along with the Visitor's laudatory comments on the impressive way that Young Socrates follows this scheme, reflects Plato's intention to promote this narrative technique as an appropriate choice for anyone who wishes to place the history of men into the framework of the universe's perpetual motion.

In a similar vein, in the *Timaeus* and *Critias* the recurring narrative scheme is shown by the composition of intensely descriptive segments both in Timaeus' account and in Critias' myth of Atlantis. We saw that both characters touch upon the difficulty that narrators are faced with in verbally conveying the world they are invited to describe. Both Timaeus' cosmological myth and Critias' story markedly differentiate themselves from their counterparts of the Platonic oeuvre due to their uniquely detailed descriptiveness. Similarly to the repetition of the alternation of present and past tenses in the myth of the *Statesman*, the two myths' descriptiveness, as a recurring narrative scheme, is foregrounded as a compositional choice attractive to narrators who are troubled with the incompleteness of verbal depictions of fictional worlds.

This function is also traced in the *Laws*, specifically in the repetition of the suspenseful structuring in the accounts on the decadence of the Doric alliance and the Persian institutions. The issue of narrative composition to which the aforementioned scheme offers a solution lies in the challenge a legislator faces in his effort to promote a certain ideological system by means of past narratives. In the first two books of the dialogue, Plato repeatedly forces the reader to realise that the stories circulating in a state must disseminate the legislator's code of principles. So, when in Book 3 Plato invites the reader to engage with the practical perplexities of the poetics of intentional history, the repetition of the suspenseful scheme conveys the message that a way in which to narrate the past through the prism of the legislator's moral doctrines is the following: to record the events of the past, lead the audience to perplexity by posing certain questions about the causes of these events, and to use the legislator's views as the source of explanation to these questions and thus as the key for the resolution of the audience's perplexity.

One further common feature of the narratives in the dialogues in question, which also differentiates these accounts from other similar ones of the Platonic corpus, lies in the fact that significant parts of them constitute *dialogic narratives*, meaning that they unfold in a dialogic form. In these segments of the accounts, the metanarrative reflections and the narrative paradigms come so close to one another that they become one. In my view, at least from a structural point of view, this is the most intimate way in which narration and metanarrative statements interact in the Platonic dialogues. Let us see how this scheme manifests itself in the two cases.

In the *Statesman*, the introductory discussion between the Visitor and Young Socrates constitutes a step by step agreement on the basic compositional choices which define the ensuing myth. The two men decide what tales they will choose and, what is more, which parts of them instead of others. In what follows, the first part of the myth in its entirety, the one about the Age of Cronus, unfolds in the form of a dialogue. In particular, as we saw, certain key questions of the boy carry forward the causal and temporal interweaving of the events in the plot. The Visitor explains why the world occasionally changes its route only after the boy's question on the matter. Afterwards, the whole causative chain that leads from the change of west and east towards the change in the way organisms die and give birth unfolds through the boy's confirmations and queries about the views exposed by the Visitor. The temporal placement of the earthborn men at the Age of Cronus is also made by the Visitor only after Young Socrates' question about how men were born at that period of time. Last, the temporal clarifications about the Age of Cronus are also offered as a response to the boy's question.

The same scheme, which is also partly oriented towards the same themes, is employed almost in all the narratives of Book 3 in the *Laws*. In this case too, the interaction of dialogue and narration is more frequent in the first part of the Athenian's story, where he presents the age of the first shepherds and the Trojan War. However, in contrast to the myth in the *Statesman*, the technique does not totally disappear but gradually fades away, as the dialogic interruptions of the narration decrease and the pure third-person narrative parts become more prominent. As in the *Statesman*, the Athenian decides together with his partners to begin the account from the very incunabula of human society. Here too, the interlocutors are concerned with the immense amount of time between their present and the starting point of their story. Also, similarly to the conversation between the Visitor and Young Socrates, they agree to shape their account in such a way that they search for the cause of the phenomenon they examine, the mutable nature of society. The selection of the exact starting point among so many other choices thus comes as the outcome of an agreement (677a8: νοή-σωμεν). Also, the information that in the age of the shepherds coastal and riparian settlements were destroyed is agreed upon (677c1 and 3: θῶμεν), and this is also the case with the temporal placement of that period in relation with the interlocutors' present through an extensive stichomythia between the main narrator, the Athenian, and the other two discussants. Even the defamiliarisation of the content of the Homeric verses is also addressed by Megillus in his brief exchange with the Athenian.

The main difference between the *Statesman* and the *Laws* lies in the fact that in the first case the discussions drive the narrator's choices not through agreements but by means of the boy's questions to him, while in the latter case the discussion takes place between peers, three wise elders, and the main narrator's choices emerge as agreed and common decisions which are defined by the knowledge and tastes of all three interlocutors. This difference can be explained by the goals which the account under construction serves in each case. In the *Statesman*, the myth aims at teaching the boy, while in the *Laws* the narratives constitute a common effort under the Athenian's guidance. In both cases, though, we are faced with narratives driven by a discussion on compositional issues between the narrator and his audience.

In the *Timaeus*, we do not find this scheme but we do find its content and, most importantly, at the point where it also appears in the *Statesman* and *Laws*. As demonstrated, in the latter two dialogues the dialogic narrative at the beginning of the account dramatises, in a step-by-step fashion, the narrator's key choices: the selection of the material and the definition of the starting point of the dramatic time. This is also the way in which, in the *Timaeus*, the Egyptians open their account. They explain to Solon that their story will refer to a period of time that is far remote from what is usually taken to be the past. Second, they consider an era which is temporally defined by a natural disaster. Third, the Egyptians too choose only one from among countless catastrophes, introducing us in this way to the issue of the selection procedure. All these similarities have already been noticed by previous scholars. What the present analysis adds is the point that they should be treated as parts of the typical features of the scheme 'metanarrative reflections and narrative paradigms', along with the rest of the patterns (dispersive statements, component-endowing statements, and recurring narrative schemes).

I would like to complete my analysis of this scheme's typicality by highlighting a pattern which does not lie in the use of a specific technique, as is the case with the aforementioned motifs, but is suggestive of the inadequacy of the way in which Plato is read by narratologists. This feature lies in the fact that this scheme always develops within the framework of a large macro-structure, which sometimes begins and ends in one and the same work (the *Laws*) or transcends the limits of a single dialogue and is materialised through intertextual cross-referencing (the *Statesman* and the *Timaeus/Critias*).

To begin with the *Statesman*, we have seen that many aspects of narrativity addressed by the Visitor are introduced in the work which serves as the methodological and thematic prelude to the *Statesman*, namely the *Theaetetus*. We cannot fully grasp the reason why the Visitor extracts from the Pelopidae myth the change of west and east instead of the golden lamb, unless we have already read Socrates' digression in the *Theaetetus*, where we learn that the examination of the nature of statesmanship requires a shift of interest from the possession of material goods towards those elements that define the nature of kingship. If we do not approach the Visitor's choice in the light of Socrates' views, we cannot apprehend that in Plato's mind the selection procedure should be defined, at the level of narrative composition, by the need to define statesmanship as a *genus*. Similarly, we are not in a position to realise the purpose in the alternation of present and past tenses, nor the repetition of the scheme '*cosmos* → human biology → politics', unless we have first read Socrates' thesis that the examination of statesmanship requires widening our gaze towards the universe. Equally incomplete is the impression we have of the Visitor's views on narrating/listening time, if we do not read them in the light of Plato's general agenda on the value of leisure of time in philosophy.

In the *Timaeus* and *Critias*, the views expressed by the characters on the construction and reception of a story cannot be fully apprehended and related to modern theories of fictional worlds, unless we read them together as parts of a unified system of speculation on the relation of fiction to truth and possibility. The emphasis on the necessity of a narrative which is not necessarily true but by all means likely can also be better explained as satisfying Socrates' demand in the *Republic* that the legislator should not so much tell the truth to the citizens but fabricate stories through which he will enhance people's patriotism and persuade them to accept the political *status quo* he aspires to impose. In the *Laws*, we cannot understand the logic latent in the poetics of intentional history proposed by the interlocutors in Book 3, if we fail to read this poetics through the prism of the cross-references between the accounts of this book and the rest of the dialogue. Weil is led to this mistake by focusing exclusively on the relationship of the Athenian's narrative with other past narratives (in Thucydides, Herodotus, etc.) and ignoring the book's place in the overall arrangement of the *Laws*.

These thoughts make it clear that any reading of Platonic passages of metanarrative content which dissociates them from their wider context, be this intra-textually or intertextually, is inadequate. Plato did not write a handbook of narrative theory or poetics — at least no such text has come to us. However, this does not mean that we are doomed to search here and there for his views on the matter and, by a process of cherry-picking, to reconstruct a hypothetical Frankenstein system of his theory of narrative. The typicality of the scheme 'metanarrative reflections and narrative paradigms' in the dialogues we have examined in this book shows, if anything, that Plato had consolidated in his mind and compositionally put into effect one solid, systematic, and structurally elaborate mode in which to express his thoughts on narratives. This mode is as carefully elaborated as modern handbooks of narratology are, with the difference being that it belongs to a literary genre different from that of a treatise on literary criticism. This scheme is incorporated into dialogues which simultaneously examine other topics as well, but not in a way that is disconnected to narrative issues. In order to apprehend not only this scheme but also all Platonic passages of metanarrative content, we should thus read them in close association with their structural and thematic contexts. This is a practice which narratologists have traditionally been indifferent to, which is why, I believe, their interest in Plato is confined to what is handed to them on a plate, such as the tripartite classification of narrative modes we read of in the *Republic*.

However, if narratology is marked by its effort to shape a solid system that aims at the conceptualisation and description of narrative phenomena, then one of the first such efforts in the history of western civilisation is evident in what Plato does in the *Statesman*, *Timaeus/Critias* and the *Laws*. In these dialogues, we witness the birth of a proto-narratology which may indeed differ in many respects from modern narratological handbooks, but still demonstrates two foundational features of narratology: (a) a conscious focus on certain aspects of narrativity and narrative phenomena; and (b) a schematised mode of interaction between metanarrative reflections and textual bodies which serve as the paradigms through which to explore the interpretive potential of these reflections. For this reason, I cannot but put it bluntly as follows: any treatise on ancient Greek theory of narrative and on the history and prehistory of narratology that does not include — apart from the *Republic* — the *Statesman*, *Timaeus/Critias* and the *Laws*, is incomplete.

4.2 Plato's sociological perspective on narrative realities

The fact that Plato standardly examines narrative issues in relation to other areas of socio-political activity leads us to the conclusion that he approaches narratives from a clearly sociological perspective. In all three case studies examined in this work (*Statesman*, *Timaeus/Critias* and *Laws*), he evidently focuses on how social circumstances under which a narrative is created affect the narrator's compositional choices and the narrative's reception by the audience. In the present analysis, we have focused mainly on two facets of a narrative's social context: first, the "narrative environment", meaning the socio-cultural setting in which an account is composed and narrated;[1] and, second, the social functions that a story aims to fulfil by its narrator within its narrative environment.[2] These factors of social framing can be described as "narrative realities".[3]

In the *Statesman*, the narrative environment is denoted by a conversation between an instructor and a young boy. The goal of this discussion, apart from leading to the definition of a concept, is that Young Socrates should be taught the ability to find solutions in case that the philosophical inquiry he participates in encounters methodological complications. This is an issue that, as demonstrated, emerges already in the *Theaetetus* and *Sophist*. The myth is presented as being an alternative method to dialogue with a therapeutic role in it. Plato's interest in this specific communicative framework constitutes the point of departure for most of the views he offers us about the aspects of narrativity addressed in the dialogue. The Visitor brings us closer to the habit of many people who have participated in philosophical discussions and felt discomforted when a discussion seemed to deviate from its main goal. Within the framework of a concern about how one should control her or himself when feeling this way, the Visitor expresses his thoughts about the nature of narrating/listening time, how its size is to be assessed, and the emotions an extensive narrative elicits when it serves as a retarding digression to the overall context within which it is framed. The emphasis given to the sense of defamiliarisation that the Visitor leads Young Socrates to feel, by employing and interpreting the mythical tradition in a different way from the way that is expected, has a further social purpose: to teach the boy how to rationally explain the meaning of myths and to draw from them what he needs in his effort to reconstruct an image of men and the world. Of course, the exegesis of myths, as a practice, is as old as the Pre-Socratics and the sophists. The Visitor not only makes some narrative choices

---

[1] The concept was first introduced and described by Gubrium/Holstein 2008, 252–256 and further developed by Gubrium/Holstein 2009. On p. 252, they concisely state: "The meanings of stories are poorly understood without careful consideration of the circumstances of their production and reception, which we broadly call their narrative environments." Cf. Hyvärinen 2016, 53–55.
[2] Hyvärinen 2016, 52 and 56, who follows the psychologists Bruner 1990 and Brockmeier 2015, as well as the sociologist Plummer 1995.
[3] Gubrium/Holstein 2009, 7–47; Hyvärinen 2016, 51–55.

but also discusses them with the boy, so that the latter is instructed how one can distil of a myth's interpretation. Last, all narrative techniques foregrounded in the *Statesman* are treated as part and parcel of a widened perspective on statesmanship, one which is focussed on how young men shape their views about legislation and political organisation.

In the *Timaeus* and *Critias*, the narrative environment is presented as defining with what ease or difficulty a fictional world is conceived of, verbally conveyed and received. As demonstrated, the portraiture of all the narrators of the Atlantis tale aim to show how the age and the social environment in which a story is preserved and reproduced defines how the content of that story is taken as true or fictional. In terms of the way a story is conceived, the inexperience of poets and sophists in social circumstances in which political practice and philosophy are combined renders them, in Socrates' mind, incapable of imagining how the philosophers-guardians of the *kallipolis* can act at war and during diplomatic negotiations. Moreover, the narrative environment in which Timaeus and Critias narrate their myths defines not only what will be discussed about the composition of a narrative world but also what will be omitted. Differently from the discussion between the Visitor and Young Socrates in the *Statesman*, in this work we are offered a discussion between mature literati, who interact as peers on all levels (such as their education, interest in philosophy, experience in method, and so on). This is why there is no need for them to explain why leisure time, and thus extensive narrating/listening time, is, if needed, a welcome *desideratum*. Each of the characters is presented as having at his disposal as much time as he needs without facing any complaints from his companions. Socrates must have dedicated many hours to the description of the ideal state on the previous day, while Timaeus proceeds with a particularly lengthy myth. This is also what Plato would have had Critias do if he had completed the eponymous dialogue. Furthermore, as it has been forcefully demonstrated by Morgan, the Atlantic story, as an encomium, compositionally and thematically adheres to norms which prevailed in panegyric speeches such as that of Isocrates.[4] Last, it is these myths' social function that leads Plato to penetrate all the issues of structuring and reception of fictional worlds: his views about them emerge from his goal to use both myths as parts of his 'noble lie' in support of the *kallipolis*.

In the *Laws*, the accounts of Book 3 are recited in a narrative environment which combines those of the *Statesman* and the *Timaeus/Critias*. On the one hand, there are three peers, as is the case with the four companions in the *Timaeus/Critias*. On the other hand, these peers do not narrate a story individu-

---

[4] Morgan 1998.

ally and separately from the others, but they build many parts of the accounts together, albeit with the guidance of the Athenian, as is the case with the dialogic narrative in the *Statesman*.[5] They do not negotiate the issue of leisure time, but instead intend to use as much time as they need. Their age affects their aesthetic choices in the process of narrating their stories and, what is more, the fact that this is a friendly and private conversation between elders means they are free to include in their accounts stories which are not allowed to be publicly narrated in Sparta, such as the shortcomings of the Cretan and Lacedaemonian laws and political institutions (634d4–635a8).[6] As for their social function, the accounts of Book 3 have a didactic role both for the interlocutors as well as for the citizens of hypothetical Magnesia and us. They teach us that a virtuous and law-abiding life leads to happiness, while, since this message is meant to be spread throughout the city, these stories shape the people's collective conscience and thus serve as pieces of intentional history.

It has been argued that there is no point in trying to reconstruct Plato's views on narratives because such issues are fleetingly addressed in the dialogues and only as parts of speculations about other subjects, which are more interesting and significant to him.[7] According to this logic, the fact that such views are subsumed within a wider thematic framework entails that Plato is not interested in examining them. In contrast, the present analysis claims exactly the opposite. We should not take it for granted that Plato's speculations about socio-political matters distract him from narrative issues. The three case studies we have examined in this book show that Plato's general philosophical agenda motivates him to systematically engage with issues of theory and reception of narrative. This is a fact that generates the need to realise that there is no point for us to seek to apprehend Plato's views about narrative unless we examine them within their socio-political context.

Discrepancies between the way that the same narrative issues are treated in different dialogues leads us to the conclusion that what is at stake in our discussion is not so much what views are expressed on a certain narrative aspect but rather what views are expressed about a narrative aspect depending on the social environment in which this aspect is presented. For example, the narrator's, performer's and audience's immersion into the fictional world represented by a narrative is approached in noticeably different ways in the *Ion* and *Timaeus*.

---

[5] Weil 1959, 39–42.
[6] Cf. Meyer 2015, 135–136.
[7] Liveley 2019, 18 on Socrates' tripartite taxonomy of narrative modes: "His principal concerns, therefore, are not with narratives but with ethics."

While in the *Ion* Socrates is presented as mocking Ion for his "insanity" of being mentally transferred into the worlds of the *Odyssey* and *Iliad* he sings about, in the *Timaeus* Socrates is presented as admitting that he found himself at the same state he accuses Ion of being at. Socrates immersed himself into the world he himself created and momentarily believed that his state is a living being that can 'move'.

Why does Plato present Socrates as mocking the state of immersion in the *Ion* and as experiencing it in the *Timaeus*? There is no need for us to conclude that this question receives only one answer. Yet from the perspective of the narrative realities in each case, this discrepancy can be explained in the following way: in the *Ion* a poet, being ignorant of the affairs he describes in his poetry, immerses himself into the worlds he recreates through his singing, and he also beguiles his audience to do so. However, in terms of the narrative environment in which this activity takes place and its social function, in this case we are faced with a communal activity which does not aim at discovering the truth about the worlds described in the epics. For Plato, the latter world includes behaviours, both of men and the gods, which are examples to avoid and, occasionally, through the form of *mimesis* (dialogue or monologue), can very dangerously lead the audience to identify with unethical figures. Ion does not intend to protect his audience from these dangerous lures, which is why he is negatively treated by Plato. On the contrary, Socrates immerses himself into a world that has no ethical flaw and is therefore absolutely beneficial for those who immerse themselves in it. This is why Socrates' wish to sway his companions into following him and immersing themselves into the *kallipolis'* world is welcomed by Plato. The same phenomenon, our immersion into a fictional world, is treated differently depending on the sociocultural circumstances. When this phenomenon manifests itself in public poetic performances by uneducated poets in front of the mob, it is rejected. On the other hand, there is nothing wrong about it, as long as it takes place in a fruitful way during private philosophical discussions between well-intentioned literati and friends.

From the same perspective one may explain the difference between, on the one hand, Socrates' criticism of the audience's moral identification with unethical characters of drama (*Rep.*) and, on the other hand, his sincere effort to help Theaetetus distinguish in his mind all the different perspectives of Protagoras, the sophists, and Socrates in the *Theaetetus*, or the Visitor's well-disposed endeavour to make Young Socrates identify with the broadened gaze of the cosmological myth in the *Statesman*. Once again, the sociocultural settings (the narrator's motives, the communicational circumstances, etc.) in which audiences are led to identify with narrators or the characters of narratives doom or justify this phenomenon.

Postclassical narratologists long ago realised that an exclusive focus on the textual features of a narrative, such as was represented by classical narrative analysis, falls short of our need to offer as comprehensive as possible an interpretation of both the form of narratives and their impact on audiences. In recent decades, the scholarly focus has now massively shifted to include more kinds of accounts which can be analysed besides literary narratives, and numerous studies today elaborate on natural-language storytelling performed in the process of dialogues or in any other context of day-to-day life (such as Plato's dialogical narratives).[8] At the same time, critics are now more interested in explaining the ways in which the sociocultural context of a story both affects its structure and is affected by its social functions.[9] 'Socio-narratology' should thus trace some parts of its origins back in Plato. On all accounts, Plato's place on the archaeological map of narratology should be incised afresh.

---

[8] Frank 2010; Fludernik 2002⁴.
[9] See nn. 2–4 above.

Bibliography

Alber, J./Fludernik, M. (2009), "Mediacy and Narrative Mediation", in: P. Hühn/J.C. Meister/
   J. Pier/W. Schmid (eds.), *Handbook of Narratology*, Berlin/New York, 174–189.
Annas, J.E./Waterfield, R. (eds.) (1995), *Statesman*, Cambridge/New York.
Appelrot, B.G. (ed.) (1893), *Aristotel: Ob iskusstve poezii*, Moscow.
Arends, J.F.M. (1988), *Die Einheit der Polis. Eine Studie über Platons Staat*, Leiden.
Arends, J.F.M. (1993), "Survival, War and the Unity of the Polis in Plato's *Statesman*", *Polis* 12, 154–187.
Arrighetti, G. (1991), "Platone fra mito, poesia e storia", *SCO* 41, 13–34.
Ashbaugh, A.F. (1988), *Plato's Theory of Explanation. A Study of the Cosmological Account in the* Timaeus, Albany NY.
Atack, C. (2019), "Tradition and Innovation in the Kosmos-Polis Analogy", in: P.S. Horky (ed.), *Cosmos in the Ancient World*, Cambridge/New York, 164–187.
Atack, C. (2020), "«An Origin for Political Culture»: Laws 3 as Political Thought and Intellectual History", *Polis* 37, 468–484.
Auerbach, E. (2003), *Mimesis. The Representation of Reality in Western Literature*, Princeton.
Ausland, H.W. (2000), "Who Speaks for Whom in the *Timaeus–Critias*?", in: G.A. Press (ed.), *Who Speaks for Plato? Studies in Platonic Anonymity*, Lanham, 183–198.
Baima, N.R. (2016), "Persuasion, Falsehood, and Motivating Reason in Plato's *Laws*", *HPhQ* 33, 117–134.
Bal, M. (1981), "Aristoteles Semioticus", *Spektator* 10, 490–495.
Bal, M. (1997²), *Narratology. Introduction to the Theory of Narrative*, Toronto.
Bartels, M.L. (2012), "*Senex mensura*: An Objective Aesthetics of Seniors in Plato's *Laws*", in: I. Sluiter/R.M. Rosen (eds.), *Aesthetic Value in Classical Antiquity*, Leiden/Boston, 133–158.
Bartels, M.L. (2020), "Plato's Seasick Steersman: On (Not) Being Overwhelmed by Fear in Plato's *Laws*", in: L. Candiotto/O. Renaut (eds.), *Emotions in Plato*, Leiden/Boston, 147–168.
Belfiore, E. (1992), *Tragic Pleasures. Aristotle on Plot and Emotion*, Princeton.
Belfiore, E. (2000), "Narratological Plots and Aristotle's Mythos", *Arethusa* 33, 37–70.
Bell, A./Ryan, M.-L. (eds.) (2019), *Possible Worlds Theory and Contemporary Narratology*, Lincoln/London.
Benardete, S. (1963), "Eidos and Diaeresis in Plato's *Statesman*", *Philologus* 107, 193–226.
Benardete, S. (1984), *The Being of the Beautiful. Plato's* Theaetetus, Sophist, *and* Statesman, Chicago.
Benardete, S. (1992), "The Plan of the *Statesman*", *Métis* 7, 25–47.
Betegh, G. (2010), "What Makes a Myth *Eikôs*? Remarks Inspired by Myles Burnyeat's *EIKÔS MYTHOS*", in: R.D. Mohr/B.M. Sattler (eds.), *One Book, the Whole Universe. Plato's* Timaeus *Today*, Las Vegas, 213–224.
Bidez, J. (1945), *Eos. Ou, Platon et l'Orient*, Bruxelles.
Blondell, R. (2002), *The Play of Character in Plato's Dialogues*, Cambridge.
Blondell, R. (2005), "From Fleece to Fabric: Weaving Culture in Plato's *Statesman*", *OSAP* 28, 23–75.
Bobonich, C. (1991), "Persuasion, Compulsion and Freedom in Plato's *Laws*", *CQ* 41, 365–388.
Bostock, D. (1988), *Plato's* Theaetetus, Oxford.
Bowery, A.-M. (2007), "Know Thyself: Socrates as Storyteller", in: G.A. Scott (ed.), *Philosophy in Dialogue. Plato's Many Devices*, Evanston, 82–110.

Brague, R. (1985), "The Body of the Speech: A New Hypothesis on the Compositional Structure of Timaeus' Monologue", in: D. O'Meara (ed.), *Platonic Investigations*, Washington D.C., 53–83.
Bremmer, J.N. (2002), "Odysseus versus the Cyclops", in: S. des Bouvrie (ed.), *Myth and Symbol. 1, Symbolic Phenomena in Ancient Greek Culture. Papers from the First International Symposium on Symbolism at the University of Tromsø, June 4–7, 1998*, Sävedalen, 135–152.
Brewer, W.F./Lichtenstein, E.H. (1981), "Event Schemas, Story Schemas, and Story Grammars", in: J. Long/A. Baddeley (eds.), *Attention and Perfomance*, vol. IX, Hillsdale NJ, 363–379.
Brewer, W.F./Lichtenstein, E.H. (1982), "Stories Are to Entertain: A Structural-Affect Theory of Stories", *Journal of Pragmatics* 6, 473–486.
Brisson, L. (1987), "Le discours comme univers et l'univers comme discours: Platon et ses interprètes néoplatoniciens", in: *Le texte et ses representations*, Paris, 121–128.
Brisson, L. (1995), "Interprétation du mythe du *Politique*", in: C.J. Rowe (ed.), *Reading the Statesman. Proceedings of the III Symposium Platonicum*, Sankt Augustin, 349–363.
Brisson, L. (2012), "Soul and State in Plato's *Laws*", in: R. Barney/T. Brennan/C. Brittain (eds.), *Plato and the Divided Self*, Cambridge/New York, 281–307.
Brisson, L./Patillon, M. (2001⁵), *Platon. Timée, Critias*, Paris.
Broadie, S. (2012), *Nature and Divinity in Plato's* Timaeus, Cambridge.
Broadie, S. (2013), "Truth and Story in the *Timaeus-Critias*", in: G.R. Boys-Stones/D. El Murr/ C. Gill (eds.), *The Platonic Art of Philosophy*, Cambridge/New York, 249–268.
Brockmeier, J. (2015), *Beyond the Archive. Memory, Narrative, and the Autobiographical Process*, Oxford.
Bruner, J. (1990), *Acts of Meaning*, Cambridge MA.
Brunschwig, J. (2018), "Διήγησις et μίμησις dans l'oeuvre de Platon", *EPh* 124, 49–60.
Brütsch, M. (2017), "How to Measure Narrativity? Notes on Some Problems with Comparing Degrees of Narrativity Across Different Media", in: P.K. Hansen/J. Pier/P. Roussin/W. Schmid (eds.), *Emerging Vectors of Narratology*, Berlin/Boston, 315–334.
Buccioni, E. (2007), "Revisiting the Controversial Nature of Persuasion in Plato's *Laws*", *Polis* 24, 262–283.
Burger, R. (1980), *Plato's* Phaedrus. *A Defense of a Philosophic Art of Writing*, Alabama.
Burnyeat, M.F. (1992), "Utopia and Fantasy: The Practicability of Plato's Ideally Just City", in: J. Hopkins/A. Savile (eds.), *Psychoanalysis, Mind, and Art*, Oxford, 175–187.
Burnyeat, M.F. (2005), "ΕΙΚΏΣ ΜΥΘΟΣ", *Rhizai* 2, 143–165.
Bury, R.G. (1937), "Theory of Education in Plato's *Laws*", *RÉG* 1, 304–320.
Bury, R.G. (2001⁸), *Laws. Plato*, Cambridge MA.
Cain, R.B. (2012), "Plato on Mimesis and Mirrors", *Philosophy and Literature* 36, 187–195.
Cambiano, G. (2012), "Platone e il governo misto", *RSI* 124, 143–164.
Campbell, L. (1883), *The* Theaetetus *of Plato*, Oxford.
Capizzi, A. (1989), "Il nesso mythos-logos in Platone", *Discorsi* 9, 309–325.
Carone, G.R. (2002), "Pleasure, Virtue, Externals, and Happiness in Plato's *Laws*", *HPhQ* 19, 327–344.
Carone, G.R. (2003), "The Place of Hedonism in Plato's *Laws*", *AncPhil* 23, 283–300.
Carone, G.R. (2004), "Reversing the Myth of the *Politicus*", *CQ* 54, 88–108.
Carone, G.R. (2005), *Plato's Cosmology and Its Ethical Dimensions*, Cambridge/New York.
Casnati, M.G. (2011), "Ψεῦδος en palabras en *República* y relato εἰκός en *Timeo*", *Nova Tellus* 29, 47–85.

Castelnérac, B. (2008), "Évolution de l'humanité et education au livre III des *Lois* de Platon", *Revue Philosophique de Louvain* 106, 695–721.
Chatman, S. (1978), *Story and Discourse. Narrative Structure in Fiction and Film*, New York/London.
Clark, R.B. (2003), *The Law Most Beautiful and Best. Medical Argument and Magical Rhetoric in Plato's* Laws, Lanham.
Clay, D. (2000), "Plato's Atlantis: Anatomy of a Fiction", in: J.J. Cleary/G.M. Gurtler (eds.), *Proceedings of the Boston Area Colloquium in Ancient Philosophy. 15, 1999*, Leiden/Boston, 1–21.
Cohn, D. (2000), "The Poetics of Plato's *Republic*: A Modern Perspective", *Philosophy and Literature* 24, 34–48.
Cole, E.B. (1991), "Weaving and Practical Politics in Plato's *Statesman*", *The Southern Journal of Philosophy* 29, 195–208.
Collins, J.H. (2012), "Prompts for Participation in Early Philosophical Texts", in: E. Minchin (ed.), *Orality, Literacy and Performance in the Ancient World*, Boston, 151–182.
Collins, J.H. (2015), *Exhortations to Philosophy. The Protreptics of Plato, Isocrates, and Aristotle*, Oxford.
Collobert, C. (2013), "La littérarité platonicienne: instances et modes narratifs dans les dialogues", *RMM* 80, 463–476.
Cooper, J.M. (1999), "Plato's *Statesman* and Politics", in: J.J. Cleary/G.M. Gurtler (eds.), *Proceedings of the Boston Area Colloquium in Ancient Philosophy. 13, 1997*, Leiden/Boston, 71–104.
Cornford, F.M. (1937), *Plato's Cosmology. The* Timaeus *of Plato*, London.
Cronk, N. (1999), "Aristotle, Horace, and Longinus: The Conception of Reader Response", in: G.P. Norton (ed.), *The Cambridge History of Literary Criticism, vol. 3: The Renaissance*, Cambridge, 199–204.
Crotty, K.M. (2009), *The Philosopher's Song. The Poet's Influence on Plato*, Lanham.
Currie, G. (2010), *Narratives and Narrators. A Philosophy of Stories*, Oxford.
Davenport, D.R. (2011), "Unravelling an Outline of the *Statesman*", *Polis* 28, 74–89.
Davis, M. (1967), "The *Statesman* as a Political Dialogue", *AJPh* 88, 319–331.
de Jong, I.J.F. (2005), "Ancient Theories of Narrative (Western)", in: D. Herman/M. Jahn/M.-L. Ryan (eds.), *Routledge Encyclopedia of Narrative Theory*, London, 19–22.
de la Fuente, H.D. (2010), "Mythische Vorbilder des sakralen Gesetzgebers bei Platon (Nomoi I–IV): eine Einführung in den religiösen Hintergrund der *Nomoi*, *Zeitschrift für Religions- und Geistesgeschichte* 62, 105–124.
de Wied, M. (1994), "The Role of Temporal Expectancies in the Production of Film Suspense", *Poetics* 23, 107–123.
Des Places, É. (1951), *Platon. Les* Lois, Paris.
Desclos, M.-L. (2006), "Les prologues du *Timée* et du *Critias*: un cas de rhapsodie platonicienne", *EP* 2, 175–202.
Destrée, P./Herrmann, F.G. (eds.) (2011), *Plato and the Poets*, Leiden/Boston.
Doležel, L. (1979), "Extensional and Intensional Narrative Worlds", *Poetics* 8, 193–211.
Doležel, L. (1988), "Mimesis and Possible Worlds", *Poetics Today* 9, 475–496.
Doležel, L. (1998), *Heterocosmica. Fiction and Possible Worlds*, Baltimore.
Doležel, L. (2019), "Porfyry's Tree for the Concept of Fictional Worlds", in: A. Bell/M.-L. Ryan (eds.), *Possible Worlds Theory and Contemporary Narratology*, Lincoln/London, 47–61.
Domanski, A. (2007), "Principles of Early Education in Plato's *Laws*", *AClass* 50, 65–80.

Dorter, K. (1994), *Form and Good in Plato's Eleatic Dialogues. The* Parmenides, Theaetetus, Sophist, *and* Statesman, Berkeley.
Dušanić, S. (1982), "Plato's Atlantis", *AC* 51, 25–52.
Dušanić, S. (2002–2003), "The Unity of the *Timaeus–Critias* and the Inter-Greek Wars of the Mid 350's", *ICS* 27–28, 63–75.
Eco, U. (1996), "Thoughts on Aristotle's *Poetics*", in: C.A. Mihailescu/W. Hamarneh (eds.), *Fiction Updated. Theories of Fictionality, Narratology, and Poetics*, Toronto, 229–243.
El Murr, D. (2010), "Politics and Dialectic in Plato's *Statesman*", in: G.M. Gurtler/W. Wians (eds.), *Proceedings of the Boston Area Colloqium in Ancient Philosophy. 25, 2009*, Leiden/Boston, 109–147.
Emlyn-Jones, C. (2008), "Poets on Socrates' Stage: Plato's Reception of Dramatic Art", in: L. Hardwick/C.A. Stray (eds.), *A Companion to Classical Receptions*, Oxford, 38–49.
England, E.B. (1921), *The* Laws *of Plato*, Manchester.
Fagan, P. (2013), "*He Saw the Cities and He Knew the Minds of Many Men*: Landscape and Character in the *Odyssey* and *Laws*", in: G.W. Recco/E. Sanday (eds.), *Plato's* Laws*: Force and Truth in Politics*, Indiana, 105–117.
Farrar, C. (2013), "Putting History in Its Place: Plato, Thucydides, and the Athenian *Politeia*", in: V. Harte/M. Lane (eds.), Politeia *in Greek and Roman Philosophy*, Cambridge/New York, 32–56.
Feddern, S./Kablitz, A. (2020), "Mimesis: Prolegomena zu einer Systematik der Geschichte ihres Begriffs", *Poetica* 51, 1–84.
Ferrari, G.R.F. (1990³), *Listening to Cicadas. A Study of Plato's* Phaedrus, Cambridge.
Ferrari, G.R.F. (1993²), "Plato and Poetry", in: G.A. Kennedy (ed.), *The Cambridge History of Literary Criticism. Volume I: Classical Criticism*, Cambridge, 92–148.
Ferrari, G.R.F. (2010), "Socrates in the *Republic*", in: M.L. McPherran (ed.), *Plato's* Republic. *A Critical Guide*, Cambridge, 11–31.
Fine, G. (ed.) (1999), *Plato 2. Ethics, Politics, Religion, and the Soul*, Oxford, 297–308.
Finkelberg, M. (1998), *The Birth of Literary Fiction in Ancient Greece*, Oxford.
Finkelberg, M. (2019), *The Gatekeeper. Narrative Voice in Plato's Dialogues*, Leiden/Boston.
Fludernik, M. (2002⁴), *Towards a 'Natural' Narratology*, London.
Fludernik, M. (2009), *An Introduction to Narratology*, London.
Folch, M. (2013), "Who Calls the Tune: Literary Criticism, Theatrocracy, and the Performance of Philosophy in Plato's *Laws*", *AJPh* 134, 557–601.
Fořt, B. (2016), *An Introduction to Fictional Worlds Theory*, Frankfurt am Main.
Fowler, H.N. (1921), *Plato. Theaetetus, Sophist*, Cambridge MA.
Fowler, R.L. (2011), "*Mythos* and *Logos*", *JHS* 131, 45–66.
Foxhall, L./Gehrke, H.-J./Luraghi, N. (eds.) (2010), *Intentional History. Spinning Time in Ancient Greece*, Stuttgart.
Frangakis, P. (2016), "Narratological Elements in Aristotle's *Poetics*", *Annual Yearbook/ University of the Peloponnese* 1, 315–323.
Frank, A.W. (2010), *Letting Stories Breathe. A Socio-Narratology*, Chicago.
Frede, D. (1989), "The Soul's Silent Dialogue. A Non-Aporetic Reading of the *Theaetetus*", *PCPS* 35, 20–49.
Friedländer, P. (1954), *Platon*, vols. I–III, Berlin.
Fuks, A. (1979), "Plato and the Social Question: The Problem of Poverty and Riches in the *Laws*", *AncSoc* 10, 33–78.
Gantz, T. (1993), *Early Greek Myth. A Guide to Literary and Artistic Sources*, Baltimore.

Gartner, C./Yau, C. (2020), "The Myth of Cronus in Plato's *Statesman*: Cosmic Rotation and Earthly Correspondence", *Apeiron* 53, 437–462.
Garvey, T. (2008), "Plato's Atlantis Story: A Prose Hymn to Athena", *GRBS* 48, 381–392.
Gaudreault, A. (2009), *From Plato to Lumière. Narration and Monstration in Literature and Cinema*, Toronto.
Gauss, H. (1961), *Philosophischer Handkommentar* zu den Dialogen Platos, vol. III.2, Bern.
Gehrke, H.-J. (2001), "Myth, History and Collective Identity: Uses of the Past in Ancient Greece and Beyond", in: N. Luraghi (ed.), *The Historian's Craft in the Age of Herodotus*, Oxford, 286–313.
Gehrke, H.-J. (2019), "Intentional History and the Social Context of Remembrance in Ancient Greece", in: W. Pohl/V. Wieser (eds.), *Historiography and Identity. 1, Ancient and Early Chistian Narratives of Community*, Turnhout, 95–106.
Genette, G. (1980), *Narrative Discourse Revisited*, Ithaca.
Gigon, O. (1954), "Das Einleitungsgespräch der Gesetze Platons", *MH* 11, 201–230.
Gill, C. (1979), "Plato's Atlantis Story and the Birth of Fiction", *Philosophy and Literature* 3, 64–78.
Gill, C. (1993), "Plato on Falsehood – Not Fiction", in: C. Gill/T.P. Wiseman (eds.), *Lies and Fiction in the Ancient World*, Exeter, 38–87.
Gill, C. (1996), "Afterword: Dialectic and Dialogue Form in Late Plato", in: C. Gill/M.M. McCabe (eds.), *Form and Argument in Late Plato*, Oxford, 283–311.
Gill, C. (2002), "Dialectic and the Dialogue Form", in: J. Annas/C. Rowe (eds.), *Perspectives on Plato. Modern and Ancient*, Cambridge MA, 145–171.
Gill, C. (2017), *Plato's Atlantis Story. Text, Translation and Commentary*, Liverpool.
Gill, M.L. (2010), "Division and Definition in Plato's *Sophist* and *Statesman*, in: D. Charles (ed.), *Definition in Greek Philosophy*, Oxford, 172–199.
Golding, N.H. (1975), "Plato as City Planner", *Arethusa* 8, 359–371.
González, F.J. (2000), "The Eleatic Stranger: His Master's Voice", in: G.A. Press (ed.), *Who Speaks for Plato?: Studies in Platonic Anonymity*, Lanham, 161–181.
González, F.J. (2013), "No Country for Young Men: Eros as Outlaw in Plato's *Laws*", in: G.W. Recco/E. Sanday (eds.), *Plato's Laws. Force and Truth in Politics*, Indiana, 154–168.
Görgemanns, H. (1960), *Beiträge zur Interpretation von Platons* Nomoi, Munich.
Gottschlich, M. (2015), "Zur Systematik des μίμησις-Begriffs in Platons Kunstbegründung", *ABG* 57, 7–55.
Gould, J. (1992), "Plato and Performance", in: A. Barker/M. Warner (eds.), *The Language of the Cave*, Edmonton, 13–25.
Greco, A. (1994–1995), "Plato on Imitative Poetry in the *Republic*", *JNS* 3, 141–161.
Grethlein, J. (2021), "Author and Characters: Ancient, Narratological, and Cognitive Views on a Tricky Relationship", *CPh* 116, 208–230.
Griswold, C.L. (1989), "Politikē epistēmē in Plato's *Statesman*", in: J. Anton/A. Preus (eds.), *Essays in Ancient Philosophy III. Plato*, New York, 141–167.
Griswold, C.L. (1996), *Self-Knowledge in Plato's* Phaedrus, New Haven/London.
Gubrium, J.F./Holstein, J.A. (2008), "Narrative Ethnography", in: S. Hesse-Biber/P. Leavy (eds.), *Handbook of Emergent Methods*, New York, 241–264.
Gubrium, J.F./Holstein, J.A. (2009), *Analyzing Narrative Reality*, Los Angeles.
Hackforth, R. (1952), *Plato's* Phaedrus, Cambridge.
Haddad, A.B. (2012–2013), "A narrativa de Critias, uma *atopia*", *Kléos* 16–17.
Hadot, P. (1983), "Physique et poésie dans le *Timée* de Platon", *RThPh* 115, 113–133.

Halliwell, S. (2000), "From Mythos to Logos: Plato's Citations of the Poets", *CQ* 50, 94–112.
Halliwell, S. (2002), *The Aesthetics of Mimesis. Ancient Texts and Modern Problems*, Princeton.
Halliwell, S. (2006), "Plato and Aristotle on the Denial of Tragedy", in: A. Laird (ed.), *Ancient Literary Criticism*, Oxford, 115–141.
Halliwell, S. (2009), "The Theory and Practice of Narrative in Plato", in: J. Grethlein/A. Rengakos (eds.), *Narratology and Interpretation. The Content of Narrative Form in Ancient Literature*, Berlin/New York, 15–41.
Halliwell, S. (2014), "Diegesis–Mimesis", in: P. Hühn/J.C. Meister/J. Pier/W. Schmid (eds.), *Handbook of Narratology*, Berlin/New York, 129–137.
Harvey, G. (2006), "Politics, Slavery, and Home Economics: Defining an Expert in Plato's *Statesman*", *Apeiron* 39, 91–119.
Harvey, G. (2009), "Technē and the Good in Plato's *Statesman* and *Philebus*", *JHPh* 47, 1–33.
Hemmenway, S.R. (1994), "Pedagogy in the Myth of Plato's *Statesman*: Body and Soul in Relation to Philosophy and Politics", *HPhQ* 11, 253–268.
Herrick, M.T. (1946), *The Fusion of Horatian and Aristotelian Literary Criticism, 1531–1555*, Urbana.
Herter, H. (1958), "Gott und die Welt bei Platon. Eine Studie zum Mythos des *Politikos*", *Bonner Jahrbücher des Rheinischen Landesmuseums in Bonn und des Rheinischen Amtes für Bodendenkmalpflege im Landschaftsverband Rheinland* 158, 106–117.
Hildebrandt, K. (1959), *Platon, Logos und Mythos*, Berlin.
Hoenig, C. (2013), "Εἰκὼς λόγος: Plato in Translation(s)", *Methodos* 13. https://journals.openedition.org/methodos/2994.
Hoffmann, M. (1993), "The "Realization of the Due-Measure" as Structural Principle in Plato's *Statesman*", *Polis* 12, 77–98.
Horn, C. (2012), "Why Two Epochs of Human History? On the Myth of the *Statesman*", in: C. Collobert/P. Destrée/F.J. Gonzalez (eds.), *Plato and Myth. Studies on the Use and Status of Platonic Myths*, Leiden, 393–417.
Howland, J. (1993), "The Eleatic Stranger's Socratic Condemnation of Socrates", *Polis* 12, 15–36.
Hyvärinen, M. (2016), "Narrative and Sociology 1", *Narrative Works* 6, 38–62.
Ionescu, C. (2014), "Dialectical Method and Myth in Plato's *Statesman*", *Ancient Philosophy* 34, 29–46.
Ionescu, C. (2016), "Due Measure and the Dialectical Method in Plato's *Statesman*", *JPhR* 41, 77–104.
Janaway, C. (1995), *Images of Excellence. Plato's Critique of the Arts*, Oxford.
Johansen, T.K. (1998), "Truth, Lies and History in Plato's *Timaeus–Critias*", *Histos* 2.
Johansen, T.K. (2004), *Plato's Natural Philosophy*, Cambridge/New York.
Johansen, T.K. (2013), "Timaeus in the Cave", in: G.R. Boys-Stones/D. El Murr/C. Gill (eds.), *The Platonic Art of Philosophy*, Cambridge/New York, 90–109.
Joly, H. (1982), "Platon égyptologue", *Revue Philosophique de la France et de l'Étranger* 255–266.
Kahn, C.H. (1995), "The Place of the *Stateman* in Plato's Later Work", in: C.J. Rowe (ed.), *Reading the Statesman*, Sankt Augustin, 49–60.
Kahn, C.H. (2009), "The Myth of the *Statesman*", in: P. Catalin (ed.), *Plato's Myths*, Cambridge/New York, 148–166.
Kaklamanou, E./Pavlou, M./Tsakmakis, A. (eds.) (2021), *Framing the Dialogues. How to Read Openings and Closures in Plato*, Leiden/Boston.
Kamtekar, R. (2004), "What's the Good of Agreeing? Ὁμόνοια in Platonic Politics", *OSAP* 26, 131–170.

Kania, A. (2005), "Against the Ubiquity of Fictional Narrators", *The Journal of Aesthetics and Art Criticism* 63, 47–54.
Kélessidou, A. (1993), "L'homme "sans industrie et sans art" (*Politique* 274c): L'idée platonicienne de la "σωτηρίας μηχανή"", *RPhA* 11, 79–87.
Kennedy, G.A. (1993²), *The Cambridge History of Literary Criticism. Volume I: Classical Criticism*, Cambridge.
Kirby, J.T. (1991), "Mimesis and Diegesis: Foundations of Aesthetic Theory in Plato and Aristotle", *Helios* 18, 113–128.
Klein, J. (1977), *Plato's Trilogy. Theaetetus, the Sophist, and the Statesman*, Chicago.
Koopman, N. (2018), *Ancient Greek Ekphrasis: Between Description and Narration. Five Linguistic and Narratological Case Studies*, Leiden/Boston.
Kripke, S. (1971), "Semantical Considerations on Modal Logic", in: L. Linsky (ed.), *Reference and Modality*, Oxford, 63–72.
Kucharský, P. (1960), "La conception de l'art de la mesure dans le Politique", *Bulletin de l'Association Guillaume Budé*, 459–480.
Laks, A. (2007), "Marionnette ou miracle? Une note sur l'interprétation ficinienne d'un passage des *Lois* de Platon (I, 644c1–645c8)", in: L. Boulègue/C. Lévy (eds.), *Hédonismes: penser et dire le plaisir dans l'Antiquité et à la Renaissance*, Villeneuve-d'Ascq, 255–260.
Lane, M. (1998), *Method and Politics in Plato's Statesman*, Cambridge/New York.
Lavocat, F. (ed.) (2010), *La théorie littéraire des mondes possibles*, Paris.
Lear, G.R. (2011), "Mimesis and Psychological Change in *Republic* III", in: P. Destrée/F.G. Herrmann (eds.), *Plato and the Poets*, Leiden/Boston, 195–216.
Lee, H.D.P. (1965), *Timaeus*, Baltimore.
Lefka, A. (1994), "Pourquoi des dieux égyptiens chez Platon? ", *Kernos* 7, 159–168.
Leibniz, G.W. (1710), *Essais de Théodicée sur la bonté de Dieu, la liberté de l'homme et l'origine du mal*, Paris.
Lewis, D. (1978), "Truth in Fiction", *American Philosophical Quarterly* 15, 37–46.
Lichtenstein, E.H./Brewer, W.F. (1980), "Memory for Goal-Directed Events", *Cognitive Psychology* 12, 412–445.
Liotsakis, V. (2021), "Introduction", in: I.M. Konstantakos/V. Liotsakis (eds.), *Suspense in Ancient Greek Literature*, Berlin/Boston, 1–28.
Lisi, F.L. (2000), "La pensée historique de Platon dans les *Lois*", *Cahiers du Centre Gustave Glotz* 11, 9–23.
Lisi, F.L. (2017), "Φύσις en el libro X de las Leyes", *ÉP* 13.
Liveley, G. (2019), *Narratology*, Oxford.
Livov, G. (2011), "The Father and the Sophist: Platonic Parricide in the *Statesman*", in: N.-L. Cordero (ed.), *Parmenides, Venerable and Awesome (Plato, Theaetetus 183e). Proceedings of the International Symposium (Buenos Aires, October 29–November 2, 2007)*, Athens/Zurich, 331–343.
Lovejoy, A.O./Boas, G. (1935), *Primitivism and Related Ideas in Antiquity*, Baltimore.
Márquez, X. (2012), "Between *urbs* and *orbis*: Cicero's Conception of the Political Community", in: W. Nicgorski (ed.), *Cicero's Practical Philosophy*, Notre Dame, 181–211.
Marshall, M./Bilsborough, S.A. (2010), "The *Republic*'s Ambiguous Democracy", *HPhQ* 27, 301–316.
Mason, A.S. (2013), "The Nous Doctrine in Plato's Thought", *Apeiron* 46, 201–228.
Mayhew, R. (2007), "Persuasion and Compulsion in Plato's *Laws* 10", *Polis* 24, 91–111.

McBride, R. (2005), *Eikos Logos and Eikos Muthos. A Study of the Nature of the Likely in Plato's Timaeus*, Milwaukee Wisc.
McCabe, M.M. (1997), "Chaos and Control: Reading Plato's *Politicus*", *Phronesis* 42, 94–117.
McCabe, M.M. (2000), *Plato and His Predecessors. The Dramatisation of Reason*, Cambridge/New York.
McEvoy, J. (1993), "Platon et la sagesse de l'Égypte", *Kernos* 6, 245–275.
Menza, V.G. (1972), *Poetry and the τέχνη. An Analysis of the* Ion *and* Republic, Baltimore.
Merrill, J.P. (2003), "The Organization of Plato's *Statesman* and the Statesman's Role as a Herdsman", *Phoenix* 57, 35–56.
Metcalf, R. (2013), "On the Human and the Divine: Reading the Prelude in Plato's Laws 5", in: G.W. Recco/E. Sanday (eds.), *Plato's Laws. Force and Truth in Politics*, Indiana, 117–132.
Meyer, S.S. (2006), "Plato on the Law", in: H.H. Benson (ed.) (2006), *A Companion to Plato*, Oxford, 373–387.
Meyer, S.S. (2015), *Laws 1 and 2*, Oxford.
Michelini, A.N. (2000), "The Search for the King: Reflexive irony in Plato's *Politicus*", *ClassAnt* 19, 180–204.
Miller, C.R. (1993), "The Polis as Rhetorical Community", *Rhetorica* 11, 211–240.
Miller, M.H. (1980), *The Philosopher in Plato's* Statesman, Hague.
Mohr, R.D. (1980), "The Sources of Evil Problem and the ἀρχὴ κινήσεως Doctrine in Plato", *Apeiron* 14, 41–56.
Mohr, R.D. (1981), "Disorderly Motion in Plato's *Statesman*", *Phoenix* 25, 199–215.
Mohr, R.D./Sattler, B.M. (eds.) (2010), *One Book, the Whole Universe. Plato's* Timaeus *Today*, Las Vegas.
Möller, A. (ed.) (2019), *Historiographie und Vergangenheitsvorstellungen in der Antike. Beiträge zur Tagung aus Anlass des 70. Geburtstages von Hans-Joachim Gehrke*, Stuttgart.
Moore, K.R. (2007), "Erôs, Hybris and Mania: Love and Desire in Plato's *Laws* and Beyond", *Polis*, 112–133.
Morales Caturla, T. (2013), "El *Timeo-Critias*, una geografia imaginaria entre la escatologia y la historia", *RF* 38, 149–168.
Morgan, K.A. (1998), "Designer History: Plato' Atlantis Story and Fourth-Century Ideology", *JHS* 118, 101–118.
Morgan, K.A. (2000), *Myth and Philosophy from the Presocratics to Plato*, Cambridge/New York.
Morgan, K.A. (2004), "Plato", in: I.J.F. de Jong/R. Nünlist/A.M. Bowie (eds.), *Narrators, Narratees, and Narratives in Ancient Greek Literature*, Leiden/Boston, 357–376.
Morgan, K.A. (2010), "Narrative Orders in the *Timaeus* and *Critias*", in: R.D. Mohr/B.M. Sattler (eds.), *One Book, the Whole Universe. Plato's* Timaeus *Today*, Las Vegas, 267–285.
Morgan, K.A. (2012), "Plato", in: I.J.F. De Jong (ed.) (2012), *Studies in Ancient Greek Narrative 3. Space in Ancient Greek Literature*, Leiden/Boston, 415–437.
Morrow, G.R. (1953), "Plato's Conception of Persuasion", *The Philosophical Review* 62, 234–250.
Morrow, G.R. (1960), *Plato's Cretan City. A Historical Interpretation of the* Laws, Princeton.
Mouracade, J.M. (2005), "Virtue and Pleasure in Plato's *Laws*", *Apeiron* 38, 73–85.
Mourelatos, A.P.D. (2010), "The Epistemological Section (29b–d) of the Proem in Timaeus' Speech: M.F. Burnyeat on *eikôs mythos*, and Comparison with Xenophanes B34 and B35", in: R.D. Mohr/B.M. Sattler (eds.), *One Book, the Whole Universe. Plato's* Timaeus *Today*, Las Vegas, 225–247.

Mourelatos, A.P.D. (2014), "The Conception of Eoikōs/Eikōs as Epistemic Standard in Xenophanes, Parmenides, and in Plato's *Timaeus*", *AncPhil* 34, 169–191.
Müller, G. (1951), *Studien zu den platonischen Nomoi*, Munich.
Müller, G. (1968), *Morphologische Poetik*, Darmstadt.
Murray, A.T. (1919), *The Odyssey*, vols. 1–2, London/New York.
Murray, P. (1992), "Inspiration and Mimesis in Plato", in: A. Barker/M. Warner (eds.), *The Language of the Cave*, Edmonton Alb., 27–46.
Naas, M. (2018), *Plato and the Invention of Life*, New York.
Naddaf, G. (1993), "Mind and Progress in Plato", *Polis* 12, 122–133.
Nagy, G. (2000), *La poésie en acte. Homère et autres chants*, Berlin.
Neiman, P. (2007), "The Practicality of Plato's *Statesman*", *History of Political Thought* 28, 402–418.
Nesselrath, H.-G. (2002), *Platon und die Erfindung von Atlantis*, Leipzig.
Nesselrath, H.-G. (2006), *Platon. Kritias. Übersetzung und Kommentar*, Göttingen.
Nichols, J.H. (1998), *Plato. Phaedrus*, Ithaca/London.
Nightingale, A.W. (1993), "Writing/Reading a Sacred Text: A Literary Interpretation of Plato's *Laws*", *CPh* 88, 279–300.
Nightingale, A.W. (1999), "Historiography and Cosmology in Plato's *Laws*", *AncPhil* 19, 299–326.
Ogata, T. (2016), "Computational and Cognitive Approaches to Narratology from the Perspective of Narrative Generation", in: T. Ogata/T. Akimoto (eds.), *Computational and Cognitive Approaches to Narratology*, Hershey, 1–74.
Osborne, C. (1996), "Space, Time, Shape, and Direction: Creative Discourse in the *Timaeus*", in: C. Gill/M.M. McCabe (eds.), *Form and Argument in Late Plato*, Oxford/New York, 179–211.
Pangle, T.L. (1974), "Politics and Religion in Plato's *Laws*: Some Preliminary Remarks", *Essays in Arts and Sciences* 3, 19.
Partee, M.H. (1973), "Plato on the Criticism of Poetry", *PhQ* 52, 629–642.
Pavel, T.G. (1975), "Possible Worlds in Literary Semantics", *The Journal of Aesthetics and Art Criticism* 34, 165–176.
Pavel, T.G. (1986), *Fictional Worlds*, Cambridge MA/London.
Pender, E.E. (2007), "Poetic Allusion in Plato's *Timaeus* and *Phaedrus*", *GFA* 10, 21–57.
Peponi, A.-E. (ed.) (2013), *Performance and Culture in Plato's* Laws, Cambridge.
Petrovsky, M. (1987), "Morphology in the Novella", *Essays in Poetics* 12, 22–50.
Petrucci, F.M. (2004), "Un dialogo aperto: il *Politico* di Platone", *SCO* 50, 107–149.
Pfefferkorn, J. (2020), "Shame and Virtue in Plato's *Laws*: Two Kinds of Fear and the Drunken Puppet", in: L. Candiotto/O. Renaut (eds.), *Emotions in Plato*, Leiden/Boston, 252–269.
Plummer, K. (1995), *Telling Sexual Stories. Power, Change and Social Worlds*, London.
Post, L.A. (1929), "The Preludes to Plato's *Laws*", *TAPhA* 60, 5–24.
Poster, C. (2005), "Framing *Theaetetus*: Plato and Rhetorical (Mis)Representation", *Rhetoric Society Quarterly* 35, 31–73.
Powell, A. (1994), "Plato and Sparta: Modes of Rule and of Non-Rational Persuasion in the *Laws*", in: A. Powell/S. Hodkinson (eds.), *The Shadow of Sparta*, Swansea, 273–321.
Pradeau, J.-F (1995), "Être quelque part, occuper une place: τόπος et χώρα dans le *Timée*", *ÉPh* 3, 375–399.
Pradeau, J.-F. (1997), *Le monde de la politique. Sur le récit atlante de Platon, Timée (17–27) et Critias*, Sankt Augustin.

Pradeau, J.-F. (2004), "L'ébrété démocratique: la critique platonicienne de la démocratie dans les *Lois*", *JHS* 124, 108–124.
Prauscello, L. (2017), "Plato *Laws* 3.680B–C: Antisthenes, the Cyclopes and Homeric Exegesis", *JHS* 137, 8–23.
Press, G.A. (2000), *Who Speaks for Plato? Studies in Platonic Anonymity*, Lanham.
Price, A.W. (2011), *Virtue and Reason in Plato and Aristotle*, Oxford.
Prince, G. (1982), *Narratology. The Form and Functioning of Narrative*, Berlin/New York/Amsterdam.
Priou, A. (2013), "The Philosopher in Plato's *Sophist*", *Hermathena* 195, 5–29.
Racionero, Q. (1997), "Logos, mito y discurso probable: (en torno a la escritura del *Timeo* de Platón", *CFC* 7, 135–155.
Racionero, Q. (1998), "Logos, Myth and Probable Discoursse in Plato's *Timaeus*", *Elenchos* 19, 29–60.
Rankin, H.D. (1958), "Toys and Education in Plato's *Laws*", *Hermathena* 92, 62–65.
Rees, B.R. (1981), "Aristotle for the Structuralist", *CR* 31, 178–179.
Regali, M. (2011), "Socrate giudice nel *Timeo* di Platone", *SCO* 57, 73–96.
Regali, M. (2012), *Il poeta e il demiurgo. Teoria e prassi della produzione letteraria nel* Timeo *e nel* Crizia *di Platone*, Sankt Augustin.
Rengakos, A. (1999), "Spannungsstrategien in den homerischen Epen", in: N. Kazazis/A. Rengakos (eds.), *Euphrosyne. Studies in Ancient Epic and Its Legacy in Honor of Dimitris N. Maronitis*, Stuttgart, 308–338.
Rengakos, A. (2006a), "Thucydides' Narrative: The Epic and Herodotean Heritage", in: A. Rengakos/A. Tsakmakis (eds.), *Brill's Companion to Thucydides*, Leiden, 279–300.
Rengakos, A. (2006b), "Homer and the Historians: The Influence of Epic Narrative Techniques on Herodotus and Thucydides, in: F. Montanari/A. Rengakos (eds.), *La poésie épique grecque. Métamorphoses d'un genre littéraire*, Vandœuves/Genève, 183–209.
Rengakos, A./Tsakmakis, A. (eds.) (2006), *Brill's Companion to Thucydides*, Leiden.
Reverdin, O. (1945), *La religion de la cite platonicienne*, Paris.
Reydams-Schils, G.J. (2011), "Myth and Poetry in the *Timaeus*", in: P. Destrée (ed.), *Plato and the Poets*, Leiden/Boston, 349–360.
Ritter, C. (1923), *Platon. Sein Leben, seine Schriften, eine Lehre, II*, Munich.
Ritter, C. (1985²), *Platos Gesetze*, vols. I–II, Aalen.
Robin, L. (1919), *Études sur la signification et la place de la physique dans la philosophie du Platon*, Paris.
Robinson, T.M. (2003), "Il *Politico* di Platone: il mito e le sue implicazioni cosmologiche", *SCO* 49, 45–57.
Rodier, G. (1911), "Note sur la politique d'Antisthene: le mythe du *Politique*", *Année Philosophique*, 1–7.
Ronen, R. (1994), *Possible Worlds in Literary Theory*, Cambridge.
Rosen, S. (1995), *Plato's* Statesman. *The Web of Politics*, New Haven.
Rosenmeyer, T.G. (1956), "Plato's Atlantis Myth. *Timaeus* or *Critias*?", *Phoenix* 10, 163–172.
Rösler, W. (1980), "Die Entdeckung der Fiktionalität in der Antike", *Poetica* 12, 283–319.
Rousseaux, M. (1970), "Une Atlantide en Méditerranée occidentale", *BAGB*, 337–358.
Rowe, C. (1995), *Statesman*, Warminster.
Rowe, C. (1997), "Why is the Ideal Athens of the *Timaeus–Critias* not Ruled by Philosophers?", *Méthexis* 10, 51–57.

Rowe, C. (1999), "Myth, History, and Dialectic in Plato's *Republic* and *Timaeus–Critias*", in: R.G.A. Buxton (ed.), *From Myth to Reason? Studies in the Development of Greek Thought*, Oxford/New York, 263–278.

Rowe, C. (2007), "Plato and the Persian Wars", in: E. Bridges/E. Hall/P.J. Rhodes (eds.), *Cultural Responses to the Persian Wars. Antiquity to the Third Millennium*, Oxford, 85–104.

Russell, D.A./Winterbottom, M. (eds.) (1972), *Ancient Literary Criticism. The Principal Texts in New Translations*, Oxford.

Ryan, M.-L. (1991), *Possible Worlds, Artificial Intelligence, and Narrative Theory*, Indianapolis.

Ryan, M.-L. (2005), "On the Theoretical Foundations of Transmedial Narratology", in: J.C. Meister (ed.) (2005), *Narratology beyond Literary Criticism. Mediality, Disciplinarity*, Berlin, 1–23.

Salem, É. (2013), "The Long and Winding Road: Impediments to Inquiry in Book 1 of the *Laws*", in: G.W. Recco/E. Sanday (eds.), *Plato's Laws. Force and Truth in Politics*, Indiana, 48–59.

Sallis, J. (2013), "On Beginning after the Beginning", in: G.W. Recco/E. Sanday (eds.), *Plato's Laws. Force and Truth in Politics*, Indiana, 75–85.

Saunders, T.J. (1970), *Plato. The Laws*, London.

Sayre, K.M. (1992), "A Maieutic View of Five Late Dialogues", in: J.C. Klagge/N.D. Smith (eds.), *Methods of Interpreting Plato and His Dialogues*, Oxford, 221–243.

Scarcella, A.M. (1987), "Attrei dell'officina platonica. Struttura narratologica e progetto ideologico del *Convito*", in: E. Mirri (ed.), *Letture platoniche*, Naples, 41–52.

Schaeffer, J.-M. (2009), "Fictional vs. Factual Narration", in: P. Hühn/J.C. Meister/J. Pier/W. Schmid (eds.), *Handbook of Narratology*, Berlin/New York, 98–114.

Schaerer, R. (1953), "L'itinéraire dialectique des *Lois* de Platon et sa signification philosophique", *RPh* 143, 379–412.

Schalcher, M.G.F.F. (1997), "Mito e participação no *Timeu* de Platão", *Kléos* 1, 157–165.

Schein, S.L. (1970), "Odysseus and Polyphemus in the *Odyssey*", *GRBS* 11, 73–83.

Schmid, W. (2010), *Narratology. An Introduction*, Berlin/New York.

Schmid, W. (ed.) (2009), *Russische Proto-Narratologie. Texte in kommentierten Übersetzungen*, Berlin.

Schofield, M. (1999), "The Disappearance of the Philosopher King", in: J.J. Cleary/G.M. Gurtler (eds.), *Proceedings of the Boston Area Colloquium in Ancient Philosophy. 13, 1997*, Leiden/Boston, 213–241.

Schofield, M. (2006), *Plato. Political Philosophy*, Oxford.

Schöpsdau, K. (1994), *Werke. Übersetzung und Kommentar. 9, 2 Nomoi (= Gesetze). Buch I–III*, Göttingen.

Schöpsdau, K. (2003), *Werke. Übersetzung und Kommentar. 9, 2 Nomoi (= Gesetze). Buch IV–VII*, Göttingen.

Schröder, M. (1935), *Zum Aufbau des platonischen Politikos*, Jena.

Schuhl, P.-M. (1932), "Sur le mythe du Politique", *Revue de Métaphysique et de Morale*, 47–58.

Schultz, A.-M. (2013), *Plato's Socrates as Narrator. A Philosophical Muse*, Lanham, MD.

Scott, S. (2020), "Loving and Living Well: The Importance of Shame in Plato's *Phaedrus*", in: L. Candiotto/O. Renaut (eds.), *Emotions in Plato*, Leiden/Boston, 270–284.

Shklovsky, V. (1929), *O teorii prozy*, Moscow.

Shklovsky, V. (1965), "Sterne's Tristam Shandy: Stylistic Commentary", in: L.T. Lemon/M.J. Reis (eds.), *Russian Formalism Criticism*, Lincoln, 25–57.

Shklovsky, V. (1990), *Theory of Prose*, Elmwood Park.

Skemp, J.B. (1989), "The *Timaeus* and the Criterion of Truth", in: P.M Huby/G. Neal (eds.), *The Criterion of Truth. Essays in Honour of George Kerferd, Together with a Text and Translation (with Annotations) of Ptolemy's* On the Kriterion and Hegemonikon, Liverpool, 83–92.

Skemp, J.B. (1992), *Plato's* Statesman. *With an Introduction by Martin Ostwald*, Indianapolis.

Skultéty, S. (2006), "Currency, Trade and Commerce in Plato's *Laws*", *History of Political Thought* 27, 189–205.

Smith, C.S. (2018), "The Groundwork for Dialectic in *Statesman*", *IJPT* 12, 132–150.

Speliotis, E.D. (2011), "Φρόνησις and Law in Plato's *Statesman*", *Ancient Philosophy* 31, 295–310.

Stalley, R.F. (1983), *An Introduction to Plato's* Laws, Oxford.

Stalley, R.F. (1994), "Persuasion in Plato's *Laws*", *History of Political Thought* 15, 157–177.

Sternberg, M. (1978), *Expositional Modes and Temporal Ordering in Fiction*, Baltimore.

Stewart, J.A. (1905), *The Myths of Plato*, London.

Taylor, A.E. (1928), *A Commentary on Plato's* Timaeus, New York.

Taylor, Q.P. (2000), "Political Science or Political Sophistry?: A Critique of Plato's *Statesman*", *Polis* 17, 91–109

Todorov, V. (1981), *Introduction to Poetics*, Brighton.

Tomasi, J. (1990), "Plato's *Statesman* Story: The Birth of Fiction", *Philosophy and Literature* 14, 348–358.

Trampedach, K./Mann, C. (eds.) (2019), *Politik und politisches Denken. Hans–Joachim Gehrke*, Stuttgart.

Trowbridge, H. (1944), "Aristotle and New Criticism", *The Sewanee Review* 52, 537–555.

Tulli, M. (1991), "Età di Crono e ricerca sulla natura nel *Politico* di Platone", *SCO* 40, 97–115.

Tulli, M. (2013), "The Atlantis Poem in the *Timaeus-Critias*", in: G.R. Boys-Stones/D. El Murr/C. Gill (eds.), *The Platonic Art of Philosophy*, Cambridge/New York, 269–282.

Vaina, L. (1977), "Les «mondes possibles» de la narration", *Langage et Littérature* 22, 355–263.

van Noorden, H. (2015), *Playing the Hesiod. The 'Myth of the Races' in Classical Antiquity*, Cambridge/New York.

Verlinsky, A.L. (2008), "The Cosmic Cycle in the *Statesman* Myth. 1", *Hyperboreus* 14, 57–86.

Verlinsky, A.L. (2009), "The Cosmic Cycle in the *Statesman* Myth. 2: The Gods and the Universe", *Hyperboreus* 15, 221–250.

Verlinsky, A.L. (2010-2011), "Theology and Relative Dates of the *Timaeus* and the *Statesman*: Some Considerations", *Hyperboreus* 16–17, 328–345.

Vickers, B. (1988), *In Defense of Rhetoric*, Oxford.

Vidal-Naquet, P. (1964), "Athènes et l'Atlantide. Structure et signification d'un mythe platonicien", *RÉG* 77, 420–444.

Vidal-Naquet, P. (1986), "Athens and Atlantis: Structure and Signification of a Platonic Myth", in: P. Vidal-Naquet (ed.), *The Black Hunter. Forms of Thought and Forms of Society in the Greek World*, Baltimore/London, 263–284 (= "Athènes et Atlantide: structure et signification d'un mythe platonicien", *RÉG* 77, 420–444.

Walsh, R. (1997), "Who Is the Narrator?", *Poetics Today* 18, 495–513.

Walsh, R. (2010), "Person, Level, Voice: A Rhetorical Reconsideration", in: J. Alber/M. Fludernik (eds.), *Postclassical Narratology. Approaches and Analyses*, Ohio, 35–57.

Walton, K.L. (1990), *Mimesis as Make-Believe. On the Foundations of the Representational Arts*, New York.

Warren, J. (2014), *The Pleasures of Reason in Plato, Aristotle, and the Hellenistic Hedonists*, Cambridge/New York.

Waterfield, R. (2002), *Plato. Phaedrus*, Oxford.
Weil, R. (1959), *L'«archéologie» de Platon*, Paris.
Welliver, N. (1977), *Character, Plot and Thought in Plato's* Timaeus *and* Critias, Leiden.
Welton, W.A. (1996), "Incantation and Expectation in Laws II", *Philosophy and Rhetoric* 29, 211–224.
Whitaker, A.K. (2004), *A Journey into Platonic Politics. Plato's* Laws, Lanham.
White, D. (2018), "Paradigm, Form and the Good in Plato's *Statesman*: The Myth Revisited", in: B. Bossi/T.M. Robinson (eds.), *Plato's* Statesman *Revisited*, Berlin/Boston, 87–105.
Willems, G. (1989), *Anschaulichkeit. Zur Theorie und Geschichte der Wort-Bild-Beziehungen und des literarischen Darstellungsstils*, Tübingen.
Willink, C.W. (1986), *Orestes*, Oxford.
Wright, M.R. (2000), "Myth, Science and Reason in the *Timaeus*", in: M.R. Wright (ed.), *Reason and Necessity. Essays on Plato's* Timaeus, Swansea, 1–22.
Wright, M.R. (2000), *Reason and Necessity. Essays on Plato's* Timaeus, Swansea.
Yunis, H.E. (1990), "Rhetoric as Instruction: A Response to Vickers on Rhetoric in the *Laws*", *Philosophy and Rhetoric* 23, 125–135.
Yunis, H.E. (2011), *Plato. Phaedrus*, Cambridge.
Zeise, H. (1938), *Der Staatsmann. Ein Beitrag zur Interpretation des platonischen* Politikos, Leipzig.
Zeyl, D.J. (2000), *Timaeus*, Cambridge MA.
Zichi, C. (2018), *Poetic Diction and Poetic References in the Preludes of Plato's Laws*, Lund.
Zipfel, F. (2014), "Fiction across Media: Toward a Transmedial Concept of Fictionality", in: M.-L. Ryan/J.-N. Thon (eds.), *Storyworlds across Media. Toward a Media-Conscious Narratology*, Lincoln/London, 103–125.
Zuckert, C.H. (2009), "Practical Plato", in: S.G. Salkever (ed.), *The Cambridge Companion to Ancient Greek Political Thought*, Cambridge/New York, 178–208.
Zuckert, M.P. (2013), "It Is Difficult for a City with Good Laws to Come into Existence: On Book 4", in: G.W. Recco/E. Sanday (eds.), *Plato's* Laws: *Force and Truth in Politics*, Indiana, 86–104.

Index Nominum et Rerum

actors/performers VIII, 81–82, 87, 208
Adeimantus XVI
anticipation, 45–50, 54
Apollo XVI, 116–117, 130, 191
Argos 133, 140, 157, 159, 181, 183, 186, 188
Aristotle VII with n. 1, XV n. 16, XXI, XXIII, 14, 112 n. 5, 172 n. 108
Athenian Visitor XXII–XXIII, 92, 108–195
Athens 55–57, 59 with n. 10, 63–65, 67, 79 n. 72, 84, 87, 97–98, 100–101, 103 with n. 118, 106, 161, 167, 187, 191, 193, 195, 199
Atlantis, account of 55–107,
Atreus 15–18, 20–21, 179
audience (mainly) 45–50, 80–88, 112–159

Bal, Mieke 24–25

Cadmus 127–128, 131
Cambyses 133, 140, 188–189
causality 24–30
Cea 138
Cephalus 55, 99 n. 110, 101
Clinias XXII, 109 with n. 3, 115–118, 122, 128, 129 n. 39, 133–134, 136, 140, 142, 161, 164, 166 n. 97, 167–168, 169 with n. 103, 170 with n. 104, 185, 187, 193
Cnossos 115–116, 142, 167
cognitive narratology IX
cognitive studies IX, 47
comedy VIII
cosmological myth in the *Statesman* XVII–XIX, 1–54
– and political theory XVII-XVIII, 7–11, 17–21
– authorial comments within the account 21–24, 27–30, 32–33, 35–36, 45–50
– introductory remarks 14–21, 24–27
– its place in the overall logic of the *Statesman* XVII
– narrative arrangement of 3–11
cosmological narratives 1–107, 166
Cresphontes 181

Crete 115–119, 149–150, 168, 169 with n. 102, 170–171, 189
Critias XXII, 55 with n. 1, 56–57, 59 with n. 10, 62–69, 74–80, 84–87, 89–91, 93–94, 96–99, 101, 103–106, 198–199, 201, 207
Critias the elder 56, 64, 89, 97, 98 with n. 107
Cronus, the age of 3–11
cross-referencing 2, 7, 28, 36, 53, 75, 111, 114, 144, 149–151, 197–200, 204
Cyclopes 161, 170–180
Cyrus 188

Darius 188–189, 191
Democritus XVIII n. 21, 172 n. 108
diegesis vs. mimesis and *showing vs. telling* IX n. 5
different kinds of narrators VIII–XI
digressions 2, 11, 23, 36–54, 131, 185, 187, 189–190, 195, 200, 204, 206
Dionysus 116, 192
dithyramb VIII, 191–193
division XVII, 26 n. 50, 37–41, 51–52
Doležel, Lubomir 55–107
Dorians 133, 161, 182–187

Egypt 56, 122–124, 130–131, 137 n. 45, 148, 150, 157, 159, 191
Egyptians of Sais 56, 64, 66, 84, 89, 90 n. 96, 98–99, 199, 203
Eleatic Visitor XVII, 1–54, 131, 163–164, 166, 179
Empedocles XVIII n. 21
emplotment XIX, 110
Epimenides 167–170
erzählte Zeit vs. Erzählzeit 36 n. 56
Eurysthenes 181

fabula XIX, 12–14, 16–17, 20–21, 23–26, 28, 164–166, 171
fictional worlds 55–107
– as products of their sociocultural background 88–99

226 — Index Nominum et Rerum

– emerging from intertextual connections 99–106
– immersion 80–88
– incompleteness of 68–80
– possibility/impossibility of 59–68
– sequels/prequels 99–106
formalist narratology 2, 11–14, 16, 26, 36, 45–50, 53–54, 108

Ganymede 119–122, 124, 127, 130, 159
Gehrke, Hans-Joachim 120
Genette, Gérard IX
Greeks XVI, XXIII, 18, 65, 132, 137, 157, 159, 161, 167, 170, 183–184, 191

Halliwell, Stephen IX, XI–XII, XIV–XV
Heracleidae 149, 184
Heraclitus XVIII n. 21
Hermocrates 55, 67, 85, 89–91, 97 n. 102, 99 n. 110
Herodotus 79 with n. 71, 161, 204
Hesiod XVII–XVIII with n. 21, XIX, 125, 168–169, 198
Homer VIII, XVI–XVIII with n. 21, 87, 117, 132, 138 n. 49, 168, 169 n. 102, 170 with n. 104, 171–180, 194, 198–199, 203
Horace VII with nn. 1–2, XV n. 16

Iliad XVI, 87, 125, 169, 174, 176 n. 112, 179–180, 209
intentional history 111, 120–121, 159–195, 201, 204, 208
interaction between metanarrative reflections and narrative paradigms
– component-endowing statements 198–200
– dialogic narratives 202–203
– dispersive statements 196–198
– recurring narrative schemes 200–201
Ion IX, 52, 81–82, 87, 94, 208–209
Isis 123–124, 130–131, 159

kallipolis VIII, XI, 55–57, 59 with n. 10, 62–63, 65, 67–69, 77–78, 81–87, 89, 91–97, 100–106, 108, 198–199, 207, 209
Kripke, Saul 58 with n. 6, 60, 63

Leibniz, Gottfried 57–58
Lewis, David 55–107
literary criticism VII, XXIII, 205
Locri 90, 96, 138
logos X, 41–42
Longinus VII
Lycurgus 187

Magnesia XXIII–XXIV, 111–112, 115, 119–121, 144, 147–150, 153, 178, 208
make-believe game 57, 81, 84–85, 87
Megillus XXII, 109 with n. 3, 116, 119, 128–129 with n. 39, 161, 166 n. 97, 167, 170–171 with nn. 105–106, 178–180, 182–183, 185, 203
Messene 133, 140, 157, 159, 181, 183, 186–188
metalepsis in Plato XIII n. 15
mimesis
– as dialogue/monologue IX n. 5, 80, 209
– as representation X with n. 8, XXI, 81, 85
Minos 115, 117 with n. 15, 120, 159, 169 n. 102
mythos X, 16 with n. 27

narrating/listening time 2, XIX, 36–50, 52–54, 108, 197, 204, 206–207
narratology VII with nn. 1 and 3, VIII–X with n. 5, XII–XIII, XV, XIX, XXI–XXII with n. 32, 2, 11–14, 16, 26, 36–37, 45–50, 53–54, 56–57, 59, 101, 106–108, 196, 203–205, 210
New Criticism VII n. 1, 58

Odysseus 171–173, 175–177 with n. 114, 200
Odyssey 87, 117, 125, 169–180, 190, 194, 199–200, 209

Parmenides 51, 104–105, 166 n. 97
Pavel, Thomas 55–107
Peloponnese 140–141, 144, 153–154, 157, 159, 184
Persian Wars 65, 133, 191, 193
Persians 65, 140, 167, 187–188, 190–191
Phaedrus XVI–XVII, 79, 120 n. 24

plot 2, 12–14, 16, 21, 35–36, 47, 53, 59, 68–69, 73, 77, 101, 103, 105, 109, 138–139, 141, 161, 164–165, 167–168, 170, 172 n. 107, 178–181, 185, 188, 190–195, 197–200, 202
poetics VII, XII, 159–195, 201, 204–205
poetry and poets VII–IX with n. 4, XXIII, 68–70, 81–82, 90 with n. 96, 91–95, 97–98 with nn. 105–106, 111, 116, 122, 125, 160, 167, 170 with n. 104, 171–172 with n. 107, 190–195, 198, 200, 207, 209
Polyphemus 171–180
possible worlds 55–107
preludes XXIII–XXIV, 109–110, 112–114, 118–119, 121, 129, 131, 136–137, 143–159, 195, 204
Pre-Socratics XVII–XX with n. 21, 206
Protagoras 10–11, 52–53, 95, 172 n. 108, 178 n. 116, 209,

Republic VIII–XII, XVI, XVIII with nn. 22–23, 55, 57, 59, 65–66, 68, 79, 84, 90 n. 96, 91, 93–94, 99 with n. 110, 100, 102–106, 108–109, 124 n. 30, 172 n. 108, 195, 198–199, 204–205
Rhadamanthys 117, 120
Ronen, Ruth 55–107
Russian Formalism XV n. 16, 13 nn. 18–19
Ryan, Marie-Laure 55–107

selectivity / selection procedure 2, 13–24, 27, 44–45, 52–53, 73–74, 110, 162–171, 197
socio-narratology 205–210
Socrates VIII–XII, XVI, XXII, 207–209 with n. 7
Solon 55 n. 1, 56, 64, 86, 89, 94, 97–99, 103, 203
sophists X n. 9, 39, 43, 51, 62, 69–70, 90, 92–95 with n. 101, 206–207, 209
space in Plato XIII n. 15

Sparta 115–117 with n. 15, 119, 133, 139, 150, 159, 167 with n. 100, 170–171, 179, 181–183, 186–187, 189, 208
sujet XIX, 12–13, 23, 25, 27–28, 164, 166, 171, 178, 180
suspense 45–50, 181–190
– coexistence of fear and hope 45–50, 183
– delay 45–50, 181–190
– 'harm anticipation' phenomenon 118
– identification of the audience's horizon of knowledge with that of the characters of a plot 182–183
– piece-meal revelation 183

Temenus 181
temporality 13 n. 21, 14, 30–36, 110, 162–171, 197
Thebes 128, 130
Thucydides XXIII, 172 n. 108, 204
Thyestes 15–18, 20–21, 179
Timaeus XII, 55–107, 197–198, 201, 207
tragedy VIII, 124, 169
Trojan War 132, 136, 138, 154, 158–159, 198, 202
Troy 87, 132–133, 137–138, 154, 159, 180, 184

who speaks for Plato X–XII

Xerxes 133, 140, 189, 191

Young Socrates XVII, 1–3, 5–8, 16–21, 23, 25, 27–39, 42–43, 45–46, 48–50, 53, 166 n. 97, 197–198, 201–202, 206–207, 209

Zeus, the age of 3–11
ἁπλῆ διήγησις VIII–X
δι' ἀμφοτέρων διήγησις VIII–X
διὰ μιμήσεως διήγησις VIII–X

Index Locorum

Aristotle
Cretan Constitution (ed.Rose)
f 611.14   117 n. 13

Ephorus (*FGrHist* 70)
F 147   117 n. 13

Homer
Il.
2.570   176 n. 112
2.712   176 n. 112
5.543   176 n. 112
5.778   174 n. 110
6.13   176 n. 112
6.391   176 n. 112
7.59   174 n. 110
9.129   176 n. 112
9.271   176 n. 112
9.323   174 n. 110
14.290   174 n. 110
17.611   176 n. 112
20.216–218   180
20.216–217   180
20.218   180
20.496   176 n. 112
21.40   176 n. 112
21.77   176 n. 112

Od.
4.342   176 n. 112
5.51   174 n. 110
9.105–566   171–180
9.106   175
9.112   174
9.113   172
9.115   174
9.116–129   172–173
9.125–129   172
9.126   173
9.129   173, 176 n. 112
9.130–141   176
9.130   176 with n. 112
9.175–176   175
9.184–185   173
9.215   175
9.219–223   173
9.219   173
9.222–223   173
9.225   173
9.232   173
9.244–249   173
9.248   174
9.247   174
9.279–280   177
9.281–282   177
9.281   177
9.297   173
9.308–309   173
9.340–341   173
9.384–388   177
9.391–394   178
9.391   178
9.393   178
9.494   175
17.133   176 n. 112
19.178–181   117
22.52   176 n. 112
22.302   174 n. 110
24.226   176 n. 112
24.336   176 n. 112

Plato
Apol.
19e1–20a4   95 n. 101
21b5–6   120 n. 25
22a8–c8   94 n. 99
40e4–41c7   110 n. 4
42a3–5   72 n. 48

Charm.
155a2–3   97 n. 105
155e5–157d8   113 n. 10
157e5–158a1   97 n. 105

Cratyl.
391d2–392b7   72 n. 48
391d3–e1   120 n. 25
400d6–401a6   71 n. 46

Critias
106a1–108d8	55
106b5–6	72
106b8–108a4	56
106b8–107e3	75
107a4–6	76
107a8–b1	75
107c1–2	75
107c4–6	75
107d1	75
107d3	75
107d6–7	75

Euthyd.
275c5–d4	26 n. 49
280b1–3	26 n. 49
290e1–291a7	26 n. 49

Io.
533c9–536d7	82–83, 87
536d8–542b4	94

Lach.
178b3–4	71 n. 46

Leg.
624a1–626c5	115
624–625	118 n. 17
624a1–625a3	117
624a7–625a4	169 n. 102
624a7	117 n. 15
625a5–b1	117
625b1–7	128 n. 38
625c9–631b2	118
625c9–626b4	133
625c10–d7	137
626a3–5	134
626c6–631b2	133
626c6–628e5	115
626d1–627d7	140
628c10–11	136
628d2–e1	136
629a1–631b2	115
629a4–5	167
629b3–5	167
630a1–b8	138
630a5–d1	155
630a7–d1	157
631b2–d1	157
631b3–650b10	116
631–632	185 n. 123, 189 n. 125
631b3–632d7	125
631b3–632b1	185
631b3–632d1	118–119, 121
631b3–d1	134, 155
631b6–d1	152, 154
631b8–c1	134
631c4–5	156
631c7–8	152
631d1–632d1	118
632c4–d1	141
632c5	141
632c6	141
633a1–636a3	119
634d1–2	128 n. 38
634d4–635a8	208
634d7–635b1	117
635a3–5	128 n. 38
636a4–c7	119
636c7–d4	119
636c7	119
636d1	119
637a3	153 n. 73
638a3–7	138
638b1–3	138
639b7	189
641c3–5	153 n. 73
641e2–642b1	167
642b2–d2	167
642d3–643a1	167–168
643b4–644b4	139
643b4–d4	139
643d6–644b4	139
643d6–644a5	135
643e3–644a5	134
644a3–4	135
644a4	135 n. 43
647a4–b7	191
649c8–d7	188
649d5–7	189
649d5–6	153 n. 73
649d6–7	188–189
653a5–c4	116, 139
653c7–664d4	122

653c7–657c2	122	664a6–7	148
653d3 ff.	192	664b3–d2	128
654e9–656c7	122	664b4–5	129
656c1–660c1	152	664b5	129
656c3–4	194	664c7–d1	130
656d1–657c2	137 n. 45	664d2–4	128
656d1–657a2	122	664d3–4	129
656d5–657b8	157	664d4	130
657a5–8	123	668b9–669b3	92
657a6	148	670e4–5	194
657a7	123 n. 30	676a1–680e5	132
657a8–9	124	676a–c	163
657a9–b1	124	676a1–c10	162–163
657b3	123 with n. 30	676a1–c4	137 n. 47
657b7–8	123	676a1–6	137 n. 45
657c3–660d10	116	676a1	164
657c3–658d9	125	676a4	164
657c3	123 with n. 30	676a6	164
657d1–6	128 n. 38	676a7	164
658–663	129	676a8–b1	164
658c10–d5	169	676a8	164
658d6–9	169–170	676b1	164
658d6–7	128 n. 38	676b4	164
658e6–663d5	125	676b7	164
658e6–659c7	192	676b9–c1	165
658e9–659a1	192	676c1–2	165
659a1–b2	192	676c6–8	139, 164
659a4–b3	193	676c6–7	164
659a5–6	192	677a1–b4	164
659c9–660a8	155	677a1	164
659d4–e5	125	677a4–5	165
659e1–2	129	677a8–b4	165
659e5–660a3	125	677a8–9	165–166
660b6–7	193	677a8	203
660d11–664d4	122	677b1–2	172
660d11–663c5	126	677b5–c9	166
660d11–662a3	134, 154, 157	677b5–6	133
660e6–662a4	152	677b6	173
661b1–2	154	677c	135
661d6–662a2	153	677c1	203
661e2	153	677c3	203
662a1	154	677c4–9	177
662a2	175	677c4–7	133
663a9–d5	126	677d7–e5	168
663d ff.	118 n. 17	678b1–3	136
663d6–664b2	126–127	678c2–3	133, 173
663e6	127	678c2	172

678c5–e5	158	682b4–5	180
678c5	175	682c6–10	137
678c6–d6	133	682c9–10	159
678c6–d3	172	682d5–e6	138
678c6–7	173	682d5–e2	154
678c7–8	173	682d7–8	139
678c7	158–159	682d7	137 n. 48, 139
678c8–d3	135	682d9	139
678c9–d1	178	682e	140 n. 53
678e2–4	133	683b1–6	181
678e9–679c8	175	683c8–693c5	133, 181–187
678e9–679b5	153	683c8–e2	181
678e9–679a4	135	683c8–d4	140, 181
678e9	136	683e3–684a2	137 n. 45, 181
679a2–3	173	683e3–6	140
679a5–7	174	683e7–684a1	140
679a5–6	173–174	684a1	148
679a6–7	174	684a2–c10	182
679b–c	158 n. 80	684b5	182
679b3–c2	135	684c1–6	182
679b3–4	158	684d1–e6	182
679b8–c2	155, 158	684d1	183
679b8–c1	153	684d4–e5	149
679b8–9	175	684d4	183
679c2–8	135	684d7	149
679c3–7	135	684d9–e2	150
679c4–5	177	684e7–8	183–184
679d4–e2	135	685a1	161, 182
679e2–3	135	685a5	183
680a3–7	174	685a6–b1	183
680a3	136	685b7–e4	157
680a5–7	136, 157	685b7–c5	184
680a6–7	174	685c5–686a6	184
680b1–d6	169–170	686a7–b7	184
680d1–3	161, 178–179	686b8–c3	137 n. 45
680d7–8	133	686c7–690c9	185
680e1–2	174	686c7–e8	185
680e2	174	686e4	157
680e6–681d5	132	687a2–688d5	157
680e6–681a1	180	687c1–3	157
681d7–682e6	133	688a1–e2	186
681d8–9	137	688a–b	185 n. 123
681d8	137	689a1–c5	186
681e1–5	180	689c6–e3	186
682a1–5	180	690a1–e6	186
682b2–5	137	691a3–9	186
682b2–3	172, 180	691a6	186–187

691b1–d6	187	702a	140 n. 53
691c1–3	153	702b4–e2	113
691c3–4	154	702c8–d5	142
691c5–d6	154	704a1–709d9	144
691c7–d1	154	705c7–707d6	161
691c7	154	707b4–6	161
691d1	154	709d10–715e2	144
691d3–4	154	712c8–9	129 n. 39
691d5–693c5	187	713a9–b3	166
693b1–c5	187	713b6–7	166
693c6–d1	187	715e3–5	144, 156
693d2–694a2	187	715e7–718a6	144, 151
694a3–698a8	133, 140, 181, 187–190	716a2–7	152
		716a2–3	152
694a3–b7	188	716a6–7	153 n. 73
694b1–7	140	716a6	154
694b2	141	716a7	153–154
694b5	141	716b1–5	154
694b6	141	716b4–5	154
694c1–3	188	716d3	152
694c5–695c2	188	717d3–6	152
694d2–7	155	717d7–e3	153
694d6	155	718a6–724b5	144, 151
695b2	155	718b5–724b5	143–144
695b3–6	189	718b5–c10	146
695b4	155	718c7–719a3	145
695b5–6	189	718d3–4	144
695d5–697c4	189	718d4	144–145
696c2	135 n. 43	718d5–6	145
697e4–698a3	190	719e7–720e5	145
698a9–701c4	133, 140	720a1	146
698a9–700d2	190	720a5	146
699b6–7	191	720d6	146
699c1–6	191	722c	113 n. 9
699c6–d2	191	722c6–d2	109, 113, 147–148
700a3–c1	191	722c7–8	115
700c1–d2	192	722d2–e1	160
700c2	192	722d5	160
700c3–d2	192	722d7–e1	160
700c5	192	726a1–734e2	151
700c6	193	726a1–727c8	156
700d2–701d4	191	726a1–727a2	154
700d2–701b3	193	726a1–6	152 with n. 71
700d2–3	193	727a4–7	152
700d3–6	193	727a7–b2	156
700d6	194	727b1–2	154
701a	135 n. 43	727b1	156

727d6–728a5	154	135a7–b2	71 n. 46
728c3	152	135b2	71 n. 46
728c9–729b2	154		
728e5–729a2	155	**Phaed.**	
730c1–d2	155	58d4–6	86 n. 88
730d2–7	152	58d8–9	71 n. 45
731b5–c8	152	61b3–7	172 n. 107
731e6	152	107c1–115a3	110 n. 4
732°	135		
732a3–4	152	**Phaedr.**	
733d7–734e2	155	227b6–7	84 n. 81
734e2	156	227d6–228d5	26 n. 49
736c7–d1	150	246a3–6	72 n. 48
736c5–d4	149–150	255c	120 n. 24
738b–c	120 n. 24	264b3–e2	24 n. 41
741a6–e6	156		
741c6–d4	157	**Prot.**	
741e7–742c6	156	318e5–319a7	95
742c6–743c4	156–157	320c	49 n. 82
742d2–e1	157	320c7–323a4	10
742d3	157	321c7–323a4	11
742e7	157		
744d2–8	157–158	**Rep.**	
744d5–7	158	368e2–369a4	106 n. 121
770a6	129 n. 39	377b11–392c5	94
780–783	150–151	392c7–397b5	VIII–X
804e4–805a3	147–148	392d3	VIII
805a3–5	148	392d5	VIII
823d3–824a9	158	392d6	VIII
823e2–5	158	392d7	XVI
823e3	158	392d8–394b3	XVI
823e4	158	393a1–c9	VIII
829c6–d4	92	393c8	VIII
839–840	148	393d6	VIII
840c1–3	148	394b1	VIII
869e10–871a1	159	394b7–c2	VIII
870–871	148	394c1	VIII
870d4–7	148	394c2–3	VIII
887c5–d5	149–150	394d1–397b5	VIII
892d2–5	128 n. 38	472d4–e5	86 n. 86
919b	158 n. 80	514a–515a	83 n. 80
930e2–931b4	149	595–608	VIII
931b5–c2	149		
		St.	
Parm.		257a1–268d4	17
126b8–c3	26 n. 49	261d6	7
134e7–8	72 n. 48	265e7	7

Index Locorum — **235**

267d8–9	7	269e5–6	5
267e1–268c11	18	269e5	5
268a2	7	269e6	5
268d2	45	270a2	5
268d5–269c2	2, 4 n. 6, 14–15	270a3–4	5–6
268d5–6	45	270a6–7	6
268d8–269c3	2	270a6	5
268d8–9	16, 44	270a7	5
268d8	14 n. 23, 49	270a9	5
268d9	17, 45	270b3–271c2	6, 27
268e4–274e3	1–54	270b1–2	35
268e8–269c2	6	270b3–5	27
268e8–269a6	17	270b3–4	28
268e8–269b4	25–26	270b3	28
268e8–10	17	270b4	28
268e8	25–26, 164	270b6	35
268e9	17, 22	270b10–d1	164
269a1–5	164	270b10–c1	28
269a1–2	28	270b10	28
269a1	28	270c6	35
269a7–8	163	270c11–d4	22
269b2–3	29	270c11–13	22
269b2	29	270c12	22
269b4	17, 26, 28–29, 164	270d1–3	22
269b5–c2	26, 163	270d1–2	22, 28
269b5–6	28	270d3	43 n. 70
269b6–7	22	270d6–271a2	31
269b6	17, 23	270d7	31
269b7–9	24	270d8–e1	32
269b7	24, 28	270e3–4	32
269b8–9	30	270e6–7	32
269b8	24	270e8–9	32
269b9–c1	24, 26	270e10–271a3	32
269b9	28	271a3–4	29
269c1–2	45	271a3	32
269c3–270b2	5	271a5–8	29
269c4–272d4	4	271a5–6	29
269c4–270b2	4, 31	271a6–7	29–30
269c4–5	31	271b3–4	30
269c5	5–6, 31	271b4	30
269c6–7	31	271c1	30
269c7–d1	5, 31	271c3–272d4	6
269d1–2	5	271c4–7	32
269d2	5	271c4–5	7
269d4	35	271c8–e3	8
269d9	5	271c8	33
269e3	5	271d3–4	7

271e2–4	22–23	277b4–6	44
271e2–3	23	277b4–5	16
271e3–5	7–8	277d1–283a8	39
271e3	23	279a7–311c10	5
271e5–272d4	8	283b1–287b3	2
272b–c	50	283b1–5	46
272b5	35, 49	283b1–3	39
272d1–5	23	283b6–287b3	37–39, 46
272d4–274e3	4	283b6–c6	42
272d4–273e4	9	283b6–c1	39
272d4–6	9	283b6–7	46
272d4	6	283c	46 n. 75
272d6–273b4	34	283c3–6	40
272d7	34	283c4	45
272e1	34	283d4–9	40–41
272e4	9	283d8–9	42
272e5–6	34	283e4–5	42
272e5	34	284a5–d9	41
272e7	9	284a5–6	42
272e8	34	284b2	42
273a1	9–10	284e6–8	44
273a4	34	285a3–4	42
273a7–b1	10	286b3–d2	42–43
273a7	34	286b6–8	46
273b3	34	286b7–8	43
273b8	34	286c1–2	46
273c1–2	34	286c1	46
273c4–e4	34	286c2–3	46
273c4	34	286d4–287b2	44
273c5	34	286d4–6	46, 48–50
273c7	10	302a	164 n. 92
273c8	6 n. 12		
273e4–6	10	**Symp.**	
273e7	10	177b5–c3	95 n. 101
273e12–274a3	23	178a1–5	26 n. 49
274a1–2	10	180c1–2	26 n. 49
274a2–3	10	202c6–d6	120 n. 25
274b1–5	23	204a1–2	120 n. 25
274b1–2	10		
274b2–4	6 n. 12	**Theaet.**	
274b3	23, 45	172c3–177c5	11
274b4–5	45	172c3–177c2	39
274d4	11	174e2–5	19
274d5	11	175b8–c8	18–19
274e1–277a2	38	175c4–6	20
275a2–3	44, 46	175c5–6	19
277a3–c6	39		

Ti.

17a1–29d6	55–107	21a7–d8	97–98
17a1–20c3	55	21c3	64
17a1–19b2	95	21c4–d3	97
17a2	99	21d5–7	64
17b1–4	95–96	21e1–23e6	98
17b1–2	96	22b ff.	164 n. 92
17b2	99	23b8	64
17b5–19b2	55	23c3–d1	65
17c4–5	96	23d4–24d6	65
19a7	99	23e5–6	65
19b3–d2	81	25b5–c6	65
19b3–c8	69	25e2	99
19b4	81	26a1–2	64
19b5	81	26a2–c5	64
19b6–7	59 n. 10, 82	26a4	99
19b6	83	26b1–2	55 n. 1
19b7–8	83	26b4	99
19b7	81	26b6	64
19b8–c1	63	26b7	64
19c1	63	26c4	99
19c2–3	83	26c6–7	64
19c2	83	26c7–d3	84
19c6	63	27a2–b6	56, 85, 103
19c8–20b7	90–91	27a3–6	80
19c8–d2	69	27a3–5	96
19d2–3	69	27a7–b6	85
19d3–e8	70	27b7–29d6	56
19d5–e2	91–92	27b7–9	73
19e6–8	62	27c1–d1	73
20a1–2	96	27c3	73
20a2–3	96	27c4	73
20a6–7	96	27c7–d1	67–68
20b1	99	28c3–5	71
20b5	63	29c4–d3	67, 71
20c1–3	84	29c5–6	67–68, 71, 74
20c6	99	38b3–5	73
20d7–26e1	56	38d6–e1	74
20d7–25d6	84	40c3–d5	72
20d7–21d8	97	48c2–e1	72
20d7	64	51c5–d2	74
20d8	64	56b–c	72
20e1–3	97	69a–b	72 n. 47
		69b–c	70 n. 44

www.ingramcontent.com/pod-product-compliance
Lightning Source LLC
Chambersburg PA
CBHW020226170426
43201CB00007B/329